Your Place In the Cards

A ♠ Your Place In the Cards

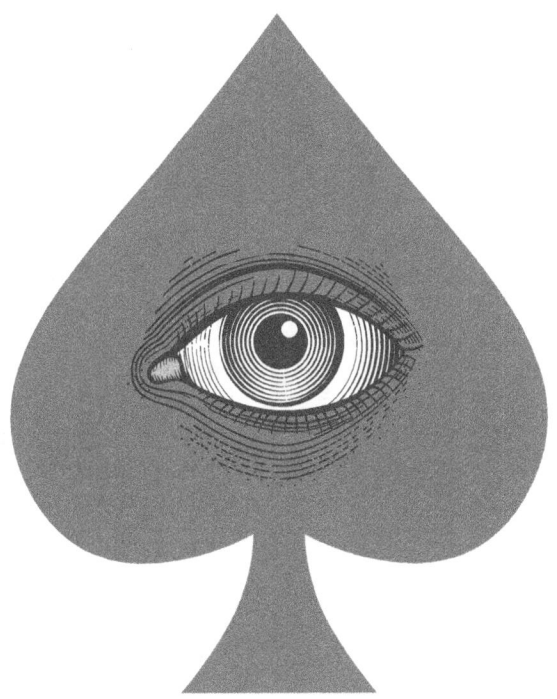

Donalie Fitzgerald

Published by Echo Point Books & Media
Brattleboro, Vermont
www.EchoPointBooks.com

All rights reserved.
Neither this work nor any portions thereof may be reproduced, stored in a retrieval system, or transmitted in any capacity without written permission from the publisher.

Copyright © 1974, 2015 by Donalie Fitzgerald
ISBN (Paperback): 978-1-62654-284-6
ISBN (Hardcover): 978-1-62654-285-3

Cover design by Rachel Boothby Gualco,
Echo Point Books & Media

Editorial and proofreading assistance by Ian Straus,
Echo Point Books & Media

Printed and bound in the United States of America

Dedicated to:

8♥ A♣ 5♣ 7♣ 8♣ Q♣

K♣ A♦ 5♦ 6♦ 10♦ 6♠ J♠ K♠

*...And to all those in the
Universe who are seeking
Knowledge and Enlightenment*

Foreword

I have come a long way since first I set out on this strange, uncertain pilgrimage. I have listened to the roar of Despair; I have held up my arms against the tide of Belief; I have walked in the valley of Pressure—to know—to not know—to question—to requestion. And I have found those things to be nothingness—like the inaccessible and unknowable God—the paradoxical fullness of the great divine Nothing. Figments of my imagination that could not translate—that could not change—that never existed, but for me at that time and place. My anxieties and my agonies were my fences around my fantasies. It kept me in a space—though not chosen by me—but comfortable as the womb.

In my travels I found the womb is not comfortable; it is reflected light. A mirror image of my mind—preconditioned to help me find the Island of Paradise, and sought by someone prior to myself. And so, like the age-old Chinese journey of a thousand miles, I had to learn to take one step at a time.

Edith L. Randall has been most patient with my walking. She is intensely grey and will admit to being "older than you think," but she is a strict and just guide and a warm and beautiful human being. She has given me strange fruit, and the juice has titillated me beyond the point of no return.

In this book, I have taken *The Sacred Symbols of the Ancients* by Edith L. Randall, to form the beginnings of a New Way. Not that it was not there to

Foreword

start with—but rather that the eyesight has recently stumbled upon a shimmering, glowing objectivity—to be understood and enjoyed by all. The New Way is for you—and for me—Edith Randall has been living this way for over fifty years.

Everyone is equipped by nature to receive and assimilate sensory experiences. Everyone is sensitive to tones, colors—to touch, taste and the feeling of space. Therefore, by nature, every person is able to participate in all pleasures of sensory experiences. Watching a flower grow consists of an inner look at one of the secrets of nature—the feeling of life before you; raising the veil of Isis. The power that the clergy calls "God"; philosophers call "law"; moralists call "precepts"; scientists call "nature"—is described by occultists as "intuition" or "understanding." For all of you who search for an answer within yourself, the principle is always the same: study the microcosm, Man, in order to understand the secrets of the macrocosm—the Universe.

Everything that is not yet known or accepted is regarded as "occult" or concealed. It is our endeavor to bring oratory to the laboratory—closing in on Initiation to reveal Inspiration. And now, it is time to penetrate the other side of the mirror.

Donalie Fitzgerald

Contents

Introduction *3*

I. Aces *23*

Ace of Hearts *24*
Ace of Clubs *32*
Ace of Diamonds *42*
Ace of Spades *52*

II. Twos *63*

Two of Hearts *64*
Two of Clubs *71*
Two of Diamonds *81*
Two of Spades *93*

III. Threes *103*

Three of Hearts *104*
Three of Clubs *111*
Three of Diamonds *120*
Three of Spades *131*

IV. Fours *141*

Four of Hearts *142*
Four of Clubs *150*
Four of Diamonds *161*
Four of Spades *172*

V. Fives *181*

Five of Hearts *182*
Five of Clubs *191*
Five of Diamonds *200*
Five of Spades *210*

VI. Sixes *221*

Six of Hearts *222*
Six of Clubs *231*
Six of Diamonds *242*
Six of Spades *251*

VII. Sevens *261*

Seven of Hearts *262*
Seven of Clubs *270*
Seven of Diamonds *281*
Seven of Spades *291*

VIII. Eights *301*

Eight of Hearts *302*
Eight of Clubs *312*
Eight of Diamonds *321*
Eight of Spades *331*

IX. Nines *339*

Nine of Hearts *340*
Nine of Clubs *348*
Nine of Diamonds *359*
Nine of Spades *369*

X. Tens *379*

Ten of Hearts *380*
Ten of Clubs *389*
Ten of Diamonds *398*
Ten of Spades *407*

XI. Jacks *415*

Jack of Hearts *416*

Jack of Clubs   *425*
Jack of Diamonds   *435*
Jack of Spades   *443*

XII. Queens   *453*

Queen of Hearts   *454*
Queen of Clubs   *462*
Queen of Diamonds   *473*
Queen of Spades   *482*

XIII. Kings   *489*

King of Hearts   *490*
King of Clubs   *500*
King of Diamonds   *510*
King of Spades   *519*

XIV. The Joker   *529*

YOUR PLACE IN THE CARDS

Introduction

The Mission of Cards as they are generally known is primarily for amusement. We "play" with these fifty-two bits of pasteboard for relaxation, for killing time or, more seriously and usually more disastrously, for testing our luck or skill in the hope of financial gain. We consult the fortune-tellers who profess a special knowledge of their power in divination because we "superconsciously" feel that there may be something more to be found than appears in the gains or losses in poker.

The use of symbolically decorated cards for fortune-telling probably preceded their use in games of chance, and later replaced the more primitive forms of divination, such as the throwing down of a bundle of sticks, or even more primitive, the inspection of entrails. Often the Gypsy would resort to an additional method such as gazing into a crystal ball, to confirm what had already been said about the Cards.

Telling fortunes with the Cards can be an amusing pastime. It can also be a deeply serious method of divination and spiritual awakening when practiced by those with the clairvoyant gifts and profound knowledge of occult symbolism. Perhaps the superconscious is wiser than some realize, for from this higher level of thinking we reach the higher level of *knowing* where—and only where—Truth is to be found. The teachings of the Wise Ones, through the Cards, are immune to the adverse opinions of the uninstructed who live behind closed doors. If symbols are a dead language to you, with no meaning other than the outline of their form, and if you have decided that spots must remain spots and that Kings, Queens and Jacks are nothing but pictures, this book is a waste of your time. From the depths of our firm faith in it as a revelation, we offer this teaching to the seekers after self-knowledge, and self and neighbor understanding. This knowledge necessitates a belief that there is no random element in anything we do; that the seemingly chance arrangement of cards is, in reality, designed by the unconscious mind—that the Mundane Spread and the Natural Spread are comprised of a strict mathematical symbology that has an exact correspondence with the mathematical laws on which the Universe was founded; so, therefore, there is no accident in the construction of the Pack of Cards, as there was no accident in the construction of the Universe.

The origin of our modern packs is still a matter of dispute and there are almost as many theories as there are devotees. Cards were known as early as 969 AD in China, and there are some theories that carry cards back to the Atlanteans and the Master Teachers who were appointed to save a remnant of the race: the initiates, in the face of the destruction of their continent, gathered together to decide which of them would be the One who would preserve the Ancient Wisdom by memorizing the knowledge from the temple libraries and go forth to the New Land to continue the teachings. When none could qualify, it was decided to symbolically enscribe the stored wisdom on a pack of papyrus cards. Some say these were the originations of the decorative and colorful Tarot Cards. A complete Tarot pack consists of seventy-eight cards, divided into four suits: Cups, Wands, Coins, and Swords. Each suit has fourteen cards and twenty-two major trumps, which is called the major arcana. These picture cards with their unusual design and bizarre titles set forth, on the Tree of Life, the Kabbalistic teachings concerning the One Source of all created things and the Universal Laws that govern them. Some Tarot packs did not include the Queen because it was thought unseemly to represent a woman in the Devil's Pack Book, as cards were often called. But as the devil can always "cite scripture for his purpose," so may we all, through ignorance or carelessness, distort and misinterpret the most sacred of symbols and the most priceless of teachings.

The Bible established the Cards as the "Little Book" in the hand of the angel (Rev. 10:4, 10, 11—Chapter V) bearing the message of the "Seven Thunders" (the Seven Planets), sealed until the time when the "Followers of the Lamb" must prophesy again before many peoples and nations and tongues and kings." The Followers of the Lamb have always held it to be a sacred book, its symbols sacred symbols. The Rosicrucians revered it and its fifty-two "chapters" as true revealers of God's Laws. We may do no harm to ourselves—and surely none to the "Little Book" by using Cards as an innocent pastime, but we are missing something valuable and important if we regard it only as a pack of cards.

The purpose of this teaching is to find a prevention and cure for the one great tragedy that accounts for all the ills of mankind and the world we have lived in from the beginning of time—what the occultist calls "The Crime of

Introduction

Separation": the Great Departure from the Divine Source of our being—followed swift on the heels of the Commandments given through the voice of Moses and of the laws set forth in the Pentateuch. We are dangerously far from that Source today. The Tarot and the "Little Book" are given as Way-Showers.

As the Tarot sets forth the pattern of the Universe and the immutable laws that govern it, man is, of necessity, included in that pattern and affected by those laws. But within that larger field he has a pattern of his own—an individualized pattern, determined and conditioned by his Numbers, his Elements and the "Seven Thunders" which surrounded him at birth. It is the "Little Book" that gives him his clue and a further extension and clarification and his own astrological and numerological maps, strictly calculated according to his elements, attitudes, emotions and reactions to all others and, most emphatically, to himself. The future lies hidden like a seed in the earth, ready to sprout, grow and flower. But if we have to use a key word, inadequate though it be, to define the purpose of this book, we would choose *illumination*, as depicted by the cover of the book. Through the Natural Spread, we shall discover that the original plan for man's life on our planet was undeviatingly sequential, with perfect harmony and stability at its center and we shall further see, through the Mundane Spread, how man himself chose to distort this Plan and disturb its harmony—and his own.

As we find our individual place in the man-made sequence and note what we have "displaced" in the God-sequence, we become more and more enlightened concerning ourselves, the One; our associates, the Many, and our universal brotherhood with the All. In holding this book at this moment, you have taken the first step in *illumination* and are well on your way to Understanding and its corollary, Tolerance. The next step ahead is universal Good Will.

In the pack of cards there are:

Two colors — red and black; positive and negative; male and female.
Four suits — Hearts, Clubs, Diamonds, Spades; the four elements; the four seasons.
Twelve court cards — Kings, Queens, Jacks; the twelve months of the year; the twelve signs of the Zodiac; the Twelve Disciples, etc.
Fifty-two pages or pieces — the fifty-two weeks.
Thirteen cards in each suit — thirteen weeks for each season.
Two special numbers — Seven and Nine:
The number Seven as the center of each suit; the seven original planets known to the Ancients; the dominical or "sacred" number that symbolizes the force, peace, and harmony that *are* at the center of the Universe; The Soul number of Man; seven days of the Week; the Seven Wonders of the World; seven virtues, etc.
The number Nine as the last single number; the Cycle of Man's experience;

the number that includes all numbers and all planets; the Universal Number.
The Joker — The "remnant of days"; the "highest" symbol in the entire pack. Usually pictured as a fool and either rejected or "played wild" in card games, its true significance is identical with that of the "Fool Card" in Tarot. It will be fully explained after the delineation of the suit cards.

Beyond the logical seven times fifty-two, to total our required 365 ¼ days for the Earth's travel in the solar year, there are 364 spots on the cards, as well, should one take the time to add them up.

Each birthdate in the year has a card that is its governor and conditioner. Each card, in turn, has a ruling planet. One of these cards is yours.

By its suit, by its planetary rulership, by its position in the Spread, by the number of its spots or the picture on its face and by its relationship to other cards in the sequence or by the card that is "displaced," you are revealed to yourself from new angles of enlightenment. You begin to understand the why of your inclinations and impulses, your emotional and psychological reactions, your attractions and repulsions and the ease or difficulty you find in living harmoniously with those in your environment.

Somewhere those individuals who touch part of your life will be found. As you gain in understanding you learn to make practical use of your knowledge. You learn the importance of choosing your vocation and developing your ability and you cease to waste your time and energy in cultivating the people and things that have no useful part in your life.

YOUR PLACE IN THE CARDS

SUITS

The order corresponds to the seasons: Hearts, Clubs, Diamonds, Spades or, Spring, Summer, Harvest, Winter.

Hearts

As source or beginning, Hearts represent the Spring of the year—the stir of all forces of nature into life; the heartbeat of the awakened rhythm. Hearts begin with the Vernal Equinox.

As Youth, Hearts represent the childhood, early associations with family and friends, the first call of love, and the urge for mating. As Fire, Hearts rule the burning devotion that leads to sacrifice for country, cause or friend. As Love, Hearts rule our nearest and dearest relationships—parent and child, lover and beloved, husband and wife, brother and sister, friend and friend. As Vocation, Hearts rule art, music, poetry, and the pursuit of beauty in any form.

The "positive" Heart is kindly, affectionate, friendly, and hospitable. The "negative" Heart is selfish, greedy, self-indulgent, and self-seeking, flirtatious and promiscuous.

The ruling Planets are Venus and Neptune.

In the Tarot, Hearts are Cups.

Clubs

Clubs represent the Summer quarter of the year. After the creative fire from the Heart of God came the animating, activating breath. Clubs correspond to the element Air: the functioning *mind* of man.

The figurative symbol is the trefoil or shamrock—the first leaf to come in the Spring, the last to go in the Fall, found all over the World. The quest of Clubs is for universal knowledge. Like the messenger of the Gods, Clubs are the link between heaven and earth, the Mind of God and the mind of man.

As Life, Clubs are the second stage—the educational or learning period, which actually lasts to the end of life, so eager and tireless is their search for knowledge. As Mind, Clubs are the guardians of intelligence and rule all mental processes, all psychological reactions, all educational interests, all inquiries, communications, and messages. They instigate arguments, debates, and disputes; they investigate, record, disseminate news, and spread propaganda; they are the brains behind the successful activities of lesser minds than their own. As Vocation, they rule all forms of education, legal matters, literature, and journalism.

The "positive" Club is brilliant, mentally magnetic, thoroughly informed, and a safe counselor. The "negative" Club is aggressive, pugnacious, tricky, and unreliable; clever in dishonesty.

The ruling Planets are Mercury and Mars.

In the Tarot, Clubs are Wands.

Diamonds

Diamonds represent the Fall quarter of the year.

"Let the Waters bring forth abundantly." "Be fruitful and multiply and have dominion." "Lay up for yourselves treasures in heaven." Abundance, with dominion over it and "treasure in heaven" sum up the mission of Diamonds.

After the Fire and the Breath, the first command for Abundance was given to Water, the Element associated with Diamonds. After the childhood of Hearts and the school days of Clubs, man must produce the Diamonds of his efforts and reap the Harvest of his sowing.

Diamonds stand for power and protection of material wealth. As a jewel, it allows the "light" to pass through with practically no loss. Jewelers look for the purity of its "water" when judging the value of the stone. The symbolism is clear. Diamonds represent the "Limitless Substance" of the Fourth Statement of the Pattern on the Trestleboard, but the Substance includes "all things needful, both spiritual and material."

Diamonds are as money; actually and more correctly they represent Values. By our conception of true values, we stand or fall. By spiritual standards, the rich man who has neglected to lay up "treasure in heaven" is a failure. As Vocation, Diamonds rule merchants, manufacturers, mine owners, operators, big business of any nature, producers, backers, investors, bankers, brokers, and world traders.

The "positive" diamond is generous, philanthropic, a power for good in any community, a dispenser of plenty, and prosperity. The "negative" is material-minded, avaricious, penurious, miserly; willing to cause hardship and misery for profit.

The ruling Planet is Jupiter.

In the Tarot, Diamonds are Pentacles—the Coin on the Magician's Table.

Spades

"And God said, 'Let the *Earth* bring forth.' " Spades represent the element Earth, the Winter of the year. Winter is a period of apparent rest, stillness, hardness, cold. Unless Labor is applied, there is no yielding of the ground nor any "bringing forth."

But underneath, at the Heart of Nature, guided by Her intelligence and blessed with Her riches, a resurrection is in the making. Only the wise know what lies behind maya, the veil of appearances.

Thus it is with Spades. The least understood of all the suits, they actually symbolize the Initiate—often the adept. Their mission is dual like their symbols, the Acorn and the Sword. Their key words are *labor* and *wisdom*.

The acorn is a symbol of death and burial—but its undying life-germ, when planted in the soil, brings forth another tree. Spades *know* that we die to free the soul and spirit for rebirth. The form of the acorn and the form of the spade are identical. Spades break the ground not only that the earth may "bring forth" but that the treasure that is buried out of sight may be released. Spades are the Diggers for Truth.

The sword in the hand of the King is but another emblem of the Spade; etymologically their meaning is the same. It is the power that compels obedience, that overcomes resistance. They came to conquer the obstacles offered by material existence, to cut down and destroy whatever would hinder the growth of the soul—even at the cost of pain, sorrow, and loss. Look at a Spade card with the point down. You will see a heart emblem, surmounted by a "cross." The earth-journey is not an easy one for Spades. To reach the goal of Wisdom and the degree of initiation to which they are entitled, they are often called upon to sacrifice ambition, personal power, and love. Their great reward lies in spiritual achievement.

Vocationally, Spades rule the world of labor, of sickness, and of death; all physicians, nurses, institutions of healing or confinement, guardians of the dead or of their goods. Also, and more importantly, all students of the Inner School, members of the Ancient Order, teachers of the Mysteries and Masters in the spiritual sense.

The "positive" Spade is self-disciplined and self-sacrificing, a tireless worker, and an example of wisdom and truth. The "negative" Spade is either in a rut of drudgery or is a bigoted and relentless disciplinarian, bent on showing his power and bending others to his will.

The ruling Planets are Saturn and Uranus.

In the Tarot, Spades are Swords.

COLORS

Regarding colors, there is a prevailing misconception. While there is an esoteric significance, the red and the black are not applicable to the life of the individual as Light and Darkness, Ease or Misfortune. For our purpose we may regard them merely as a pair of opposites under the Law of Polarity.

COURT CARDS

Four Kings, four Queens, and four Jacks establish the twelve-symbol throughout the pack. The trinity of Father-Mother-Son, Positive-Negative-Neutral is four times repeated by the four suits. Twelve stands for the "House of the Lord"—the "many mansions" which await His children—the "Houses" of the Zodiac.

As groups of three, the Court Cards are all rulers in their own right. Kings rule as Kings, to be sure, and stand at the head of the pack, but Queens are ever beside him as co-rulers and exemplars of the fact that no Positive can exist without a corresponding Negative, no action can take place without reaction and the genus Male cannot persist without the Female.

As Principle, Kings represent the Positive and Active, Queens, the receptive; Jacks, being both active and receptive, represent the Neutral.

In the Bible many of the correspondencies speak for themselves:

Disciples: In the three calls of the original Twelve, we recognize the King-Queen-Jack "stages"—Peter, Andrew, James, and John; Philip, Bartholomew, Matthew, and Thomas; Simon, Jude, James the Lesser, and Judas. Twelve Disciples.

Gospels: In Matthew, Mark, Luke, and John we have the four Kings. In Matthew, the businessman, collector of the taxes, we see the King of Diamonds; in Mark, the Evangelist, writer and recorder for Paul and Barnabas on their journeys, the King of Clubs; in Luke, the physician, the King of Spades; in John, the Beloved, the King of Hearts.

Your Place in the Cards

The Four Marys: Mary, Mother of Jesus; Mary Magdalene; Mary, Sister of Martha; and Mary, Mother of James the Lesser are the four Queens at the foot of the Cross.

The Epistles: Preachers of the new gospel, writers of the new ideas are the four Jacks who are to "Go into all the world and preach the gospel to every creature."

In history and in the lives of great men and women of other days and these days, you will find these symbols unfailingly applicable. You will recognize Kings, Queens and Jacks as such only to discover that the card that belongs to them appears as the Birth Card, as "displacement" or in the sequence established by their date of birth.

Court cards, while not the only rulers and leaders in the affairs of men are always such by "divine right" and when they do not measure up to their high calling, they have failed in their appointment.

NUMBERS

The significance of numbers is in the "spots." Cards are inseparable from the Numbers on their faces. In your Birth Card you will find a correspondence in your numerological pattern—a designed correspondence that gives emphasis and importance to the particular number designated. The same holds true of any card in your sequence (a term to be explained in full later) if it falls in the cycle from one to ten. The Court Cards are special and although they, too, have their numerological correspondence in eleven, twelve, and thirteen, we are here concerned with the Numbers of the spots:

1

Positive	Negative
Individualization	Self(ishness)
Leadership	Dictatorship
Progress	Laziness

ACES

Desire	Self

2

Positive	Negative
Cooperation	Toadying
Friendliness	Indifference
Diplomacy	Lying

TWOS

Union	Dependence

3

Positive	Negative
Happiness	Jealousy
Optimism	Worry
Sociability	Intolerance

THREES

Right Choice	Indecision

4

Organization	Carelessness
Self-discipline	Restriction
Service	Destruction

FOURS

Results	Incompletion

5

Adaptability	Aloofness
Versatility	Triviality
Change	Restlessness

FIVES

Expressiveness	Crosses

6

Responsibility	Interference
Love	Criticism
Harmony	Anxiety

SIXES

Adjustment	Monotony

Your Place in the Cards

7

Spirituality   Melancholy
Mental keenness   Coldness
Peace and silence   Skepticism

SEVENS
Spiritual victory   Obstacles

8

Power   Scheming
Material Freedom   Materiality
Philanthropy   Bullying

EIGHTS

Power   Domination

9

Humanitarianism   Selfishness
The Higher Law   Emotionalism
Universal Love   Dissipation

NINES
Fulfillment   Disappointment

10

Divinity of man   Exploitation
Universal progress   Promotion
Universal Ideals   Ambition

TENS
Success   Egotism

JACKS
Corresponding to number 11, they are linked to inspiration and ideas; negatively, they represent laziness and immaturity.

12

QUEENS

As number 12, they have power in their own right (1) and receptivity (2); negatively, they are lazy, selfish and/or drudges.

KINGS

Represent principles; negatively, fixation. As number 13, they are the One Force (1) behind the Trinity (3). In 13, whose digits added up becomes 4, they have the power of the Master number, 22.

PLANETS

While we need but little knowledge of the scientific art of astrology to understand this teaching, it is essential to be familiar with the general means and influence of the planets and signs. This system deals only with the seven original "Wanderers" known to the Ancients and the order followed is in accordance with their relative distance from the Sun.

Mercury

This planet closest to the sun, represents the mind in general and all our mental processes. It is, therefore, education, the exchange of ideas, communication, messages, things that come quickly and go quickly, flashes from the brain that direct impulses, and all stimulants to words and action. Mercury ties come and go. There is no permanence with Mercury ties.

Venus

Called the planet of Love and Marriage, Venus is guardian of all affectional ties, heart-desires and the satisfaction that ensues from accomplished objectives. It is the planet of art and beauty, idealism and harmony. It governs social contacts and family relationships. It is also the feminine principle and rules women and the things in which they are interested.

Mars

Mars is the planet of physical energy and vitality; of the human will and its resultant action; of initiative and purpose—for good or ill. It is dynamic in friendship or aggressive in war. It rules arguments, debates, quarrels and law suits. It represents the masculine principle.

Jupiter

Called the Great Benefic, Jupiter is the bringer of good fortune, commonly known as wealth, possessions, and tangible assets. In the larger sense it is all good and the protecting love of the Father. It is the ruler of business returns, of the source of income—and its disposition; of professions and higher education; of religion and the Higher Law (also the Higher Mind). It rules the judges who decide all legal questions and relationships with men of high standing. Negatively, it is greed and acquisitiveness for personal purpose, self-indulgence and self-aggrandizement. It is the "fat" that wrecks the health.

Saturn

Saturn is the planet of Karma—of the results of past actions, of debts formerly contracted to be paid now. Saturn is called the Reaper, Collector of Taxes, the Guardian of the Threshold which we may not cross until our account is cleared. He is, in reality, the symbol of wisdom, the great educator and schoolmaster who deals out strict justice in reward or punishment— according to our merited desserts. He is the inevitable effect of causes we have voluntarily created. Because of this, Saturn represents limitations, hardship, sorrow, loss, ill health, and poverty—*if earned.* Conversely, Saturn brings us to recognition and honor through a process or testing, deepening and strengthening whatever of worthiness lies within us; through creating in us balance and stability, loyalty and integrity, and through teaching us the wisdom that overcomes all obstacles. The Wise Man learns—and only through Saturn—to welcome his problems and to pile up no further debts through wrong thinking, wrong eating, and ungoverned emotions. By paying for the past we can earn our freedom for the future.

Uranus

This New Age planet, Uranus, has charge of the trend of evolution. If tradition interferes with progress, it must go; the way must be cleared for the New, even at the cost of dire destruction. Uranus is the messenger of the "magical" will that is determined that we shall go forward; in that sense it is an emissary of fate. It is the guardian of new ideas, scientific discoveries, original methods of application, and the hitherto untried and unknown universal brotherhood.

Neptune

Neptune is called the planet of the Soul. It rules inspiration, idealism, and utopian objectives. It drops a veil over reality and deflects the mind from practical, down-to-earth considerations. It therefore represents illusion and delusion. Negatively, our response is lying, deceiving, trickery, and the evil side of subtlety. It is ruler of liquids and gases, medicines and drugs, commerce and shipping—all things at a distance.

On the following page, you will find the Birthdate Chart. This will give you the governing Card for each day of the year. Find the desired month at the top. Find the desired date in the left-hand column. If you want to know what other dates are governed by the same Card, consult the actual Cards themselves. Here you will find that of the 365 birthdates, Hearts will rule fifty-two, Clubs rule 133, Diamonds rule 131, and Spades rule forty-nine. December 31 does not appear on any of the suit charts. This last day of the year is ruled by the Joker and is the only date under this rulership. The teaching concerning the Joker is given at the end of the Chapter on Kings.

THE SPREAD CHARTS

The Natural Spread

This is the natural sequence, beginning with the Ace of Hearts in the first row at the right and running through clubs and diamonds to the Ten of Spades on the last row at the left—keeping strictly to the prescribed order—hearts, clubs, diamonds, and spades and laid in rows of seven.

Always read from right to left.

The remaining three cards of the Spade suit are placed at the top, above the first row, in the center of the Spread. These are the Crown Cards. Their position denotes Initiation.

The entire picture of this "Natural" Spread is a statement of God's Plan—an orderly, sequential Pattern for man's life. It is the Divine Spread. This is the chart where you will find your "Displacement Card."

The Mundane Spread

This is actually man's distortion of God's Plan. It is plain to see that here we have no sequence by suit or number; no order (except the inescapable "seven" in rows—horizontal and vertical) and no harmony. But it is the Pattern man has chosen to operate under and is but another evidence of what we mentioned earlier, the "Departure" or "The Crime of Separation."

This Spread was arrived at through a system of quadration—an exact mathematical quartering of the circle of 360 degrees and an equally exact method of timing.

The seven rows follow the order of the seven (ancient) planets: Mercury, Venus, Mars, Jupiter, Saturn, Uranus, and Neptune. Thus, the Three of Hearts begins the Mercury line; the Seven of Hearts begins the Venus Line; the King of Hearts, the Mars Line; the Six of Diamonds, the Jupiter Line; the Queen of Diamonds, the Saturn Line; the Queen of Spades, the Uranus Line; and the Four of Hearts, the Neptune Line.

Each line follows the same order. The Three of Hearts is the Mercury Card in the Mercury Line; Ace of Clubs is the Venus Card in the Mercury Line; Queen of Clubs is the Mars Card—Ten of Spades, the Jupiter Card; Five of Clubs, the Saturn Card; Three of Diamonds, the Uranus Card; the Ace of Spades, the Neptune Card—all in the Mercury Line. Follow the same order

Your Place in the Cards

CARDOLOGY BIRTHDATE CHART

Abbreviations: S = Spades D = Diamonds C = Clubs H = Hearts

Day	Jan.	Feb.	Mar.	Apr.	May	June	July	Aug.	Sept.	Oct.	Nov.	Dec.
1	KS	JS	9S	7S	5S	3S	AS	QD	10D	8D	6D	4D
2	QS	10S	8S	6S	4S	2S	KD	JD	9D	7D	5D	3D
3	JS	9S	7S	5S	3S	AS	QD	10D	8D	6D	4D	2D
4	10S	8S	6S	4S	2S	KD	JD	9D	7D	5D	3D	AD
5	9S	7S	5S	3S	AS	QD	10D	8D	6D	4D	2D	KC
6	8S	6S	4S	2S	KD	JD	9D	7D	5D	3D	AD	QC
7	7S	5S	3S	AS	QD	10D	8D	6D	4D	2D	KC	JC
8	6S	4S	2S	KD	JD	9D	7D	5D	3D	AD	QC	10C
9	5S	3S	AS	QD	10D	8D	6D	4D	2D	KC	JC	9C
10	4S	2S	KD	JD	9D	7D	5D	3D	AD	QC	10C	8C
11	3S	AS	QD	10D	8D	6D	4D	2D	KC	JC	9C	7C
12	2S	KD	JD	9D	7D	5D	3D	AD	QC	10C	8C	6C
13	AS	QD	10D	8D	6D	4D	2D	KC	JC	9C	7C	5C

Introduction

```
14  KD  JD  9D  7D  5D  3D  AD  QC  10C 8C  6C  4C
15  QD  10D 8D  6D  4D  2D  AD  KC  JC  9C  7C  5C  3C
16  JD  9D  7D  5D  3D  AD  KC  QC  10C 8C  6C  4C  2C
17  10D 8D  6D  4D  2D  AD  KC  QC  JC  9C  7C  5C  3C  AC
18  9D  7D  5D  3D  AD  KC  QC  JC  10C 8C  6C  4C  2C  AC  KH
19  8D  6D  4D  2D  AD  KC  QC  JC  10C 9C  7C  5C  3C  AC  KH  QH
20  7D  5D  3D  AD  KC  QC  JC  10C 9C  8C  6C  4C  2C  AC  KH  QH  JH
21  6D  4D  2D  AD  KC  QC  JC  10C 9C  8C  7C  5C  3C  AC  KH  QH  JH  10H
22  5D  3D  AD  KC  QC  JC  10C 9C  8C  7C  6C  4C  2C  AC  KH  QH  JH  10H 9H
23  4D  2D  AD  KC  QC  JC  10C 9C  8C  7C  6C  5C  3C  AC  KH  QH  JH  10H 9H  8H
24  3D  AD  KC  QC  JC  10C 9C  8C  7C  6C  5C  4C  2C  AC  KH  QH  JH  10H 9H  8H  7H
25  2D  AD  KC  QC  JC  10C 9C  8C  7C  6C  5C  4C  3C  AC  KH  QH  JH  10H 9H  8H  7H  6H
26  AD  KC  QC  JC  10C 9C  8C  7C  6C  5C  4C  3C  2C  AC  KH  QH  JH  10H 9H  8H  7H  6H  5H
27  KC  QC  JC  10C 9C  8C  7C  6C  5C  4C  3C  2C  AC  KH  QH  JH  10H 9H  8H  7H  6H  5H  4H
28  QC  JC  10C 9C  8C  7C  6C  5C  4C  3C  2C  AC  KH  QH  JH  10H 9H  8H  7H  6H  5H  4H  3H
29  JC  10C 9C  8C  7C  6C  5C  4C  3C  2C  AC  KH  QH  JH  10H 9H  8H  7H  6H  5H  4H  3H  2H
30  10C 9C  8C  7C  6C  5C  4C  3C  2C  AC  KH  QH  JH  10H 9H  8H  7H  6H  5H  4H  3H  2H  AH
31  9C  8C  7C  6C  5C  4C  3C  2C  AC  KH  QH  JH  10H 9H  8H  7H  6H  5H  4H  3H  2H  AH  Joker
```

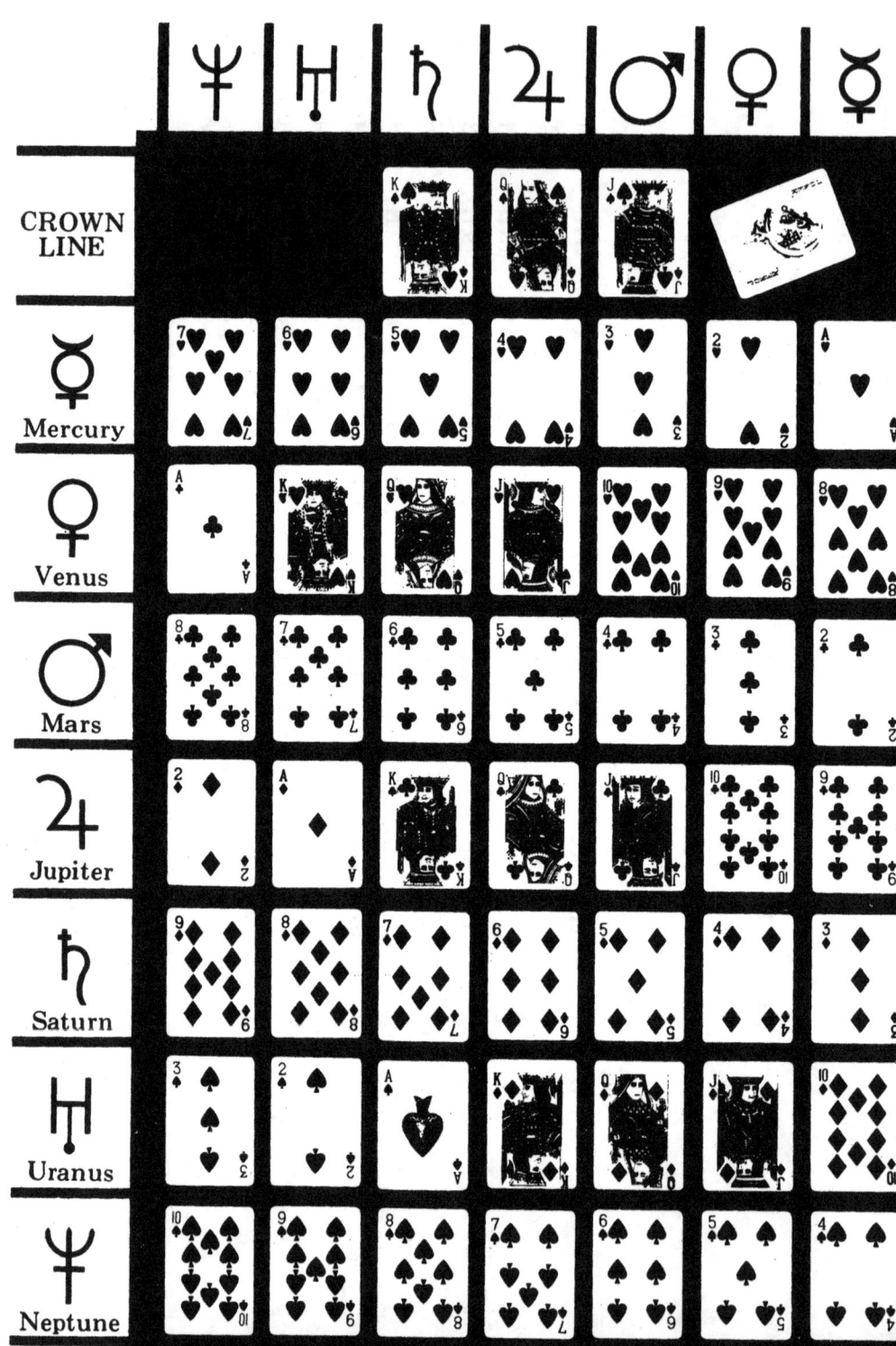

NATURAL SPREAD

MUNDANE SPREAD

throughout the other rows—Seven of Hearts is the Mercury Card in the Venus Line; Seven of Diamonds, the Venus Card in the Venus Line, etc.

You will note the Ten of Diamonds lies in the exact center of the Mundane Spread—the Jupiter Card in the Jupiter Line. Man has centered his *values* (Diamonds) on money—and in the acquisition and power of money he counts his blessings (Jupiter) and builds for his success (Ten).

Now turn to the corresponding position in the Natural, or "God's Plan," Spread and see what has been displaced. We find the Queen of Clubs is the pivotal point in this Spread—the Intuition (Queen) and Awareness (Clubs). The Quest for Truth and the knowledge of divine laws is the focal point in the Divine Plan; the Quest for Money and its employment for personal place and power is man's "distortion." The Ten of Diamonds is the strongest of the money cards; the Queen of Clubs is the strongest of the intuitional.

Adjacent to the Ten of Diamonds in its four corners are (1) the Two of Diamonds at the upper left—which represents bargaining; (2) the Six of Hearts at the upper right—the "higher plane" symbol of the Christ Principle—in its mundane aspect, this card embodies the ability to compromise; (3) the Nine of Hearts at the lower left—usually interpreted as a "lower plane" symbol, indicating a loss of time in the pursuit of love; (4) the Three of Clubs at the lower right, representing a conflict of ideas—man at the crossroads, not sure of himself but free to choose Love, the gospel of all religious concepts.

THE THREE FIXED CARDS IN THE MUNDANE SPREAD

In the process of quadration, referred to above, regardless of the number of times this is executed, there are three cards that always retain their original position—the Jack of Hearts, the Eight of Clubs, and the King of Spades. These three cards represent Fixed Principles; these people *know*.

Jack of Hearts — Always the middle card in the second line.
Eight of Clubs — Always the last card in the third line; in other words, the Neptune Card in the Mars Line. This is power in knowledge. These people are always protected.
King of Spades — Always the third card at the top (left). This is the highest degree of Power through Wisdom.

Find your Birth Card on the Birth Chart and consider its suit. Are you a lover? (Heart) Are you a seeker? (Club) Are you a reaper? (Diamond) Are you a knower? (Spade)

This will give you the trend of your life and will help you to focalize your natural aptitudes and show you how you relate to those around you. See if you have been following your own or trying to work on a tangent. Consider its number. Are you using it positively or negatively?

Introduction

PERSONALITY CARDS

Women

In the case of a woman, you can choose to operate under your Personality Card—the Queen of the same suit as your Birth Card—instead of under the Birth Card itself. You may find many of the people you are associated with both personally and impersonally involved with you under your Personality Card sequence. While the Personality Card is a woman's legitimate choice, it is often found to be a weakening influence (in which case it should not be chosen), and it's never as important as the prescribed Birth Card. The Personality Card is the side that you show the outside world. This is not the real you—you can never get away from your Birth Card, but sometimes, if those people in your life are creating hardships for you and your own Spread is too difficult, it is better to operate under your Personality Card.

Men

A man may choose either the Jack or the King of his Birth Card suit under which to operate. In many cases, this may be a strengthening influence. The Jack represents mental attitudes; the King represents the personality side shown to the world.

If an individual falls in your sequence under your Personality Card, the relationship or association is never as close or as important as when it falls in your own Birth Card sequence.

READING YOUR PLANETARY SEQUENCE IN THE MUNDANE SPREAD

The Horizontal Line is read first; these relationships are the most important to you. The Vertical Line is read second, and the Diagonal Lines, third. Always read the Horizontal Line from *right to left*—the direction of the Planetary Sequence. Unless your Birth Card falls in the Vertical Neptune Line (extreme left of the Mundane Spread), your horizontal relationships will be divided between two lines.

The first card to the left of your Birth Card is your Mercury Card; the second is your Venus Card; the third is your Mars Card, etc., following the original design of the Seven Thunders (Seven Planets and their actual distances from the sun.

For example, if you are a Seven of Diamonds (Venus Card in the Venus Line), your first card (Mercury Card) will be the Five of Spades. The second card (Venus Card) will be the Jack of Hearts; the Nine of Clubs is your Mars Card.

A birthdate governed by the Queen of Hearts will jump up to the Crown Line and the first card (Mercury Card) will be the Ten of Clubs; the Venus

Card will be the Eight of Diamonds, the Mars Card is the King of Spades. Now, still reading from right to left, we go to the Mercury Line and the Three of Hearts becomes the Jupiter Card; the Saturn Card is the Ace of Clubs; the Uranus Card, the Queen of Clubs, and the Neptune Card, the Ten of Spades.

The Vertical Line is always read from your Birth Card up—and then from the bottom of the same line, up to the Birth Card. In this case, the Vertical Line of the Seven of Diamonds is the Venus Line. The Ace of Clubs would be in the Mercury Line to the Seven of Diamonds; the Four of Diamonds would be in the Neptune Line; the Jack of Clubs in the Uranus Line, etc. For the Queen of Hearts, the Jack of Diamonds is in the Uranus Line; the Five of Diamonds in the Saturn Line; the Ace of Diamonds is in the Jupiter Line, etc. All Birth Cards appearing in the Mars, Jupiter, and Saturn Vertical Lines must also include the three cards in the Crown Line in their sequence; these cards are power in their own right and can only enhance the life of the individual Birth Card.

The Diagonal Lines work differently in that all Cards in the Upper Diagonal Lines will affect your lives more than those in the lower Diagonal Lines—but each remains important in its own right. It is not unusual for a card to fall into two phases of your sequence; e.g., the King of Hearts is the Uranus Card in the Mercury Line to the Seven of Diamonds on the Horizontal Line, and also affects the Seven of Diamonds on the Diagonal Line by its position on the Mars and Mercury Lines. This places a double emphasis on all relationships with a King of Hearts—or any male Heart Birth Card who may be operating under the King.

Those whose birthdates correspond to your Mercury Card (or Mercury Line influence) will have a mental affiliation with you; to your Venus, an affectional or emotional; to your Mars, a stimulating or aggressive; to your Jupiter, a beneficial; to your Saturn, a limiting and restrictive, or a connection with illness; to your Uranus, a progressive, unusual, or undefinable; to your Neptune, an idealistic, confusing, mistaken, or psychic.

See from what angle others touch your life, and what you can do to keep the relationship positive and constructive.

Aces

Aces represent Desire. Man is an emotional animal. His feelings and desires constitute his first reactions. In the beginning, a howl of protest for having been born at all; next, a reaching out for something he desires.

This continues throughout his life, and the chief characteristic that distinguishes the individual "animal" from all others is the nature of his desires. This, *Your Place in the Cards* clearly defines.

    Hearts – Desire for Love
    Clubs – Desire for Knowledge
    Diamonds – Desire for Wealth
    Spades – Desire for Wisdom

Aces are ones–the Individual Self–the eternal *I am*. All Aces are concerned with their own Plan of Life. Through it they take the various initiations–on the emotional, mental, physical or spiritual planes.

Ace of Hearts

Hearts — Emotions
Ace of Hearts — Desire for Affection
One in Hearts — *I am* Love

The Uranus Card in the Jupiter Line. Displaces the **Ace of Diamonds** in the Natural Spread.

From the standpoint of numbers or numerology, Aces are ones. Always with Aces there are desires. This is a wish. This is concern with the individual self-expression. Actually, subconsciously or in the superconsciousness, this is the *I am*.

Hearts rule the home, emotions, friends, so with the Ace of Hearts, there is the desire for harmony. The Ace of Hearts is concerned with keeping harmony.

The original position of the Ace of Hearts in the Mundane Spread is the Uranus Card in the Jupiter Line, which displaces the Ace of Diamonds in the Natural Spread. This ensures a very close relationship between these two cards, and, if you check the Mundane Spread, you will find that the Ace of Diamonds is also the Mercury Card to the Ace of Hearts in the Horizontal Line. This accentuates or emphasizes the relationship, and the Mercury influence brings the qualities of the Ace of Diamonds into the open. It is also important to note that the Ace of Hearts position in the Original Plan, or the Natural Spread, was the beginning of all the calculations. The First Step. The Displacement Card for the Ace of Hearts in the *Mundane Spread* is the Three of Hearts. This displacement would give those bearers of the Ace of Hearts' card a certain amount of indecision and uncertainty about love, marriage, and children—family and affectional ties in general.

Planetary Sequence

			K♠	8♦	10♣			
A♠	3♦	5♣	10♠	Q♣	A♣	3♥		Mercury
2♥	9♠	9♣	J♥	5♠	7♦	7♥		Venus
8♣	J♠	2♦	4♣	6♥	K♦	K♥		Mars
A♦	A♥	8♠	10♦	10♥	4♠	6♦		Jupiter
Mercury								
5♦	7♣	9♥	3♠	3♣	5♥	Q♦		Saturn
	Neptune	Uranus	Saturn	Jupiter	Mars	Venus		
J♦	K♣	2♣	7♠	9♦	J♣	Q♠		Uranus
Q♥	6♠	6♣	8♥	2♠	4♦	4♥		Neptune

Neptune Uranus Saturn Jupiter Mars Venus Mercury

Mundane Spread

Although an Ace of Hearts desires harmony and peace, he also is conscious of money-emphasis. A desire to stand well with people. Money may be and often is desired for unselfish reasons, but these are overshadowed by the fact that this is an Ace. Number One. The Self. Motives may be less utilitarian than personal.

The Uranus position gives evidence that there is a desire for occult communication. But here again, owing to the Ace of Diamonds displacement card, it must be tangible and proven. And, as the Uranus Card in the Jupiter position, astrologically this is equivalent to a trine between Uranus and Jupiter—an individual who is concerned with Uranian things—a new order of thinking.

Inasmuch as there is only one birthdate for the Ace of Hearts and it is Capricorn, ruled by Saturn, this is a serious-minded person who can also be in conflict with himself because Saturn represents the old and well-established, while Uranus is the planet of progress—exactly contrary to Saturn. In this case an Ace of Hearts can be either very conservative, dogmatic and bigoted or extremely broad. It would depend on the environment and understanding of the individual as to how he would operate. These natives have a deep-seated desire for peace. They want protection, and it is always based on one desire—to stand well. Since Jupiter and Saturn are the planets of the soul and Jupiter actually rules the living, this is an Ace of Hearts who has been out in the Universe and who has a very humanitarian focus on life.

If a woman, the Personality Card of the Ace of Hearts is the Queen of Hearts. It is a mothering card—friendly, kind, warm and perhaps oversolicitous. On the negative side, flirtatious and not concerned with anything else. The Queen is also all Neptune (in the Mundane Spread), so there is mysticism or, negatively, insidious selfishness.

If a man, the Ace of Hearts' Personality Card could either be the King of Hearts or the Jack of Hearts. Operating under the King, the Ace of Hearts could be a good father but not necessarily a good husband. Under the Jack of Hearts, he could make sacrifices that would not necessarily be of benefit to his family or friends. It is always important to check the individual charts of the Personality Cards in order to determine if you—as an Ace of Hearts—are operating under your Personality Card rather than your Birth Card.

An Ace of Hearts wants comfort and is an ambitious person who is concerned with where he stands, in relationship to the rest of the world. Not necessarily commercially, but if he is in the commercial field, then the desire for money may well dominate him and his thinking. This is also a card of writers. And there is a decided interest in metaphysics, but sometimes the study of it brings disappointment. An Ace of Hearts is inclined to be secretive and actually does not talk too much. He talks on the surface for the most part. Travel is more unexpected than planned, and you can usually count on an Ace of Hearts having a dollar for a rainy day.

Ace of Hearts people do not like menial work. They don't want to get out and scrub, cook, do housework, mow lawns, or carry out the garbage. They are best suited as professional people.

BIRTHDATE RULED BY THE ACE OF HEARTS

DECEMBER 30–CAPRICORN–RULED BY SATURN

This is the only date ruled by the Ace of Hearts. Should avoid connection with illness, hospitals, etc. as a profession. Can succeed with land, real estate, products of the earth and under the earth. Should hold to well-established interests and not strive for innovations. Are good counselors and educators. Should avoid nagging.

ACE OF HEARTS–PLANETARY SEQUENCE OF PERSONAL RELATIONSHIPS

Horizontal Lines–Jupiter and Saturn

ACE OF DIAMONDS–MERCURY CARD IN THE NEPTUNE LINE
(Ace of Hearts Displacement Card)

You possess some of the same qualities and are inextricably tied to this native because of the displacement. Communications with Aces of Diamonds should be good–don't believe in all their business ventures, but know that if their goal is money, they will undoubtedly make it, and there can be some successful business ventures for you both. Romantically, this Ace is not recommended. You could be madly in love with each other, but if that's the case, neither one of you will be making a living. If you're both doing well financially, there won't be enough love left to keep a cinder glowing. A Karmic relationship in any event.

Ace of Diamonds birthdates: January 26, February 24, March 22, April 20, May 18, June 16, July 14, August 12, September 10, October 8, November 6, December 4

QUEEN OF DIAMONDS–VENUS CARD IN THE MERCURY LINE

There is a natural attraction to these natives, but you may find them a little too hard-nosed for your way of thinking. They have a great deal to offer you in strength and determination but are better suited for you in a not-so-close involvement.

Queen of Diamonds birthdates: January 15, February 13, March 11, April 9, May 7, June 5, July 3, August 1

FIVE OF HEARTS–MARS CARD IN THE VENUS LINE

You could meet this person while traveling–or decide to take a trip with him. Keep it that way. Any personal, romantic situation would almost certainly end in unhappiness and/or divorce. Five of Hearts natives will undoubtedly be stimulating to you, and the sex drive will tend to dominate, but keep a cool head. This person simply isn't for you.

Five of Hearts birthdates: October 30, November 28, December 26

THREE OF CLUBS–JUPITER CARD IN THE MARS LINE

This is a friend you will probably never quite understand. The basic difference is that you want to know where you stand, and this native is always uncertain of where he stands. This will cause aggravation to you. You can help Three of Clubs (especially after their twenty-seventh birthdays when they begin to feel a little more secure with themselves) by subtly introducing them to your own "new order of thinking" along the metaphysical line.

Three of Clubs birthdates: May 29, June 27, July 25, August 23, September 21, October 19, November 17, December 15

THREE OF SPADES–SATURN CARD IN THE JUPITER LINE

Here is another difficult situation for you, and yet you will feel drawn to this native. Don't feel masochistic—consider it as it really is—a Karmic tie. It's important to you to know these people to better understand yourself. An approach to this native on the metaphysical plane might be too difficult a problem for you. Try business ventures—Threes of Spades have a certain amount of protection in business, but be prepared to take charge of the situation if a headache keeps them from attending an all-important meeting. Romanticism is better forgotten.

Three of Spades birthdates: January 11, February 9, March 7, April 5, May 3, June 1

NINE OF HEARTS–URANUS CARD IN THE SATURN LINE
(Double Saturn Lines on the Diagonal)

A relationship with this person can only bring you disappointment after disappointment. Most of them coming after you had renewed your faith in your Nine of Hearts and suddenly he disappoints you again. The one exception (and it's a rare exception) might occur if you were ill and your problem difficult to diagnose. A Nine of Hearts doctor *might* be the one to come up with the answer. For the most part, take a pass on any kind of involvement.

Nine of Hearts birthdates: Ausust 30, September 28, October 26, November 24, December 22

SEVEN OF CLUBS–NEPTUNE CARD IN THE URANUS LINE
(Saturn Line on the Vertical)

You will feel opposition with this native. If you say "yes," this Seven of Clubs would say "no." Go easy—and remember, the Seven of Clubs is not for romance—for you.

Aces

Seven of Clubs birthdates: March 29, April 27, May 25, June 23, July 21, August 19, September 17, October 15, November 13, December 11

Vertical Line—Uranus

JACK OF SPADES—MARS LINE

This card has as its Displacement Card in the Natural Spread the Seven of Clubs, so many of the same problems that you would encounter with that native, you would encounter here. Some of the exceptions would be an understanding inherent to the Jack of Spades that would attract you, stimulate you, but probably ultimately irritate you. His values are not on the main line with yours, and they may seem to be a little too shiftless for your own ideas.

Jack of Spades birthdates: January 3, February 1

NINE OF SPADES—VENUS LINE

Here is one of the best romantic combinations you could find. When you find your Nine of Spades, encourage him to continue and keep up with his work, whatever it may be. He will have a tendency to drop everything if this match between the two of you is struck. If he forgets his work, he may ultimately forget you. Remember this. These natives have the power to overcome their problems (which sometimes seem to be many), and they will always appreciate flowers and candles for a late dinner or a barefoot walk on a warm moonlit beach. A long and happy love life is almost assured if you keep yourself and your Nine of Spades on a positive plane.

Nine of Spades birthdates: January 5, February 3, March 1

THREE OF DIAMONDS—MERCURY LINE

Stimulation might be the key word here. This native might be able to give you ideas that you could go out and commercialize, but don't necessarily expect him to, and try not to get locked into a close involvement. Better to use the ideas and pay him a royalty than be subjected to a day-to-day relationship. Nix on romance—you probably wouldn't be his first—or last—spouse.

Three of Diamonds birthdates: January 24, February 22, March 20, April 18, May 16, June 14, July 12, August 10, September 8, October 6, November 4, December 2

SIX OF SPADES—NEPTUNE LINE

Avoid romance here, even though it seems to be there—and seems to be comfortable. These are interesting people for you to know, and they can be most fulfilling in your quest for metaphysical knowledge; they will keep you

29

going when you may want to give up prematurely. They have this kind of gift. But living together is something else. Your inborn need for some form of materialism will not fit into their lifestyle. Recognize the relationship and enjoy it for what it really is.

Six of Spades birthdates: January 8, February 6, March 4, April 2

KING OF CLUBS—URANUS LINE

This is an unavoidable relationship that could turn into a long and lasting one. You will find many things to be learned from this native, and you will never cease to be surprised, for both good and ill. The involvement is not without problems, but most of them will probably emanate from you. This native will test and strengthen your good points—but he will also bring out your negative side. Learn to discredit and discard this negativity, and happiness can be found on some level with a King of Clubs.

King of Clubs birthdates: January 14, February 12, March 10, April 8, May 6, June 4, July 2

SEVEN OF CLUBS—SATURN LINE: SEE HORIZONTAL LINE

Diagonal Lines

EIGHT OF CLUBS—MARS AND NEPTUNE LINES

A dynamic friendship can be found with this native, who possesses a great flow of ideas. Don't give in to a feeling of being argumentative because he seems to know more than you. He probably does. Use this relationship in a totally positive manner; the Eight of Clubs may be able to tell you things of which others have only dreamed.

Eight of Clubs birthdates: March 28, April 26, May 24, June 22, July 20, August 18, September 16, October 14, November 12, December 10

NINE OF HEARTS—DOUBLE SATURN LINES: SEE HORIZONTAL LINE

SEVEN OF SPADES—URANUS AND JUPITER LINES

You may fall in love with this person before you're aware of it yourself, and by no means will you be disappointed. But keep a watchful eye. The problem you both may encounter will concern your individual values. Though the Seven of Spades' search is probably on another plane, you are essentially seeking and wanting similar material things. If you are not financially comfortable together, you should be. You are both capable, so re-evaluate your approaches. Money and love can never be denied either of you, so go after what you want.

Seven of Spades birthdates: January 7, February 5, March 3, April 1

TWO OF SPADES—NEPTUNE AND MARS LINES

This is *not* someone for you, romantically. These natives will seem to drag you down and dump all their problems in your lap and then turn around and probably be angry with you for not understanding them better. You will feel a great deal of energy and drive coming from them, but you will feel it is misdirected for the most part. Hold your temper—just try not to spend too much time around this native.

Two of Spades birthdates: January 12, February 10, March 8, April 6, May 4, June 2

FIVE OF DIAMONDS—SATURN AND NEPTUNE LINES

You will find this native easy to talk to when you're discussing money. You both know pretty much what you're talking about. Be aware that the Five of Diamonds has another facet to his diamond that he may not wish to show you. If you're romantically inclined to this native (which is not necessarily recommended), you should pursue this other side. It could lead to metaphysical discussions, in which you, yourself, have had some interest. Business with these natives could be very good—but double-check all deals and contracts to make sure they are as represented.

Five of Diamonds birthdates: January 22, February 20, March 18, April 16, May 14, June 12, July 10, August 8, September 6, October 4, November 2

TWO OF DIAMONDS—MARS AND SATURN LINES

If you were the leader of a debate team, this native would be a worthy opponent. And be prepared to lose. This relationship could be very good for business (if you're on the same side, of course—and disastrous for love. If you need a nurse or a doctor, a Two of Diamonds would be your best choice.

Two of Diamonds birthdates: January 25, February 23, March 21, April 19, May 17, June 15, July 13, August 11, September 9, October 7, November 5, December 3

JACK OF HEARTS—VENUS AND JUPITER LINES

Here is that irresistible "someone." And if it were any other card in the pack, it might be an idealistic love affair or marriage forever. That doesn't mean to say that it can't be so with the Jack of Hearts. The "cross" formed with the Jack of Hearts—if you'll check the Mundane Spread, you'll see that not only is it a fixed (not displaced) card, but it lies directly in the center of the "cross"—signifies impersonal love. So this card probably cannot give you the personal love that *you* require. The natives who are not operating through an impersonal love are often too irresponsible and thoughtless for you to tolerate for too long. You'll love this person—but know what's in store for you, and remember—it's your choice.

Jack of Hearts birthdates: July 30, August 28, October 24, November 22, December 20.

QUEEN OF CLUBS—MERCURY AND MARS LINES

If this native is your lawyer, you have probably picked the best counselor available to you at any time or place. He is dynamic, forceful and able to put his point across. These traits are, of course, good for any other profession, but especially law. A personal friendship would be exciting with this native, but perhaps a little wearisome to you. And as far as romance is concerned—find it somewhere else.

Queen of Clubs birthdates: January 28, February 26, March 24, April 22, May 20, June 18, July 16, August 14, September 12, October 10, November 8, December 6

ACE OF HEARTS FAMOUS BIRTHDATES

December 30   Sandy Koufax
        Rudyard Kipling

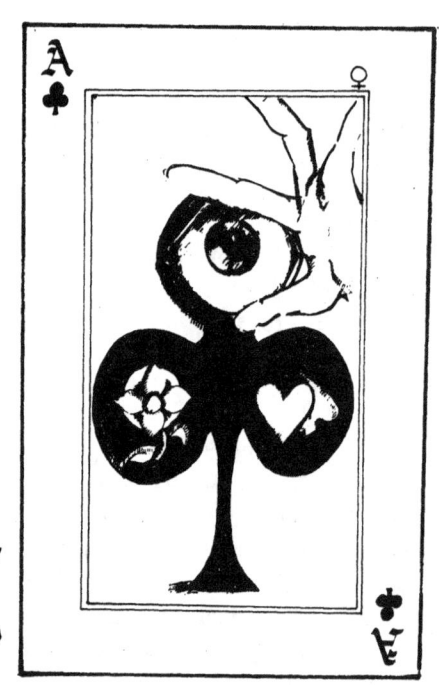

Ace of Clubs

Planetary Sequence

				K♠	8♦	10♣	
A♠	3♦	5♣	10♠	Q♣	A♣	3♥	Mercury
Saturn	Jupiter	Mars	Venus	Mercury			
2♥	9♠	9♣	J♥	5♠	7♦	7♥	Venus
					Neptune	Uranus	
8♣	J♠	2♦	4♣	6♥	K♦	K♥	Mars
A♦	A♥	8♠	10♦	10♥	4♠	6♦	Jupiter
5♦	7♣	9♥	3♠	3♣	5♥	Q♦	Saturn
J♦	K♣	2♣	7♠	9♦	J♣	Q♠	Uranus
Q♥	6♠	6♣	8♥	2♠	4♦	4♥	Neptune
Neptune	Uranus	Saturn	Jupiter	Mars	Venus	Mercury	

Mundane Spread

Clubs — Mental Attitudes
Ace of Clubs — Desire for Knowledge
One in Clubs — *I am* Intelligence

The Venus Card in the Mercury Line. Displaces the **Two of Hearts** in the Natural Spread.

In addition to an insatiable thirst for knowledge, the association with the Two of Hearts gives these people a desire for union (two) with one who is emotionally compatible. These two cards are so bound together that at no time do they fail to be associated. They want to know the reasons for relationships with people—their attractions and repulsions, and they want love (as the Venus Card) for their hearts as well as knowledge for their brains.

In the Natural Spread the true position for the Ace of Clubs is the Neptune Card in the Venus Line. Here is introduced the idealistic element so characteristic of Aces of Clubs. They are always looking for the "soul mate"; they believe true marriages are made in heaven. In the midst of their yearnings, however, they never forget to use their minds—and here is where the conflict comes in.

Because of their desire to know, they seek many channels of expression. If they find one that is satisfactory, they will stay with it and improve it; if not, they will soon abandon it and seek something else.

The Ace of Clubs is a better card for a man than a woman. If undeveloped, the women become busybodies and gossip-mongers—or flirtatious, even promiscuous, until the right mate is found; after that, they are usually faithful to the end. The women have masculine minds and are often so dominated by them that the emotional life is not satisfied and men are repelled. Both sexes have splendid brains. Both are restless and demand a change if a rut seems likely or interest wanes.

Usually there are ample funds at these natives' disposal. They either inherit money or make considerable amounts through their own efforts. They are capable of attaining wonderful results, but the Mercury influence inclines them to pass on quickly, once their objectives are established. With the Mercury Line and the Venus position and Neptune in the True Place, Aces of Clubs are always subject to an elusive ideal to which they must apply their wits and ingenuity.

They are highly emotional, often temperamental. Their illnesses are hard to diagnose because they are affected by their emotions. Physical disturbances are either chronic or unusual. They should strive to build up a strong physique and maintain good mental balance.

The early or middle years are usually the best unless they prepare for their material security and search for truth as eagerly as they do for knowledge. Spirituality is not outstanding, but it can—and should—be cultivated. They desire to know all causes and have a keen curiosity about what makes the Universe "tick," but they never find their answers in orthodox religion and are rather fearful (because of the Two of Hearts displacement) of adopting Universal Love.

Aces

BIRTHDATES RULED BY THE ACE OF CLUBS

MAY 31–GEMINI–RULED BY MERCURY

Apt students. Learn fast. Work hard mentally if interested, but not otherwise. Witty; quick at repartee. Good reporters, news commentators, correspondents. Not attracted to salesmanship. Prefer to talk or make contacts. Good at statistics, census data. If work is boring, will seek escape. Must have home roots but are wanderers. Need many changes in environment, variety. Like to make frequent changes of furniture. Change their minds about people. Can write, talk or promote but require change of subject. If a man, will go further when working under the King of Clubs, using the Ace of Clubs in combination. A woman working under the Queen of Clubs will be doubly undecided about people.

JUNE 29–CANCER–RULED BY THE MOON

Too mystical to be practical; imagination overdeveloped. Need a firm hand in youth to curb erratic tendencies. Dwell in the past and refer everything to it. Need strong home roots and understanding associations. Should learn to serve and get away from self. Interests usually confined to a narrow circle. Usually have strong psychic power. Need a business that is definite but does not require responsibility. Lack ability to concentrate. Music a fine outlet when emotionally disturbed. Color sense accurate and good. Public spirited and willing to work for causes–public health, civic improvement, welfare. Usually more successful in public services than in business. Cannot sustain long, drawn-out effort.

JULY 27–LEO–RULED BY THE SUN

Want to live well and associate with people of importance. Not always contented because of strong drive for power. Are generous and open-hearted. Should have own business or be in undisputed authority. Usually have one great love affair–often secret. People very important but want to escape from home ties. Must be careful to keep the reputation unassailable. Successful in merchandising. Also make good lawyers, art dealers, theatrical directors. If artistically gifted, are good sculptors and can commercialize their work. There may be a tendency to "rule or ruin" which must be checked. Should guard against developing a condescending manner and a superiority complex.

AUGUST 25–VIRGO–RULED BY MERCURY

Highly intellectual. Interested in laboratory work and research. Good technicians. Attracted to botany and forestry, from a scientific angle. Experiment with chemicals, compounds and combinations, especially for soil and gardens. Skilled in X-rays. Should cultivate breadth of vision; easily become narrow and negative in thinking. Inclined to work for others rather than run own business. Interested in brains—but not as psychiatrists.

SEPTEMBER 23—VIRGO OR LIBRA—RULED BY MERCURY OR VENUS

This birthdate may fall under either of these signs but is influenced by both. Want professional success but often interfere with it through their own emotions. Self-indulgent; like ease and comfort and may be lazy. Deal successfully with women. Have pleasing personalities; popular. Cannot save money but keep enough to be comfortable. May become interested in law but take nothing too seriously. If finances become stringent, may worry themselves into illness. Require change, activity and self-expression. Emotions play a vital part. Love art but cannot commercialize it. Live on the physical plane; grow younger with the years. Are clever at adapting ideas of others. Do well in partnerships. Interested in travel. Can throw off trouble.

OCTOBER 21—LIBRA—RULED BY VENUS

Have more talent than September 23 and can commercialize their work. Apt to change occupation after thirty. Are truthful, but secretive. Can manage to sublimate disappointment and grow from the experience. Open to enlightenment, which brings peace of mind. Homes often broken up through outside interference. May travel for a living. Make good friends. Cater to the opposite sex; expressive and convincing. Successful in an artistic career—singing, dancing, music, acting. Good at lecturing. Should cultivate self-discipline to overcome obstacles. Subject to overturning of plans.

NOVEMBER 19—SCORPIO—RULED BY MARS

Versatile. Successful in many different lines. Dissatisfied, restless, aspiring; always seeking. Fixed in ideas, despite urge for enlightenment. Skeptical but optimistic. Ask and give no quarter. Interested in business on a large scale. Like to tackle problems, institute improvements and reforms. When all is running smoothly, lost interest. Dislike interference, criticism—unless self-inflicted. Long for peace of heart; expect to find it through love but are often disappointed. Clever with tools. Will disregard own health if service needed or work to be done. Highly magnetic; can persuade or convince others of anything. Wide choice of occupation.

DECEMBER 17—SAGITTARIUS—RULED BY JUPITER

Nervous and impatient. Unsettled about business; find it difficult to choose one that is congenial. Subject to fluctuations, usually due to outside conditions. Better in merchandising than manufacturing. Despite insecurity, make enough money to get along. Seek partnership but are not secure in it. Natural financiers. Should strive to be practical and level-headed—not eccentric. Can succeed in real estate, produce business, timberlands, livestock. Fond of horses and may be connected with them. Good travel agents. Should cultivate strict honesty. Have periods of spending and saving. Dislike the beaten track. Take their pleasures away from home.

ACE OF CLUBS—PLANETARY SEQUENCE OF PERSONAL RELATIONSHIPS

Horizontal Lines—Mercury and Venus

QUEEN OF CLUBS—MERCURY CARD IN THE MARS LINE

There is apt to be an immediate feeling of unfriendly competition if this person is a man; if a woman, you may feel she comes on a little too strong; both lack of experience as far as you're concerned, but you should have a respect for their judgment. It's usually reliable.   Queen of Clubs birthdates: January 28, February 26, April 22, May 20, June 18, July 16, August 14, September 12, October 10, November 8, December 6

TEN OF SPADES—VENUS CARD IN THE JUPITER LINE

A good chance for a great love affair including marriage. Watch out that your lady Ten of Spades doesn't lapse into a routine of cooking and cleaning, and forget you. If a man, the opposite could happen: his business may take full charge of him and *he* might forget. These natives can give you the love you want and need. Just keep giving them a nudge when they seem to fall into a mediocre style of living.

Ten of Spades birthdates: January 4, February 2

FIVE OF CLUBS—MARS CARD IN THE SATURN LINE

You might have the urge to *be* this person or have the energy to go out and do something about your own life after meeting this individual, but don't go running off without the facts. The truth is, you'll find the Five of Clubs too restless as opposed to too busy, too skeptical as opposed to too probing, and too insecure for you to identify with him in any way. You will appreciate those who specialize in a particular profession, but their constant changes (in work and love) will be an irritating factor. Not a recommended relationship—especially romantic.

Five of Clubs birthdates: March 31, April 29, May 27, June 25, July 23, August 21, September 19, October 17, November 15, December 13

THREE OF DIAMONDS–JUPITER CARD IN THE URANUS LINE

A good native for work; his insecurity and worry will drive him forward in business, thus helping your own drive for success. Only good things can come from this involvement, and don't be surprised if love is one of them—although there are better combinations for you.

Three of Diamonds birthdates: January 24, February 22, March 20, April 18, May 16, June 14, July 12, August 10, September 8, October 6, November 4, December 2

ACE OF SPADES–SATURN CARD IN THE NEPTUNE LINE

You may feel you can't believe anything this native says—or that he doesn't know what he's talking about. Because of this aura of distrust, you will definitely know that the relationship is not worth the price. It's Karmic, so it's inevitable at some level—just keep trusting your own good intuition and work it out on a positive plane.

Ace of Spades birthdates: January 13, February 11, March 9, April 7, June 3, July 1

SEVEN OF HEARTS–URANUS CARD IN THE MERCURY LINE
(Venus and Mercury Lines on the Diagonal)

This native could stimulate you by his work and progress; you will like his charm, but it would be better to steer clear of a personal involvement. You could be "swept off your feet" only to be disenchanted by this native's suspicion and jealousies, or so it seems. And it probably will be so. Sooner or later that "caged" feeling will ruin whatever relationship you might have had.

Seven of Hearts birthdates: September 30, October 28, November 26, December 24

SEVEN OF DIAMONDS–NEPTUNE CARD IN THE VENUS LINE
(Venus Line on the Vertical)

This could be an idealistic situation for you, in love and work, but these natives will keep you hopping to keep up with both. A Seven of Diamonds' need for love can fulfill your desire if you can meet and sustain your relationship on some kind of middle ground, satisfactory to you both. For good or ill, you may tend to paint a picture of this native (Neptunian influence) that may not in fact, be fact. Enjoy the surprises, illusions and love he has to offer you.

Seven of Diamonds birthdates: January 20, February 18, March 16, April 14, May 12, June 10, July 8, August 6, September 4, October 2

Aces

Vertical Line—Venus

FOUR OF DIAMONDS—NEPTUNE LINE

Here is probably a quick meeting that will not turn out as expected. But don't necessarily give up. Communications are good, and you will have more insight when the affair or friendship seems to be in the past.

Four of Diamonds birthdates: January 23, February 21, March 19, April 17, May 15, June 13, July 11, August 9, September 7, October 5, November 3, December 1

JACK OF CLUBS—URANUS LINE

A romantic interest that will intrigue you even more after you get to know them. Knowledgeable, active and outgoing—everything that you essentially like. Good for business and friendship, but be careful in the romance department. The probability is that once you're closely involved, you won't see this native so often. He cannot supply your need for love, so don't wear your heart on your sleeve or you'll lose it—in vain.

Jack of Clubs birthdates: January 29, February 27, March 25, April 23, May 21, June 19, July 17, August 15, September 13, October 11, November 9, December 7

FIVE OF HEARTS—SATURN LINE

Not a good match in your personal life. These people are too unsettled emotionally for you and too forceful in what you may think are the wrong directions for business, as well. At best it would take a lot of effort to make anything positive out of this combination.

Five of Hearts birthdates: October 30, November 28, December 26

FOUR OF SPADES—JUPITER LINE

This person could be "the one"—the soul-mate you seek. Try not to dissuade him from his own knowledge; he usually knows what it is he has to do. A good work relationship as well. Fours of Spades have the minds you admire so much. The love department may not be as passionate as you may have visualized, but they will see that you have everything else. A definite *yes* in any kind of involvement.

Four of Spades birthdates: January 10, February 8, March 6, April 4, May 2

KING OF DIAMONDS—MARS LINE

These people are on a materialistic trip as far as you're concerned, and, therefore, you may find them on the obnoxious side. Don't turn your back on the possibility of business. You don't have to love someone to make money with him. Trust these natives' financial judgment; they rarely make mistakes. But also make sure of your own position in the business arrangement and that everything is defined on paper. You may need it.

King of Diamonds birthdates: January 14, February 12, March 10, April 8, May 6, June 4, July 2

SEVEN OF DIAMONDS—URANUS CARD IN THE VENUS LINE: SEE HORIZONTAL LINE

Diagonal Lines

FIVE OF SPADES—VENUS AND MARS LINES

This could be a fast love affair that quickly falls into a rut. Ultimately you will not like the changes that these people will try to inflict upon you, but they might make good traveling companions for short trips. Don't look for anything long-term; *you* will not want to sustain the relationship.

Five of Spades birthdates: January 9, February 7, March 5, April 3, May 1

FOUR OF CLUBS—MARS AND JUPITER LINES

You could fall in love with this person only to find that his own state of discontentment may create arguments between the two of you. You'll like his verbal ability, but you'll also think he talks too much. Even when the subject is interesting, it will be overkill to you.

Four of Clubs birthdates: April 30, May 28, June 26, July 24, August 22, September 20, October 18, November 16, December 14

EIGHT OF SPADES—JUPITER AND SATURN LINES

This native will take care of you, sometimes whether you want it or not. (Secretary, nurse, etc.) You'll appreciate his strength and stamina but not necessarily approve of his way. But accept it anyway. He won't hurt you—unless you try to marry him.

Eight of Spades birthdates: January 6, February 4, March 2

SEVEN OF CLUBS—JUPITER CARD IN THE SATURN AND URANUS LINES

This is a good friend who can inspire you and others. It will seem discouraging to have to stand by and watch him plunge into an unwise investment, but you'll understand. Enjoy the good things that can and will come of this relationship, and though it sometimes seems burdensome, live through the many little surprises that the Seven of Clubs tends to spring on you. They're mostly good.

Seven of Clubs birthdates: March 29, April 27, May 25, June 23, July 21, August 19, September 17, October 15

JACK OF DIAMONDS—URANUS AND NEPTUNE LINES

You will feel confused, never knowing whether this native is judging you (and others) for what you can do for him, or whether he actually likes you. Chances are it will seem to be the latter, but don't count on it, until this native is past thirty-five years of age. Before this, he is usually trying to keep up with the Joneses and probably wanting your friendship for what he can get.

Jack of Diamonds birthdates: January 16, February 14, March 12, April 10, May 8, June 6, July 4, August 2

TEN OF CLUBS—CROWN LINE

You will admire but probably not be overly fond of these people. And this is a shame because they have much to offer you. Communication with this native should be good, though sometimes irritating. This could be a sign of your own immaturity. Know that he is a knowledgeable human being and can bring this knowledge to you and others—with great passion. On anything personal, pass.

Ten of Clubs birthdates: January 30, February 28, March 26, April 24, May 22, June 20, July 18, August 16, September 14, October 12, November 10, December 8

SEVEN OF HEARTS—VENUS AND MERCURY LINES: SEE HORIZONTAL LINE

ACE OF CLUBS FAMOUS BIRTHDATES

May 31	Walt Whitman
	Don Ameche
	Joe Namath
	Prince Rainier III
July 27	Leo Durocher
August 25	Sean Connery
	George C. Wallace
	Leonard Bernstein

Your Place in the Cards

September 23	Ray Charles
	Mickey Rooney
November 19	Dick Cavett
	President James Garfield
December 17	Erskine Caldwell
	Arthur Fiedler
	Ludwig van Beethoven
	John Greenleaf Whittier

Planetary Sequence

			K♠	8♦	10♣		
A♠	3♦	5♣	10♠	Q♣	A♣	3♥	Mercury
2♥	9♠	9♣	J♥	5♠	7♦	7♥	Venus
8♣	J♠	2♦	4♣	6♥	K♦	K♥	Mars
A♦	A♥	8♠	10♦	10♥	4♠	6♦	Jupiter
5♦	7♣	9♥	3♠	3♣	5♥	Q♦	Saturn
Neptune	Uranus	Saturn	Jupiter	Mars	Venus	Mercury	
J♦	K♣	2♣	7♠	9♦	J♣	Q♠	Uranus
Q♥	6♠	6♣	8♥	2♠	4♦	4♥	Neptune

Neptune • Uranus • Saturn • Jupiter • Mars • Venus • Mercury

Mundane Spread

Your Place in the Cards

Diamonds —Values
Ace of Diamonds —Desire for Money
One in Diamonds —*I am* Worth

The Neptune Card in the Jupiter Line. Displaces the **Two of Diamonds** in the Natural Spread.

This Ace's association with the Two of Diamonds creates a conflict between the ideals and the practical values.

In the Natural Spread the position of the Ace of Diamonds is the Uranus Card in the Jupiter Line—values, yes, but their rightful place is found through higher guidance and the cultivation of intuition. Emotions from the Two of Diamonds play a large part in this Ace's life, and it becomes a race between love and money. One—not both—must win first place, so if love becomes absorbing, money flies out the window, and vice versa.

In either event, contacts are important, likewise secrecy in connection with associations, either business or personal. Ambition often dominates, and then the emotions are sure to suffer. In general, this is a card of sorrow that is usually hidden, because of the Two of Diamonds displacement. The entire sequence falls in the Saturn Line, bespeaking a life of obstacles and difficulties—Karmic debts. The positive natives learn to overcome their handicaps and develop strong minds and firm purpose; the negatives usually knuckle under and submit to failure.

The early years will count most for development and future success. If wisdom is cultivated and the value of love realized, peace of mind may be secured before these natives reach thirty years of age. Experiences come into the life, even in the early years, that requires strength of character to handle successfully. If personal ambition or a false sense of values is dominant, seeds are sown early for defeat—in love, in marriage, and in business.

This is a safer and easier card for a man than for a woman. The man can always choose to operate under the Jack of Diamonds or the King of Diamonds, but the woman has no other choice than the Queen of Diamonds, her Mercury Card in the Mercury Line. Her mental reactions are too quick and ill-considered; her natural ambitions are too easily thwarted; and her eagerness to project herself (from ulterior motives) too likely to meet with insurmountable obstacles.

BIRTHDATES RULED BY THE ACE OF DIAMONDS

JANUARY 26—AQUARIUS—RULED BY URANUS

Should avoid dealings in real estate. Need an occupation which gives freedom of action and promises adequate returns. Make good investment counselors, investigators, manufacturers of electrical machinery, managers of travel bureaus, especially air travel, research specialists in science or medicine.

Drawn to psychicism but develop an antagonism toward it, being unwilling to persist in investigation. Work better for others than themselves.

FEBRUARY 24—PISCES—RULED BY NEPTUNE
Interested in oils, chemicals, and drugs. Usually make less and spend more than is figured on. Prefer a business connected with water or travel. Could represent oil interests or deal in cosmetics and perfumes. Are more inclined to service than the other Ace of Diamonds birthdays.

MARCH 22—ARIES—RULED BY MARS
Through indecision and doubt make many unnecessary and unfortunate changes. Should avoid law and politics as professions. These people have a considerable store of knowledge, but do not always know what to do with it. Can succeed at architecture and building. These people have come to be humanitarians but are often too self-concerned to devote their lives to it. Should restrain their nervousness, impetuousness and irritability. They have an unusual amount of power but are unpredictable in their use of it. Should guard against a tendency to be dictatorial and self-important.

APRIL 20—ARIES OR TAURUS—RULED BY MARS OR VENUS
Here lie progressive ideas and strong creative ability. These people need contacts and are successful with them. Any musical ability should be cultivated, if not as a profession, then as a hobby. The greatest success is found in fields which give service. Subject to frequent changes in life. Never sure of people and apt to have burdens in connection with them as soon as the relationship becomes personal. Can manage shops that handle artistic and beautiful things; can lecture, preach, teach, or act. Should learn to conquer dissatisfaction and rise above burdens.

MAY 18—TAURUS—RULED BY VENUS
Make friends easily, but marriage with these people is apt to be a gamble, since they sometimes marry for reasons of expediency. Money is an important factor. Can succeed at interior decorating, clothes designing, textiles, and weaving. They are more patient, faithful, and affectionate than many of the Aces of Diamonds.

JUNE 16—GEMINI—RULED BY MERCURY
Should be allowed freedom of movement in any occupation—no routine desk job, but work best in a well-ordered and well-organized business. Are good personnel directors or hotel managers. Can become valuable secretaries

or aides in a medical or dental office. The women are apt to be too positive and self-centered and should guard against abusing their position. They love luxury and money. If psychic gifts are evident, they should not be commercialized; if they are, the power is lost. Both sexes are wary of marriage but want its protection. Are quick-witted and entertaining.

JULY 14–CANCER–RULED BY THE MOON

Sensitive, nervous, self-indulgent—often lazy. Make too frequent changes, usually due to discontent. For accomplishment, they are lacking in stability. Urge for diversion scatters forces which could be turned to good account. They are ambitious but dislike the hard work that could realize ambitions. Are best adapted to an occupation that keeps them on the move: traveling salesman, agent, demonstrator. Can succeed as trial lawyers or in any line of work connected with food, supplies or home commodities—*if* it is sufficiently varied.

AUGUST 12–LEO–RULED BY THE SUN

Make good actors, writers, or agents for advertising and publishing concerns. Love display and carry an air of prosperity. Have lively imaginations and can commercialize them. Are magnetic and popular. If a woman, most of her earnings are spent on clothes and "front"—and the men are not far behind in this respect. They consider the show of poverty a disgrace. Are proud and protective, sometimes generous. Willing to work in projects for civic welfare—but want credit for it.

SEPTEMBER 10–VIRGO–RULED BY MERCURY

A very exacting birthdate. These people are sensitive and intuitive, have high standards of honesty, and insist that others live up to them. Make able leaders, commanders, and technicians, also good office managers and confidential secretaries. Clever at raising money for causes. Have a sense of loneliness. Should cultivate some talent as a sideline and outlet.

OCTOBER 8–LIBRA–RULED BY VENUS

Can convert anything into money. Their efforts must produce tangible results, or they will abandon them. They love beauty but want evidence of its costliness. They should be in the countryside part of the year. The personality is attractive and friendly. They are generous in giving to projects or institutions—not to individuals. Have considerable magnetic power and should be careful to use it constructively. Make good lawyers, counselors, managers, department heads, or agents. Will go far if engaged in work where personality counts. The women usually have good looks and make excellent models.

NOVEMBER 6—SCORPIO—RULED BY MARS

This birthdate has two major fears: being obliged to live in the poorhouse or with their children. Money is important as a bulwark against these possibilities. Pride is strong—also a love of independence. Often lack inner resources and hate to be alone; women often great flirts. If developed, have much power and magnetism. Will not take orders or endure criticism. Attracted to sculpture (all art forms) and the theatre. Good leaders, commanders, practitioners.

DECEMBER 4—SAGITTARIUS—RULED BY JUPITER

Men of this birthdate are apt to be dominated by their wives or mothers. Make good managers—away from home. Can succeed in real estate. Are good organizers, especially in a large business. Usually suffer in the love life—but in silence. Are often found as musicians, especially in technique. Are nervous and overstimulated. Should avoid alcohol and all other stimulants.

ACE OF DIAMONDS—PLANETARY SEQUENCE OF PERSONAL RELATIONSHIPS

Horizontal Line—Saturn

QUEEN OF DIAMONDS—MERCURY CARD IN THE MERCURY LINE

If you are a woman, you will identify with this person (your Personality Card), but with either sex you will find it difficult to have an involved relationship of any kind, for his problems will seem to equal yours, therefore making it hard for you to be of help to each other.

Queen of Diamonds birthdates: January 15, February 13, March 11, April 9, May 7, June 5, July 3, August 1

FIVE OF HEARTS—VENUS CARD IN THE VENUS LINE

A love affair with this person is almost inevitable, but in the long run it will only bring unhappiness. You both share a common hang-up: love or money, but seldom both at the same time.

Five of Hearts birthdates: October 30, November 28, December 26

THREE OF CLUBS—MARS CARD IN THE MARS LINE

This would be a frustrating situation for you, and about as easy as pushing a steam roller uphill. Negative on a close personal involvement if possible. If not, develop your muscles.

Three of Clubs birthdates: May 29, June 27, July 25, August 23, September 21, October 19, November 17, December 15

THREE OF SPADES—JUPITER CARD IN THE JUPITER LINE

You will be automatically drawn to these people, but you probably will feel that they don't do well enough financially for you. For a meaningful relationship, you must understand that their set of values may be different.

Three of Spades birthdates: January 11, February 9, March 7, April 5, May 3, June 1

NINE OF HEARTS—SATURN CARD IN THE SATURN LINE

This is probably one of the worst combinations in the pack for you. Nines of Hearts will expect more from you than you are probably able to give. If they are doing well financially, the kind of love that you will want from them will be practically nil. Take a pass if you can, although you may not be able to. In friendship, they will probably dump all their problems on you, expecting you to understand; do your best—but avoid them as much as possible.

Nine of Hearts birthdates: August 30, September 28, October 26, November 24, December 22

SEVEN OF CLUBS—URANUS CARD IN THE URANUS LINE
(Saturn and Uranus Lines on the Diagonal)

You will appreciate the activity connected with this person; he may keep you too confused and nervous, however, to produce a healthy personal friendship, but he certainly will make an interesting friend.

Seven of Clubs birthdates: March 29, April 27, May 25, June 23, July 21, August 19, September 17, October 15, November 13, December 11

FIVE OF DIAMONDS—NEPTUNE CARD IN THE NEPTUNE LINE
(Saturn Line on the Vertical)

This person may be too wrapped up in himself and his problems to give you the love you need. Although there will be ups and downs, he will provide financially, if you are willing to pay the price that goes with it. Be sure to evaluate these natives properly, and don't rely on first impressions.

Five of Diamonds birthdates: January 22, February 20, March 18, April 16, May 14, June 12, July 10, August 8, September 6, October 4, November 2

Vertical Line—Neptune

EIGHT OF CLUBS—MARS LINE

This person is your teacher. Though information may come in spurts and you may not always agree, it will still be knowledge to which you might never have had access otherwise. Listen and learn. A personal relationship might be irritating.

Eight of Clubs birthdates: March 28, April 26, May 24, June 22, July 20, August 18, September 16, October 14, November 12, December 10

TWO OF HEARTS—VENUS LINE

A dynamite relationship could result with this person—except that just when you think everything is fine, your Two of Hearts will start to get cold feet. This doesn't mean that the affection has cooled, only that skepticism has set in. The Two of Hearts wants the relationship as much as you, but it will be up to you to make it happen.

Two of Hearts birthdate: December 29

ACE OF SPADES—MERCURY LINE

You will not have much patience with this person. You have your own Crosses to bear and will not be able to tolerate too many of his. If you are interested and/or involved in metaphysics, this native could be a real challenge for you.

Ace of Spades birthdates: January 13, February 11, March 9, April 7, May 5, June 3, July 1

QUEEN OF HEARTS—NEPTUNE LINE

If you are a man, you will like this lady. She may not turn out to be everything you want in a woman, but her charm will compensate. If you are a lady and the Queen of Hearts is a man, you will probably think he is weak and not facing up to reality.

Queen of Hearts birthdates: July 29, August 27, September 25, October 23, November 21, December 19

JACK OF DIAMONDS—URANUS LINE

These people work very hard for everything they get, and you will and a woman with a pushy drive. Either situation will probably turn you off eventually.

Jack of Diamonds birthdates: January 16, February 14, March 12, April 10, May 8, June 6, July 4, August 2

FIVE OF DIAMONDS—SATURN LINE: SEE HORIZONTAL LINE

Diagonal Lines

JACK OF SPADES—MARS AND URANUS LINES

This could be a difficult relationship, for it may prove to be hard for you to understand what makes this person tick. Inasmuch as you are essentially traveling different roads, being together may prove to be discomforting for you.

Jack of Spades birthdates: January 3, February 1

NINE OF CLUBS—VENUS AND SATURN LINES

You will like and appreciate this person. His ability to buy things that he doesn't need may be disturbing to you, and you may feel that he extends his charm a little too freely. But if you are willing to enter into a relationship knowing these things, the end result could be very good for you.

Nine of Clubs birthdates: January 31, February 29, May 27, April 25, May 23, June 21, July 19, August 17, September 15, October 13, November 11, December 9

TEN OF SPADES—MERCURY AND JUPITER LINES

A romantic involvement with this native would be almost impossible for you. When he is doing well in business, you will have little or no home life and vice versa. As a friend, he will be able to give you good judgment, so stick with a platonic involvement, if possible.

Ten of Spades birthdates: January 4, February 2

TEN OF CLUBS—CROWN AND MARS LINE

Stubbornness will be the only problem you'll encounter with these people. You will tend to want to push them, but it's not necessary. They'll get there, and with you—if your frustrations hold out.

Ten of Clubs birthdates: January 30, February 28, March 26, April 24, May 22, June 20, July 18, August 16, September 14, October 12, November 10, December 8

SEVEN OF CLUBS—SATURN AND URANUS LINES: SEE HORIZONTAL LINE

TWO OF CLUBS—URANUS AND SATURN LINES

You will like this person, but your life will probably have to be completely rearranged in order to create a romantic situation. And it still will probably not be comfortable. Walk cautiously. It will not be an easy relationship, but it could be worthwhile, so don't pass it up.

Two of Clubs birthdates: May 30, June 28, July 26, August 24, September 22, October 20, November 18, December 16

EIGHT OF HEARTS—NEPTUNE AND JUPITER LINES

Talk about being swept off your feet. This card can do it. These natives can weave a spell of love in and around you—but beware. It's not really in the cards for you. Just as great as this person can seem to be—he can also be as difficult for you. He can argue you down and then take off, leaving you in a cloud of confusion.

Eight of Hearts birthdates: August 31, September 29, October 27, November 25, December 23

ACE OF DIAMONDS FAMOUS BIRTHDATES

January 26	Douglas MacArthur Eartha Kitt Paul Newman
March 22	Marcel Marceau
April 20	Lionel Hampton Adolf Hitler Prophet Mohammed
May 18	Perry Como Dame Margot Fonteyn Omar Khayyam Bertrand Russell
July 14	Polly Bergen Ingmar Bergman Ann Landers Terry-Thomas
August 12	Cecil B. DeMille Diamond Jim Brady
September 10	Arnold Palmer
October 8	Juan D. Peron Eddie Rickenbacker
December 4	Maria Callas

Ace of Spades

Spades — Labor and Wisdom
Ace of Spades — Desire for Enlightenment
One in Spades — *I am* Service

The Neptune Card in the Mercury Line. Displaces the **Seven of Hearts** in the Natural Spread.

This is a very powerful card. Spiritually this card can represent a Master who does not realize it. Negatively, this is a card of secrecy, of one who plots, one who is scheming all the time as to how to outwit the other person. Spiritually, it is the desire for secret wisdom. If there were a key phrase for this card, it would be "Let there be Light." Although few of its natives are aware of its inner symbolism (and still fewer are able to live up to it), the Ace of Spades represents the Initiate, about to become the Adept.

Unrelated and most unknown to the individual, the Ace of Spades is the symbol of the Order of the Magi, the "trademark" of many of the ancient, secret orders and mystery schools throughout history. Behind the Ace of Spades stands a definite knowledge of spiritual values; instruction in the Law, the deathlessness of the soul; the inevitability of Karma and the certainty that we "die" in our earth experiences but to live eternally in spirit.

Personal happiness is not usually in the cards for the Ace of Spades. Disappointments come through treachery of people; the childhood is often disturbed with family complications; and there is sometimes sickness or poverty. If the natives accomplish nothing and are mediocre in their field of endeavor, it is because they have allowed the materialism to drown out

Planetary Sequence

			K♠	8♦	10♣			
A♠	3♦	5♣	10♠	Q♣	A♣	3♥	Mercury
2♥	9♠	9♣	J♥	5♠	7♦	7♥	Venus
Neptune	Uranus	Saturn	Jupiter	Mars	Venus	Mercury	
8♣	J♠	2♦	4♣	6♥	K♦	K♥	Mars
A♦	A♥	8♠	10♦	10♥	4♠	6♦	Jupiter
5♦	7♣	9♥	3♠	3♣	5♥	Q♦	Saturn
J♦	K♣	2♣	7♠	9♦	J♣	Q♠	Uranus
Q♥	6♠	6♣	8♥	2♠	4♦	4♥	Neptune
Neptune	Uranus	Saturn	Jupiter	Mars	Venus	Mercury	

Mundane Spread

spiritualism. If they become interested in business on a large scale, they are always distrustful of people and will never be satisfied and content no matter how much money they make. This negativity opens the door for others to walk in and actually take the fortune away.

On a material plane, the Ace of Spades is very nearly always in trouble. People are unreliable; money is unreliable. Tempers usually flare and die down quickly. Sacrifices for family occur more often than not.

Concentration should be placed on these natives' ability to touch the Other World and call upon their own inner strength. The right teacher is important—one who can teach them that there is One way—and only One—of overcoming their difficulties.

The enlightened Ace of Spades knows all this and accepts his difficult lot in life as a purging preparation for his future freedom. He has come to discharge his Karma, and he is willing and eager to free his soul from the "Wheel of Necessity." He devotes his life to a search for the true Light—the reality behind the veil. He knows he must labor unceasingly, suffer emotionally and endure without complaint whatever vicissitudes his personal Karma prescribes—even to the point of hardship and privation.

For the individual, this is the ultimate—and, in reading about any of the seven birthdates under the rule of the Ace of Spades, you may not be able to recognize a single one of these high requirements. In the majority of cases the individuals themselves do not recognize them either. There may be—and often is—an intuitive or subconscious awareness of their destiny, but unless they cultivate and strengthen this awareness, they remain blinded and overwhelmed by their difficulties and disappointments. Their lot is a hard one, to be sure, but they have the power to overcome their obstacles through a sincere quest for enlightenment. Too often there is no interest or desire to make the effort, and the net result is that one trouble after another pursues Aces of Spades.

Their life pattern includes a doubled emphasis on frustration and a doubled warning to live the Law. The need for self-discipline is usually disregarded, and resentment over their own hard lot is often visited upon those in their environment.

If they are ever so little "on the way," blessings and protection surround the life at certain periods; they do not *hold*, however, unless the "way" is persistently followed. The lives of the Aces of Spades smooth down a bit after the forty-ninth year, when the natives begin to realize that out of disappointment come fulfillments.

BIRTHDATES RULED BY THE ACE OF SPADES

JANUARY 13—CAPRICORN—RULED BY SATURN

Must work hard to get any tangible results. If living negatively, may go from one menial position to another. Health is largely dependent on the state of mind; if depressed and unwilling to rise above it, a chronic condition may result. May become materialistic and bitter. Can work well in hospitals or in connection with the ground—soil, minerals, excavations, archeology. Are valuable in the field of orthodox religion or religious institutions. Should be content to work behind the scenes.

FEBRUARY 11—AQUARIUS—RULED BY URANUS

Experiment with new lines of thought; dislike orthodoxy. Averse to physical labor and are most contented in metaphysical or occult investigation. Are willing to serve without remuneration. Make good religious leaders; may choose law, politics or science—and have ability in all.

MARCH 9—PISCES—RULED BY NEPTUNE

Will make many sacrifices for religion or for service to the sick.

Many nuns, priests, and acolytes are found under this birthdate—likewise workers in the Salvation Army. May be highly nervous but are patient and kind-hearted. Will assume the responsibilities of parenthood with seriousness.

APRIL 7—ARIES—RULED BY MARS

Spiritual leaders among the underprivileged. Organizers of boys clubs, reforms, and the like. Become tired of routine and are apt to step out and leave the management to others. Are usually impervious to criticism. Good promoters, pioneers in new fields. Are often found behind the scenes—but not from choice. Should guard against aggressiveness.

MAY 5—TAURUS—RULED BY VENUS

A very stubborn card. Will not be driven or coerced. Home ties strong but will not be bound by them. Fond of diversion—also of public acclaim. Are very ambitious. Fixed—but ready to change if expedient. Make good actors, producers, directors. Also dressmakers and clothes designers. Will faithfully discharge obligations but do not seek responsibility.

JUNE 3—GEMINI—RULED BY MERCURY

Restless and spasmodic. Will seek diversion in some mental pursuit—study courses, attend lectures, as an escape from boredom. Travel is sought as a cure for restlessness, but is seldom satisfactory. Usually have good manners and present a pleasing appearance. Easy talkers; make easy contacts. Can sell, publish, write articles, and review books. Successful as interviewers; persuasive.

Your Place in the Cards

JULY 1—CANCER—RULED BY THE MOON

Should guard against laziness and selfishness. Will seldom make the effort to use the knowledge they have. Avid for money, which they never consider sufficient. Not well-adapted for partnerships. If willing to serve, make good physicians or nurses—but want to be in full charge. Can succeed in commodities or necessities—any small articles with large sales. Sympathetic, but not always popular, with children.

ACE OF SPADES—PLANETARY SEQUENCE OF PERSONAL RELATIONSHIPS

Horizontal Line—Venus

SEVEN OF HEARTS—MERCURY CARD IN THE MERCURY LINE

Romantically, this native would drive you crazy. A compliment to your secretary on a well-typed letter would mean a love affair as far as the Seven of Hearts is concerned, if she were married to you. And your own secret nature would only reinforce her suspicions—about everything. These natives like groups of people; you prefer aloneness. Communication can be good, but don't expect much of anything else.

Seven of Hearts birthdates: September 30, October 28, November 26, December 24

SEVEN OF DIAMONDS—VENUS CARD IN THE VENUS LINE

This is an attraction that can (and probably will) stay with you throughout your life. These people are not easy for you to know. They are split in their desires, and you probably have no wish to explore those particular desires in the first place. Money is not your main drive (though sometimes it seems as if it has to be) and you are apt to scoff at metaphysics. An evolved Seven of Diamonds could be of great benefit to you, so if you're *in*-volved with one, relax and make an effort to *e*-volve with one, as well.

Seven of Diamonds birthdates: January 20, February 18, March 16, April 14, June 10, July 8, August 6, September 4, October 2

FIVE OF SPADES—MARS CARD IN THE MARS LINE

First of all, don't consider romance. This card will push you into things that you are probably ready for, but will balk at, insisting that you're not really ready. Even if you give in, it won't stop there. This native will try to help you live all your lives in this one. It can only result in unhappiness for you and frustration for him. In friendship he can stimulate you and perhaps get you started where someone else might find it more difficult to persuade you.

Five of Spades birthdates: January 8, February 7, March 5, April 3, May 1

JACK OF HEARTS—JUPITER CARD IN THE JUPITER LINE

If you are (or have been) romantically involved with a Jack of Hearts, you already know some of the heartaches of this association. Your difficulties can be compounded by the lifestyle of this native. There is one exception—and this exception could bring you a kind of happiness that would otherwise be unknown to you. If you are working on your positive side and are genuinely seeking enlightenment, the Jack of Hearts could lead the way—if he, too, is working on his positive side. This relationship could bring you love and fulfillment. Negatively, it would bring ruts, disappointments and two people who feel sorry for themselves and their lots in life. Be careful with this involvement. There is no middle ground.

Jack of Hearts birthdates: July 30, August 28, September 26, October 24, November 22, December 20

NINE OF CLUBS—SATURN CARD IN THE SATURN LINE

A Karmic association. Inevitably you will wind up in some kind of a relationship with at least one of these natives. The best situation (no other is recommended) is probably business. You might be able to make a lot of money quickly with this person—but first understand what it is you're investing in, and double-check all contracts. These natives won't cheat you, but they won't pay enough attention to the "fine print" either. Remember, too, don't invest with this native unless you've got it to lose in the first place.

Nine of Clubs birthdates: January 31, February 29, March 27, April 25, May 23, June 21, July 19, August 17, September 15, October 13, November 11, December 9

NINE OF SPADES—URANUS CARD IN THE URANUS LINE
(Venus and Uranus Lines on the Diagonal)

These natives always keep you wondering as to what will happen next, and much of it can be positive and loving. This is a good person for you—in friendship or romance. Be careful that you don't add to these people's worries by being too skeptical. Give them their heads and walk proudly with them. They can be of great value to you.

Nine of Spades birthdates: January 5, February 3, March 1

TWO OF HEARTS—NEPTUNE CARD IN THE NEPTUNE LINE
(Venus Line on the Vertical)

You will probably never quite know where you stand with these people. When everything seems to be going along smoothly, suddenly it will seem the opposite. They have enough of their own fears about love, and unless you're very careful, you will seem too negative and frighten the Two of Hearts away.

Two of Hearts birthdate: December 29

Your Place in the Cards

Vertical Line—Neptune

QUEEN OF HEARTS—NEPTUNE LINE

You will find a great deal of understanding from a Queen of Hearts, no matter which sex, but chances are if you are a female, you won't want to marry a male Queen of Hearts. You will feel that he often drags his feet, and you know that your own feet are heavy enough. This could be a good and active association through church or other religious groups. A Queen of Hearts will be easy for you to confide in.

Queen of Hearts birthdates: July 29, August 27, September 25, October 23, November 21, December 19

JACK OF DIAMONDS—URANUS LINE

If you're a woman and this is your man, you can always depend on him to see that you will be provided for. In any case, this is a good match for you for love or friendship. Follow these natives' advice; they tend to be a little more successful in their business ideas, and they can help to open some of those doors to your soul—if you give them a chance. It certainly should not be a damaging relationship in any way—unless you want it to be.

Jack of Diamonds birthdates: January 16, February 14, March 12, April 10, May 8, June 6, July 4, August 2

FIVE OF DIAMONDS—SATURN LINE

This native is another story for you. A personal involvement will probably leave you angry with the Five of Diamonds most of the time. Money will be the major source of irritation in any kind of relationship, so if you are involved, try to keep your discussions away from finances of any kind.

Five of Diamonds birthdates: January 22, February 20, March 18, April 16, May 14, June 12, July 10, August 8, September 6, October 4, November 2

ACE OF DIAMONDS—JUPITER LINE

Money is a problem here as well, but it won't be so all-consuming and irritating. You will also like and be automatically drawn to this native if both of you don't become too consumed with your individual selves and forget about taking care of each other. Take a chance; you might find a fulfilling relationship. The aspects are certainly on the good side. If this person is a member of your family, you will probably feel a closer relationship with the Ace of Diamonds than with any other family member.

Ace of Diamonds birthdates: January 26, February 24, March 22, April 20, May 18, June 16, July 14, August 12, September 10, October 8, November 6, December 4

EIGHT OF CLUBS—MARS LINE

Here is one of your teachers, although you may find so much inborn resistance that it will be difficult for you to learn anything. Try very hard. You will feel as if he is "putting upon you"—and he may very well be doing just that, but the knowledge he has to impart will be worth the irritation. Forget about a close relationship of any kind, but don't try to avoid this involvement. It will happen anyway, so listen and learn.

Eight of Clubs birthdates: March 28, April 26, May 24, June 22, July 20, August 18, September 16, October 14, November 12, December 10

TWO OF HEARTS—VENUS LINE: SEE HORIZONTAL LINE

Diagonal Line

NINE OF SPADES—VENUS AND URANUS LINE: SEE HORIZONTAL LINE

TWO OF DIAMONDS—MARS AND SATURN LINES

Although you will feel a strong sexual attraction with a Two of Diamonds of the opposite sex, it is unlikely that it will (or should) develop into anything else. These natives irritate you, and you will give in to their wishes only to find that you are both in danger of slipping into a routine with each other that eventually will only produce more irritations. So, no personal involvements, please. It is also unlikely that you will find yourself spending very much time with this native on any other level.

Two of Diamonds birthdates: January 25, February 23, March 21, April 19, May 17, June 15, July 13, August 11, September 9, October 7, November 5, December 3

TEN OF DIAMONDS—DOUBLE JUPITER LINES

If there is a card in the pack that stands out as a person for you to make money with, this is it. Not only does this card represent (by itself) a great deal of money, but the planetary influences should be extremely good for you. Your financial investments with this native will receive special protection, and you will feel the strength to pursue each endeavor. You might even become involved personally or romantically. These aspects are also good, except in a close one-to-one involvement you can expect a certain amount of arguments. Watch your temper and make a special effort to bend his way. Tens of Diamonds have inborn good business sense and a form of good judgment that many other people are never able to acquire, no matter how hard they work at it—so utilize your position with this person.

Tens of Diamonds birthdates: January 17, February 15, March 13, April 11, May 9, June 7, July 5, August 3, September 1

Your Place in the Cards

THREE OF CLUBS—SATURN AND MARS LINES

There will be something about this native that you cannot help but like, and yet you'll feel hesitant to become involved. Follow this intuition, for this native's life pattern is as heavy a burden as you have to carry, and there is no real reason for you to compound your problems. Should you both become involved in metaphysics, this could reverse the patterns, and happiness could then be found with each other. The probability is slight, but the opportunity is certainly there—if you are both willing to work and earn that happiness.

Three of Clubs birthdates: May 29, June 27, July 25, August 23, September 21, October 19, November 17, December 15

JACK OF CLUBS—URANUS AND VENUS LINES

It would be better if you didn't even utter the first hello to this card, but you will do it anyway, inasmuch as it is a Karmic relationship for you. But don't get involved, or you could find yourself in a relationship that will create such a burden on you that you may not even be able to function at times.

Jack of Clubs birthdates: January 29, February 27, March 25, April 23, May 21, June 19, July 17, August 15, September 13, October 11, November 9, December 7

FOUR OF HEARTS—NEPTUNE AND MERCURY LINES

This native will delight you and keep you entertained. His bright, personality will, for the moment, help you to escape from your seemingly humdrum existence. This could be a fine friendship, but don't be too critical, even if these natives seem to be terribly sure of themselves. What does it really matter? Enjoy them; they can bring you many happy hours.

Four of Hearts birthdates: October 31, November 29, December 27

ACE OF SPADES FAMOUS BIRTHDATES

January 13	Horatio Alger
	Robert Stack
February 11	Eva Gabor
	Thomas A. Edison
March 9	Mickey Spillane
April 7	David Frost
	Ravi Shankar
	Walter Winchell
	William Wordsworth

May 5	Karl Marx
June 3	Tony Curtis
	Maurice Evans
	Allan Ginsberg
July 1	Olivia De Haviland
	Charles Laughton

Twos

TWOS represent Union—the Father-Mother Principle—hence, association and cooperation. As Two is the Carrier or Bearer, it is representative of messages and communications. As the Mother member of the Father-Mother union, it symbolizes all pairs of opposites—male and female, light and darkness, heat and cold, wet and dry, action and reaction.

Two is a complement, the other half, but not the whole; so there is always a fear of aloneness or lack of support from another; an eternal search for a counterpart, a complement, the Other Self.

In the twos of all suits, *people* are essential:

Hearts seek Union in Love
Clubs seek Kindred Minds
Diamonds seek Helpful Partnerships
Spades seek Congenial Co-Workers or Students of the Occult

All are sensitive to the reactions of others and the impression made upon others. All become ill or unhappy when there is lack of harmony or evidence of disapproval.

It is important to give these people the right start in life. In the Heart, great harm can be done if there is a lack of love in the early years at home. In the Club, a sympathetic and understanding teacher in the learning years is essential for the establishment of mental processes that are to remain balanced and normal. When it comes to assuming their own place in the world, Diamonds find little chance for success unless there is someone by their side to encourage, advise, and support them. In the quest for wisdom, Spades find no urge for independent investigation, and some Master or guru or guide must point the way.

Union is their weapon against fear.

Two of Hearts

Hearts — Emotions
Two of Hearts — Union in Love
Two in Hearts — Cooperation with Loved Ones

The Neptune Card in the Venus Line. Displaces the **Ace of Clubs** in the Natural Spread.

By position, the Two of Hearts is influenced by Venus and Neptune, which affect the entire outlook and viewpoint when applied to the emotional life and ideals of the Two of Hearts. The negative side of all Twos is Fear. Therefore, the conflict for the Two of Hearts is to harmonize—to want love, but to fear that it can't be had.

Two of Hearts people have an idealism about human relations. Like a Piscean moon, they tend to build things up in their minds the way they want to see them, and then everything falls short. They invariably will take people too much for granted and actually be nosy and concerned with what goes on all the time.

If the card belongs to a woman, she will be concerned with marrying a diamond man, because the King of Diamonds is her Venus Card. The man will be financially comfortable but not necessarily well educated, for a Two of Hearts woman will feel that she can "teach him something" and, therefore, will "work with him."

Two of Hearts men are very touchy and hot-tempered, even though their

Planetary Sequence

			K♠	8♦	10♣			
A♠	3♦	5♣	10♠	Q♣	A♣	3♥		Mercury
2♥	9♠	9♣	J♥	5♠	7♦	7♥		Venus
8♣	J♠	2♦	4♣	6♥	K♦	K♥		Mars
Neptune	Uranus	Saturn	Jupiter	Mars	Venus	Mercury		
A♦	A♥	8♠	10♦	10♥	4♠	6♦		Jupiter
5♦	7♣	9♥	3♠	3♣	5♥	Q♦		Saturn
J♦	K♣	2♣	7♠	9♦	J♣	Q♠		Uranus
Q♥	6♠	6♣	8♥	2♠	4♦	4♥		Neptune
Neptune	Uranus	Saturn	Jupiter	Mars	Venus	Mercury		

Mundane Spread

temperaments are sometimes buried under the personality. There are usually two marriages—the first one a sudden, early one. These men make good fathers but have no patience in handling their children.

For both sexes there is always great interest in people and curiosity regarding their emotional lives. These natives' ideals of love are very high, and disappointment in marriage is often the result—since few can live up to them. Believing that man or woman was not meant to live alone, the Two of Hearts would rather experiment and meet with disappointment than die an old maid or old bachelor. Neptune, however, is never far away, and since it works both ways, confusion, illusion and disillusion often result from the union.

There is great interest in foreigners and foreign countries and a great desire to establish a lively correspondence with those who live at a distance.

Closely knit to the love life is a search for knowledge (from the Ace of Clubs Displacement Card), and the one frequently interferes with the other. If the emotions become too involved, both education and business are checked or become stagnant. When this is recognized, there is regret or remorse—for this two of all others has a strong mental bent and a subconscious realization that cultivation of the mind is a part of the destiny. On the other hand, the Two of Hearts who devotes himself to education at the expense of his heart is in a sorry state indeed and feels that he has lost the best there is in life. With such a person a neurosis may develop, and melancholia may result in the later years.

BIRTHDATES RULED BY THE TWO OF HEARTS

DECEMBER 29—CAPRICORN—RULED BY SATURN

This is the only birthdate for the Two of Hearts. Since the sign is Capricorn and the rulership Saturn, these natives should strictly avoid a tendency to become mercenary. Must never be too demanding about money. There is plenty of foundation for the recognition of true values—but the fear of not being able to pay their debts makes these people very self-protective where money is concerned. Sometimes, also, this interferes with a willingness to share—hence, the reason behind the Challenge. Their motto should be, "Give and ye shall receive," and the Law of Compensation works in all cases in which they apply it. They are best suited for an occupation that deals with products of the earth or under the earth—farming, mining, real estate, forestry. They are also successful if associated with the government—secret service, diplomacy, statesmanship. The better the educational preparation, the more likely are they to attain an important position. Can become civil engineers or mathematicians.

Twos

TWO OF HEARTS—PLANETARY SEQUENCE OF PERSONAL RELATIONSHIPS

Horizontal Line—Mars

KING OF HEARTS—MERCURY CARD IN THE MERCURY LINE

You will find a great deal of communication with this native, though you may find what he has to say interesting, but not necessarily what you want to learn about. You will like this King a great deal, feel a friendship or fatherly attraction but probably not a romantic involvement. But if it is romance, by all means, don't pass it up.

King of Hearts birthdates: June 30, July 28, August 26, September 24, October 22, November 20, December 18

KING OF DIAMONDS—VENUS CARD IN THE VENUS LINE

When you meet this person, stop looking—it's all over. He is capable of fulfilling what you want. Remember, he's a diamond and on a different trip so don't ride him about being late for dinner because of work or being on the pushy side when it's necessary to your economic welfare. Your life will never be better so count your blessings that you found this native.

King of Diamonds birthdates: January 14, February 12, March 10, April 8, May 6, June 4, July 2

SIX OF HEARTS—MARS CARD IN THE MARS LINE

Don't expect so much of this person or you will be setting yourself up for fall. He is not really as active as you—and does not need to be. As a result of this friendship (and it should be only that), you will feel even more active—more anxious to "get going" to do some of the things you've maybe been putting off. Use the relationship constructively. Don't try to push a square cube into a round hole.

Six of Hearts birthdates: October 29, November 27, December 25

FOUR OF CLUBS—JUPITER CARD IN THE JUPITER LINE

This person can give your King of Diamonds a run for his money in the romance department, or in a deep friendship. These natives have some of the knowledge you seek; they may tend to turn you off by telling you about what they know, but this is trivial in comparison to the happiness they can bring to you. A definite yes to any kind of relationship.

Four of Clubs birthdates: April 30, May 28, June 26, July 24, August 22, September 20, October 18, November 16, December 14

TWO OF DIAMONDS—SATURN CARD IN THE SATURN LINE

If this is a friendship, it will probably be a once-a-month, on-the-telephone kind. You will find these natives too difficult and inflexible for much else. It's a Karmic friendship, it will exist, but make it easy on yourself and don't try for communication in areas where there never will be any.

Two of Diamonds birthdates: January 25, February 23, March 21, April 19, May 17, June 15, July 13, August 11, September 9, October 7, November 5, December 3

JACK OF SPADES—URANUS CARD IN THE URANUS LINE
(Mars and Uranus Lines on the Diagonal)

You will never understand this native, and you could drive yourself crazy trying. Therefore, a close personal involvement should not be attempted. On an acquaintance-friendship basis, these natives will prove to be among some of the most interesting people you know and will ripen even more as the years go by.

Jack of Spades birthdates: January 3, February 1

EIGHT OF CLUBS—NEPTUNE CARD IN THE NEPTUNE LINE
(Mars Line on the Vertical)

These natives can influence you a great deal, and in the majority of cases, it will be for the better. They have a great deal of knowledge and will gladly give of themselves and their time to a curious mind such as yours. But if they give an inch, don't try to take a mile—don't expect more from them than what they are prepared to do for you at a particular time. They are good friends and valuable to your own growth. But don't set them up so that you will wind up being the disappointed one. Enjoy the relationship and learn.

Eight of Clubs birthdates: March 28, April 26, May 24, June 11, July 20, August 18, September 16, October 14, November 12, December 10

Vertical Line—Neptune

ACE OF SPADES—MERCURY LINE

Communications are good with these natives. You may not get together for long periods of time, but you will probably find the brief encounters that you do have rather interesting. Don't try romance unless it is blatantly there—these people don't have any more luck in their love lives so why double your problems?

Ace of Spades birthdates: January 13, February 11, March 9, April 7, May 5, June 3, July 1

QUEEN OF HEARTS—NEPTUNE LINE

A man would find a Queen of Hearts woman to be almost what he is seeking, idealistically and romantically. But beware. The only stimulation you may get from the lady may be sexual, which doesn't necessarily stand alone over the long pull. As a female Two of Hearts, you will undoubtedly be attracted to these natives, but the association will be too weak for you. Don't spend too much time in finding this out. For both sexes these natives are wonderful friends.

Queen of Hearts birthdates: July 29, August 27, September 25, October 23, November 21, December 19.

JACK OF DIAMONDS—URANUS LINE

You could fall into the lap of this native literally and perhaps eventually spiritually. You'll feel strength and be titillated—and sometimes irritated—by the unexpected things these natives do. It's a difficult relationship for marriage and should be avoided if possible, but enjoy the other aspects of an interesting friendship.

Jack of Diamonds birthdates: January 16, February 14, March 12, April 10, May 8, June 6, July 4, August 2

FIVE OF DIAMONDS—SATURN LINE

Here is a relationship that may prove to be one of the better ones for you. Though the road will get a little rough at times, stick with it and help to keep your Five of Diamonds there by encouraging him. You can present far more problems for him than he for you. Suggest that he read a little more—study a little more to further his own goals, and this will bring a closeness for you both because of your own inborn curiosity for learning. Friendship is best—marriage will be rough, but whatever happens, don't miss the opportunity.

Five of Diamonds birthdates: January 22, February 20, March 18, April 16, May 14, June 12, July 10, August 8, September 6, October 4, November 2

ACE OF DIAMONDS—JUPITER LINE

If you are working for, or with, an Ace of Diamonds, you will probably not find a better relationship. The problem is your recognizing it and using it to its fullest potential. You may feel that these natives impose tasks on you that should be given to others—or tasks that even seem to be next to the impossible. You may be right. But know that only good things are in store for you when you face and meet these challenges. Don't think about love, although you will be tempted. An Ace of Diamonds will make the first move, if it's to be made—and it probably will be in some form:

Ace of Diamonds birthdates: January 26, February 24, March 22, April 20, May 18, June 16, July 14, August 12, September 10, October 8, November 6, December 4

EIGHT OF CLUBS–MARS LINE: SEE HORIZONTAL LINE

Diagonal Lines

THREE OF DIAMONDS–MERCURY AND URANUS LINES

You'll be intrigued by this native's ability to communicate, and on several different levels, depending on his individual awareness. This person could be a friend, an associate, someone you do business with. This is not necessarily a long-term association, so don't look for any involvement to last.

Three of Diamonds birthdates: January 24, February 22, March 20, April 18, May 16, June 14, July 12, August 10, September 8, October 6, November 4, December 2

JACK OF SPADES–MARS AND URANUS LINES:
SEE HORIZONTAL LINE

EIGHT OF SPADES–JUPITER AND SATURN LINES

If any relationship was "meant to be"–here is a strong tie. A great deal of love can be exchanged between the two of you; you will never feel better and probably never experience more understanding and rapport from another person. This is truly an involvement you will enjoy. So take the time–don't expect everything at once, and you both can be richly rewarded in just knowing each other.

Eight of Spades birthdates: January 6, February 4, March 2

THREE OF SPADES–SATURN AND JUPITER LINES

Although you probably won't have the feelings to start with anyway, don't even attempt a personal involvement with this native. Marriage is out; love will be difficult, and he will always seem to fall short, in some way, of your expectations or aspirations for him. Do yourself a favor and try to stay uninvolved.

Three of Spades birthdates: January 11, February 9, March 7, April 5, May 3, June 1

NINE OF DIAMONDS–URANUS AND MARS LINES

This is a difficult relationship also–though these natives will be very good for you. Sometimes generous to a fault, they will expect something in return, so if you're involved, be prepared to pay some kind of price. Romance and friendship are both possible–just keep your eyes open and know (as well as you can) what's expected of you.

Nine of Diamonds birthdates: January 18, February 16, March 14, April 12, May 10, June 8, July 6, August 4, September 2

FOUR OF DIAMONDS—NEPTUNE AND VENUS LINES

There is a Karmic tie with this card that will force you together in some way. Hopefully, it will not be a close involvement of any kind. These natives have as many Crosses to bear as you, and together you would be compounding the problems rather than complementing each other. Work out the relationship as harmoniously as is possible for you and have no regrets when your paths don't run together any longer.

Four of Diamonds birthdates: January 23, February 21, March 19, April 17, May 15, June 13, July 11, August 9, September 7, October 5, November 3, December 1

TWO OF HEARTS FAMOUS BIRTHDATES

December 29   Pablo Casals
               Andrew Johnson

Clubs — Knowledge
Two of Clubs — Union in Mental Interests
Two in Clubs — Mental Cooperation

The Saturn Card in the Uranus Line. Displaces the **Ace of Spades** in the Natural Spread.

This is the most difficult and the least cooperative of all the twos. The key to the life lies in the Displacement Card, the Ace of Spades, but while divine knowledge would give these natives the solution to all their problems, they are so fearful of what any metaphysical truths might reveal to them, they seldom go near them.

Two of Clubs people, on the material plane, are afraid of the unknown, and they are never content until they get into some study of philosophy or metaphysics. Those who do not, are beset with fear all of their lives. There is another side to the Two of Clubs: people who get into secret types of work—the F. B. I., the police department, foreign work. Still another side is politics, and the most constructive side is psychology. All have the ability, with the Saturn-Uranus position, to tap the unknown sources.

Twos of Clubs put up a very aggressive and self-confident front, but as a matter of fact, they *fear* everything—themselves included. Of all the Twos this is the least representative of Union—and the most in need of it. The well-worn term, *defense mechanism,* applies to these natives perfectly and accounts for a tendency to contention and dispute, sudden flashes of anger, and lack of control. It must be understood that this does not apply to individuals who are highly developed and self-disciplined, but it does apply to the majority.

The nature is impulsive and hot-headed; conclusions are too speedily arrived at—with no patience or inclination to reason things out to a logical end; the first reaction is always for the opposite side of the argument. If a Two of Clubs is ill, he thinks the worst; if trouble does not actually exist, he'll borrow it; if the future is uncertain, it is black.

These people are clever and quick witted—never lacking for an answer and very positive (apparently) in their own opinions. If they seem to agree with an expressed viewpoint, it is usually for the purpose of drawing out the antagonist and making him commit himself to something he does not intend. They are skilled at ferreting out secrets—and, if unscrupulous, these twos will use the information against you. They seldom give you the benefit of the doubt and usually suspect your motives. It is easy for them to misrepresent facts—for they fear the consequences of Truth.

Strictly on the negative side, a Two of Clubs person operates with extreme secrecy and unreliability. There is no smooth path for the person who is working on the negative side. The negative Two of Clubs will use other people. When the card belongs to a man, his mind is on himself. He is concerned with what he thinks and how he can use it to the best advantage.

It all boils down to the Two of Clubs inherent psychology of *fear,* and the tragedy reaches back to the childhood, to impulses allowed to run wild, to concealments that should have been brought to the surface, and to an unusually keen mind and a cleverness that was encouraged as cute instead of being checked as dangerous. These children must be taught not to fear the dark or the parents' displeasure, not to conceal their own feelings until they are too overgrown or violent to handle, and not to feel that the whole world is against them and that they must strike the first blow to fight it.

The Two of Clubs soul wants divine wisdom; the heart yearns for cooperation, although these natives do little to earn it; the realm of spirit—where they really belong—is unknown and intangible, and they are afraid of the "dark."

Two of Clubs people have a source they can tap, but they have to be aware of it, to be able to recognize it. The potential for the Two of Clubs is very great for this reason. They marry rather suddenly. There is also a possibility of divorce. The keynote for the Two of Clubs can go two ways: One is the ability to use knowledge for the good of others, and the other is the ability to use knowledge for themselves. So in many cases, they are not interested in a formal education.

After forty they lose the desire to dominate. Once they recognize their inner strength, they eagerly seek the workings of the higher mind; many of them, in the later years, become members of secret orders and attain a high place in them. The Two of Clubs needs an *outlet* for his rare abilities—a talent cultivated or a hobby enjoyed.

BIRTHDATES RULED BY THE TWO OF CLUBS

MAY 30—GEMINI—RULED BY MERCURY

Great talkers—not always constructive. Choose the easiest way and shun responsibility. Should be careful not to misrepresent. Should cultivate good sportsmanship. Can adapt the knowledge of others to own needs. If not watchful, may become lazy and self-satisfied. Make good agents, promoters, lecturers; also salesmen—especially insurance. Many are found as court stenographers.

JUNE 28—CANCER—RULED BY THE MOON

If fear dominates, will make little progress. Want to express but are often inarticulate. Absorbed by home and want comfort in it. Have difficulty in putting themselves over. Actual power is blocked by concealed sense of inferiority. Dwell in the past. Have psychic power but will not cultivate it. Want personal freedom; hate restraint. Attracted to occupations that deal with healing. Make good nurses, art dealers, cartoonists. Can succeed in clothing, mechanical toys, home commodities. Have some outstanding peculiarity.

JULY 26—LEO—RULED BY THE SUN

Make others comfortable and do considerable entertaining, mainly for business reasons. If attracted to the theater, can succeed as directors, producers, sometimes as actors. If follow the law, become judges; if work in a bank, become president or director. Always attracted to large concerns. Want appearance of wealth; love display. Slated for success because of their drive for power. Sometimes wear loud clothes, big diamonds. Insist upon a position of authority.

AUGUST 24—VIRGO—RULED BY MERCURY

Desire for knowledge; love of home. Have a strong sense of responsibility and can capitalize on it. Get along best when taking orders; are not pioneers. Unhappy alone and should marry young—but many bachelors are found among the men because of their shyness. Must be given a plan with which to work. Should cultivate positiveness. Interested in furniture, ceramics, gadgets, and systems. Shine better at home than elsewhere. Make good teachers of the young. Should have some emotional outlet for expression.

SEPTEMBER 22—VIRGO—RULED BY MERCURY

More nervous and high-strung than the other Virgo. Cannot endure uncertainty. Have power and high ideals—practical visionaries. Have inspiration but should not depend upon impulse. Strong humanitarian inclinations. Want improvement and general welfare. If teachers, have a new and progressive program. Promote music and art as a universal language. Need people, but do better without close associations. Make good architects, draftsmen, corporation lawyers. Always raise the standard of whatever they undertake.

OCTOBER 20—LIBRA—RULED BY VENUS

Should avoid being negative and vacillating. Need constant approval and cooperation. If highly evolved, can branch out for themselves and make great progress. Cultured; inclined to self-indulgence. Duality in interests and associations. Make good teachers—or preachers; art dealers and connoisseurs; can succeed in politics (have great tact and diplomacy).

NOVEMBER 18—SCORPIO—RULED BY MARS

Very powerful card. These people can succeed in anything they undertake. Have determination and persistence. Sure of themselves and believe in their own mental attitudes. Never baffled by failure—and never admit it. Have the least fear of all the Twos. Will investigate sources. Always manage to live well. Interested in minerals. Always just and fair. Marriage important, but demand independence. Can succeed in law, politics, religion, philosophy, teaching.

Your Place in the Cards

DECEMBER 16—SAGITTARIUS—RULED BY JUPITER

Dislike changes and uncertainty. Will brook no interference in money matters or their own position. Like to travel by sea and prefer their own ships. Will save and spend all on one trip. Clever and intellectual. Good gamblers. If not rovers (and many are), are attracted to science, shipping, research. If a woman, attracted to nursing, cosmetics, perfumes, scientifically or for beauty. Both sexes can succeed at law. Not always given the credit they merit.

TWO OF CLUBS—PLANETARY SEQUENCE OF PERSONAL RELATIONSHIPS

Horizontal Lines—Uranus and Neptune

KING OF CLUBS—MERCURY CARD IN THE URANUS LINE

This is a mental attraction—if you're up to it. Don't come on as if you're a mental superior; it might be the other way around, but a true King will never be obvious about it. You'll just lose the relationship and never know why. Until later years this could be a difficult relationship for you, but most rewarding, so don't pass it up—at any age.

King of Clubs birthdates: January 27, February 25, March 23, April 21, May 19, June 17, July 15, August 13, September 11, October 9, November 7, December 5

JACK OF DIAMONDS—VENUS CARD IN THE NEPTUNE LINE

There's no question that this could be an immediate love affair including marriage—while you're young. The problems arise when you're older in this case. Most Jacks of Diamonds, in later years, turn to some form of religion, and this may not be where you wish to be. However, with a little investigation the relationship could be the most wonderful experience of your life.

Jack of Diamonds birthdates: January 16, February 14, March 12, April 10, May 8, June 6, July 4, August 2

FOUR OF HEARTS—MARS CARD IN THE MERCURY LINE

You probably cannot help but feel that this native has some ulterior motive for a relationship with you. It's doubtful. Fours of Clubs are more open and eager in all their involvements than you, so relax and enjoy this (usually) happy person. Romance can work for a while, but marriage probably won't work at all.

Four of Hearts birthdates: October 31, November 29, December 27

FOUR OF DIAMONDS–JUPITER CARD IN THE VENUS LINE

This relationship is not only important—it's a must, and it will probably happen whether you want it to or not. With opposite sexes, it's surely romance, and with all others it's the same warm feeling of another kind of love. Difficulties can (and probably will) arise when your Four of Diamonds fails to apply himself to his work as you think and know he can. Hold your tongue—keep the love alive through the crises, and you can experience a beautiful relationship.

Four of Diamonds birthdates: January 23, February 21, March 19, April 17, May 15, June 13, July 11, August 9, September 7, October 5, November 3, December 1

TWO OF SPADES–SATURN CARD IN THE MARS LINE

If you want to be irritated beyond belief, spend some time with this native—it will be like mixing oil and water. You will see some of the traits you dislike most about yourself in this native. And, in this case, use the information constructively and learn from the negative side. Don't attempt any involvement that doesn't have to exist.

Two of Spades birthdates: January 12, February 10, March 8, April 6, May 4, June 2

EIGHT OF HEARTS–URANUS CARD IN THE JUPITER LINE
(Neptune and Jupiter Lines on the Diagonal)

You will like and want to know more about this friendly person. His probing mind and active life will titillate you, but don't throw the gauntlet down—you will only find yourself running for cover—and unnecessarily. Any kind of involvement is possible. But the success of it will be largely up to you and your positive attitude, for an Eight of Hearts, no matter how negatively he is operating, will have little or no negativity in close associations.

Eight of Hearts birthdates: August 31, September 29, October 27, November 25, December 23

SIX OF CLUBS–NEPTUNE CARD IN THE SATURN LINE
(Neptune Line on the Vertical)

You will feel that this native is offbeat—perhaps too involved in seemingly unimportant things that don't relate to you. On the other hand, a Six of Clubs may be simply attempting to escape from the frenetic personality some Twos of Clubs have. Friendship of some kind could be useful. Personal involvements should be out.

Six of Clubs birthdates: March 30, April 28, May 26, June 24, July 22, August 20, September 18, October 16, November 14, December 12

Your Place in the Cards

Vertical Line—Saturn

NINE OF HEARTS—SATURN LINE

If you decide to take on a personal involvement with a Nine of Hearts, you may just as well take your shirt off and have someone give you forty lashes with a leather whip. You have too many problems—and this Nine has more, none of which is related to you in any way. Be nice to yourself and avoid this one. Even a long distance friendship can be difficult—perhaps interesting—but better if avoided.

Nine of Hearts birthdates: August 30, September 28, October 26, November 24, December 22

EIGHT OF SPADES—JUPITER LINE

Here is the person who can bring you peace and love. But not without a great deal of effort on your part. He has the wisdom you seek and the spiritual qualities that intrigue you so—yet keep you at a distance. Swallow all the words that lump in your throat; let him take your hand—and take a chance. If you try, you can be happier than you've ever dreamed.

Eight of Spades birthdates: January 6, February 4, March 2

TWO OF DIAMONDS—MARS LINE

Another pass on an involvement. You'll feel energy from this native—almost as if you could run right out and do all those things you've wanted to do for years, especially in finances. This native will seem to make everything simple—to the point of oversimplification. Use the energy, but check your impulses. You may be running down a wrong road. Forget personal relationships if possible.

Two of Diamonds birthdates: January 25, February 23, March 21, April 19, May 17, June 15, July 13, August 11, September 9, October 7, November 5, December 3

NINE OF CLUBS—VENUS LINE

Although the attraction here will be incredibly strong for romance, it is not among your better relationships. With this native you could fall into the problem area of playing games with each other—resulting only in name-calling matches and hot tempers flaring. Take it slow and easy, to determine the qualities of the individual and perhaps keep the relationship on a pure friendship level, which is better for you both.

Nine of Clubs birthdates: January 31, February 29, March 27, April 25, May 23, June 21, July 19, August 17, September 15, October 13, November 11, December 9

FIVE OF CLUBS—MERCURY LINE

This native will never really open up to you—and when he does even a little, you won't be that pleased with what is there. You will find a Five of Clubs somewhere in your lifetime as a Karmic tie, but keep it on a straight communication level and enjoy the relationship more.

Five of Clubs birthdates: March 31, April 29, May 27, June 25, July 23, August 21, September 19, October 17, November 15, December 13

KING OF SPADES—CROWN LINE

You'll never know what to expect from a King of Spades—but just knowing one will make your life more interesting. What these natives say will have little or no effect on you; this is unfortunate because no matter how fanatical they may seem, there's always something of value, so open up a little and don't be so close-minded, around this native especially.

King of Spades birthdates: January 1

SIX OF CLUBS—NEPTUNE LINE: SEE HORIZONTAL LINE

Diagonal Lines

SEVEN OF CLUBS—SATURN AND URANUS LINES

This is a difficult involvement for you both. In any kind of involvement—other than a detached, noncaring kind—you will feel certain vibrations about these natives and their lives that will probably force you to seek the true answers. But the true answers may turn out to be skeletons in their closets that could have little or no bearing on your relationship. By then, it won't matter—you will already have nailed the Seven of Clubs to the cross. Don't press and don't get involved.

Seven of Clubs birthdates: March 29, April 27, May 25, June 23, July 21, August 19, September 17, October 15, November 13, December 11

ACE OF DIAMONDS—JUPITER AND NEPTUNE LINES

Love and romance will gleam from both your eyes and the eyes of this native on first meeting—but you will probably wind up giving him a much harder time than he to you. If you really want those good feelings, don't stand in the way of these natives' ambitions. You won't stop them, and you'll only lose in the end. And most of all—give them love, affection, and understanding. The rewards are well worth the price.

Ace of Diamonds birthdates: January 26, February 24, March 22, April 20, May 18, June 16, July 14, August 12, September 10, October 8, November 6, December 4

EIGHT OF HEARTS—NEPTUNE AND JUPITER LINES: SEE HORIZONTAL LINE

SIX OF SPADES—NEPTUNE AND URANUS LINES

Don't get any romantic aspirations, or you could be disappointed. It would be difficult for this relationship to work, as the pace in which you live your life is vastly different from this native's. You can take a problem to a Six of Spades and find a friend and advisor, but don't expect much of anything beyond.

Six of Spades birthdates: January 8, February 6, March 4, April 2

THREE OF SPADES—SATURN AND JUPITER LINES

A Las Vegas quickie type marriage to this native may happen before either of you knows what hit you. Although you both have good instincts, sustaining the relationship may be difficult. But certainly not impossible. You will find many things in common, but you may also find that you and your Three of Spades are in a rut. Keep yourselves vital and alive in outside interests, and you'll find happiness—on some level. Friendship is even better, but if you're picking a business partner, stay away from this native.

Three of Spades birthdates: January 11, February 9, March 7, April 5, May 3, June 1

TEN OF HEARTS—JUPITER AND MARS LINES

This could be a love affair that could go on down in the annals of your family history. But you probably won't want most people to know about this screaming-loving-touching, love/hate relationship that probably will never bear your name on a marriage contract. When it's all over, you'll probably bleed mentally, far more than the Ten of Hearts will—so forget the past and keep your memories in your scrapbook, cherished and secret.

Ten of Hearts birthdates: July 31, August 29, September 27, October 25, November 23, December 21

KING OF DIAMONDS—MARS AND VENUS LINES

Here's another romantic shouting match, but the King of Diamonds will not enjoy it quite as much as the Ten of Hearts, so the affair will probably be shorter. If you're smart, you'll keep *this* involvement strictly business and profit by the association.

King of Diamonds birthdates: January 14, February 12, March 10, April 8, May 6, June 4, July 2

SEVEN OF HEARTS—VENUS AND MERCURY LINES

You might call this love at first sight. If you want to win the Seven of Hearts, show your approval and don't forget to tell him how important he is to you. Suppress your aggressive side temporarily until this native knows that you also have a tender side. You can bring great happiness to each other if you take the time to care—and let each other know. Good for all involvements.

Seven of Hearts birthdates: September 30, October 28, November 26, December 24

TWO OF CLUBS FAMOUS BIRTHDATES

May 30	Benny Goodman, Cornelia Otis Skinner, Clint Walker
July 26	Jason Robards, Jr., Carl Jung, George Bernard Shaw, Aldous Huxley
September 22	Alfred G. Vanderbilt
October 20	Art Buchwald, Mickey Mantle, Bela Lugosi
December 16	Sir Noel Coward

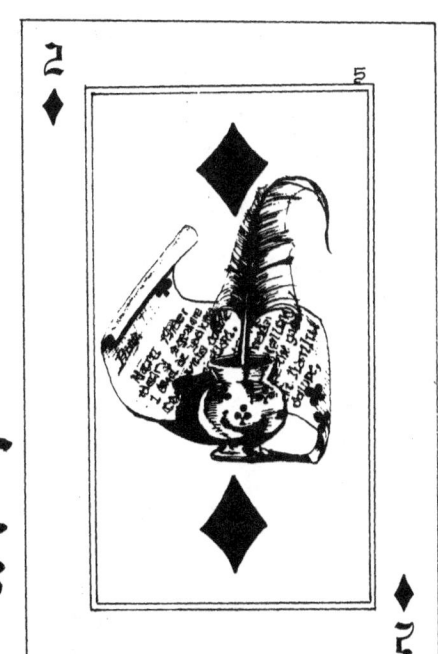

Two of Diamonds

Planetary Sequence

		K♠	8♦	10♣			
A♠	3♦	5♣	10♠	Q♣	A♣	3♥	Mercury
2♥	9♠	9♣	J♥	5♠	7♦	7♥	Venus
8♣ (Venus)	J♠ (Mercury)	2♦	4♣	6♥	K♠	K♥	Mars
A♦	A♥	8♠ (Neptune)	10♦ (Uranus)	10♥ (Saturn)	4♠ (Jupiter)	6♦ (Mars)	Jupiter
5♦	7♣	9♥	3♠	3♣	5♥	Q♦	Saturn
J♦	K♣	2♣	7♠	9♦	J♣	Q♠	Uranus
Q♥	6♠	6♣	8♥	2♠	4♦	4♥	Neptune

Neptune · Uranus · Saturn · Jupiter · Mars · Venus · Mercury

Mundane Spread

Diamonds — Wealth
Two of Diamonds — Compromise
Two in Diamonds — Cooperation for Security

The Saturn Card in the Mars Line. Displaces the **Six of Clubs** in the Natural Spread.

The Two of Diamonds, in itself, is concerned with business transactions on the one side. On the other side, these natives are interested in the healing arts or in serving humanity. This card belongs to people who are quite successful in dealing with others. Much of the fear and vacillation of the Two is dispelled here by the Displacement Card, the Six of Clubs. All sixes are Universal; all have a mission rather than a vocation. It is therefore easier for the Two of Diamonds to work on the higher levels of thinking than for the Two of Hearts or the Two of Clubs—both of which displace Aces, which are always less concerned with the Universe than with themselves.

This is an entirely different type of Two than the preceding Twos. This Mars-Saturn trine means that these natives are not actually thwarted. They have a tenacity about them, and they have terrific intuition.

The Two of Diamonds is more aware, and if awareness is used, mistakes are rare; if principles are adhered to, success is assured, even though there is always some concern about money—as is the case with all diamonds. The True Place is the Neptune Card in the Jupiter Line (in the Natural Spread) and this, in itself, is an indication of protection as well as a pull toward idealism.

Being a Saturn-Mars-Neptune combination, however, there is always an element of conflict in the life—often through illness or disability—which is apt to interfere, on occasion, with the activities or ambitions. It is an excellent card for physicians as it gives them the ability to diagnose correctly. If not concerned with medicine, there is a great power for healing, whether or not it is ever recognized or used.

Like all Twos, the Two of Diamonds feels much concern about people, there is a continuous flow of messages, telephone calls, communications, and interviews. A good half of his business seems to be transacted by mail, telegraph, or telephone.

The Two of Diamonds is a rather powerful card, and the people who do not live up to it are not operating under the Two of Diamonds. If the native is a man, he could be operating as the King of Diamonds, which is good. But operating under the Jack of Diamonds would be less positive than operating under the Birth Card. Two of Diamonds people are always attracted to those who are mentally alert. Men with this birthdate get interested in groups; they join political organizations and service clubs. There is power available for whatever line of activity is chosen, perhaps a position of leadership and authority; the power even extends to the social life. The women seem to know all the "worthwhile" people; the men either become important themselves or are surrounded with those who have "arrived." They also may try to talk you out of your ideas and take you over. They are smart, and they need smart people around them. Twos of Diamonds should have a good education and they hate stupidity. If they are well-educated, they want to associate with people who know more than they do. But few Twos of Diamonds can be pushed into anything by anyone.

These natives are always positive and self-assured. They never yield an inch in an argument. Because their Displacement Card is a six, they are fixed and may develop fixations instead of the higher wisdon—depending entirely upon how it is handled by the individual. The inclination of the Two of Diamonds is toward fixation, and the majority are in danger of becoming so satisfied with what they do and how they think that they forget to work with the principles that give the key to their highest attainment.

This card is not too bad for marriage provided there is a mental rapport established. Twos of Diamonds need it. They are very honest and are sticklers for justice. They do not necessarily want an eye for an eye, but they want to have the last word. All Twos of Diamonds have a front to show the world, but they know what is inside and why this front is put out. This is typical of the Birth Card for both men and women. The men are excellent traders and merchants. If they follow an artistic line, they are less apt to give evidence of their inherent power and will often end up drifting or being content with a mediocre performance. This is not so true of the women. All need a definite goal in life—a positive form of expression that will bring out their true worth and allow them to use it for universal benefit.

BIRTHDATES RULED BY THE TWO OF DIAMONDS

JANUARY 25—AQUARIUS—RULED BY URANUS

Here is a tendency to negativity—"riding along between the shafts" and perhaps depending on gifts or support from others—especially from women. Should cultivate independence and positiveness. Can deal successfully with real estate, products of the earth, manufacturing, or contracting. Are often endowed with psychic gifts but should not dabble in phenomena.

FEBRUARY 23—PISCES—RULED BY NEPTUNE

If the Neptune of the astrological chart is well-aspected, there is a chance for outstanding success. In any case, there is power in this date and the ability to overcome obstacles if the native is ready to accept necessary changes. Sometimes a desire is mistaken for a talent, and a stubborn adherence to its pursuit may block off more practical opportunities. Great interest in color and tone—but not necessarily artistic. Succeed best in occupations that involve travel, shipping, or distant interests. The psychic gifts must not be neglected, but handled with care.

MARCH 21–ARIES–RULED BY MARS

Good promoters. Work better for others than for themselves. Not too sure of their ground and easily lose interest. If interest is not held, will walk out; will start and let others finish. Have keen minds and easy flow of expression. Can work skillfully with sharp instruments or machinery. Often make good engineers. Interested in art but don't have the patience to study techniques. Can succeed in publishing, book concerns, writing.

APRIL 19–ARIES–RULED BY MARS

A more exacting birthdate than the March Aries. Nineteen is a Karmic number and demands settlement of all debts and justice in all dealings. Apt to run the gamut of emotional experience with frequent disappointment. More restless than March twenty-first. Make good salesmen. Should be allowed to be active, not confined to a desk. Can deal in radio, publishing, travel, all moving things. Impulsive and spasmodic–but determined. Must cultivate balance.

MAY 17–TAURUS–RULED BY VENUS

Usually interested in religion. Have positive and definite goals. Demanding and possessive. Want home as a center. Like to have working groups there. Very interested in young people and their education. Enthusiastic about parent-teacher associations, Scout clubs, helping underprivileged children. Make good teachers–of kindergarten, primary grades especially. Good organizers and financiers, bankers. Can always choose the right vocation if they allow the intuition to work. Can make considerable money, save for a while, and then spend extravagantly. Generous sponsors of art but more interested in a productive business than art as a career.

JUNE 15–GEMINI–RULED BY MERCURY

May encounter opposition in early life, but succeed by their own merits later on. Attracted to art, music, and beauty in all forms. Have interest and curiosity about things and people. Do not like responsibility and will not assume it unless obliged to. Like events to move rapidly. Usually assured of success after thirty-six years of age, but may arrive much earlier. Make friends easily. Do better with a professional career than in business. Make good lawyers, pleaders, writers, speakers. Can buy or sell jewelry or other articles of adornment. Make good interior decorators. If they choose business, it is good to cultivate a talent on the side.

JULY 13–CANCER–RULED BY THE MOON

Want money but have to work for it. Thirteen is a testing number, and those who have not developed a strong character may crumple under it; if they do, become consumed with self-pity. The life is not easy, but when problems are met squarely and strongly, great success may ensue. Should follow a line they feel best adapted for and not be forced into an uncongenial occupation. Often become outstanding educators or religious leaders. May have interference from some male member of the family. Interested in the ground and gardens. Can succeed in foods and home commodities. Should cultivate tolerance and unselfishness.

AUGUST 11–LEO–RULED BY THE SUN

This date is slated for success—usually in a professional line. Excellent promoters of the line in which they are most interested. Often attracted to the stage as musicians, composers, or actors. May be outstanding as statesmen or government officials. Must always dominate and will not be dictated to. Are nervous; energies and interests often fluctuating, but can sometimes make a success of two lines of activity pursued at the same time. Should always have an important hobby as an outlet for their duality of interest.

SEPTEMBER 9–VIRGO–RULED BY MERCURY

Have high standards of perfection—for themselves and others. May become overmeticulous and fussy. Power is increased by broadening outlook and humanitarian interests. Tendency to be self-centered. Good lawyers, teachers, linguists. Best in a mental or merchandising occupation.

OCTOBER 7–LIBRA–RULED BY VENUS

A birthdate of spiritual power. If they learn to use it, can become outstanding in the religious world. Must learn early to distinguish between the true and the false. Should avoid self-indulgence and secretiveness. Very deliberate in thinking and action. Good educators, writers, sponsors of just causes. An element of drama leads some of them to the theater or screen. Love art, beauty, poetry; can write poetry themselves. Often have strong intuitions and a prophetic gift.

NOVEMBER 5–SCORPIO–RULED BY MARS

Deep and keen thinkers; diggers for facts. If there is a talent for drama, make outstanding actors. Become valuable and important in any business undertaken. Want all or nothing in terms of accomplishment. Expressive and dynamic, often critical and sarcastic. If self-indulgent, may take to drink as an escape from emotional frustration. Good lawyers, negotiators, statesmen, leaders in large businesses.

DECEMBER 3–SAGITTARIUS–RULED BY JUPITER

Friendly and popular. Can always get help from others. Inspire confidence. Have power in words. Can commercialize art—as dealer, connoisseur or performer. May marry a well-traveled or wealthy person. Have optimistic temperament; make good companions. Good critics, but usually kindly ones. More expressive in public than at home. Friends and social contacts necessary for contentment. Women should cultivate definite interests or may become butterflies and gossips.

TWO OF DIAMONDS—PLANETARY SEQUENCE OF PERSONAL RELATIONSHIPS

Horizontal Lines—Mars and Jupiter

JACK OF SPADES—MERCURY CARD IN THE URANUS LINE

On some levels you will find great rapport with these natives, and you might find you could talk for hours and hours, but the overall picture does not include this card in your close personal life. These people's feet will seem to be a little farther off the ground than you want to be.

Jack of Spades birthdates: January 3, February 1

EIGHT OF CLUBS—VENUS CARD IN THE NEPTUNE LINE

This is one of your best possibilities for a lasting and loving relationship that will also turn you on mentally. You'll feel acutely aware—probably more so with this native than others. But don't let him inhibit you. He will enjoy you more when you use your mind—even if you think he is smarter than you. He doesn't wish to be around people who don't use their minds.

Eight of Clubs birthdates: March 28, April 26, May 24, June 22, July 20, August 18, September 16, October 14, November 12, December 10.

SIX OF DIAMONDS—MARS CARD IN THE MERCURY LINE

Communication here will be more on the material level than the in-depth kind of discussions you seek and ultimately enjoy most. Keep these natives from talking about money, and you will like the friendship. Personal and romantic involvements don't stand up well over time.

Six of Diamonds birthdates: January 21, February 19, March 17, April 15, May 13, June 11, July 9, August 7, September 5, October 3, November 1

FOUR OF SPADES—JUPITER CARD IN THE VENUS LINE

There is no question about the feeling that will happen between the two of you in this case. It's love at whatever level you find it, and you better pursue it because it may never pass your way again. Whatever the case, this native can always bring good things your way. Don't expect money consciousness to any great extent. The long drive up the hill to the big mansion is not what these natives are looking for—and you might find it's not so important to you, either.

Four of Spades birthdates: January 10, February 8, March 6, April 4, May 2

TEN OF HEARTS—SATURN CARD IN THE MARS LINE

If you meet this native and he is of the opposite sex, don't get involved—or at least don't get romatically involved. This is that whirlwind affair which not only leaves your pockets emptier but also leaves—you. Use your fine intuition, and enjoy the acquaintance, but don't read anything into a relationship that has no real basis.

Ten of Hearts birthdates: July 31, August 29, September 27, October 25, November 23, December 21

TEN OF DIAMONDS—URANUS CARD IN THE JUPITER LINE
(Double Jupiter Lines on the Diagonal)

Any kind of new business with this native will probably prove to be profitable—new ideas or items in a business with which you are already familiar would be ideal. This is a good working relationship; if you try to squeeze it into a romantic involvement; it probably wouldn't work over the years.

Ten of Diamonds birthdates: January 17, February 15, March 13, April 11, May 9, June 7, July 5, August 3, September 1

EIGHT OF SPADES—NEPTUNE CARD IN THE SATURN LINE
(Jupiter Line on the Vertical)

These natives will seem too lazy for your way of life, and the chances are strong that you're right. However, the tie with this card can be very strong. You are both healers—you could work effectively together in the fields of medicine or science. Don't be misled by what appears on the outside. Underneath is an important person for you to know. Don't think about love unless it's thrust upon you, and then a long courtship is in order.

Eight of Spades birthdates: January 6, February 4, March 2

Vertical Line—Saturn

NINE OF CLUBS—VENUS LINE

You'll be able to see through this person while you're still shaking hands and saying hello. You'll like him but feel emotionally that he is not for you. Stay friends; he can keep you informed on many interesting subjects. (Though you won't always want the information, it can't hurt you.) Try not to get personally involved; this cannot be a lasting relationship without a great deal of effort on your part.

Nine of Clubs birthdates: January 31, February 29, March 27, April 25, May 23, June 21, July 19, August 17, September 15, November 11, December 9

FIVE OF CLUBS–MERCURY LINE

An immediate attraction; these natives will especially like your sure-footed attitude. The glitter tarnishes when you cease to entertain them and must dig back into your work. Their restless nature will leave you in the same place they found you—but wiser. Don't look for any long-term romance or relationships of any kind; just enjoy what you have when you have it.

Five of Clubs birthdates: March 31, April 29, May 27, June 25, July 23, August 21, September 19, October 17, November 15, December 13

KING OF SPADES–CROWN LINE

You may find it very difficult to agree with anything these natives have to say. Make every effort to close your mind to what irritates you about them—even if they seem a little far-out in their way of thinking. The problem here is that you both have much to give to each other, but if you (or this native) are operating on a negative level, you will both be blind to each other, and the result will be a lot of knowledge and wisdom lost to both of you. Definitely not for marriage, and other relationships are most difficult unless much effort is made and maintained.

King of Spades birthdate: January 1

SIX OF CLUBS–NEPTUNE LINE
(Two of Diamonds Displacement Card)

This person can never hurt you seriously—for he is a part of you as your Displacement Card. Getting into a personal relationship will be difficult (though you'll be seriously tempted). The difficulty becomes obvious when your Six of Clubs tries to dominate you by subtly placing you in his way of life—which probably will be too inactive for you. These natives can be good friends, and this is where you should stay.

Six of Clubs birthdates: March 30, April 28, May 26, June 24, July 22, August 20, September 18, October 16, November 14, December 12

TWO OF CLUBS–URANUS LINE

This relationship, no matter what kind, will not only displease you—you will wind up hoping your paths never cross again. You may feel as if an encounter is like a weight around your neck—something you have to do—and this could be pretty accurate. Dealing on a positive plane with this native will further your own thinking and goals for many years to come. Don't let yourself get into a vulnerable position at any time, which means no personal involvements.

Two of Clubs birthdates: May 30, June 28, July 26, August 24, September 22, October 20, November 18, December 16

NINE OF HEARTS–SATURN LINE

This native will definitely be more attracted to you than vice versa. But if you attempt to become emotionally involved, you will find every possible brick wall standing in your way. Listen to your inner voice—and don't bother. Once the romantic attraction is out of the way, you'll find a bright, interesting person who can always keep you intrigued just by his way of life.

Nine of Hearts birthdates: August 30, September 28, October 26, November 24, December 22

EIGHT OF SPADES–JUPITER LINE: SEE HORIZONTAL LINE

Diagonal Lines

ACE OF HEARTS–JUPITER AND URANUS LINES

You will probably feel superior to this native and that, in itself, is a danger sign. Though you may well be superior, it is your obligation to relate on a level the other person can understand. Universal discussions may not be important to this native, so don't hit on areas that may be uncomfortable or impossible. Aces of Hearts can help you and be your friends, they will never knowingly hurt you. This is an exceptionally good business relationship, so capitalize on that. Romantically, it's not ideal, but not impossible. Just remember only to expect that which is available or conceivable in the first place.

Ace of Hearts birthdates: December 30

FIVE OF DIAMONDS–SATURN AND NEPTUNE LINES

No matter what you do, you may not be able to escape this native. And he will feel a strong attraction to you. If it's a close personal involvement, don't probe into areas that don't affect your relationship—just enjoy the great romantic love you can give each other. You will be somewhat of a stabilizing factor for him, so don't be surprised when it happens. This is the way it's supposed to be, the way it will work best.

Five of Diamonds birthdates: January 22, February 20, March 18, April 16, May 14, June 12, July 10, August 8, September 6, October 4, November 2

JACK OF HEARTS—VENUS AND JUPITER LINES

Not only will you have to be very careful when you meet this native, but if you are a female, you will have to be careful of meeting *any* Heart-card man who may be operating under the Jack as his Personality Card. This is a card of love for you, but these natives (operating under their Birth Card) usually have little or no personal love life. The best way to recognize the danger signs for personal love would be to come to a decision on whether your Jack of Hearts is more interested in his friends and humanity in general, or you. Be very realistic—you could be innocently deceived and emotionally disappointed.

Jack of Hearts birthdates: July 30, August 28, September 26, October 24, November 22, December 20

QUEEN OF CLUBS—MERCURY AND MARS LINES

This is someone you will probably admire and not want to admit it. Ideally, for romance you would be female and your Queen of Clubs a male, but in any case, you will both have irritations (mostly minor) in any kind of relationship. Marriage is not recommended, but possible. The best involvement would be friendship—someone you see occasionally, whose opinion not only stimulates you, but garners respect from you as well. Don't be so know-it-all with these people. *They* know better.

Queen of Clubs birthdates: January 28, February 26, March 24, April 22, May 20, June 18, July 16, August 14, September 12, October 10, November 8, December 6

NINE OF SPADES—VENUS AND URANUS LINES

You could find romance with this person where you would least expect it. And it could work well. Especially if you are male and your Nine of Spades female. In either case, these natives will keep life interesting for you. Business involvements are not recommended unless you are doing the selling, and they, the creating.

Nine of Spades birthdates: January 5, February 3, March 1

ACE OF SPADES—MERCURY AND NEPTUNE LINES

You are apt to fall in love with an Ace of Spades without ever knowing what he looks like in the sunshine. And it can work—especially if you tend to be somewhat domineering. These natives will be enchanted with your capabilities, and this can dispel some of the fear they carry around. If you are involved with this Ace in any area, permit him his secretive side; it probably won't be worth the effort of investigation and will give him a certain amount of pleasure.

Ace of Spades birthdates: January 13, February 11, March 9, April 7, May 5, June 3, July 1

TEN OF DIAMONDS—DOUBLE JUPITER LINES: SEE HORIZONTAL LINE

THREE OF CLUBS—SATURN AND MARS LINES

Here is another strong romance card, but a romance is not recommended. The heavy influence of Saturn and Mars will bring problems to a personal involvement, problems that you wouldn't have to go through with another card. Be friends—but at a distance; otherwise you will feel drained every time you are around this native.

Three of Clubs birthdates: May 29, June 27, July 25, August 23, September 21, October 19, November 17, December 15

JACK OF CLUBS—MARS CARD IN THE URANUS AND VENUS LINES

You can do business with these natives and make a lot of money (providing you have a good attorney). Don't be surprised if they cut corners—even if you happen to be one of the corners. It's possible and probable. In the words of Teddy Roosevelt, "Speak softly, and carry a big stick." Know what you're doing, and don't get personally involved under any circumstances. Your sex life may be fantastic, but this native won't be around when it really counts.

Jack of Clubs birthdates: January 29, February 27, March 25, April 23, May 21, June 19, July 17, August 15, September 13, October 11, November 9, December 7

FOUR OF HEARTS—NEPTUNE AND MERCURY LINES

This native could be one of the best friends you'll ever have. And it would be best to keep it that way unless you have an undiscovered yearning for a life of romanticism (which is not probable). Don't be misled by his smug facade; he can only bring happiness to you.

Four of Hearts birthdates: October 31, November 29, December 27

TWO OF DIAMONDS FAMOUS BIRTHDATES

January 25	William Somerset Maugham
February 23	Peter Fonda
March 21	John D. Rockefeller III Flo Ziegfield Joseph Pulitzer
April 19	Don Adams Hugh O'Brien

August 11	Mike Douglas
October 7	June Allyson
	Andy Devine
November 5	Roy Rogers
December 3	Andy Williams

Two of Spades

Spades – Labor; Enlightenment
Two of Spades – Fear of the Will of God
Two in Spades – Union and Rhythm in Work

The Mars Card in the Neptune Line. Displaces the **Six of Spades** in the Natural Spread.

This is the first instance where the Horizontal Line in the Planetary Sequence carries up to the Crown Line (the three top cards). This gives the Two of Spades a special significance as well as a more exacting requirement than the other Twos. Regardless of the nature of the cards themselves or of

Planetary Sequence

			K♠ Neptune	8♦ Uranus	10♣ Saturn			
A♠	3♦	5♣	10♠	Q♣	A♣	3♥		Mercury
2♥	9♠	9♣	J♥	5♠	7♦	7♥		Venus
8♣	J♠	2♦	4♣	6♥	K♦	K♥		Mars
A♦	A♥	8♠	10♦	10♥	4♠	6♦		Jupiter
5♦	7♣	9♥	3♠	3♣	5♥	Q♦		Saturn
J♦	K♣	2♣	7♠	9♦	J♣	Q♠		Uranus
Q♥ Jupiter	6♠ Mars	6♣ Venus	8♥ Mercury	2♠	4♦	4♥		Neptune

Neptune Uranus Saturn Jupiter Mars Venus Mercury

Mundane Spread

their planetary rulership, as soon as the Sun realm is reached, there is additional power and spiritual strength. It becomes, therefore, all the more important for these natives to cultivate awareness of their true destiny as seekers of wisdom and messengers of Light. The main difficulty with the majority of the Spade cards is their lack of this awareness. Life is never a bed or roses for any of them, and unless and until they begin to operate on the "upper levels," they will remain so engrossed in the struggle to overcome their material and emotional handicaps and the misunderstanding to which they are usually subjected, they will have little time or courage left for the cultivation of their spiritual powers.

This doesn't have to happen at all. It is the Spades who become great spiritual leaders and come as close to adeptness as is possible in the earth experience. This state is never reached without great sacrifice and the achievement of impersonality, and spades always have to struggle against apparently unmerited odds and other people's misunderstanding of their motives.

The task of the Two of Spades is to live on a strictly constructive basis; to avoid self-indulgence at the expense of work or duty; to be willing to serve—regardless of remuneration; and not to spare himself hard work, which is one phase of the mission he has come to fulfill.

Practicality and common sense must be instilled early. These natives can easily be thrown off balance, lost in daydreaming and a realm of unreality. Later in life they may develop a neurosis that might have serious consequences. So great is the power of the Two of Spades that those who are deliberately headed for evil become the so-called "Black Magicians."

The Two of Spades is a card of fear, but this is a whining kind of fear. The April birthdate, accentuated by the Mars position, especially whines a lot. Two of Spades are interested in music and art, and they also have their hand on the pulse of the public. They can touch the "higher forces"; they make good doctors and are very kind as a rule, but fearful.

Intuitional force in the highest degree is at their disposal—but it requires an earnest desire plus steady application to establish a clear channel. Those who are able to bring to their conscious minds their subconscious knowledge of who they are, know the right direction to take and the answers to their problems.

In practical affairs, Two of Spades people make good buyers and traders; they have an interest in foreign places and people and become successful foreign agents and negotiators. There is a fine balance to be sought between spiritual ideals and sound business tactics. With the right cooperation (and all Twos need it) this balance can be—and often is—found.

There is a tendency to willfulness—with consequent self-undoing. They want their own way and often mislead themselves by their adherence to it. They also have the ability to dramatize, and many actors are Twos of Spades.

The women should strive to know the men with whom they are closely associated; they may easily become a burden and a problem.

Most Twos of Spades like diversion and good company. They are genial

Your Place in the Cards

and popular, easy drinkers and lively entertainers. Although, like all Twos, they want home roots, they are often obliged to work away from home. Circumstances drive them to stand on their own feet—usually the hard way. When they do, and make a success of it, they develop a strength of character that helps them overcome their material obstacles.

BIRTHDATES RULED BY THE TWO OF SPADES

JANUARY 12—CAPRICORN—RULED BY SATURN
There is no laziness in this birthdate, but rather a willingness to work hard—often too hard—to obtain the desired place. Ambition is strong, often so dominating that it obscures more worthy objectives. The attraction is usually to a business career—merchandising or building, contracting or land transactions. Whatever these natives undertake must pay, even if they choose to direct their talent to writing or the theater. Success is practically assured.

FEBRUARY 10—AQUARIUS—RULED BY VENUS
To be satisfied, these natives must deal with people, either by direct contact or through work that has a public appeal. Aquarians are always free lancers and from a wide choice select the occupation that most appeals to them—as long as it promises good returns. Writers, actors, clergymen, statesmen, or counselors and group leaders can succeed.

MARCH 8—PISCES—RULED BY NEPTUNE
These natives have a strong sense of service and an urge to make known the ideals to which they are dedicated. There is usually great attraction for the sea, and many are successful in commerce, naval affairs, and foreign trade. Good diagnosticians, dealers in cosmetics and perfumes, or oil operators are found here—also writers and philosophers.

APRIL 6—ARIES—RULED BY MARS
Enthusiastic and impetuous, but often beset with obstacles and disappointments owing to their tendency to choose the easiest way. Subject to many changes caused by circumstances. Make good writers, lecturers, journalists—sometimes actors or artists. Are able as trial lawyers. Not sufficiently patient or far-sighted to become counselors or trustees.

MAY 4—TAURUS—RULED BY VENUS
Are public spirited and philanthropic. Want peace and security and strong home roots, with luxurious surroundings. Are successful in land deals, horti-

culture, and anything concerning natural products and resources. Love of nature is strong, and they should live in the countryside part of the year. Many poets and authors are found under this date. If attracted to public life, they make good politicians and government officials. In business can succeed as heads of large manufacturing concerns.

JUNE 2—GEMINI—RULED BY MERCURY

Restless and active; always have more than one iron in the fire. Both social and business contacts are successful; must always have an audience. Have easy flow of words; make good journalists, columnists and correspondents. Many are attracted to science (mainly by curiosity) and the church (mainly by their sense of drama). They move quickly and change frequently—in a search for improvement. If there is any monotony, it comes early in life.

TWO OF SPADES—PLANETARY SEQUENCE OF PERSONAL RELATIONSHIPS

Horizontal Lines—Neptune and Crown

EIGHT OF HEARTS—MERCURY CARD IN THE JUPITER LINE

This native is a "good-time Charlie" to you, and if you really wanted to pursue a relationship on a deeper level (which you probably won't), you would find someone who could be extremely helpful in your own spiritual growth. It would be best to be friends or lovers (no business ventures) if you can truly accept these natives as they are.

Eight of Hearts birthdates: August 31, September 29, October 27, November 25, December 23

SIX OF CLUBS—VENUS CARD IN THE SATURN LINE

Marriage or a lasting relationship with this native is entirely possible and probable. You may have a tendency to feel negative—but don't. Sixes of Clubs have many things to teach you and the patience it takes to do so. Relax. Let them do most of the talking.

Six of Clubs birthdates: March 30, April 28, May 26, June 24, July 22, August 20, September 18, October 16, November 14, December 12

SIX OF SPADES—MARS CARD IN THE URANUS LINE
(Two of Spades Displacement Card)

Eventually a close association here will probably wind up with the two of you in a rut. This person doesn't have enough action for you, and even though it may seem to be a new way of life that you haven't tried before—

resist it. You'll feel driven toward some kind of involvement, but you'll end up bored and probably in a subservient position.

Six of Spades birthdates: January 8, February 6, March 4, April 2

QUEEN OF HEARTS—JUPITER CARD IN THE NEPTUNE LINE

This native can be a lot of fun for you, but when you feel it's time for the party to be over for a while, your Queen of Hearts will still be whooping it up. You are a little too practical for this relationship although you won't be able to resist this (usually) delightful, fun-loving person.

Queen of Hearts birthdates: July 29, August 27, September 25, October 23, November 21, December 19

TEN OF CLUBS—SATURN CARD IN THE MARS LINE
(Crown Line on the Vertical)

If you could apply yourself to the knowledge this native has to offer, you could overcome many of the obstacles you will inevitably encounter on a practical level. Follow their suggestions, even if they are relegated only to recommend books for you to read. It is the Ten of Clubs' Karmic debt not to steer you wrong. Close involvements will be difficult and are not conducive to happiness with this native.

Ten of Clubs birthdates: January 30, February 28, March 26, April 24, May 22, June 20, July 18, August 16, September 14, October 12, November 10, December 8

EIGHT OF DIAMONDS—URANUS CARD IN THE JUPITER LINE

Stick to business with this native, and you can't go wrong—especially in a new or contemporary type of business that could have wide appeal. Any problems here could be with you. Don't buck this native by insisting you're right without the facts to back you up. Chances are you may not be completely accurate—without knowing it. A love association will not be nearly so important as money in this relationship, so take full advantage.

Eight of Diamonds birthdates: January 19, February 17, March 15, April 13, May 11, June 9, July 7, August 5, September 3, October 1

KING OF SPADES—NEPTUNE CARD IN THE SATURN LINE

If you ever meet a King of Spades, take as much time as you can afford to discover the intricacies of this amazing person. It could mean a dynamic change in your life, or it could represent all the things you don't want to be—but in either case, you will come away from the relationship a much wiser human being. Don't miss the opportunity. A romantic involvement is virtually impossible unless you are willing to submit totally to this individual. (And, in this case, it wouldn't hurt you—only elevate your spirituality to a level you may have only dreamed of.) Be sure-footed in any decision; it's important for your growth.

King of Spades birthdate: January 1

Vertical Line—Mars

NINE OF DIAMONDS—URANUS LINE

A great struggle could exist in a close relationship with this native; even though he could open many new doors for you, the whole thing will be short-lived. Although you will be interested in his money-making abilities, you will probably clash head-on when it comes to the practicalities of living. You both want your own way, and you both can be extremely verbal about this. Take a pass on anything but a brief encounter.

Nine of Diamonds birthdates: January 18, February 16, March 14, April 12, May 10, June 8, July 6, August 4, September 2

THREE OF CLUBS—SATURN LINE

Here is a Karmic tie—particularly romantic—that you could be much better off without. The Three of Clubs uncertainty of his own position in life will only compound your own fears of the future. It's a weak relationship at best and should be kept (if at all) at twenty paces.

Three of Clubs birthdates: May 29, June 27, July 25, August 23, September 21, October 19, November 17, December 15

TEN OF HEARTS—JUPITER LINE

Your eyes will lock, and you'll know it's love—but it couldn't be farther from the truth. Unless your concept of love is for the moment, which it isn't. Your need of roots will make you very possessive of this individual; then he will run like a red-handed bandit. And you will be the loser. Don't consider anything other than friendship, and even that could pose certain problems. Be careful—the eight hours aren't worth the eight seconds.

Ten of Hearts birthdates: July 31, August 29, September 27, October 25, November 23, December 21

SIX OF HEARTS—MARS LINE

This is a similar relationship, yet radically different. This native won't hurt you as the Ten of Hearts will—but the result can be somewhat similar. This native is a true friend, capable of encouraging you to continue those unfinished projects, but never making you feel guilty that you didn't. Don't look for love—you could be disappointed. Sixes of Hearts are more universally oriented and love many people. If love happens to be there on a personal level, accept it as it is; it could be a beautiful experience.

Six of Hearts birthdates: October 29, November 27, December 25

FIVE OF SPADES—VENUS LINE

This is another problem card for you. No matter how you conduct yourself, this native will make some effort to rearrange your life. As a Saturn Card, it's his obligation, so there's not much you can do about it. Try a lightweight relationship—remote but within hearing distance. These natives *do* have something to say.

Five of Spades birthdates: January 9, February 7, March 5, April 3, May 1

QUEEN OF CLUBS—MERCURY LINE

This native could sell you a lucrative piece of real estate or conduct an E.S.P. session with you—both productive and positive. Or he could even be a lawyer who settles a case for you in an unusual way. In any situation this is a good relationship for you—preferably friendship or business. The Queen of Clubs' thinking is on a different plane than yours for a successful personal involvement.

Queen of Clubs birthdates: January 28, February 26, March 24, April 22, May 20, June 18, July 16, August 14, September 12, October 10, November 8, December 6

TEN OF CLUBS—CROWN LINE: SEE HORIZONTAL LINE

Diagonal Lines

JACK OF CLUBS—URANUS AND VENUS LINES

If you have a quick love affair with this native, and he doesn't answer your phone calls afterwards, you have only yourself to blame. This relationship—whatever it is—should be considered temporary, something different and perhaps sensual, but the emphasis is on *temporary*. Don't look for anything else in any kind of involvement. It's like two ships in the night—you touch, you do what you can for each other, and you continue on your separate ways. Don't have any regrets.

Jack of Clubs birthdates: January 29, February 27, March 25, April 23, May 21, June 19, July 17, August 15, September 13, October 11, November 9, December 7

QUEEN OF DIAMONDS–SATURN AND MERCURY LINES

You will never lack financial security with this mate, but the price may be on the heavy side. Some of it could be practical such as short illnesses and large doctor bills, and some could be spiritual with as "simple" a problem as an inability to relate on that level. In any event, the involvement is certainly worth investigation.

Queen of Diamonds birthdates: January 15, February 13, March 11, April 9, May 7, June 5, July 3, August 1

SEVEN OF SPADES–URANUS AND JUPITER LINES

It may be difficult for you to keep up with this native, and you may feel it's not worth the effort—but it is. Make every effort, as a matter of fact, at any kind of involvement—it could be an important relationship. Don't try to force your knowledge on these natives; it may be relative in any event.

Seven of Spades birthdates: January 7, February 5, March 3, April 1

NINE OF HEARTS–DOUBLE SATURN LINES

Any attraction with this native should be suppressed. The double Saturn emphasis places heavy burdens on any kind of involvement; coupled with your own material and spiritual obstacles, you would only be involved with a duplicate of yourself. Relationships should be based on enhancing weaknesses, so this card should be avoided, no matter how strong the inclination may be toward (what may seem to be) a serious situation.

Nine of Hearts birthdates: August 30, September 28, October 26, November 24, December 22

ACE OF HEARTS–JUPITER AND URANUS LINES

You may feel good all over when you meet this native—but don't let that feeling lead you to the altar. Divorce would almost be inevitable; your goals, ideals, and ambitions in life simply don't mix. Keep the relationship in its proper perspective and enjoy this native and the many little pleasing surprises that he will give to you, making a portion of your life that much easier.

Ace of Hearts birthdates: December 30

EIGHT OF CLUBS–MARS AND NEPTUNE LINES

When you meet this native, be prepared to keep your mouth closed and your ears open. You won't agree most of the time—you'll feel as if he is not being truthful, but set that aside. Here is an opportunity to feel the passion of a conviction—it can only be good for you.

Eight of Clubs birthdates: March 28, April 26, May 24, June 22, July 20, August 18, September 16, October 14, November 12, December 10

Your Place in the Cards

TWO OF SPADES FAMOUS BIRTHDATES

January 12   John Hancock
                    Jack London

February 10   Jimmy Durante
                    Leontyne Price
                    Robert Wagner

April 6   Andre Previn
                    Henry Houdini

June 2   Johnny Weissmuller

Threes

THREES represent a divided path, the Middle Way with a fork in the road—hence Indecision.

If there is enough enlightenment to go straight ahead, there will be no deviation from the Middle Way—the One Path that leads to the Source of Light.

Three, as the number of the Trinity, *is* the Light Bearer—but when there is deviation and the pursuit of temptation, the Light that is three becomes destructive dynamite, and we have but another example of *separation* from the Source of our good.

The Indecision that besets the individuals whose birthdates are ruled by threes is but a product of their own faulty judgment of lasting values and abiding Truth.

Three scatters and diffuses, wasting time, energy, and *words* (its greatest power) in an uncertain three-dimensional world. Although the basic symbol is the triangle, it is by no accident that the Masters of old gave to the threes a straight line, without deviation or uncertainty. He who goes *directly* and follows the line straight *up* will have no problems in life, no failure in the attainment of his goal. This is the Via Media of the Tarot—"the straight and narrow path" from Malkuth, the Kingdom, to Kether, the Crown.

The usual Three is uncertain and diffused; the positive, Light-bearing Three knows the Straight Line and follows it—even though there is invariably a choice and a major decision to be made in some department of the life.

Many of our outstanding authors, religious leaders, and actors are Threes— the actors being, as a rule, of the more serious and message-bearing type. No man can ever lose his spark of divinity; the Three is the closest of all to the Source, if he did but know it.

Hearts are uncertain about Love
Clubs must choose between the Higher and the Lower Mind
Diamonds are in doubt about Values
Spades must choose between Matter and Spirit

Three of Hearts

Hearts — Love
Three of Hearts — Uncertainty in Personal Relations
Three in Hearts — Happiness in Contacts

The Mercury Card in the Mercury Line. Displaces the **Ace of Hearts** in the Natural Spread.

In the Mundane Spread the Three of Hearts is the "first step out"—the first departure from God's Plan, the original parent of all the mistakes that follow, the Adam that symbolizes the fall of Man. The desire for love (the Ace of Hearts being the Displacement Card) rules the lives of the Threes of Hearts, who have mental uncertainty about love in general and love of what or whom in particular. Perhaps it is the subconscious realization of this great error that so often makes the love life of the Three of Hearts an unsatisfying—or tragic—thing, and causes the eternal quest for the perfect love—and the doubt of it when found.

As far as the emotions are concerned, life for the Three of Hearts is a series of trials and errors. Threes go in one direction and then the other. They either stand in the center and reach up or reach down. A Three of Hearts can either work entirely on the material plane or work on the spiritual plane.

The Three, itself, represents the Trinity—the Father, the Son and the Holy Ghost. The Three of Hearts is expression of it, or it can be scattering, the

Planetary Sequence

			K♠	8♦	10♣			
A♠ Uranus	3♦ Saturn	5♣ Jupiter	10♠ Mars	Q♣ Venus	A♣ Mercury	3♥	Mercury
2♥	9♠	9♣	J♥	5♠	7♦	7♥ Neptune	Venus
8♣	J♠	2♦	4♣	6♥	K♦	K♥	Mars
A♦	A♥	8♠	10♦	10♥	4♠	6♦	Jupiter
5♦	7♣	9♥	3♠	3♣	5♥	Q♦	Saturn
J♦	K♣	2♣	7♠	9♦	J♣	Q♠	Uranus
Q♥	6♠	6♣	8♥	2♠	4♦	4♥	Neptune

Neptune · Uranus · Saturn · Jupiter · Mars · Venus · Mercury

Mundane Spread

majority of Threes being very indecisive people. They do not know which way to go.

There is no lack of activity in the Threes of Hearts' quests. Their fellow men never give them a crown of fidelity, but it is not so much a question of fickleness or promiscuity in their case as an inner need for the love that satisfies the Self (again from the Ace as Displacement Card). The pity of it is that the critical faculty of Mercury steps in and sows the seeds of questioning and doubt.

Socially, these natives are usually charming and attractive people—welcome guests and perfect hosts; it is only in the closer relationships that the strain becomes a break. Three of Hearts people are concerned with knowing where they stand as to emotions. Their lives are very changeable because of their discontent. On the other hand, if they were contented, they probably wouldn't reach out to know where they stood.

They are always intelligent and informed, but since their uncertainty extends to their mental processes, they do not always distinguish clearly between right and wrong, truth and falsehood—unless the early training has fixed the distinction for them. They are often dominated in youth by the mother, later by the wife and therefore have the best chance for self-development away from home. They should never marry anyone who interferes with their freedom—even in its uncertainty or misuse.

There are only two birthdates ruled by this card, only two types of people to consider—the Sagittarian (November 30) and the Capricorn (December 28).

BIRTHDATES RULED BY THE THREE OF HEARTS

NOVEMBER 30—SAGITTARIUS—RULED BY JUPITER

Good sportsmanship and popularity belong to this birthdate. Clever with words, but seldom show their hand. Have great influence with crowds; understand mass psychology. Good orators, writers, statesmen; often have inventive gifts.

DECEMBER 28—CAPRICORN—RULED BY SATURN

Have fits of stubbornness but are actually concerned about their future. Fear insecurity. Should avoid medicine as a career; dislike physical contacts. Interested in large enterprises; ambitious. May become political leaders, statesmen. More faithful than November 30.

THREE OF HEARTS — PLANETARY SEQUENCE OF PERSONAL RELATIONSHIPS

Horizontal Lines—Mercury and Venus

ACE OF CLUBS—MERCURY CARD IN THE VENUS LINE

A possible romance, but don't expect anything permanent. Great relationship if the two of you don't mess it up by constant questioning and re-questioning of each other's love. If you want it, accept it as is, and insist that the Ace of Clubs do the same. Friendship good.

Ace of Clubs birthdates: May 31, June 29, July 27, August 25, September 23, October 21, November 19, December 17

QUEEN OF CLUBS—VENUS CARD IN THE MARS LINE

A stimulating, probably sexually oriented love affair which will overpower and dominate you eventually. (The Queen of Clubs is the Three of Hearts' Displacement Card in the Natural Spread). This native is a good friend who will always be there in time of need and who will probably tell you how to avoid the problem in the future. Don't make too many demands on him—he already does that himself.

Queen of Clubs birthdates: January 28, February 26, March 24, April 22, May 20, June 18, July 16, August 14, September 12, October 10, November 8, December 6

TEN OF SPADES—MARS CARD IN THE JUPITER LINE

Home life would be nil with this native if he is financially successful to any degree. Arguments and irritations will be prevalent in a close involvement. Good for business, so stop that pessimistic attitude.

Ten of Spades birthdates: January 4, February 2

FIVE OF CLUBS—JUPITER CARD IN THE SATURN LINE

A Karmic relationship that can never work for you romantically. These natives will drive you crazy wondering about the why's, how's and where's of who they are. And don't ever think you can find out. This is not a relationship to upset you when it is over, and you probably will profit by the association.

Five of Clubs birthdates: March 31, April 29, May 27, June 25, July 23, August 21, September 19, October 17, November 15, December 13

Your Place in the Cards

THREE OF DIAMONDS—SATURN CARD IN THE URANUS LINE

A definite Karmic relationship; be careful of negative influence. What you are in doubt about is not related to this native—better to listen to one with a different approach, more akin to your own way of thinking and feeling.

Three of Diamonds birthdates: January 24, February 22, March 20, April 18, May 16, June 14, July 12, August 10, September 8, October 6, November 4, December 2

ACE OF SPADES—URANUS CARD IN THE NEPTUNE LINE

Not good for emotional involvements because of conflicting insecurities. Never underestimate this native; he'll keep you guessing. Friendship best of all involvements.

Ace of Spades birthdates: January 13, February 11, March 9, April 7, May 5, June 3, July 1

SEVEN OF HEARTS—NEPTUNE CARD IN THE MERCURY LINE
(Venus Line on the Vertical)

Confusing relationship; these natives' emotional and romantic involvements fluctuate and will make you want to run the other way. (If you don't feel this way, take another look.) May tend to reveal to you too many of your own problems. Their jealousy will turn you off.

Seven of Hearts birthdates: September 30, October 28, November 26, December 24

Vertical Line—Mercury

FOUR OF HEARTS—NEPTUNE LINE

A quick not-what-it-seemed-to-be involvement; someone you can talk to, but someone whom you have chased away romantically by not fully believing him. Be friends—this native can help to right your head about your own love life.

Four of Hearts birthdates: October 31, November 29, December 27

QUEEN OF SPADES—URANUS LINE

Surprises are in store when you really get involved with this native. Be prepared for a lackadaisical attitude toward their mode of living—but an interesting love and intellectual relationship.

Queen of Spades Birthdate: January 2

QUEEN OF DIAMONDS—SATURN LINE

Don't get romantically involved, or you'll wind up in a courtroom. Chances are you won't even give each other long enough to get to know your last names, and it's just as well. A possible Karmic involvement, but try to stay clear of this native—more problems for you than he's worth.

Queen of Diamonds birthdates: January 15, February 13, March 11, April 9, May 7, June 5, July 3, August 1

SIX OF DIAMONDS—JUPITER LINE

Nothing but good can come of this involvement. Friendship and business are probably best, but don't overlook romantic overtones. An important relationship.

Six of Diamonds birthdates: January 21, February 19, March 17, April 15, May 13, June 11, July 9, August 7, September 5, October 3, November 1

KING OF HEARTS—MARS LINE

A Karmic tie that will probably have a strong influence on you—perhaps your father or older brother, if either is of the heart suit. A burden to you that can create frustrations and angry outbursts. Know that whatever is done in this relationship, is done in love—and handle accordingly.

King of Hearts birthdates: June 30, July 28, August 26, September 24, October 22, November 20, December 18

SEVEN OF HEARTS—VENUS LINE: SEE HORIZONTAL LINE

Diagonal Line

SEVEN OF DIAMONDS—DOUBLE VENUS LINES

This native will really excite you, but the relationship will probably be short-lived. If your seven is financially struggling, you'll think your love life couldn't be better. But you'll still doubt it—only to confirm your doubts when he begins making money again. Don't think about making any permanent plans.

Seven of Diamonds birthdates: January 20, February 18, March 16, April 14, May 12, June 10, July 8, August 6, September 4, October 2

SIX OF HEARTS—DOUBLE MARS LINES

Dynamic romance—sexually oriented relationship that can prove fulfilling if you try to understand these natives' winning personalities as they really are. Nice people who wouldn't and couldn't willingly hurt you. Great for friendship; business aspects good.

Six of Hearts birthdates: October 29, November 27, December 25

TEN OF DIAMONDS–DOUBLE JUPITER LINES

Terrific for business; you can only profit by this association. Friendship okay, except under close circumstances—the Ten of Diamonds' values are different from yours, and this can create arguments. Not good for love life.

Ten of Diamonds birthdates: January 17, February 15, March 13, April 11, May 9, June 7, July 5, August 3, September 1

NINE OF HEARTS–DOUBLE SATURN LINES

Heavy burden of responsibility to this card through Karma—but this nine brings answers otherwise unsought and unsolved. Too difficult a life for the two of you, romantically—but friendship should prove rewarding.

Nine of Hearts birthdates: August 30, September 28, October 26, November 24, December 22

KING OF CLUBS–DOUBLE URANUS LINES

Another Karmic tie that can be fulfilling. Probably represents a "club man" who will teach you new and important things—even though it will be difficult, it's most important. Stay away from close personal involvements.

King of Clubs birthdates: January 27, February 25, March 23, April 21, May 19, June 17, July 15, August 13, September 11, October 9, November 7, December 5

QUEEN OF HEARTS–DOUBLE NEPTUNE LINES

Will never fulfill your expectations and can never live up to the illusion you have of them. Could represent your mother or sister if either is a "heart" person." Enjoy these natives—they are nice people and can bring much happiness to you—in their own way.

Queen of Hearts birthdates: July 29, August 27, September 25, October 23, November 21, December 19

THREE OF HEARTS FAMOUS BIRTHDATES

November 30	Efrem Zimbalist, Jr.
	Winston Churchill
	Mark Twain (Samuel Clemens)
December 28	Woodrow Wilson

Three of Clubs

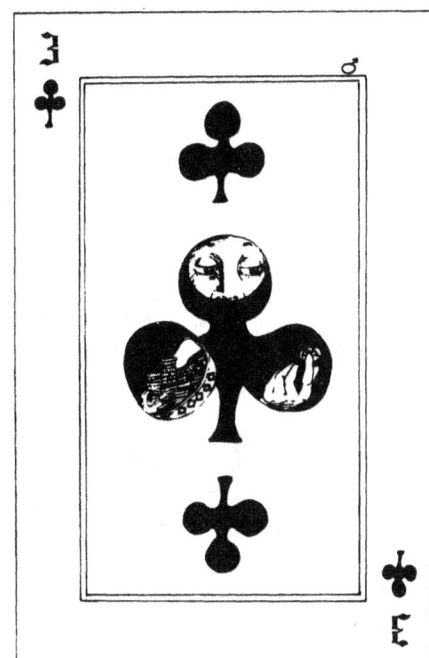

Clubs — Mental Attitudes
Three of Clubs — Uncertainty in Beliefs
Three in Clubs — Ideas from Kindred Minds

The Mars card in the Saturn Line. Displaces the **Five of Diamonds** in the Natural Spread.

This card carries a heavy burden of Three—with a strong emphasis on "heavy," since the card falls in the Saturn Line under the emphatic influence of Mars. Two Threes fall together—the card itself and its Mercury Card, the Three of Spades. Its True Place is in the Mars Line, so a Mars-Saturn conjunction defines the undercurrent throughout this native's life. Perhaps a slight saving grace lies in the fact that the True Place is in the Venus position—but doubt about the choice or stability of love relationships is likely to be as disturbing as the shifting mental attitudes. The cry for Peace seems never to be answered for these people until they learn to depend solely upon themselves and their inner resources.

The displacement of the Five of Diamonds bespeaks money as a major factor in uncertainty. Periods of steady and dependable income are few and far between. There is often a change—or several changes—in occupation in the hope of finding means of increasing the income.

Despite the shifts in viewpoint, Threes of Clubs seldom desire to change themselves or their own established concepts and intolerance of the new and untried. This is caused partly by the inability to decide on the right course, partly by stubbornness. All Clubs feel that their mental attitudes are right. They do have an inner knowledge—but they don't always use it.

Planetary Sequence

			K♠	8♦	10♣		
A♠	3♦	5♣	10♠	Q♣	A♣	3♥	Mercury
2♥	9♠	9♣	J♥	5♠	7♦	7♥	Venus
8♣	J♦	2♦	4♣	6♥	K♦	K♥	Mars
A♦	A♥	8♠	10♦	10♥	4♠	6♦	Jupiter
5♦ (Jupiter)	7♣ (Mars)	9♥ (Venus)	3♠ (Mercury)	3♣	5♥	Q♦	Saturn
J♦	K♣	2♣	7♠	9♦ (Neptune)	J♣ (Uranus)	Q♠ (Saturn)	Uranus
Q♥	6♠	6♣	8♥	2♠	4♦	4♥	Neptune
Neptune	Uranus	Saturn	Jupiter	Mars	Venus	Mercury	

Mundane Spread

These natives are usually willing to acknowledge their mistakes and willing to try again—but with no confidence in the new effort; mentally, they are beaten before they start.

The more developed ones—those who are aware of their intuitive gifts and of their inheritance of knowledge—will invariably turn to metaphysics for their solution. And they will find it. Then they become secure and they abandon the role of "Doubting Thomas."

Threes of Clubs experience some misfortune connected with death and inheritance; something may interfere with receiving their rights, payment of debts owned them, or money that is legally their own. There is also some danger of accident in these birthdates—Mars-Saturn being a combination to watch, and uncertainty of direction is a menace at all times.

Decisions should be made carefully and slowly—then believed in and held to. These natives should be willing to abandon tradition in this changing world and to accept new values in the name of growth. They should strive, through meditation and the cultivation of their own spiritual power, to work with what the soul knows from past experience, not against it.

BIRTHDATES RULED BY THE THREE OF CLUBS

MAY 29—GEMINI—RULED BY MERCURY

High-strung, restless and nervous. Constantly on the go. Have at least two irons in the fire at a time. Should cultivate a hobby or sideline that holds their interest. Are adaptable and versatile, but don't stick to anything very long unless interested in a cause or an individual. Well suited to public life—stage, politics, lecturing. Clever and good investigators—but not researchers. Good at salesmanship if allowed to travel; should never be tied to a desk or a boring occupation. Skillful with their hands.

JUNE 27—CANCER—RULED BY THE MOON

Can deal successfully with children. The women make good nurses, devoted and motherly. Home is their center. Will take many responsibilities of others on their own shoulders. Willing to sacrifice for loved ones. Like to be before the public or be considered the center of some branch of public life. Have a strong sense of drama and appreciation of music. Can succeed at teaching, direction, dressmaking, millinery.

JULY 25—LEO—RULED BY THE SUN

Have more power and strength than the other Threes of Clubs, and they are aware of it. Have a law unto themselves, not usually orthodox. Dictatorial in own line of work. Best of all professions for them is the theater—but not necessarily acting. Make good directors and producers. May attain a high place if willing to work hard and stick to their decisions. Ill health may interfere with work. Good executors, statesmen, leaders. Fundamentally spiritual, but not always considered so. Can commercialize art.

AUGUST 23—LEO—OR VIRGO—RULED BY THE SUN OR MERCURY

Want power but prefer to leave responsibility to others. If in the army, will always "pass the buck." If Leo predominates, may be performers—actors, musicians, etc. If Virgo, good scientists—especially chemists. Can be very calculating. Can succeed in banking, real estate, or as professors and teachers of adults. Investigating turn of mind; often have wanderlust—from mental curiosity. Subject to nervous indigestion and should be careful of diet. Good in the publishing field, preferring educational books. Many are successful writers.

SEPTEMBER 21—VIRGO—RULED BY MERCURY

Sensitive and nervous. Dissatisfied with own accomplishment; need praise and approval. Have keen minds and high ideals. Should guard against depression and discouragement. Long for success and try many ways of attaining it—not fully trusting any of them. Inclined to belittle their own abilities. Great readers and investigators. The most spiritually minded of the Threes of Clubs. Discriminating in taste. Writers, publishers, investigators. More concerned with the interests of others than their own. Often talented in art but cannot commercialize it. Lack self-assurance.

OCTOBER 19—LIBRA—RULED BY VENUS

Independent, inclined to self-indulgence. Should guard against selfishness. Original in thought. Life often disturbed by outside interference. Can commercialize art. Successful at law, music, plastics. Writers—sometimes poets. Want harmony and like to please, but not given to sacrifice unless obliged to.

NOVEMBER 17—SCORPIO—RULED BY MARS

After the twenty-eighth year usually develop strength and decision. More powerful than the other Three of Clubs. Interested in the occult—but must handle it carefully. The realm of "Magic" is dangerous for this card; can misuse the knowledge. Interested in causes and hidden truths. Very magnetic and hypnotic. Have healing power. Deep thinkers. Must have large enterprises. Hate inferiority. Dramatic. Can succeed in the theater or on the public platform.

DECEMBER 15–SAGITTARIUS–RULED BY JUPITER

Home and emotional life very important. Work best if married. Never learn by rule; only by observation and absorption. Usually have one main objective and will stick to it. Intuitive and inventive. Extravagant and generous–but also inclined to be selfish. Want own business and can make money at it. Attracted to outdoor occupations and must have freedom of action. Interested in horses and horse racing. Should avoid law as a profession, although often attracted to it.

THREE OF CLUBS – PLANETARY SEQUENCE OF PERSONAL RELATIONSHIPS

Horizontal Lines–Saturn and Uranus

THREE OF SPADES–MERCURY CARD IN THE JUPITER LINE

Friendship is about all you can afford with this native; good exchange of ideas–a definite influence to some degree, but probably a brief relationship or a series of small encounters over a period of time. Don't attempt to attach permanence–it isn't worth all the effort.

Three of Spades birthdates: January 11, February 9, March 7, April 5, May 3, June 1

NINE OF HEARTS–VENUS CARD IN THE SATURN LINE

A romantic attraction but more problems than you've ever dreamed of. A twosome with this card will bring you obstacles in almost everything you do; nothing will come easy, and these natives' great need for love will leave you in a quandary as to how you really feel. Too difficult a relationship for any practical purpose.

Nine of Hearts birthdates: August 30, September 28, October 26, November 24, December 22

SEVEN OF CLUBS–MARS CARD IN THE URANUS LINE

Definitely not a card of agreement for you; the conflict may be between the new ideas that these natives press upon you and your adherence to the older "safer" methods. You can receive much energy from this native–he'll always be on the go in some exciting way–but romantic love leading to marriage should not even be considered.

Seven of Clubs birthdates: March 29, April 27, May 25, June 23, July 21, August 19, September 17, October 15, November 13, December 11

FIVE OF DIAMONDS—JUPITER CARD IN THE NEPTUNE LINE

There's something about these natives that will hold your interest. If it's romance, make sure you're not too surprised after the wedding bells stop tolling. Know what you're getting—it could be a beautiful experience if you accept their problems along with them. But for your own happiness, see them as they truly are.

Five of Diamonds birthdates: January 22, February 20, March 18, April 16, May 14, June 12, July 10, August 8, September 6, October 4, November 2

QUEEN OF SPADES—SATURN CARD IN THE MERCURY LINE

A Karmic relationship—perhaps a dictatorial teacher you once disliked, although you learned more in his class than in any other. Good for communications—someone who has come into your life to give you information. Reject personal involvements; it's too heavy an experience on a close basis.

Queen of Spades birthdate: January 2

JACK OF CLUBS—URANUS CARD IN THE VENUS LINE
(Uranus and Venus Lines on the Diagonal)

A likeable business associate/friend who can help you get things together. Use the relationship to your full advantage, and it can be profitable to you. Don't worry about the outcome—just make sure you are fully legally protected prior to the association. Romantic love possible but be cautious. Chances are you'll give much more of yourself to him than he to you.

Jack of Clubs birthdates: January 29, February 27, March 25, April 23, May 21, June 19, July 17, August 15, September 13, October 11, November 9, December 7

NINE OF DIAMONDS—NEPTUNE CARD IN THE MARS LINE
(Uranus Line on the Vertical)

You'll never understand these people, but they will probably know right where you are. A difficult relationship because of your own uncertainties—this involvement will only compound the problems. Guard against this native's taking advantage of you.

Nine of Diamonds birthdates: January 18, February 16, March 14, April 12, May 10, June 8, July 6, August 4, September 2

Vertical Line—Mars

TEN OF HEARTS—JUPITER LINE

Quick love affair that could leave your head reeling—a "here today, gone tomorrow" involvement. Don't worry about it; enjoy it while you have it and kiss it off as a nice memory when it's gone. Undoubtedly good for friendship and a longer-lasting involvement on that level. Someone you can really like for varied reasons.

Ten of Hearts birthdates: July 31, August 29, September 27, October 25, November 23, December 21

SIX OF HEARTS—MARS LINE

A sexual involvement that can eventually fall into a routine or pattern that will make you uncomfortable. You two are best as friends—extremely good and conscientious.

Six of Hearts birthdates: October 29, November 27, December 25

FIVE OF SPADES—VENUS LINE

Another physical stimulant who can give you that appropriate shove when you need it most. Love life could end disastrously, but you can profit from a friendship—if you'll make the effort to listen.

Five of Spades birthdates: January 9, February 7, March 5, April 3, May 1

QUEEN OF CLUBS—MERCURY LINE

A good relationship that will only help you in your learning of values; especially good for business. Romance should be short-term but cannot hurt you in any event. Enjoy this native.

Queen of Clubs birthdates: January 28, February 26, March 24, April 22, May 20, June 18, July 16, August 14, September 12, October 10, November 8, December 6

TEN OF CLUBS—CROWN LINE

A Karmic tie—a teacher. The responsibility is up to you to listen. A hard relationship to maintain, but work at it for it is important to you. No personal involvements would be best.

Ten of Clubs birthdates: January 30, February 28, March 26, April 24, May 22, June 20, July 18, August 16, September 14, October 12, November 10, December 8

TWO OF SPADES—NEPTUNE LINE

A dramatic acquaintance that you can always expect to be exaggerated—a figment of the imagination or just plain unreality. Too difficult for personal involvements.

Two of Spades birthdates: January 12, February 10, March 8, April 6, May 4, June 2

Your Place in the Cards

NINE OF DIAMONDS—URANUS LINE: SEE HORIZONTAL LINE

Diagonal Lines

SEVEN OF SPADES—URANUS AND JUPITER LINES

You'll feel more security with this card than with probably any other. Whatever dealings you have, though surprising at times, will turn out for the better. Great for business; probably temporary for romance. But a good all-around relationship in any event.

Seven of Spades birthdates: January 7, February 5, March 3, April 1

SIX OF CLUBS—NEPTUNE AND SATURN LINES

A romantic relationship that may suddenly be in front of you before you know it. These natives have the ability to make your life much easier, so take advantage—love them as mates and/or friends—but love them without doubt. They have much to offer you.

Six of Clubs birthdates: March 30, April 28, May 26, June 24, July 22, August 20, September 18, October 16, November 14, December 12

FOUR OF SPADES—JUPITER AND VENUS LINES

A healthy relationship that can go in almost any direction. Don't give up so easily with these natives; they will help you, even if you are a burden to them—which you could be. Know that they are good people and can only bring good things to you.

Four of Spades Birthdates: January 10, February 8, March 6, April 4, May 2

KING OF HEARTS—MARS AND MERCURY LINES

A love relationship that could bring you a few problems. You would love this person but have to know that he has a certain fear of new ideas and therefore might become a little lazy. A dynamic card—urge him to follow his ideals and dreams—even if only as an avocation.

King of Hearts birthdates: June 30, July 28, August 26, September 24, October 22, November 20, December 18

JACK OF CLUBS—URANUS AND VENUS LINES: SEE HORIZONTAL LINE

FOUR OF HEARTS—NEPTUNE AND MERCURY LINES

An overabundance of love that will frighten you away. But take advantage—it's a warm, loving relationship on a romance and/or friendship level.

Four of Hearts birthdates: October 31, November 29, December 27

TEN OF DIAMONDS—DOUBLE JUPITER LINES

Fabulous association for business; these natives lean to the materialistic side, but this should afford needed security to you. Good for any involvements, but don't look for anything long-term.

Ten of Diamonds birthdates: January 17, February 15, March 13, April 11, May 9, June 7, July 5, August 3, September 1

TWO OF DIAMONDS—MARS AND SATURN LINES

A sexual attraction, but a difficult relationship—this card could wind up taking care of you the rest of your life, thus stifling his own dreams and ambitions and creating frustrations which could be erroneously blamed on you. Suppress any personal feelings. Friendship is fine—but try to keep it at a distance if you want to remain good friends.

Two of Diamonds birthdates: January 25, February 23, March 21, April 19, May 17, June 15, July 13, August 11, September 9, October 7, November 5, December 3

NINE OF SPADES—VENUS AND URANUS LINES

Don't get swept off your feet by this romanticist, or you're in trouble. Once into this unworkable combination, you may be hesitant to try again. Keep the association strictly as friendship.

Nine of Spades birthdates: January 5, February 3, March 1

ACE OF SPADES—MERCURY AND NEPTUNE LINES

Good rapport as long as you're talking about mutual interests, such as homes and families. A sympathetic friend who will be there when you need him. Church or organization oriented, and you may never know why—it may not be important. Good for friendship, but expect a spiritual sacrifice on your part if you become romantically entwined.

Ace of Spades birthdates: January 13, February 11, March 9, April 7, May 5, June 3, July 1

THREE OF CLUBS FAMOUS BIRTHDATES

May 29	Bob Hope
	Patrick Henry
	John Fitzgerald Kennedy
June 27	Helen Keller
July 25	Walter Brennan

Your Place in the Cards

August 23	Gene Kelly
September 21	H. G. Wells
November 17	Rock Hudson
December 15	Nero

Diamonds — Values
Three of Diamonds — Uncertainty in Money Conditions
Three in Diamonds — Worry; Waste of Best Self
　The Uranus Card in the Mercury Line. Displaces the **Six of Hearts** in the Natural Spread.

Planetary Sequence

		K♠	8♦	10♣			
A♠ Mercury	3♦	5♣	10♠	Q♣	A♣	3♥	Mercury
2♥	9♠ Neptune	9♣ Uranus	J♥ Saturn	5♠ Jupiter	7♦ Mars	7♥ Venus	Venus
8♣	J♠	2♦	4♣	6♥	K♦	K♥	Mars
A♦	A♥	8♠	10♦	10♥	4♠	6♦	Jupiter
5♦	7♣	9♥	3♠	3♣	5♥	Q♦	Saturn
J♦	K♣	2♣	7♠	9♦	J♣	Q♠	Uranus
Q♥	6♠	6♣	8♥	2♠	4♦	4♥	Neptune
Neptune	Uranus	Saturn	Jupiter	Mars	Venus	Mercury	

Mundane Spread

The Three of Diamonds is a card that can be interpreted two ways. One side is very materially minded and concerned with insecurity. The other side is the Displacement Card—the Six of Hearts, which represents a person who has a message to give the others.

If the Three of Diamonds is working strictly on the material plane, then it becomes secretive—a closed mind. It makes its own decisions without anyone else's knowing what they are.

In no event is the Three of Diamonds a smooth pattern. Problems always come with the family, and when these natives marry, if they do, it is not often satisfactory. And there is usually more than one marriage. These people need outlets of self-expression—they need to let go a lot. They are subject to making up their minds unexpectedly, and they take many short journeys.

They usually have to learn things the hard way and for the most part are set in their ideas. This may be their biggest handicap. They can be martyrs, or they can take responsibility and work things out because they feel it is simply what they have to do. If the card belongs to a woman, she will most likely sacrifice for her family—sometimes in such a way that she runs her family too much and feels that she is called upon to support or to help them in some way. There is usually some problem with children, most likely with a son. A Three of Diamonds man might feel that his wife or mother is too dominant.

Threes of Diamonds need people, and the challenge in life would be to go out and meet them—not to seclude themselves. It sometimes takes these natives a long time to find themselves, and although the life pattern, as mentioned, is not smooth, if the natives become well grounded in philosophy or metaphysics, they can handle themselves in bringing out their best. Inwardly, they are old souls. In the "fruit of the spirit," their security is assured.

BIRTHDATES RULED BY THE THREE OF DIAMONDS

JANUARY 24—AQUARIUS—RULED BY URANUS

Attracted to politics or matters of public or national interest—education, welfare, economics. Must have a vital concern for their work or lose interest and become bored and indifferent. Need encouragement to keep them going. Are ambitious and self-interested. Can succeed as bankers and trustees, ambassadors, or leaders. If they can write, usually choose subjects that are weighty rather than imaginative.

FEBRUARY 22—PISCES—RULED BY NEPTUNE

Deeply concerned with human needs and ills. Often are martyrs to a cause. Always willing to serve and sacrifice. Always conscious of a message to be given. Sensitive and poetic. Are depressed by opposition and become secretive, but do not abandon their efforts. Work well with men. Well suited to public life and may become famous. Good diplomats, leaders, writers, philosophers—often actors. Usually not physically strong; recuperate slowly from illness. Given to worry. Travel not satisfactory.

MARCH 20–PISCES–RULED BY NEPTUNE

Illness may interfere with work and success. More aggressive than February 22. Always worried about finances. Novelists, playwrights, artists (especially singers), educators. Also good diplomats, secret service operators. Interested in reform. Often very religious. Should guard the health.

APRIL 18–ARIES–RULED BY MARS

Impulsive, hasty, unobservant. Should guard against accidents through carelessness. Have great drive and energy. Reckless in spending—of money and their own efforts. Never know where their funds have gone. Scatter their forces; too diffusive. Ardent about causes; natural reformers. Want to do something about existing evils. Never take advice. May become good orators, lawyers, or pleaders—but are seldom adequately paid for their efforts. Marriage not favored for this birthdate. Have great force and power, but do not mix with others. Drive hard and push toward an objective but easily influenced and distracted. Success may be outstanding—but not usually lasting.

MAY 16–TAURUS–RULED BY VENUS

Like good surroundings and will sacrifice for them. Attract friends and partners that are not always reliable. Want to stand well with others. Apt to make more money than other Three of Diamonds. Can succeed as merchants, bankers, or manufacturers; also on the stage or in the educational and literary fields. Always conscious of appearances and like to outshine others. Often have artistic talent and unusual acting ability.

JUNE 14–GEMINI–RULED BY MERCURY

Restless and uncertain. Have great desire for self-expression. Work best on the mental plane but are more attracted to the dramatic and spectacular. Have a tendency to concealment; may lead a double life. Not always stable or loyal. Are gifted and inspirational. Dislike routine and obscurity. Greatly influenced by their associations.

JULY 12–CANCER–RULED BY THE MOON

Fear insecurity. Very dependent upon others; want comfort and cannot always earn enough to assure it. Do not take kindly to interference but will sacrifice for loved ones. Demand a home but dislike any limitation in it. Dominated by a desire for love but are often disappointed. Given more to philosophy and theories derived from tradition and past experience than to progress and changes. Are useful in a public capacity—as politicians, welfare workers, reformers (according to orthodox rules). Like a position of prominence but need support from others.

AUGUST 10—LEO—RULED BY THE SUN

Are natural leaders and promoters but have a sense of isolation when they become prominent. Love deeply and are loyal; when the idol is broken, have no desire to rebuild. Too sensitive for their own good. Public spirited; able and successful in public life. Self-protective because uncertain of the future. Succeed best as heads of own businesses. Are dynamic writers, good propagandists. Can succeed in merchandising and manufacturing. Are dramatic and effective.

SEPTEMBER 8—VIRGO—RULED BY MERCURY

More materially minded and less aware of their true destiny than many other Threes of Diamonds. Apt to be swamped with detail and have a narrow viewpoint. Can become penurious if they are not watchful. Analytical and meticulous. Neglect no small points but often lose the larger vision. Can succeed as public servants, writers, or lawyers (corporation, not trial). Good researchers. Want practical results and good return for their efforts.

OCTOBER 6—LIBRA—RULED BY VENUS

Want peace and easy conditions, but uncertainty interferes with contentment. More protected than many Threes of Diamonds but always fearful of the poorhouse. Are intuitive and find many answers—then doubt them. Attracted to the limelight and can become good actors, playwrights, or lecturers. Good hosts and entertainers. Love the countryside and even go in for sports to keep themselves in the open—although better adapted for an artistic or literary career. Very vacillating in opinions and incapable of firm decisions.

NOVEMBER 4—SCORPIO—RULED BY MARS

Like all threes, have doubts and indecision but give the impression of being very set and sure of themselves. Suffer through love but remain loyal and continue to sacrifice. Keep their troubles to themselves. Have a keen understanding of human foibles and a set philosophy to apply to them. Often attracted to drugs or medicine and can succeed in all branches of healing. Keen searchers for Truth and supporters of causes. Outwardly critical. Good at manual arts—sculpture, modeling in clay.

DECEMBER 2–SAGITTARIUS–RULED BY JUPITER

Want success and will make frequent changes to obtain it. Need congenial surroundings and harmony in associations. Sensitive and magnetic—often very aware spiritually. Must never deviate from their ideals or will end in failure. Inwardly know the Law but fear it—and fear not to follow it. Meet many disappointments and frustrations. Often put in a position that is foreign to their nature or beyond their ability. Good writers.

THREE OF DIAMONDS–PLANETARY SEQUENCE OF PERSONAL RELATIONSHIPS

Horizontal Lines—Mercury and Venus

ACE OF SPADES–MERCURY CARD IN THE NEPTUNE LINE

This native will be a close friend—someone whom you may feel can keep your innermost secrets. Perhaps you may become involved in church organizations or metaphysical discussions with an Ace of Spades—in any case you will feel a definite rapport. Not especially good for romantic involvements.

Ace of Spades birthdates: January 13, February 11, March 9, April 7, May 5, June 3, July 1

SEVEN OF HEARTS–VENUS CARD IN THE MERCURY LINE

Here is a romantic involvement for you—but not without a number of emotional problems, especially jealousy or unfaithfulness. One of the major problems can be that you both will want to give and give to each other. This can be frustrating if no one ever enjoys receiving.

Seven of Hearts birthdates: September 30, October 28, November 26, December 24

SEVEN OF DIAMONDS–MARS CARD IN THE VENUS LINE

Though you'll be tempted romantically, a marriage with this person will probably end unhappily. You have many of the same problems, notably the extreme choice of operating on the spiritual or material planes, and unless you are both highly evolved, this could be a love-hate relationship that cannot be constructive.

Seven of Diamonds birthdates: January 20, February 18, March 16, April 14, May 12, June 10, July 8, August 6, September 4, October 2

FIVE OF SPADES–JUPITER CARD IN THE MARS LINE

This is a friend and traveling companion. He likes to go as much as you do, even if you don't always agree on where, how and when. Bend a little; the

125

irritations are slight by comparison to the sights you'll see and the fun you'll have with this native.

Five of Spades birthdates: January 9, February 7, March 5, April 3, May 1

JACK OF HEARTS–SATURN CARD IN THE JUPITER LINE

These people may seem to be immovable, and most likely, they are just that. Good friends, but they are searching for things that may be of no importance to you right now. Try to accept them as they are even though they may seem not to care about you. Know that they do—but perhaps on a more impersonal level that you may not find satisfactory. Any kind of involvement cannot harm you, but a romantic situation might be fruitless.

Jack of Hearts birthdates: July 30, August 28, September 26, October 24, November 22, December 20

NINE OF CLUBS–URANUS CARD IN THE SATURN LINE
(Venus and Saturn Lines on the Diagonal)

This native will show you many sides and may keep you forever guessing as to who he really is. A surprise could actually turn out to be a burden to you—such as a live puppy on your birthday when you're living in a small apartment that doesn't permit dogs. Although this native is an attractive person to you, you will find that any kind of close attachment will probably affect you more negatively than it would him. Not really recommended for true personal happiness.

Nine of Clubs birthdates: January 31, February 29, March 27, April 25, May 23, June 21, July 19, August 17, September 15, October 13, November 11, December 9

NINE OF SPADES–NEPTUNE CARD IN THE URANUS LINE
(Venus Line on the Vertical)

As a woman with a male Nine of Spades, you might see him as a father figure, one who would take care of you—up to a point. Male or female, this native is an individual with whom you may take chances. But be cautious—here is that situation where those "chances," and even the person himself, may not turn out as anticipated. Double-check all business dealings and try not to get too closely involved, or you may find yourself tied up like a bundle of yesterday's newspapers. Aspects for love are not impossible but not probable because of these natives' unexpected moments of deep depression.

You can help them to understand that through disappointment comes fulfillment.

Nine of Spades birthdates: January 5, February 3, March 1

Vertical Line—Uranus

SIX OF SPADES—NEPTUNE LINE

You might find this person monotonous. But don't stop with this one opinion. There are far deeper caverns to explore that can actually help, and sometimes be a guide, in your goals and desires. Neither of you has an easy road to follow, but through a better understanding of metaphysics (which is the best kind of relationship for the two of you), you have a great deal to offer each other. Push your Six of Spades a little. He needs it and will ultimately be grateful if you're gentle.

Six of Spades birthdates: January 8, February 6, March 4, April 2

KING OF CLUBS—URANUS LINE

If you can handle your own life and try to keep it much more simplified, you might find a King of Clubs roosting on your doorstep and have an experience with him that you will cherish. This native will willingly help you rearrange certain aspects of your lifestyle that will make things easier for you—but don't push too many problems on these natives. They're Kings, but they have their own Crosses, and you could frighten them away.

King of Clubs birthdates: January 27, February 25, March 23, April 21, May 19, June 17, July 15, August 13, September 11, October 9, November 7, December 5

SEVEN OF CLUBS—SATURN LINE

This native will probably "rub you the wrong way" on your first encounter—if you even stay interested long enough to acquire any kind of feeling. Your on-the-go nature would find this native negative, discouraging, and probably frustrating.

Seven of Clubs birthdates: March 29, April 27, May 25, June 23, July 21, August 19, September 17, October 15, November 13, December 11

ACE OF HEARTS—JUPITER LINE

Although both of you and the Ace of Hearts are burdened with uncertainties, this could still work as a good match for you. You will have many things in common—the need and desire to present yourselves well in the eyes of others, an interest in the study of metaphysics. Your Ace of Hearts may talk of dreams and desires—try not to discourage him by being flexible. Aspects are good for a warm and meaningful relationship.

Ace of Hearts birthdate: December 30

JACK OF SPADES—MARS LINE

This person is really not the type you are looking for—unless you need a doctor. Romantically, you will be running and he will be sitting. You'll bring home the paycheck, and he'll greet you with sleepy eyes and a half-read book—neither of which ever will have earned him (or you) a quarter. As friends, these natives may have many things to say that could be beneficial to you, but chances are that their other traits will block your ears, and whatever wisdom they have to impart will be lost to you.

Jack of Spades birthdates: January 3, February 1

NINE OF SPADES—VENUS LINE: SEE HORIZONTAL LINE

Diagonal Lines

TWO OF HEARTS—VENUS AND NEPTUNE LINES

You may find that the emotional strength of this person may not be sufficient for a romantic involvement with you. These natives may tend to jump into a serious involvement, regarding it (in the back of their minds) as an experiment—and hope that it works. But you will feel the insecurity of this kind of situation, which will create emotional problems for the relationship. Two of Hearts can be good friends and good advisors on affairs of the heart—to you and to others.

Two of Hearts birthdate: December 29

KING OF SPADES—CROWN AND SATURN LINES

Great communications with this native—who can understand some of your most inner feelings—nothing you would normally show the outside world. Difficult relationship only if you permit it to be. Keep it impersonal on all levels and enjoy it more.

King of Spades birthdate: January 1

NINE OF CLUBS—VENUS AND SATURN LINES: SEE HORIZONTAL LINE

FOUR OF CLUBS—MARS AND JUPITER LINES

This could be a good relationship, you won't accept the know-it-all attitude of these natives. You have your own ideas and are not so sure that the Four of Clubs has better ones. In a close personal involvement. You could live under one roof and be happy—but the Four of Clubs would cover up any problems, and you would probably suffer through them. Keep a watchful eye that the two of you don't get into a rut.

Four of Clubs birthdates: April 30, May 28, June 26, July 24, August 22, September 20, October 18, November 16, December 14

TEN OF HEARTS—JUPITER AND MARS LINES

Charm is the byword here. You'll see a flashing smile, feel a warm hand, and think you're in Nirvana. But by no means is this shadow going to be on your wall without more problems than you've ever dreamed of. Your emotional life could be secure, but when the wedding flowers wilt, you may find yourself spending many hours alone—even when your Ten of Hearts is within touching distance. Remember the laws of Polarity with this native. Emotional highs may be fabulous—but the lows that will accompany them may be the absolute bottom. Know what you're getting into.

Ten of Hearts birthdates: July 31, August 29, September 27, October 25, November 23, December 21

FIVE OF HEARTS—SATURN AND VENUS LINES

At first you might find a rapport with this native, inasmuch as you like to keep active and this native requires changes. The two desires may seem to be one and the same—but they're most definitely not. If you're a lady and your husband is a Five of Hearts, this relationship could fall into the typical "girl puts husband through college; husband becomes successful, divorces girl" routine. The reverse could also be true if the husband sacrifices for his wife's career or education. Although it may be tempting, the relationship is recommended only on an arm's length practical friendship basis—and questionable even then.

Five of Hearts birthdates: October 30, November 28, December 26

QUEEN OF SPADES—URANUS AND MERCURY LINES

A lady Queen of Spades in business with a male Three of Diamonds could prove to be a most beneficial relationship if you (the Three of Diamonds) could listen and learn. This would not be an easy relationship for you because she will probably be right most of the time, and you will tend to be very stubborn in taking her advice. She is stubborn, too, with fixed ideas. For both sexes, this is a learning time and cannot harm you. Try to bend more than usual, or you may not be able to have any kind of relationship at all.

Queen of Spades birthdate: January 2

THREE OF DIAMONDS FAMOUS BIRTHDATES

January 24	Maria Tallchief
February 22	George Washington

Your Place in the Cards

March 20	Carl Reiner
	Sergei Rachmaninoff
April 18	Leopold Stokowski
	Clarence Darrow
May 16	Henry Fonda
	Woody Herman
	Liberace
	Honoré Balzac
June 14	Gene Barry
	Burl Ives
July 12	Milton Berle
	Andrew Wyeth
	Henry Thoreau
	Julius Caesar
August 10	Jimmy Dean
	Eddie Fisher
	Rhonda Fleming
	Herbert Hoover
September 8	Sid Caesar
	Peter Sellers
November 4	Walter Cronkite
	Gig Young
December 2	Julie Harris

Three of Spades

Spades — Labor; Wisdom
Three of Spades — Difficulty in finding Solutions and Illumination
Three in Spades — Expression of the Law

The Jupiter Card in the Saturn Line. Displaces the **Six of Diamonds** in the Natural Spread.

In this Jupiter-Saturn conjunction the key to the pattern of the card is evident. Well established in the Saturn Line, the way of life for these natives is not an easy one. Saturn is the Guardian of the Threshold, the Keeper of the Gate Out—the "Ring Pass Not." Not until the conditions of Saturn have been met and declared paid in full will these natives be free from the obstacles and disciplinary tribulations that are the harvest of their sowings.

In many of the Spade birthdates there is an aura of heaviness. These natives know they have come to *labor* for whatever achievement is theirs, and unless they are willing to struggle for the enlightenment that will free them, they stay in a rut and resign themselves to drudgery.

As in the case of the Three of Diamonds, the card that is displaced is a six. This always means *cosmic* responsibility (a Karmic debt), but six also stands for love, harmony, and beauty; these are the sure rewards of those who meet the responsibility and dicharge it willingly.

Unlike the other Threes, this card has a Jupiter position—a protection in itself; so even though the displaced six is a Diamond and the insecurity of the three extends primarily to finances, the Jupiter Line gives blessings if the card makes the right decisions about *values*.

With any strong Saturn emphasis health is always a problem. Here, because of the alliance with the six, a health condition, if not headed off or treated at once, may become chronic or of long duration. It is only common sense, when any Birth Card falls in the Saturn Line, to live sanely and eat wisely; and when the uncertainty of the Three is also there to deal with, living this way is imperative.

A good education is necessary for the Three of Spades. Fear should not be allowed to enter in so that the health will not be disturbed psychologically. Three of Spades children profit more from the mother than they do the father. The father's attitude may be a little bit stern, or he may not take the responsibility he should. The Three of Spades is always in doubt about physicians, usually making many changes and experiments with them and the medicines prescribed. As a rule the majority fare better with natural methods and physiotherapy than with drugs. Spades belong to the earth; they are close to the heart of Mother Nature herself.

If the card belongs to a woman, she depends upon herself; she works for herself. She usually gets a job that requires a lot of hard work and will go on to a key position. As the Jupiter Card, there is always good attached to this three, and if the card belongs to a man, chances are he will marry a woman who will be good for him. The male Three of Spades will profit from some woman, whereas the woman will profit from her own personality.

The main obstacle for these natives to overcome is doubt, as a bulwark against disappointment. Once they make up their minds, they have enough inherent tenacity to abide by the decision. The trouble lies in an unwillingness to stop and analyze, then choose. The displaced Six of Diamonds bids them wait, balance and judge, but they are quite too apt to "leap" first.

One of the hardest lessons they have to learn is to achieve impersonality. The Cosmic Responsibility must come first. The personal aims, drives, and desires become sublimated when it does. A wise man said, "Not to desire is to have"—and so it is with the Three of Spades. They have come to be "Laborers in the vineyards of the Lord"; they need not be laborers in the fields or the ditches.

BIRTHDATES RULED BY THE THREE OF SPADES

JANUARY 11–CAPRICORN–RULED BY SATURN

Nervous, inspired, ambitious. This date has produced many keen thinkers, loyal patriots and outstanding public servants. They are well suited to government positions and will work without sparing themselves for any cause in which they believe. The outstanding fault is intolerance. Despite elements of greatness, narrowness and pettiness often creep into personal relationships; they will not tolerate anyone who outshines them or questions their authority—and may go to some lengths to discredit anyone who interferes with them. The basis of their insistence on their own place and power is fear. They need to cultivate their inner security and not be dependent upon the opinion of others. Through worry they may become very irritable and hard to live with. Serious, often depressed. Writers, orators, philosophers, psychologists. Like to be in the public eye.

FEBRUARY 9—AQUARIUS—RULED BY URANUS

The mental balance here is much less secure than in the Capricorn birthdate. Steadiness and self-control should be instilled early. Apt to allow their own temperament to run away with them. When there is real talent, the theater offers the best outlet. They want variety, excitement, and frequent changes. Should not become involved with women in business unless they are thoroughly reliable. Impractical but often very gifted; often become famous. Should seek a profession rather than a commercial line.

MARCH 7—PISCES—RULED BY NEPTUNE

Sense of service less evidenced here than with many Pisceans; prefer to express their own talents but are glad to have the public profit by them. Many make a valuable contribution to music, painting, or writing. The less ambitious make good nurses, community doctors, workers in institutions. Keen and inquiring minds; seldom lazy. Have power in mental cases.

APRIL 5—ARIES—RULED BY MARS

Progressive and dynamic. Eager to try new ventures but will abandon those which do not offer an opportunity to express their talents. Often great awareness in these people. Can succeed brilliantly in the dramatic world—especially cinema. Scientists, educators, and philosophers belong here; also explorers, discoverers, pioneers.

MAY 3—TAURUS—RULED BY VENUS

Need cooperation for best success but cannot always secure it. Will work hard to accumulate for security. Are attracted to artistic pursuits or will patronize the arts. Good decorators, painters, designers. Interested in the underpriveleged; will work for them if given a position of authority. Writers, scientists.

JUNE 1—GEMINI—RULED BY MERCURY

Most indecisive of all the Threes of Spades. Need contacts and variety—but never satisfied. Constantly seeking new people, new scenes, new interests. Never finish what they start; never quite know what they want. Best suited to traveling, acting, selling (from door to door or over a wide territory). Good as foreign correspondents, journalists, traveling lecturers, itinerant preachers. Should strive to use the information they accumulate.

THREE OF SPADES — PLANETARY SEQUENCE OF PERSONAL RELATIONSHIPS

Horizontal Lines—Saturn and Uranus

NINE OF HEARTS—MERCURY CARD IN THE SATURN LINE
Make life easier for yourself and keep this involvement as Mercurial as it is meant to be. You'll have things to talk about, but the conversation won't take you anywhere—the more time you spend, the more time you waste.

Nine of Hearts birthdates: August 30, September 28, October 26, November 24, December 22

SEVEN OF CLUBS—VENUS CARD IN THE URANUS LINE
Not only will you like this native, but you'll probably pursue him as well. Take your time and make sure the friendship or love affair is worth the price. Businesswise, the relationship works but won't make you an overabundance of money.

Seven of Clubs birthdates: March 29, April 27, May 25, June 23, July 21, August 19, September 17, October 15, November 13, December 11

FIVE OF DIAMONDS—MARS CARD IN THE NEPTUNE LINE
You may think this is blatant materialism and even become hostile toward this native. Another look from the positive side will tell you otherwise. Use the energy that they can spark within you, but don't get romantically involved—no matter what.

Five of Diamonds birthdates: January 22, February 20, March 18, April 16, May 14, June 12, July 10, August 8, September 6, October 4, November 2

QUEEN OF SPADES—JUPITER CARD IN THE MERCURY LINE
As a female you will be almost immediately attracted to this female. They offer you wisdom, and you'll listen. For a man the story is quite different. A male Three of Spades would be bored and probably aggravated by the Queen—to the point of self-inducing headaches—just to stay out of this native's company. In either case, the relationship is good and can influence you extremely well in many areas. Give it every chance.

Queen of Spades birthdate: January 2

JACK OF CLUBS—SATURN CARD IN THE VENUS LINE

A love affair you can't escape if you try. And it would be better for you if you tried. A burden, a hardship—and definitely leading you to a fall and disappointment. Take it lightly. The Jack will.

Jack of Clubs birthdates: January 29, February 27, March 25, April 23, May 21, June 19, July 17, August 15, September 13, October 11, November 9, December 7

NINE OF DIAMONDS—URANUS CARD IN THE MARS LINE
(Uranus and Mars Lines on the Diagonal)

Immediate dislike—especially if this card belongs to a female. But remember —even this native's domineering side can help you a step closer to where you want to go, who you want to be.

Out of negatives can come positives. Nines of Diamonds have new things to say; listen but don't get involved—unless it's on an impersonal businesslike basis.

Nine of Diamonds birthdates: January 18, February 16, March 14, April 12, May 10, June 8, July 6, August 4, September 2

SEVEN OF SPADES—NEPTUNE CARD IN THE JUPITER LINE
(Uranus Line on the Vertical)

A good relationship if you can ever get together and get something accomplished without your or this native's being sick at those important times. Brush aside any feelings of these Sevens' not being capable. They most assertedly are—especially in business, and you'll always be able to trust them. Any kind of involvement is worth the effort, but don't fool yourself. See the relationship (and the native) as it truly is.

Seven of Spades birthdates: January 7, February 5, March 3, April 1

Vertical Line—Jupiter

TEN OF DIAMONDS—JUPITER LINE

Great for business, and you'd be foolish to pass up the opportunity. But don't confuse money with values. These natives are interested in money first. Not too spiritually inclined so not necessarily good mates—but certainly can solve many of your financial problems if you give them the lead.

Ten of Diamonds birthdates: January 17, February 15, March 13, April 11, May 9, June 7, July 5, August 3, September 1

FOUR OF CLUBS—MARS LINE

If these natives ever stop talking long enough, you'd probably like to hug or kiss them. A dynamic sexual attraction that will probably not be mutual.

Threes

You may seem to be an unwise investment to them. Great for friendship—even if they're irritating at times.

Four of Clubs birthdates: April 30, May 28, June 26, July 24, August 22, September 20, October 18, November 16, December 14

JACK OF HEARTS–VENUS LINE

Don't be romantically driven to this native—although the physical attraction is certainly here. Best for friendship. Try not to be too harsh on his individual philosophies. Forget any business ventures—even if you're tempted.

Jack of Hearts birthdates: July 30, August 28, September 26, October 24, November 22, December 20

TEN OF SPADES–MERCURY LINE

Good friendship—good relationship on any level. The two of you can grow and have a fine life together if the accentuation is on togetherness as opposed to the Golden Calf. A straight business venture could suffer but won't damage you (won't make you a lot of money, either).

Ten of Spades birthdates: January 4, February 2

EIGHT OF DIAMONDS–CROWN LINE

A good business card for you, but the price of worry and frustration may be too much for the value received. Know your individual; he has the ability. Also know the inevitability of some kind of relationship with this card—but for happiness, keep it light.

Eight of Diamonds birthdates: January 19, February 17, March 15, April 13, May 11, June 9, July 7, August 5, September 3, October 1

EIGHT OF HEARTS–NEPTUNE LINE

You may never have more fun with anyone than this card. You'll love being with him but don't complain so much about the fast pace. It'll be a refreshing change and maybe the only opportunity in your life to enjoy a relationship this frivolous. Too difficult and confusing an involvement for anything other than an occasional get-together.   NO

Eight of Hearts birthdates: August 31, September 29, October 27, November 25, December 23

SEVEN OF SPADES–URANUS LINE: SEE VERTICAL LINE

Diagonal Lines

TWO OF CLUBS–URANUS AND SATURN LINES

The first words out of this native's mouth will leave you wondering if he's for real. You probably won't like him but will find him interesting. If you permit yourself to get too closely involved, this relationship could create illness for you. Keep it in its proper perspective and say "hi" once in a while.

Two of Clubs birthdates: May 30, June 28, July 26, August 24, September 22, October 20, November 18, December 16

SIX OF SPADES–NEPTUNE AND URANUS LINES

If you marry this native—and the chances are strong that you will—he will not have any sympathy for the health problems you may encounter, maybe even going so far as to believe the problems are psychosomatic. Learn to handle yourself in a positive way and keep your mental spirits up, through your work. And most of all, understand this Six's resiliency. He will help you in many ways and—most of all—love you in return.

Six of Spades birthdates: January 8, February 6, March 4, April 2

TEN OF HEARTS–JUPITER AND MARS LINES

This friend can tell you all about your problems and help you to understand them, and the reverse is also true. But don't look for anything long-term—and especially don't try to create romance. You're the only one who'll suffer in this case.

Ten of Hearts birthdates: July 31, August 29, September 27, October 25, November 23, December 21

KING OF DIAMONDS–MARS AND VENUS LINES

Probably the most dynamic love affair, sexual attraction, or marriage that you can make. A real provider who'll pay your bills, love you (when he's not out making money), and irritate you—all at the same time. If this card belongs to a woman and you're a guy, you've really got a driver on your hands. Encourage her—she's happier this way—and learn to live with the situation. You might surprise yourself at how happy you can be.

King of Diamonds birthdates: January 14, February 12, March 10, April 8, May 6, June 4, July 2

SEVEN OF HEARTS–VENUS AND MERCURY LINES

You'll really wish you could do something for this native, but he'll seem too much off to himself—incommunicado. And it won't seem to be that important. A good friend to whom you can talk if you make the effort—but don't try any business ventures.

Seven of Hearts birthdates: September 30, October 28, November 26, December 24

NINE OF DIAMONDS—URANUS AND MARS LINES: SEE HORIZONTAL LINE

FOUR OF DIAMONDS—NEPTUNE AND VENUS LINES

A beautiful love affair and marriage can happen here providing you take the time to really see the person and know that his life isn't any easier than yours. But he's willing to work to make both lives happier. Your love will be returned. In the case of friendship, it will be close and lasting. Business will not be so good with the one exception that hard work can make it profitable.

Four of Diamonds birthdates: January 23, February 21, March 19, April 17, May 15, June 13 and July 11, August 9, September 7, October 5, November 3, December 1

EIGHT OF SPADES—JUPITER AND SATURN LINES

A short-term business arrangement can work satisfactorily—or any other business venture where communications are important. Friendship fine but might be occasionally irksome. Personal involvements should be out. Listen. These natives have worthwhile things to say.

Eight of Spades birthdates: January 6, February 4, March 2

JACK OF SPADES—MARS AND URANUS LINES

This person will probably like you a great deal more than you think. But work on it. It can be of great benefit to you. He has much to teach you—but don't be shocked by the methods. This native could be an older brother who's walked a little farther than you—so give a listen. Personal involvements are definitely possible but not probable.

Jack of Spades birthdates: January 3, February 1

TWO OF HEARTS—VENUS AND NEPTUNE LINES

You could be turned on by this native, but his own lack of effort will probably irritate you. A difficult personal relationship at best—but business might work out well if everything's defined in front.

Two of Hearts birthdate: December 29

THREE OF SPADES FAMOUS BIRTHDATES

February 9	Mia Farrow
	Ronald Colman
March 7	Antony Armstrong-Jones
	Luther Burbank

Your Place in the Cards

April 5   Bette Davis
                   Gregory Peck
                   Melvyn Douglas
                   Spencer Tracy

May 3   Samantha Eggar
                   William Inge
                   Golda Meir

June 1   Pat Boone
                   Andy Griffith
                   Marilyn Monroe
                   Brigham Young

Fours

FOURS represent Enclosure, Completion, *Foundation.* The pattern is the square—or the three-dimensional square, the cube. Four is our Fenced Field, our Security—and therefore our Protection.

"Sentinels" are at the four corners of the field, assuring our safety within it; the field itself is ours—to *build* in.

Four is the symbol for earth, the fourth "element." We "fell" into matter that we might *work* our way out of it, so we know that despite the security and protection that surrounds us, there is to be no idleness within the God-given enclosure that is Four. We are to build a firm and unassailable foundation; we are to labor with concentration and diligence and secure for ourselves the right to work out our pattern in freedom from unconquerable obstacles, poverty, heartache, and failure. We must bear in mind that four is the number of Saturn, who hands out the rewards if and when they are earned—and only then.

As Birth Cards, Fours are among the most favorable. They give us a wonderful start—with protection, security, sufficiency; but like every other card and every birth pattern, the course of our lives and their *finish* is up to us. Of the four spots or "sentinels," two are matter and two are spirit; in Four they are united. He who attempts to separate them builds his foundation on sand, and the wind and floods sweep it from under him. He finds himself in an empty field, save for Saturn.

The fourth Sphere on the Tree of Life is Chesed—Mercy—the realm of Jupiter. The fourth Statement in the Pattern on the Trestleboard is, "From the Limitless Substance I draw all things needful, both spiritual and material."

To the Pythagoreans four was the Sacred Number, for its elements—one, two, three, and four—when summed up are equal to ten, "which is so perfect that we can go no further, but to increase we must return to the Monad."

For our Fours, then, the prime admonition is to *build*.

Hearts are to build their security on love for their fellow man if they may hope for love in their own lives.
Clubs are to build on knowledge to be shared and disseminated for the profit, education, and growth of all.
Diamonds are to build on values that are everlasting.
Spades are to labor, with hands and hearts and minds, for the wisdom that is of God. That is their foundation and security. Their mission is to shed the Light they have found on every dark corner, on all blind eyes, and every burdened heart.

As in the Tarot, the Four is an Emperor. Fours have come to be and can be in command of every situation that arises. Their task is organization. They are dealing with practicalities—and they have the power to glorify them.

Four of Hearts

Planetary Sequence

			K♠	8♦	10♣ Neptune		
A♠	3♦	5♣	10♠	Q♣	A♣	3♥	Mercury
2♥	9♠	9♣	J♥	5♠	7♦	7♥	Venus
8♣	J♠	2♦	4♣	6♥	K♠	K♥	Mars
A♦	A♥	8♠	10♦	10♥	4♠	6♦	Jupiter
5♦	7♣	9♥	3♠	3♣	5♥	Q♦	Saturn
J♦	K♣	2♣	7♠	9♦	J♣	Q♠	Uranus
Q♥	6♠	6♣	8♥	2♠	4♦	4♥	Neptune
Uranus	Saturn	Jupiter	Mars	Venus	Mercury		

Neptune, Uranus, Saturn, Jupiter, Mars, Venus, Mercury

Mundane Spread

Hearts — Love
Four of Hearts — The Marriage Card
Four in Hearts — Protection in Relationships

The Mercury Card in the Neptune Line. Displaces the **Four of Spades** in the Natural Spread.

The three planetary rulers in this case are Mercury, Neptune, and Jupiter. The Mercury influence is especially strong since the True Place falls in the Mercury Line. If handled wisely, this is a wonderful combination. Love (hearts) is to be the ruling motive of the life—love that is raised to the plane of idealism (Neptune) but is devoid of Neptunian confusion, since judgment and discrimination (Mercury) are such strong factors. Over all, there is the protection of Jupiter in the position of the True Place. If family ties are not strong and the emotional life not satisfactory for the Four of Hearts, it would seem that he has only himself to blame. For *all* Hearts, people are important, and relationships that are friendly and harmonious are essential to happiness. Those Heart people born on a birthdate ruled by Mercury would create things along the intellectual line; those Heart people born with a Venus ruler would be artistic; Jupiter-ruled, attuned for business, patronage, philanthropy, and benefits in general—for themselves or for others; Uranus-ruled, friendly dealings with groups and organizations, new ideas for progress and culture, the promotion of universal brotherhood; and with Neptune as a ruler, service and willing sacrifice, poetry, mysticism, and idealism.

All Fours of Hearts will have a strong attraction for the theater—and even with but a small amount of talent, a measure of success is assured.

Business associates should be chosen among those who are of kindred minds and wholly congenial; this is often more important than efficiency—providing there is a willingness to work hard for results.

In all but the Four of Diamonds, there is a gift of healing. When enhanced by the magnetism inherent in all Hearts, many cures and "restorations" are accomplished.

The pitfall of this card is self-satisfaction. The negative Four of Hearts can become very smug, giving all the credit for his success to himself. In this event success is not likely to be lasting; self alone has no power in this combination of matter and spirit. These natives must be watchful, too, of quitting a given task because of waning interest. They should never ask, "What can this person (this job or this project) do for me?" But rather, "What can I put into it?" They have more than most people have to give, and if they'd only realize it, their satisfaction in accomplishment is based upon the amount of their giving.

In the Four of Hearts there is a strong sense of fairness and justice, tolerance and understanding. These desirable traits, coupled with these natives, natural mental balance and sense of discrimination, make them good judges and counselors, leaders and directors.

In the event of any trial, there is always compensation.

Fours

BIRTHDATES RULED BY THE FOUR OF HEARTS

OCTOBER 31–SCORPIO–RULED BY MARS

For those who have chosen to devote themselves to public interests and the cause of humanity, marked success is indicated. These are the searchers for the Truth and the Light—be it in science, religion, or literature. They succeed as educators, reformers, authors, or physicians.

NOVEMBER 29–SAGITTARIUS–RULED BY JUPITER

Discoverers and explorers belong to this card, true humanitarians who "go into all the world and preach the gospel to every creature." Nervous, restless, and inquiring, they seek to make the world a better place to live in. Their best success lies in activities or interests far removed from the place of birth. Good judges, lawyers, educators, and publishers. Their principal task in life is broadcasting.

DECEMBER 27–CAPRICORN–RULED BY SATURN

Level-headed and practical. Ambitious and eager to attain a high place. Succeed in life before the public; science is a good field.

FOUR OF HEARTS–PLANETARY SEQUENCE OF PERSONAL RELATIONSHIPS

Horizontal Lines–Neptune and Crown

FOUR OF DIAMONDS–MERCURY CARD IN THE VENUS LINE

Though you may find many things in common with this native and may intuitively know that this is a Karmic tie, this is still not the love union you seek. You will always feel an undertow of restlessness that you don't wish to—and don't have to—deal with. These natives can be valuable personal friends, and your happy nature can be even more valuable to them—if you can communicate without trying to impress each other with your own importance. Relax. You're both Fours. You both *know* your importance, so don't talk about it or show it unnecessarily.

Four of Diamonds birthdates: January 23, February 21, March 19, April 17, May 15, June 13, July 11, August 9, September 7, October 5, November 3, December 1

Your Place in the Cards

TWO OF SPADES—VENUS CARD IN THE MARS LINE

Here is a real quest for you. Drawn like a magnet to a nail, you'll find an overactive sex drive that might lead to more responsibility than even you will want to handle. On the one hand, you'll have a lot of fun together and you'll both be popular. On the other, you'll probably drink too much together, and before you know it, you'll be completely involved in the Two of Spades' problems, and neither one of you will be doing anything besides running around in circles. (And maybe not even together.) This *could* be a good relationship, but you must be prepared to take it on. You have the ability but make sure you re-evaluate your stamina.

Two of Spades birthdates: January 12, February 10, March 8, April 6, May 4, June 2

EIGHT OF HEARTS—MARS CARD IN THE JUPITER LINE

Look out. You may have met your match. But not in the way you may wish it to be. These natives want love as much or maybe more so than you. But just as "man cannot live by bread alone," you and your Eight of Hearts cannot live by love alone. This relationship will be one of touching, loving, being together, combined with philosophical and metaphysical theories—none of which will pay the rent. As an occasional lover or personal friend—great. But don't try marriage, unless you're ready for the possible ramifications.

Eight of Hearts birthdates: August 31, September 29, October 27, November 25, December 23

SIX OF CLUBS—JUPITER CARD IN THE SATURN LINE

Intuitively you know that this native is a good person for you. And you will like Sixes of Clubs even if the friendship is difficult for you to maintain. You will want to "play" more than they—and if the friendship is to be sustained, you must permit them to operate under their own banner and at their own speed. Don't splash too much love on them too quickly and encourage their intuitive powers—which *you* know are already there.

Six of Clubs birthdates: March 30, April 28, May 26, June 24, July 22, August 20, September 18, October 16, November 14, December 12

SIX OF SPADES—SATURN CARD IN THE URANUS LINE

A Karmic relationship. Anything you try to accomplish with this native will seem to move at a snail's pace to you. Though practically inevitable, try to keep from having a close involvement, especially in business. It will be very difficult for you to find successful business ventures with the Six of Spades except by a pure stroke of luck.

Six of Spades birthdates: January 8, February 6, March 4, April 2

QUEEN OF HEARTS—URANUS CARD IN THE NEPTUNE LINE

Here is another drinking partner for you. You can't help but have a good time together, and there's nothing wrong with enjoying the company of another person—but in this situation it is more escapism than just a good time. You will like each other, and you will have every reason to, but try not to make a regular thing of it—a happy, carefree relationship could turn into a sloppy and irresponsible situation for you both.

Queen of Hearts birthdates: July 29, August 27, September 25, October 23, November 21, December 19

TEN OF CLUBS—NEPTUNE CARD IN THE MARS LINE

This person can spur your thinking into areas that you may have only entertained before—especially, but not restricted to, the metaphysical realm. You have the power, and they have the ability so enjoy the relationship in any form that it comes to you.

Ten of Clubs birthdates: January 30, February 28, March 26, April 24, May 22, June 20, July 18, August 16, September 14, October 12, November 10, December 8

Vertical Line—Mercury

QUEEN OF SPADES—URANUS LINE

You may find a harshness here that is a little more than you want or need in your life. This native has the knowledge but may tend to cram it down your throat without giving your happy-go-lucky nature the slightest consideration. Queens of Spades can be excellent guides for you—both mentally and spiritually, but you will have to let them be the boss.

Queen of Spades birthdate: January 2

QUEEN OF DIAMONDS—SATURN LINE

The points of this Diamond will dig deeply into your "soft" heart. This native can lead you around with a ring in your nose, and you might find the value received worth a little nose-pulling. These people can offer you a lot if your values come anywhere near close—but it's doubtful that they ever will.

Queen of Diamonds birthdates: January 15, February 13, March 11, April 9, May 7, June 5, July 3, August 1

SIX OF DIAMONDS—JUPITER LINE

You are immediately at odds with this native. Your first and foremost thought concerns fulfillment of your emotions, while the first and foremost thought of the Six of Diamonds is on a financial plane. You can sit back and objectively tell these natives what they have to do to reach their financial goals, but their answer to you will be that they don't want to know *how*—but *when*. A romance is practically out of the question, and only your tolerance can maintain a friendship.

Six of Diamonds birthdates: January 21, February 19, March 17, April 15, May 13, June 11, July 9, August 7, September 5, October 3, November 1

KING OF HEARTS—MARS LINE

This person could be a friend for life. You will find kindness, stimulation, energy—sometimes disagreements, but rarely arguments. You won't have to thank these natives for what they do for you, but don't ever lie to them. You will definitely feel a natural affinity toward all Kings of Hearts.

King of Hearts birthdates: June 30, July 28, August 26, September 24, October 22, November 20, December 18

SEVEN OF HEARTS—VENUS LINE

If you know yourself well enough to know how important a true love in your life is to you—you won't find it with this person. Sevens of Hearts will misunderstand your show of warmth to others, and the resulting jealousies would ruin any kind of relationship. Another Karmic tie, but try to not become personally involved.

Seven of Hearts birthdates: September 30, October 28, November 26, December 24

THREE OF HEARTS—MERCURY LINE

There is no happiness in a romantic union here, either. Mostly this relationship will be a social, country-club or bingo-night buddy. You can have many good times together, but you could be a helpful friend as well. These natives never know quite what they have until they've lost it. Your own knowledge is more secure. Try to advise them to not doubt things so much. You have the ability and the power.

Three of Hearts birthdates: November 30, December 28

Diagonal Line

JACK OF CLUBS—URANUS AND VENUS LINES

You will never cease to be amazed with a Jack of Clubs. He will blurt out the most incredible information—and sometimes at the most incredible times. You will undoubtedly like these natives and can learn from them, but you can't get too close (or as close as a Four of Hearts wants to be). Not recommended romantically because the personality will not be one that you would want to "take home to mother."

Jack of Clubs birthdates: January 29, February 27, March 25, April 23, May 21, June 19, July 17, August 15, September 13, October 11, November 9, December 7

THREE OF CLUBS—SATURN AND MARS LINES

Following the butterflies in your belly will more than likely get you into trouble with this card. You will have difficulty in understanding that your loving nature cannot help these people. They must find their contentment within themselves first, and you're likely to overwhelm them. It's a heavy trip for you and not really necessary.

Three of Clubs birthdates: May 29, June 27, July 25, August 23, September 21, October 19, November 17, December 15

TEN OF DIAMONDS—DOUBLE JUPITER LINES

Here is a financially protected involvement. You should not have too many problems in making money with this native. Though he may seem to have an extremely direct approach to business that may irritate you, keep your personality warm *and showing,* and trust in the somewhat better business acumen of the Ten of Diamonds.

Ten of Diamonds birthdates: January 17, February 15, March 13, April 11, May 9, June 7, July 5, August 3, September 1

TWO OF DIAMONDS—SATURN AND MARS LINES

You'll appreciate this person and like him—from a distance. This can be a friend whom you don't see too often, mostly because that is the way you prefer it. You'll *feel* these natives' difficulties with their lives and therefore not wish them to be too close a part of your life. When you need a doctor, a Two of Diamonds would be an excellent choice for you.

Two of Diamonds birthdates: January 25, February 23, March 21, April 19, May 17, June 15, July 13, August 11, September 9, October 7, November 5, December 3

NINE OF SPADES—URANUS AND VENUS LINES

It is inevitable that in some way, at some point, you will find a Nine of Spades in your life. Preferably, the tie won't be romantic because you will find that maintaining the relationship will be almost entirely on your shoulders—at times a hardship for you. On the other hand, the Displacement Card of the Nine of Spades is the Personality Card of a male Four of Hearts (the King of Hearts) if you are a man and your Nine of Spades is a lady, you might find the exciting, stimulating romance you seek—providing you can (and want to) be fatherly toward her at times. Other relationships are possible through working for the good of others. Don't try to avoid some kind of relationship. It's Karmic.

Nine of Spades birthdates: January 5, February 3, March 1

ACE OF SPADES—NEPTUNE AND MERCURY LINES

You will probably never understand this native. Every attempt at conversation will probably seem as if both of you are speaking a language the other person can't understand. It's hardly worth the effort unless you are willing to work at it. And remember, you'll be amazed at what you will discover about this person—when and if you discover anything.

Ace of Spades birthdates: January 13, February 11, March 9, April 7, May 5, June 3, July 1

FOUR OF HEARTS FAMOUS BIRTHDATES

October 31	Chiang Kai-shek
	Ethel Waters
November 29	Louisa May Alcott
December 27	Marlene Dietrich
	Louis Pasteur

Four of Clubs

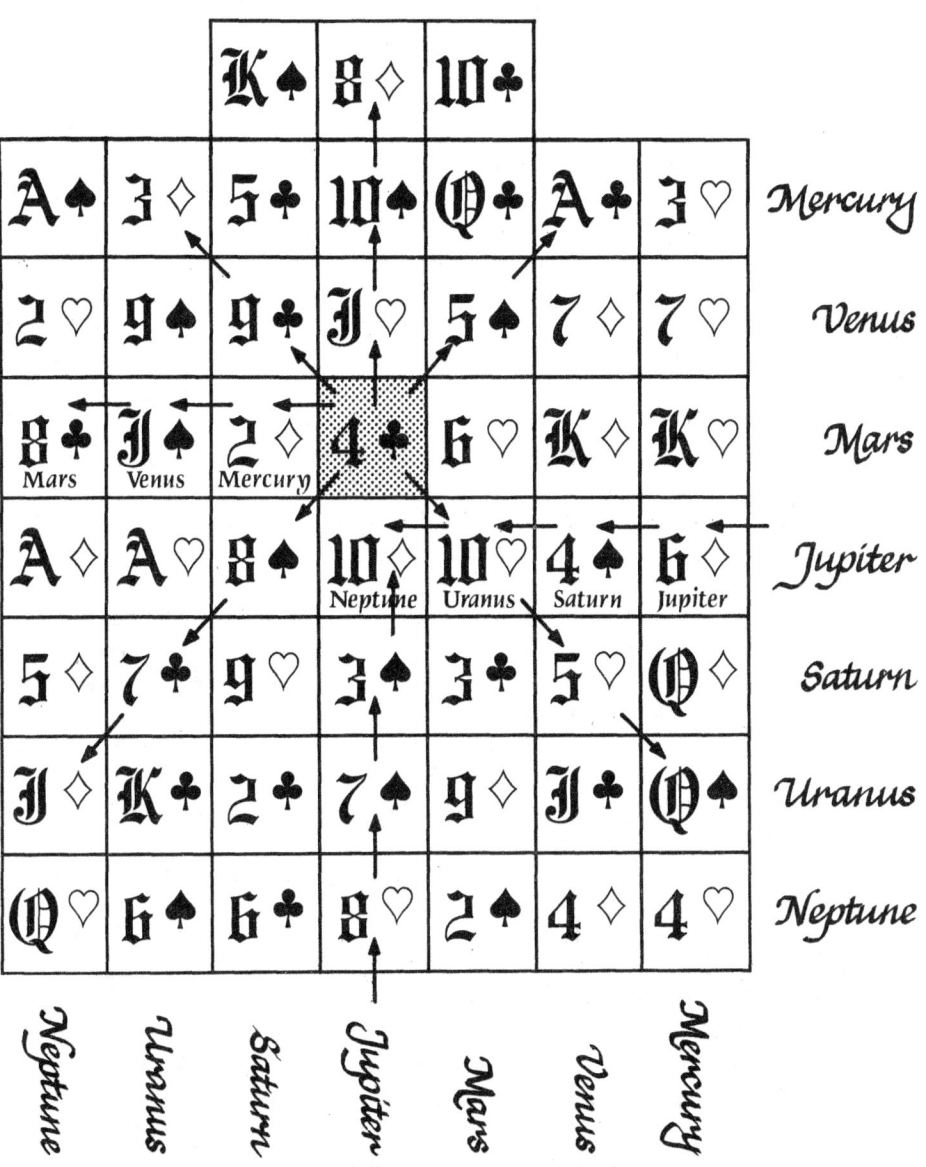

Clubs — Mental Attitudes
Four of Clubs — Good Judgment; Discrimination
Four in Clubs — Concentrated Mental Work

The Jupiter Card in the Mars Line. Displaces the **Five of Clubs** in the Natural Spread.

The card that is displaced in this birthdate indicates restlessness, changeability and dissatisfaction with the type of education sought and the decisions made. This, however, prevails only when there is insufficient knowledge to support the judgment. This kind of restlessness, in connection with this card, indicates also that the Birth Card will try to cover up the faults of the Displacement Card (the Five of Clubs); the Four of Clubs will make an effort *not* to let others know of this restlessness. On the other hand, the Five of Clubs *may* indicate merely a wholesome desire for change in the name of progress. There is no lack of activity, for the True Place of this card is in the Mars position in the Mars Line; the only trouble is that the activity may be too diffused. There is a desire to experiment in mental realms—a "divine discontent" with the knowledge acquired and an eagerness to find something that is definite and stabilizing. As the character develops, wisdom and experience correct this fault—if fault it be, and the majority make a valuable contribution to literature, philosophy, and education in general.

These people make good propagandists in lines which interest them. The Four of Clubs can be very smug about what he knows even though the judgment is usually sound and the appeal is to those of intelligence and common sense. There is a tendency to cling to tradition and principle, but not to an extent that interferes with progress. This is one of the patriot cards inasmuch as there is no departure from fundamentals. These natives will fight for their interpretation of the law if they believe it is a good law to start with.

Between the men and women Personality Cards there is a basic equality. The Queen of Clubs is as powerful in her way as either the King or the Jack; her judgment is usually as sound and her intuition superior. Then, too, she occupies the central position in the Natural Spread, and in this age of intuition and extrasensory perception, she is given her place of equality. In the realm of politics and political economics she is, in many instances, usurping the place formerly held exclusively by men, and it is her job, as the Four of Clubs, to prove she can hold it and perhaps improve upon it. The Jupiter position bespeaks its blessing on this situation because it is evolutionary. The keynote for this man-woman combination is cooperation. Together they will gain more wisdom than would be possible separately.

The keen intelligence of the Four of Clubs' Mars-Jupiter conjunction makes these people intolerant of stupidity and triviality; these natives are fundamentally mental, and they realize that growth and expansion are possible only through constant mental activity.

The undeveloped ones are apt to talk much and say little. Their right to the Four of Clubs as a Birth Card gives them a hearing, but unless they have learned to clarify and organize their ideas, they will not hold their audience.

These are the arguers and debaters—the lawyers with voluminous briefs, the speakers with lengthy paragraphs, the writers whose introductions are longer than the subject matter. Unless they are lazy and careless, which is rare, they are concerned only with matters of importance. They are seldom willing to waste their time or brains on inconsequentials. The Four of Clubs people also have, at some point in their lives, a drinking problem to some degree.

They are good travelers and interesting companions—always ready to point out something everybody else has missed. They are, of necessity, usually attracted to professions and mental pursuits—teaching, lecturing, philosophy, education, politics, and economics. If in business, they want their independence and an opportunity to project their own ideas. Only in rare cases are the women domestically inclined; their best expression is in an independent business or in the literary or educational fields.

BIRTHDATES RULED BY THE FOUR OF CLUBS

APRIL 30–TAURUS–RULED BY VENUS

Natural artists or musicians; appreciative critics. Influenced by family opinions and ties. Want authority in business and not too much responsibility. Intuitive. Want full credit for what they do. Cooperative if marry early; if late, may become self-centered. Uncertain conditions in the early years. Can succeed at banking, promotion, organizing. Must guard against revengefulness.

MAY 28–GEMINI–RULED BY MERCURY

Good agents and go-betweens. Keen, inquiring minds. Must have occupation that moves fast. Should avoid medicine as a career except as mental or nerve specialists. Good talkers, lecturers. Interested in law, diplomacy, or the market. Can succeed as engineers or scientists. Should guard against superficiality, procrastination. Apt to scatter their forces. Work best with others.

JUNE 26–CANCER–RULED BY THE MOON

Self-indulgent. Usually put on much weight. Must take good care of the teeth—may tend to crumble. Natural ability for dealing with others. Often talented in singing or working in metal or clay. Successful in work with the ground—raising commodities, growing flowers, profiting by oil. May become food experts, dieticians, prize-winning chefs. May have talent for the theater.

JULY 24–LEO–RULED BY THE SUN

Responsible leaders. Want public life or prominence. Dramatic, spectacular. Actors, playwrights. Want to discover or initiate something of importance. May become public philanthropists, welfare promoters, art sponsors. Charitable–but want their gifts publicized.

AUGUST 22–LEO OR VIRGO–RULED BY THE SUN OR MERCURY

Less spectacular than July 24, but often better balanced and equally gifted. May become outstanding in dramatic or musical field. May devote their lives to a cause; have strong opinions and beliefs. Love the countryside, children, and dogs. Sensitive and idealistic, but remain practical. Excellent parents.

SEPTEMBER 20–VIRGO–RULED BY MERCURY

Have intuition and inspiration, but fight them; want to remain practical. Often choose the easiest way because of laziness or expedience. If remain true to the best of themselves, can accomplish much. May be drawn to law, counseling, psychology, research–especially of disease. Want personal freedom. Should choose an occupation that is mental. If tied to home, should have a hobby.

OCTOBER 18–LIBRA–RULED BY VENUS

Friendly, popular. Business interests advanced by personality. Can become a power in groups. Like to shine–as socialites, entertainers, artists. Usually well groomed. Women succeed as stylists, models, beauticians. Work best if married or in partnership. May meet opposition from family. Can succeed as lawyers or politicians.

NOVEMBER 16–SCORPIO–RULED BY MARS

Set and fixed in ideas. Want to promote what they believe in. Will espouse causes; public spirited. Intense and dramatic; usually have musical talent. Not always successful in marriage; have ideals and want others to live up to them. Good government officials, statesmen. Have a long-range vision. Men (especially–should guard against self-indulgence.

DECEMBER 14–SAGITTARIUS–RULED BY JUPITER

Born speculators, but often bound to a routine occupation. A Karmic date; have come to settle obligations. Honest but reckless, careless of consequences. Nervous and tense. Can write, lecture, sell, but only if interested. Philosophical in later years.

Fours

FOUR OF CLUBS—PLANETARY SEQUENCE OF PERSONAL RELATIONSHIPS

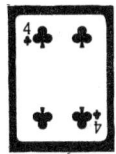

Horizontal Lines—Mars and Jupiter

TWO OF DIAMONDS—MERCURY CARD IN THE SATURN LINE

Activities can be continuous with this native. You'll never have a communication problem; even if you aren't wild about what is actually being said, you will understand. If you're in the field of medicine, an association with a Two of Diamonds (also in the medical field) could be most rewarding and profitable. Not fantastic for your love life, but not impossible. A relationship that requires work—but can bring satisfactory results.

Two of Diamonds birthdates: January 25, February 23, March 21, April 19, May 17, June 15, July 13, August 11, September 9, October 7, November 5, December 3

JACK OF SPADES—VENUS CARD IN THE URANUS LINE

A Jack of Spades can physically turn you on, but his intense search for the unknown may make you weary. This relationship can open new vistas of thinking for you (just when you thought you were content)—so don't pass it up. And your own interest in metaphysics may be just the ticket to a good and lasting romance. A Four of Clubs female will probably be more attracted to an older Jack of Spades male.

Jack of Spades birthdates: January 3, February 1

EIGHT OF CLUBS—MARS CARD IN THE NEPTUNE LINE

You will have great admiration for this person and feel great stimulation emanating from him. You may feel that he's not always right, and you may probe to find the real person. It's not necessary. What you see is what you get with these natives. You can learn from them so stop creating challenges, however insignificant they may seem to be. Enjoy time spent with this native. Stay away from romance—it's not likely to work out, even if you are attracted sexually.

Eight of Clubs birthdates: March 28, April 26, May 24, June 22, July 20, August 18, September 16, October 14, November 12, December 10

SIX OF DIAMONDS—JUPITER CARD IN THE MERCURY LINE

This is a friend who can learn from *you*. You can show him many new ideas and ways of doing things, and although it may seem to be a little difficult, don't hold back. This native will hear everything, and although it may be a delayed reaction, time spent with him can be well worth the effort. A romantic involvement can be good for both of you but preferably if you are male and the Six of Diamonds, female.

Six of Diamonds birthdates: January 21, February 19, March 17, April 15, May 13, June 11, July 9, August 7, September 5, October 3, November 1

FOUR OF SPADES–SATURN CARD IN THE VENUS LINE

A Karmic relationship (which may be one of the reasons you are also attracted to the Ten of Clubs—the Four of Spades' Displacement Card). If a business involvement, there will be overtones that indicate a closer involvement—or a desire for a closer one. If a straight love affair, it cannot be without difficulties. In either case, it's best not to think in terms of a lasting relationship—it may prove to be too much for both of you. This could be a natural escapist relationship for you as well—be careful the two of you aren't involved in drinking sprees, etc., too often.

Four of Spades birthdates: January 10, February 8, March 6, April 4, May 2

TEN OF HEARTS–URANUS CARD IN THE MARS LINE
(Jupiter and Mars Lines on the Diagonal)

You'll find things to talk about; these natives will never cease to surprise you; you'll be sexually drawn to each other—but keep them out of your personal life if you can. It won't be easy, but it will save you some grief in the future. On a platonic level, these people will willingly give you their time and energies, and you can help set their heads on a little straighter—but romantically, this is a bigger bite than is necessary to take. Use the "ten-foot pole" and enjoy them; they are good people to be around.

Ten of Hearts birthdates: July 31, August 29, September 27, October 25, November 23, December 21

TEN OF DIAMONDS–NEPTUNE CARD IN THE JUPITER LINE
(Jupiter Line on the Vertical)

This is one of your best relationships—especially if you are female and your Ten of Diamonds is male. His Displacement Card is your Personality Card (Queen of Clubs), which will put his head into thinking along some of the same lines that you do. He is much more interested in making money than you are, but that will make your life more comfortable, and you can constructively use your Five of Clubs Displacement Card and have the time to seek the many facets of knowledge you know are available to you. In both sexes the relationship is good even though things may not always be as they appear—they won't harm you, and they will always work out for the best. A definite "go ahead" for whatever involvement occurs.

Ten of Diamonds birthdates: January 17, February 15, March 13, April 11, May 9, June 7, July 5, August 3, September 1

Vertical Line—Jupiter

JACK OF HEARTS—VENUS LINE

You'll like these natives but not necessarily be interested in them. It's conversation—hearing what they have to say—enjoying perhaps a different point of view, not necessarily buying it—but not being adverse to it either. These are friends—don't try to make them into something other than that.

Jack of Hearts birthdates: July 30, August 28, September 26, October 24, November 22, December 20

TEN OF SPADES—MERCURY LINE

A definite romantic card for you, but the romance could turn out to be a drain. You two can meet and quickly find that you have many things in common—one of them could be too much partying or just the social activities of drinking. Too much of this and all the romance is gone; it goes without saying. You both have good judgment, so keep everything on the positive plane. If your Ten of Spades seems irresponsible to you, don't nag. This involvement could work out well if you both make the effort.

Ten of Spades birthdates: January 4, February 2

EIGHT OF DIAMONDS—CROWN LINE

You probably won't be attracted to these natives, unless it's just a passing fancy. You won't like their ability to turn a certain amount of ruthlessness on and off. It's just as well. They're definitely not for romance—friendships could be irritating to you, and you won't feel as if Eights of Diamonds have anything to share with you mentally. The one positive situation that can develop is a financial one. You might be able to make money through this person. But for the most part, keep him at arm's length and enjoy knowing him more.

Eight of Diamonds birthdates: January 19, February 17, March 15, April 13, May 11, June 9, July 7, August 5, September 3, October 1

EIGHT OF HEARTS—NEPTUNE LINE

Romance—not necessarily the wild, uncontrolled, heart-throbbing, time-stopping kind, but don't be surprised if it turns into that. You will really have to be on your toes for this one because these natives can be gone as quickly as they came—to the point where it may seem to have been a dream. They will woo and win you—and *then* examine you with a magnifying glass. You can handle it—just be your natural and sure-footed self.

Eight of Hearts birthdates: August 31, September 29, October 27, November 25, December 23

SEVEN OF SPADES—URANUS LINE

A male Seven of Spades will probably feel an automatic attraction for you inasmuch as you are Venus to his Displacement Card (King of Diamonds), but don't be misled. Although this is a Karmic tie and you will unquestionably find a Seven of Spades somewhere in your past, present, or future relationships—be aware that it will not necessarily be a successful involvement. The greatest personal success you can have with these natives will be to understand them. Don't deny the involvement; just be prepared.

Seven of Spades birthdates: January 7, February 5, March 3, April 1

THREE OF SPADES—SATURN LINE

These natives will be both a challenge and a frustration for you. You will feel that your knowledge is exactly what they need to overcome some of their difficulties—and you may be right, but convincing them is something else. Don't work too hard—it could be an impossible task, and there are many other relationships in your Spread that can be much easier and more rewarding.

Three of Spades birthdates: January 11, February 9, March 7, April 5, May 3, June 1

TEN OF DIAMONDS—JUPITER LINE: SEE HORIZONTAL LINE

Diagonal Lines

NINE OF CLUBS—VENUS AND SATURN LINES

You will especially enjoy talking to these natives; they are flashy and seem to lead interesting lives. Eventually your interest will probably decline, as you will feel that they spend far too much time on unimportant things. It's a relationship that can drain you if you permit it to happen. Keep them on a more positive plane if you want the involvement at all.

Nine of Clubs birthdates: January 31, February 29, March 27, April 25, May 23, June 21, July 19, August 17, September 15, October 13, November 11, December 9

THREE OF DIAMONDS—MERCURY AND URANUS LINES

A romantic involvement that will be enhanced by your conscious level of understanding. You will like these natives, have good rapport and could even find yourself happily married to one. They have worries—mostly financial, some of which are more imagined than real, but you have the ability to make a problem seem as if it's not a problem at all. You would be very good for a Three of Diamonds—and you might even enjoy the whole thing.

Three of Diamonds birthdates: January 24, February 22, March 20, April 18, May 16, June 14, July 12, August 10, September 8, October 6, November 4, December 2

TEN OF HEARTS—JUPITER AND MARS LINES: SEE HORIZONTAL LINE

FIVE OF HEARTS—VENUS AND SATURN LINES

This is a romance that will happen to you immediately, and you will find it almost impossible to resist. There are similarities in each of you that will draw you together. (Your Displacement Card is the Five of Clubs; the Displacement Card of the Five of Clubs is the Five of Hearts.) However, this situation is not without difficulties, and most of them will be on the side of the Five of Hearts. It will be difficult to get him settled or concentrating in any one area. He may be anxious to earn money—but too scattered to make it really happen. Your good foundation of fundamental knowledge will keep this relationship alive—if you want to put in the time and energy.

Five of Hearts birthdates: October 30, November 28, December 26

QUEEN OF SPADES—MERCURY AND URANUS LINES

This could be an instant dislike for you. You will feel that there is no rapport and nothing to be gained from these natives. You will probably be right as far as you are concerned. If there is a glimmer of positiveness, give them a chance. They *do* have something to say, to offer, but are simply not so as articulate as you. If you aren't interested, don't press the relationship. Take a pass.

Queen of Spades birthdate: January 2

FIVE OF SPADES—VENUS AND MARS LINES

This could be a highly stimulating relationship for you—either romance or friendship. The two of you could certainly keep each other entertained with a great deal of movement going on. In this person, you may find many of the qualities you have sought in others, it could be an exciting involvement. Don't fail to make the most of it.

Five of Spades birthdates: January 9, February 7, March 5, April 3, May 1

ACE OF CLUBS—VENUS AND MERCURY LINES

There's a lot of love here, and you will probably not hesitate in telling this native so. You could feel as if you've known him for a long time—but it's really all those good feelings coming through. Communication is extremely good, but don't frighten your Ace of Clubs away with overkill. He will want to hear everything in time, so forget that need to babble it all out immediately. A definite "must try" in the romance department and a "don't miss" for friendship.

Ace of Clubs birthdates: May 31, June 29, July 27, August 25, September 23, October 21, November 19, December 17

EIGHT OF SPADES—JUPITER AND SATURN LINES

A good working relationship that may not earn you as much money as satisfaction. You'll feel good communications; whatever point you try to make will eventually be understood by this native. The reverse can also be true so give him opportunities to be heard. Not an impossible romantic involvement but not really where it's at.

Eight of Spades birthdates: January 6, February 4, March 2

SEVEN OF CLUBS—SATURN AND URANUS LINES

An automatic attraction that you should not permit to invade your personal life too much. The nervousness of this native could rattle your life to the point where neither one of you is productive. In a business involvement always be prepared for the unexpected that these natives can impose upon you.

Seven of Clubs birthdates: March 29, April 27, May 25, June 23, July 21, August 19, September 17, October 15, November 13, December 11

JACK OF DIAMONDS—URANUS AND NEPTUNE LINES

If this person comes running to you and tells you of the best business deal of your life, put your money there—but not without checking it out thoroughly first. Once it's confirmed on paper to be what this native says it is, you'll probably make a lot of money. Keep the relationship on a stockbroker-client, salesman-buyer level. Romance with this native probably won't work out over the long pull. And personal friendship is only a little less difficult.

Jack of Diamonds birthdates: January 16, February 14, March 12, April 10, May 8, June 6, July 4, August 2

FOUR OF CLUBS FAMOUS BIRTHDATES

April 30   Queen Juliana of the Netherlands

Fours

May 28	Ian Fleming
June 26	Pearl S. Buck
July 24	Amelia Earhart
September 20	Sophia Loren
October 18	Melina Mercouri George C. Scott Pierre Elliott Trudeau
November 16	Burgess Meredith
December 14	James H. Doolittle Patty Duke

Four of Diamonds

Planetary Sequence

			K♠	8♦ Neptune	10♣ Uranus			
A♠	3♦	5♣	10♠	Q♣	A♣	3♥		Mercury
2♥	9♠	9♣	J♥	5♠	7♦	7♥		Venus
8♣	J♠	2♦	4♣	6♥	K♦	K♠		Mars
A♦	A♥	8♠	10♦	10♥	4♠	6♦		Jupiter
5♦	7♣	9♥	3♠	3♣	5♥	Q♦		Saturn
J♦	K♣	2♣	7♠	9♦	J♣	Q♠		Uranus
Q♥ Saturn	6♠ Jupiter	6♣ Mars	8♥ Venus	2♠ Mercury	4♦	4♥		Neptune

Neptune · Uranus · Saturn · Jupiter · Mars · Venus · Mercury

Mundane Spread

Fours

Diamonds — Values
Four of Diamonds — Financial Protection through Hard Work
Four in Diamonds — Concentration on Security

The Venus Card in the Neptune Line. Displaces the **Five of Spades** in the Natural Spread.

Work is important for all Fours; this is especially true of the Four of Diamonds. The financial situations of many of the natives of these birthdates prove it. There is inherent protection, power, and success in all Fours—but these are potentials; they do not become actualities until stirred into life by diligent and concentrated effort. If not, poverty and failure—in varying degrees—are the sure results.

The Displaced Card is the Five of Spades—a Cross in Labor. The Four of Diamonds has an inherent dislike of strict application, an unwillingness to be tied down, and a restlessness and dissatisfaction with his "lot" in life because money is not at his disposal unless he makes an effort to earn it—and then to keep it.

Labor is not always with the hands; earning is not always connected with a clerical or managerial job. A Four of Diamonds woman, for example, may marry a man who has plenty—but if she is to have any freedom of her own with it, she will have to do something to earn or deserve it. The husband may be difficult or uncongenial; running a house may be distasteful and burdensome; what is demanded of her may be intolerable; but she must work at it if she hopes to profit by what doesn't actually belong to her. It is often a heavy price to pay for financial freedom—especially when the personal need for variety has to be sacrificed.

There is a certain churning in all Fours of Diamonds all the time. These people have a burden—there is no question about it, in some way. This is also a person who can be very sure of himself. In a Monterey, California, cemetery one of the old gravestones reads, "She was always right"—her birthday shows that she was a Four of Diamonds.

The Personality Card is important for these natives. For the men both the King and the Jack have good sequences; not so with the women. The Queen of Diamonds, the Mercury Card in the Saturn Line, has many obstacles in her path—all under the heavy hand of Saturn. Four of Diamonds women should be very careful not to live their lives under their personality ray, not to depend upon their charm and femininity to get them by, not to evade work. A good earning capacity belongs to the card; no one need become a victim of poverty or failure unless he so chooses.

The True Place of the Four of Diamonds is Venus, in the Saturn Line—another testimony to the fact that work is a requirement.

This is by no means an easy card with which to deal. With the majority of the cards in the Neptune Lines, there are sure to be confusing experiences and unaccountable developments in associations. The displaced Five of Spades

Your Place in the Cards

indicates delusion and disappointment in affectional matters, in finances and business dealings. As a compensation, however, the Four of Diamonds' planetary sequence has two cards in the Crown Line—a strong call to the "higher mind."

The Four of Diamonds is a card of overcoming—and as in all other cases, spiritual understanding is the solution to difficulties. The truly evolved Fours of Diamonds lead happy and useful lives; the "negatives" are less fortunate.

BIRTHDATES RULED BY THE FOUR OF DIAMONDS

JANUARY 23–AQUARIUS–RULED BY URANUS

Good understanding of human nature. Successful planners. Have vision of things to come; want progress and improvement. Should follow a mental pursuit. Are inclined to somewhat reckless beginnings; then lose interest and become indifferent. Can succeed with property transactions—real estate, building. Have originality and good taste. Dynamic and dramatic; may be attracted to the stage or pictures.

FEBRUARY 21–PISCES–RULED BY NEPTUNE

Often confused or misdirected in seeking the proper vocation. Apt to follow inclination rather than fitness. Can succeed in own business (better than working for others)—especially insurance, annuities, trust funds, and the like. Often attracted to the theater but do better as directors, dramatists, or producers than as actors. If inclined to medicine, make good researchers and discoverers. Objectives must be well defined; otherwise drift or chase rainbows.

MARCH 19–PISCES–RULED BY NEPTUNE

More sure of themselves than the other Pisces. Usually have more artistic talent—singing, acting, designing. Interested in righting wrongs and correcting abuses. Good workers for prison reform, improvement for hospitals. Ambitious—but less avid for money than many Fours of Diamonds.

APRIL 17–ARIES–RULED BY MARS

Sure of themselves and their beliefs. Very ambitious; willing to work hard to get to the top. More self-disciplinary than many Fours of Diamonds. Have a keen sense of values and always get their money's worth. Good for dealing with foreign countries—shipping, commerce, travel bureaus. Enjoy travel.

Given to starting large projects—then leaving them for others to finish. If the "finishers" are capable, the projects may become highly important. Many are attracted to the law and banking.

MAY 15–TAURUS–RULED BY VENUS

Home and business easily combined. Work best with friends and family. Dislike changes. Willing to take responsibility in the name of service. Should always marry and have a home of their own. Capable and well balanced in whatever line they follow. Good business sense but do not like business responsibility. May have strong religious inclinations. Good religious leaders, preachers, lecturers, writers.

JUNE 13–GEMINI–RULED BY MERCURY

Keen minds; clever judges of people on first sight. Interested in scientific experiments—but not as patient researchers. Good personalities; deal successfully with employees. Interested in many lines. Will try anything once. Do best in an occupation that taxes their mental faculties. Can succeed in business, if fast moving, but not as well adapted for it as for a profession. Make good trial lawyers. Like changes, entertainment, excitement. Should cultivate any latent talent.

JULY 11–CANCER–RULED BY THE MOON

Very emotional, self-concerned. When they forget themselves, become successful in business, useful in the community. Concerned with homes, families, housing. Can deal in commodities that the public needs and wants. Paternal (or maternal) and protective. Like to shine as public benefactors. Nervous and restless; never feel they are fully appreciated. Have a sense of service but are often too lazy to let it manifest. Want comfort without effort.

AUGUST 9–LEO–RULED BY THE SUN

Very keen for success. Do well in business if already established. But want it on a large scale. Always want value received. Are either self-centered or just the opposite—humanitarian and self-sacrificing. May be attracted to religious groups; if the self-seeking type, can make the connection pay. Are good organizers. Can succeed as actors, but an equal number do just as well as merchants and manufacturers. Are sympathetic—sometimes patronizing.

SEPTEMBER 7–VIRGO–RULED BY MERCURY

Inclined to science and research. Should follow a line that requires good judgment and a keen mind. May be fussy and too meticulous if not careful, also petty in personal relationships. Sharp and clever—sometimes too much so. If religiously inclined, want demonstrations. *Can* be very high-minded. Good writers, teachers, educators; often have keen sense of humor. Should avoid working for expediency rather than mutual benefit.

OCTOBER 5—LIBRA—RULED BY VENUS

Performers, artists, writers. Much attracted to the stage or screen. Want to be a power in their own circle. Make good lawyers, politicians, leaders. Good agents and go-betweens. Are friendly and cooperative. Have strong metaphysical inclinations. Emotional and self-indulgent; if they overcome those traits, can develop much soul-force. Always have an eye for beauty; always present a good appearance. Need many contacts and changes to keep interest alive.

NOVEMBER 3—SCORPIO—RULED BY MARS

Much financial power in this birthdate, but many prefer the easiest way and will not make the necessary effort. Should avoid getting into a rut. Can gain much hidden knowledge if they seek it. Fixed and set in their thinking; hard to convince. Have inner fear of lack of money, but do little to forestall it. Can succeed in big business—especially manufacturing. Have a gift for writing but must cultivate it. Many of the deep thinkers become poets or composers.

DECEMBER 1—SAGITTARIUS—RULED BY JUPITER

Some woman may be very influential in this life. Dependent upon close associations and will take responsibility for them. Nervous about making changes, so apt to remain in one place for a long time. Want freedom and independence in finances; willing to work hard to stay that way. Good for travel business, foreign connections, law, or diplomacy. Good foreign correspondents. Can become able and popular leaders.

FOUR OF DIAMONDS—PLANETARY SEQUENCE OF PERSONAL RELATIONSHIPS

Horizontal Lines—Neptune and Crown

TWO OF SPADES—MERCURY CARD IN THE MARS LINE

An acquaintance—someone who works for you, or someone with whom you may be involved on an impersonal level—is the best combination here. You should get along fine as long as you don't try to get too close.

Two of Spades birthdates: January 12, February 10, March 8, April 6, May 4, June 2

EIGHT OF HEARTS—VENUS CARD IN THE JUPITER LINE

You will dearly love this person but probably find it difficult to live with him. Your organizational ability could be thrown out of kilter in a close association with an Eight of Hearts who always seems to be running in dozens of different directions. Try to work it out; there's lots of love waiting for you if you can live with it.

Eight of Hearts birthdates: August 31, September 29, October 27, November 25, December 23

SIX OF CLUBS—MARS CARD IN THE SATURN LINE

"If he could move a little faster, maybe he could get his work done—and then maybe he would stop worrying about getting his work done" is probably your reaction to this native. Don't be too harsh; he may not like some of your traits, either. Stay away from anything personal.

Six of Clubs birthdates: March 30, April 28, May 26, June 24, July 22, August 20, September 18, October 16, November 14, December 12

SIX OF SPADES—JUPITER CARD IN THE URANUS LINE

You'll feel similarly about this native as you do about the Six of Clubs— except you'll probably like and admire this Six more. You'll feel sympathetic to his plight, but that doesn't mean a personal involvement. Romance won't hurt you—but won't necessarily make you happy, either. Think twice about it.

Six of Spades birthdates: January 8, February 6, March 4, April 2

QUEEN OF HEARTS—SATURN CARD IN THE NEPTUNE LINE

A working relationship is possible here if you have the patience to stay after this native constantly. He could be a fabulous salesman for you—but just as these people sell extremely well, they will tend to paint the same rosy pictures to you, but the results may not always be as anticipated. The relationship is inevitable on some level, and it's better on an employee-employer basis than romantically. You would find (in love) that you can't live within painted pictures.

Queen of Hearts birthdates: July 29, August 27, September 25, October 23, November 21, December 19

TEN OF CLUBS—URANUS CARD IN THE CROWN LINE

These people have information to give to you, much of it in the form of ideas or things you had not previously known about. If you are operating on a positive level, you will use this new-found knowledge and convert it into a money-making idea.

Ten of Clubs birthdates: January 30, February 28, March 26, April 24, May 22, June 20, July 18, August 16, September 14, October 12, November 10, December 8

EIGHT OF DIAMONDS—NEPTUNE CARD IN THE CROWN LINE

Ideal business partners, providing that when they try to run you, you don't resent it too much and ruin the relationship. The Eight of Diamonds is more in tune with a spiritual side so there is much to learn from him besides business. Even though you are also "in balance," don't ever underestimate (or overestimate when they are young) this native's abilities.

Eight of Diamonds birthdates: January 19, February 17, March 15, April 13, May 11, June 9, July 7, August 5, September 3, October 1

Vertical Line—Venus

JACK OF CLUBS—URANUS LINE

Nothing that you've ever done will be forgotten by these natives. They, too, are business associates—but ones you have to be a little more careful about. They will be forceful and even revolutionary in some of their thoughts and ways, but don't run down the garden path after them. If the situation doesn't work, you'll be hurt a great deal more than they—financially, and physically. Communications are good.

Jack of Clubs birthdates: January 29, February 27, March 25, April 23, May 21, June 19, July 17, August 15, September 13, October 11, November 9, December 7

FIVE OF HEARTS—SATURN LINE

Fall in love with this native (and you'll be tempted), and you're in for problems. While you're running around working your head off to help pay the bills, this native will be busy wondering if this is the life he really wants. You really don't have the time for this native, and it would make life easier for you if you would look elsewhere for a mate. Friendship is fine and probably will last—but these natives cannot help but drain you of energies you know you need to put elsewhere.

Five of Hearts birthdates: October 30, November 28, December 26

FOUR OF SPADES—MARS CARD IN THE JUPITER LINE

This could be a sexual experience you would never forget—or the friend who keeps prodding you to keep going when things look grimmest. In either case it is an exciting relationship that should not include marriage.

Four of Spades birthdates: January 10, February 8, March 6, April 4, May 2

KING OF DIAMONDS—JUPITER CARD IN THE MARS LINE

If this is a man-to-man relationship, you couldn't get much closer to perfection as far as business involvements are concerned. You can amass a fortune through this man—if you lose that know-it-all attitude and listen to him. If this native is a woman and you are a man, it would be quite difficult—society has probably educated you to discount her—even when she's right. In any event, this is a great combination for making money and a possible happy romance if you are a woman and this native a man. It's not an easy relationship—on any level—but well worth the effort.

King of Diamonds birthdates: January 14, February 12, March 10, April 8, May 6, June 4, July 2

SEVEN OF DIAMONDS—SATURN CARD IN THE VENUS LINE

You'll always like this person—maybe even think romantically about him if the situation is right—but always wonder why your paths keep crossing. The relationship is Karmic, and if you truly studied the card, you would find you could make a lot of money from the association. Don't get involved romantically—this native would only add to your own difficulties, but you might consider the business aspects.

Seven of Diamonds birthdates: January 20, February 18, March 16, April 14, May 12, June 10, July 8, August 6, September 4, October 2

ACE OF CLUBS—URANUS CARD IN THE MERCURY LINE

These people will say the darndest things at the most inappropriate times as far as you're concerned—it might even feel embarrassing at times, but don't get bogged down with that. Utilize their need to learn, and you'll find your own mind taking a refreshing shower occasionally. Don't look for anything permanent. There's really not enough going between the two of you to sustain a relationship—unless you create it, which is not that advisable.

Ace of Clubs birthdates: May 31, June 29, July 27, August 25, September 23, October 21, November 19, December 17

Your Place in the Cards

Diagonal Lines

QUEEN OF SPADES—MERCURY CARD IN THE URANUS AND MERCURY LINES

Here is another temporary relationship; these natives can take you down another path of learning, certainly one you should be somewhat curious about—your spiritual side. Their attitudes will help you better understand your contemporaries. Don't be too harsh about their daily living habits. You're not living with them—and if you are, it will be unusual if it lasts.

Queen of Spades birthdate: January 2

NINE OF DIAMONDS—URANUS AND MARS LINES

Another Mercurial relationship, but one that you will not mourn when it's gone. In fact you could even be pleased. You may find that these natives have represented themselves to be capable of things that don't come to pass; don't be hard on them should this happen—they have ability, and you can pull it out of them. Don't be personally involved. It's not worth it.

Nine of Diamonds birthdates: January 18, February 16, March 14, April 12, May 10, June 8, July 6, August 4, September 2

THREE OF SPADES—SATURN AND JUPITER LINES

This is a love relationship, but this native could possibly hold back some of your own personal desires for yourself, by his fear and uncertainty. You could also find yourself working and working to just pay off doctor and dental bills. So be careful about any personal involvements—make *sure* before you leap.

Three of Spades birthdates: January 11, February 9, March 7, April 5, May 3, June 1

EIGHT OF SPADES—JUPITER AND SATURN LINES

A dynamic relationship, one you'll never forget. Hopefully, it's on a friendship level; this will prove to be a strong involvement that will not only stimulate you—keep you going when you're down, but will create many good happenings in your life. This person can't hurt you in any way, but marriage should not be foremost in your mind if it's romance you seek—even though you might think there will never be another human being like this in your life. You're probably right, so keep him in your life—but don't marry him.

Eight of Spades birthdates: January 6, February 4, March 2

JACK OF SPADES—MARS AND URANUS LINES

Another friend who can be of great benefit to you in your personal life. This native can open doors you've only dreamed of. Romance is possible and probable—with success especially in the later years. Enjoy the relationship and work at it.

Jack of Spades birthdates: January 3, February 1

TWO OF HEARTS—VENUS AND NEPTUNE LINES

Any romantic attraction you feel for this native would be better suppressed and kept on a platonic level. You can never prove to these natives that you love them, especially when you really don't feel it's necessary to prove anything—if you already show it, they should know it. But they don't know it, and you won't show it, so you are defeated with this card before you start. Some kind of relationship is inevitable, but try to make it easy on yourself.

Two of Hearts birthdate: December 29

FOUR OF DIAMONDS FAMOUS BIRTHDATES

January 23	Randolph Scott
	Edouard Manet
March 19	Ursula Andress
	Earl Warren
April 17	James Garner
	William Holden
May 15	Errol Garner
June 13	Basil Rathbone
	William B. Yeats
July 11	Yul Brynner
	Tab Hunter
August 9	Bob Cousey
September 7	Taylor Caldwell
	Elia Kazan
	Peter Lawford
	Queen Elizabeth I of England
December 1	Woody Allen
	Mary Martin

Four of Spades

Spades — Labor; Wisdom
Four of Spades — Peace of Soul through Work
Four in Spades — Labor for Duty

The Venus Card in the Jupiter Line. Displaces the **Ten of Clubs** in the Natural Spread.

Of all the fifty-two patterns, this is one of the most fortunate—at least in terms of "heritage." It would seem that these natives had earned the right to a certain amount of security (providing, of course, that the requirement of work is met) and that no long periods of hardship or material lack would be their lot. This does not mean, however, that there are no problems to be solved, no heartaches through personal relationships, and no thorny paths to travel on the road to achievement. There is an inner awareness of destiny in spades, and although it does not always reach the conscious mind, it manifests itself in the life experience in the form of tests and trials.

The Four of Spades is a very powerful card, if it is used right. If not, it can be just the opposite. This native's problem is rarely financial; when it is, it is usually of brief duration. A desire for money exists, but unless the desire develops into greed, there is sufficient power to satisfy it. The problem is more apt to be emotional. Someone near and dear proves disappointing—unwilling, perhaps, to improve or elevate himself or to cooperate with the native in his own efforts at self-development. Disappointments in people cause Fours of Spades to seek isolation rather than cope with their fear of not living up to the psychological demands put upon them. The weaker Fours of

Spades drop down to the lower levels; the stronger continue their task alone but suffer for those they have left behind. Awareness and the development of intuition give the solution. If the stronger natives cannot manage to pull the weaker loved ones up to their own levels, they can adjust themselves to emotional loneliness and accept it as their prescribed experience.

The Four of Spades applies his knowledge well. He must hold to what he knows and be unmoved. Through work, completeness and satisfaction *can* be attained—but the wise ones know it takes constant application to keep their benefits intact. These natives are independent in thinking, fixed in their mental attitudes. It is hard to persuade them to any course but the one they decide upon for themselves. Indeed, no such effort should be attempted; they are their own guides and their own critics. If they remember who they are, they will go further without any interference from the outside world. The True Place is the Mercury Card in the Neptune Line. If they hold fast to the idealism of Neptune, they will free themselves from its confusions.

The men of these birthdates seem to find themselves earlier than the women—but peace of soul and satisfaction in work are indicated for both sexes during their active lifetime.

Parents should teach their children, from the time they can walk or think, the value and dignity of work. Parents are piling up a heavy debt for themselves if they spoil their children or bring them up in idleness.

A firm health foundation is a great asset for these people—but that, too, requires effort in many cases. Nature's laws are the best to follow. Spades are *earth*.

BIRTHDATES RULED BY THE FOUR OF SPADES

JANUARY 10—CAPRICORN—RULED BY SATURN

Ambition is the ruling drive for this birthdate. They work primarily for money, and while their aim in this direction is very high, they are pleased with any and all returns—and unhappy without them. Their fondest hopes are seldom realized since the dimensions are out of line. There is a laudable desire, however, to make something of themselves as individuals, and they work hard to become outstanding in their line. Many are attracted to the theater and acquit themselves well. The majority are better adapted to business, however, and become good managers and executives.

FEBRUARY 8—AQUARIUS—RULED BY URANUS

Inspiration and creative ability belong to this date. Intuition is strong, and there is often evidence of direct guidance from higher sources. With many there is a sixth sense and a gift of prophecy—especially among the women.

Few of this date are unsuccessful, and many have become famous. Their talents are varied—they can succeed as military men of high rank; as explorers and discoverers; as composers, dancers, artists or writers; as clergymen and philosophers; as actors, directors or theater managers; as scientists or inventors; or as business magnates.

MARCH 6—PISCES—RULED BY NEPTUNE

Musicians, poets, painters, actors, and dancers head the list of occupations for this date—but these by no means exhaust it. If forced by circumstances to seek an occupation in less glamorous fields, there is always a yearning for some form of self-expression that gives scope to their imagination and an outlet for their emotions. In this date there is decided talent, and it should be discovered and expressed. There is also an urge for service and a willingness to assume responsibility. The women make excellent nurses; the majority in either sex have an ability for writing, music, painting, or some allied form of art.

APRIL 4—ARIES—RULED BY MARS

These are the real go-getters among the Fours of Spades. They know what they want, go after it, and succeed at it—even against odds. There is much concentrated force here and a determination that wins. A strong streak of practicality makes them good managers and executives. The stage has a strong attraction—or some connection with the entertainment world in a business capacity. They are playwrights, dramatic teachers, coaches, or managers. They likewise can make fine success of a business that is pioneering and progressive.

MAY 2—TAURUS—RULED BY VENUS

These people want luxury, security—and prominence. Are dependable and responsible, public spirited and charitable, affectionate and loyal. There is often a streak of shyness that makes them appear aloof—but it is mainly for the preservation of their dignity, which is important. They are good actors, judges, writers.

FOUR OF SPADES—PLANETARY SEQUENCE OF PERSONAL RELATIONSHIPS

Horizontal Lines—Jupiter and Saturn

TEN OF HEARTS—MERCURY CARD IN THE MARS LINE

The charm and witticism of this native will be amusing to you, but the chances of your falling for his line are slim. You may even feel that he should get down to business a little more and stop fooling around so much.

Ten of Hearts birthdates: July 31, August 29, September 27, October 25, November 23, December 21

TEN OF DIAMONDS—VENUS CARD IN THE JUPITER LINE

Romance, marriage—the works—are not only possible, but probable with this card. You will admire this native's abilities, and the two of you can accomplish almost anything together. A great relationship on any level—if you find each other, you should never lack for anything, with one exception: Spiritual awareness will not be a part of your lives, and this may be too great a sacrifice for you.

Ten of Diamonds birthdates: January 17, February 15, March 13, April 11, May 9, June 7, July 5, August 3, September 1

EIGHT OF SPADES—MARS CARD IN THE SATURN LINE

You will have met your match with this native and could even fall prey to him—finding yourself in a position you totally dislike. There is no real reason why you couldn't use a friendship with this person to your advantage. Meet him on equal ground with openness and sincerity, and you could find someone who could be most beneficial to you in your lifetime. No personal attachments and you're better off.

Eight of Spades birthdates: January 6, February 4, March 2

ACE OF HEARTS—JUPITER CARD IN THE URANUS LINE

You'll be drawn to these natives, probably thinking that you can help them in some way—which is true, if it doesn't turn out to detract you too much from what you want to do. Romance is all right, but there are much better aspects in your Pattern.

Ace of Hearts birthdates: December 30

ACE OF DIAMONDS—SATURN CARD IN THE NEPTUNE LINE

You probably know at least two or three Aces of Diamonds now and have known these people for most of your life. These natives are people to whom you have old obligations—but don't mislead yourself. You've probably paid the debt five times over. No need to continue any of these relationships on their current level—unless you want to.

Ace of Diamonds birthdates: January 26, February 24, March 22, April 20, May 18, June 16, July 14, August 12, September 10, October 8, November 6, December 4

Fours

QUEEN OF DIAMONDS—URANUS CARD IN THE MERCURY LINE
(Saturn and Mercury Lines on the Diagonal)

Good communications, but a person with too many problems for you to get involved. This is a situation where you could melt into the fixtures with this native and find yourself struggling right alongside him—without cause or reason. Take a pass on anything other than a slight acquaintance.

Queen of Diamonds birthdates: January 15, February 13, March 11, April 9, May 7, June 5, July 3, August 1

FIVE OF HEARTS—NEPTUNE CARD IN THE VENUS LINE
(Saturn Line on the Vertical)

This native will appear to be free, fun-loving, and perhaps full of surprises—but don't put your money or your life on the line because it won't be that way. You are far too stability conscious to bring him happiness—or he, to you. Keep the whole relationship as a fantasy and you're way ahead of the game.

Five of Hearts birthdates: October 30, November 28, December 26

Vertical Line—Venus

KING OF DIAMONDS—MARS LINE

You'll probably feel that this native is too material-minded, and you will take a pass on any relationship. You can talk to him, so find out for sure before you make any radical decisions.

King of Diamonds birthdates: January 14, February 12, March 10, April 8, May 6, June 4, July 2

SEVEN OF DIAMONDS—VENUS LINE

This is love and there's no escaping it. This card is not only your Venus Card, but it's in the double Venus Lines. You will adore these natives and probably overlook the faults, problems and obstacles that they must sometimes endure. Be prepared to support them financially, or at least contribute. They can do well financially, but it will be more difficult with all the love you have to give them.

Seven of Diamonds birthdates: January 20, February 18, March 16, April 14, May 12, June 10, July 8, August 6, September 4, October 2

ACE OF CLUBS—MERCURY LINE

This relationship could wind up disappointing you—especially if you are sexually attracted. It is not a good involvement; try to bypass it. There will always be irritating factors—the way these people talk, the things they say, how they say them, etc. Don't bother unless you have to—and if so, keep everything at a low level.

Ace of Clubs birthdates: May 31, June 29, July 27, August 25, September 23, October 21, November 19, December 17

FOUR OF DIAMONDS—NEPTUNE LINE

Ideally, this is an employee on whom you can depend (even if you have to push him a little). Don't always believe everything these natives say but know that it will never be meant to hurt you. Don't get personally involved, or you'll find yourself running to the beat of their drums. You can find more happiness elsewhere.

Four of Diamonds birthdates: January 23, February 21, March 19, April 17, May 15, June 13, July 11, August 9, September 7, October 5, November 3, December 1

JACK OF CLUBS—URANUS LINE

Somewhere, sometime, you will meet a Jack of Clubs, and you could spend a half a lifetime listening to him—only to wind up being drained yourself. These people have knowledge, but so do you. Use what you can of what they offer but eliminate a close relationship. The price could be exorbitant.

Jack of Clubs birthdates: January 29, February 27, March 25, April 23, May 21, June 19, July 17, August 15, September 13, October 11, November 9, December 7

FIVE OF HEARTS—SATURN LINE: SEE HORIZONTAL LINE

Diagonal Lines

KING OF HEARTS—MARS AND MERCURY LINES

Here is your top salesman or the teacher you like some days and can't stand the next, or someone you work for whose door is always open to you even though you don't always get that raise. This person will briefly influence your life; then you may never see him again. Use the influence well—these are good, endearing people.

King of Hearts birthdates: June 30, July 28, August 26, September 24, October 22, November 20, December 18

THREE OF CLUBS—SATURN AND MARS LINES

Talking to this person could be like talking to a stone wall, but don't hold it against him. Not only is he uncertain of what you said, but probably uncertain of why you said it. Don't be concerned and don't get involved. The result will not be worth the effort.

Three of Clubs birthdates: May 29, June 27, July 25, August 23, September 21, October 19, November 17, December 15

SEVEN OF SPADES—URANUS AND JUPITER LINES

Good for romantic involvement—the mate who stands behind proudly while you shine before others. Better if you are male and your Seven of Spades female because of social pressures, but it can work well in either case. Much love and exciting new experiences to be shared with this card.

Seven of Spades birthdates: January 7, February 5, March 3, April 1

SIX OF CLUBS—NEPTUNE AND SATURN LINES

You'll be irritated with this card because you'll feel he is not living up to his full capacity. You're probably right, but it's not your job to take that problem on. Marriage will probably end in divorce, and you'll come out of the whole thing more of a loser than the Six of Clubs. Friendship is possible, but, again, probably irritating and tiresome most of the time. Encourage these natives to develop their intuition—the whole relationship will improve considerably.

Six of Clubs birthdates: March 30, April 28, May 26, June 24, July 22, August 20, September 18, October 16, November 14, December 12

QUEEN OF DIAMONDS—SATURN AND MERCURY LINES: SEE HORIZONTAL LINE

SIX OF HEARTS—DOUBLE MARS LINES

This person has been, is, or will be a teacher to you. You won't particularly agree—you might even violently disagree, but remember—it is only information for you to disseminate and use at your own discretion. Chances are this native has sacrificed some of his own desires in order to teach you. No close involvements.

Six of Hearts birthdates: October 29, November 27, December 25

JACK OF HEARTS—VENUS AND JUPITER LINES

You are capable of many powerful things with this combination. First and foremost, it is love—but the love could be of an impersonal nature. Even if you are personally involved with, or married to, this native, the same could be true. That's not to say that he doesn't love you—he does, but you must share his love. This person could be your Master, your guru, your minister, priest, or rabbi, and if you become a worker for one of those causes or similar ones, you would do great things. A dynamic love (in the true sense of the word) relationship.

Jack of Hearts birthdates: July 30, August 28, September 26, October 24, November 22, December 20

FIVE OF CLUBS—MERCURY AND SATURN LINES

A fast, in-and-out kind of relationship that will leave you wondering where this native has gone. And you'll probably never find out. Avoid it if you can—especially marriage—even though it's tempting.

Five of Clubs birthdates: March 31, April 29, May 27, June 25, July 23, August 21, September 19, October 17, November 15, December 13

FOUR OF SPADES FAMOUS BIRTHDATES

January 10	Ray Bolger
	Gypsy Rose Lee
	Frank James
February 8	Jack Lemmon
	James Dean
	Lana Turner
	Evangeline Adams
March 6	Lou Costello
	Elizabeth Barrett Browning
	Arthur Murray
May 2	Bing Crosby
	Hussein I of Jordan
	Catherine the Great of Russia

Fives

FIVES represent Changes, Variety, Opportunity, Travel, Escape, and Fluctuating Life Experience.

Look carefully at the formation of the spots on the cards, and you will see that Five is a cross. This is logical enough when we reflect that Five is the Number of Man and his original five senses.

Life experience is of necessity a cross. Changes and surprises we regard with disfavor since it is but human to fear the unfamiliar or unknown. We may regard Five solely in this light if we choose to—but the wise ones recognize change as growth, the release from the well-worn rut as opportunity.

Whatever our point of view, the Five natives are restless and usually dissatisfied. They want change because they do not want what they have, but as soon as the change is made—still fearful of what lies ahead—they want to change the change. There is always the chance that more freedom lies ahead—and freedom is their battle-cry.

It is difficult for these people to concentrate. They stand in the center and strive to reach all corners at the same time. They are much like the mythical knight of old who mounted his horse and rode off in all directions. Fives are always seeking new places and new faces, new occupations and new loves, new experiences and new *changes*.

This is by no means the whole story of the Fives. While the choice is for experience rather than achievement, a Five gains great understanding of his fellow man; he is strictly honest and strictly just (unless operating wholly negatively), for his *sixth* sense tells him that only thus may he expect honesty and justice from others. He understands the five progressions in the scheme of creation—stone, plant, animal, man, God—and he feels that if he seeks far enough and keeps moving and observing, he will reach the topmost.

The Fives' discontent is not always "divine"; it easily descends to chronic disaffection with people, surroundings, and life in general. Abhorring routine, disclaiming responsibility, fearful of any inroad on their personal freedom, they are not always dependable or faithful; their sense of justice does not extend to ties that could—and perhaps should—bind them. Their own growth is vital, but they should realize that it is not a very laudable type of growth when it is achieved at the expense of those to whom they are obligated.

Hearts have the problem of unsatisfied emotions
Clubs of a chronic mental restlessness—and no peace
Diamonds of money that is never enough
Spades of ill-paid labor

Fives must realize the difference between good and bad restlessness. Changes imposed from without, in accordance with evolutionary law, carry us *up* the spiral. Voluntary changes from a sense of discontent deprive us of our right to final peace.

Five of Hearts

Planetary Sequence

K♠	8♦	10♣	

A♠	3♦	5♣	10♠	Q♣	A♣	3♥	Mercury
2♥	9♠	9♣	J♦	5♠	7♦	7♥	Venus
8♣	J♠	2♦	4♣	6♥	K♦	K♥	Mars
A♦	A♥	8♠	10♦	10♥	4♠	6♦	Jupiter
5♦	7♣	9♥	3♠	3♣	5♥	Q♦	Saturn
Saturn	Jupiter	Mars	Venus	Mercury			
J♦	K♣	2♣	7♠	9♦	J♣	Q♠	Uranus
					Neptune	Uranus	
Q♥	6♠	6♣	8♥	2♠	4♦	4♥	Neptune

Neptune / Uranus / Saturn / Jupiter / Mars / Venus / Mercury

Mundane Spread

Hearts — Love
Five of Hearts — Emotional Restrictions
Five in Hearts — Changeable Affections

The Venus Card in the Saturn Line. Displaces the **Four of Diamonds** in the Natural Spread.

There are only three Fives of Hearts—Scorpio, Sagittarius, and Capricorn. This card shows many disappointments and heartaches. Most Fives of Hearts have confusion in accumulating money and must come to learn the value of it. The unsettled emotional situation of the Five of Hearts is closely linked to a money card—the Four of Diamonds, its Displacement Card. Money problems are sure to be tangled up with affection and desire; either too much money or not enough causes separation of lovers in youth—if they yield to expediency and marry for money, they'll wish they hadn't. If they marry without it, "love flies out the window" nine times out of ten. If some wise teacher or parent or friend could but explain the significance of that displaced Four of Diamonds, the chance for happiness would be much greater for these natives. Settle down, says the Four; stick to the job and give it a chance; learn to count your blessings—here and now. Because it is a four and because it is a diamond, the power of money is at its disposal. Will the Five of Hearts pay the price of concentrated effort? Rarely, if ever.

Fives want complete satisfaction—no half measures. It seems never to be at hand, so it must be elsewhere. They seek and change and experiment and scatter their forces. Their position in the Saturn Line brings obstacles and difficulties. These they charge to environment or association and fondly imagine they can escape them by moving on. Never too robust in health, they are forever taxing it by overexertion in the wrong directions.

There is no inherent weakness in this card, no lack of intelligence; the True Place is in the Mercury Line—but again in the Saturn position. Fives of Hearts have to work for what they get—and work is distasteful because it interferes with freedom.

It is better for these people to work under their Personality Cards. In all Heart personalities there is a certain amount of charm and magnetism; if the sequences of the King, Queen or Jack are followed, the road is an easier one than the sequence for the Five of Hearts. The difficulties are less personal. This does not guarantee an evasion of destiny—nothing ever does—but the cultivation of a suave and pleasing manner, a friendly approach, and a determined contentment serves to attract from the outside benefits that are lacking in the Five of Hearts Sequence itself. This is especially true for the women, whose emotional difficulties are always more devastating than the men's. The trouble is, the women don't always bother to put their best foot forward, to go out of their way to make friends—or stick to those they already have.

Among these natives there are, of course, wise ones who accept their circumstances and make the best of them. There are also "lucky" ones who profit by gifts and inheritance—but in this case it is usually because they have made an effort to be helpful, dutiful, and loyal and have earned the right to recompense.

Fives of Hearts should cultivate emotional responsibility; they are wonderful people when they do.

BIRTHDATES RULED BY THE FIVE OF HEARTS

OCTOBER 30—SCORPIO—RULED BY MARS

Less changeable than the other Five of Hearts birthdates. Are sincerely seeking values and make many of their changes in associations for that reason. Difficulties are caused by illness or disability of some member of the family— usually one who is not congenial but has some inescapable claim on the native. Likely to become interested in metaphysics and occultism—which solves many of their problems. Usually have a gift for writing, especially dramatic. Can succeed in the theater, often brilliantly. Well adapted to public life.

NOVEMBER 28—SAGITTARIUS—RULED BY JUPITER

Like the rest of the Fives of Hearts, are restless and changeable, but manage to get more pleasure from moving from place to place than the others. Should have an occupation that keeps them in the open much of the time. Should live in the countryside the greater part of the year. Should guard against accidents—especially through speed and carelessness. Have ambition to excel and will make sacrifices for it. Love beauty but cannot create it. Highly nervous. Unconventional and unorthodox. Can write, but have difficulty in expression. Good critics; often have talent for musical composition. Make good theater directors.

DECEMBER 26—CAPRICORN—RULED BY SATURN

Better adapted to big business than the other Fives of Hearts; more likely to stay with it. More money conscious and more apt to accumulate money by their own efforts. Can succeed in real estate, mining, oil or farming. Good writers and speakers; good public servants. Unlike the others, have a good sense of organization, if necessary, and can lead and direct others effectively. Always want a position of authority and recognition for their efforts. Not always willing to grant freedom to others—especially those in their employ.

Your Place in the Cards

FIVE OF HEARTS—PLANETARY SEQUENCE OF PERSONAL RELATIONSHIPS

Horizontal Lines—Saturn and Uranus

THREE OF CLUBS—MERCURY CARD IN THE MARS LINE

The best thing the two of you could do together would be to talk about your problems. To attempt any other kind of involvement would only drag you both down. Keep conversations not so much on past problems and how they're affecting you, but rather on what you both can do to eliminate them.

Three of Clubs birthdates: May 29, June 27, July 25, August 23, September 21, October 19, November 17, December 15

THREE OF SPADES—VENUS CARD IN THE JUPITER LINE

You could have an excellent romance and/or friendship with this native—if the two of you ever wade through the exterior problems and reach the center together. Your respective Displacement Cards are the answer: Your Four of Diamonds tells you to be content and happy *now;* the Three of Spades' Six of Diamonds tells him to wait and use his (otherwise) good judgment. With rational intellect, this relationship can really work for you. Take your time . . . both of you.

Three of Spades birthdates: January 11, February 9, March 7, April 5, May 3, June 1

NINE OF HEARTS—MARS CARD IN THE SATURN LINE

You won't want to spend more than the first five minutes meeting time with this card. Here again, you'll be subjected to hearing about problems—all his. Reject those hostile feelings; they won't do either of you any good. And above all, don't get involved with this native on any level.

Nine of Hearts birthdates: August 30, September 28, October 26, November 24, December 22

SEVEN OF CLUBS—JUPITER CARD IN THE URANUS LINE

This card can be a good friend whose problems may be a little more out in the open so you can identify openly. Though their own lives are never easy, these natives (especially the educated ones) usually have good judgment. So far, in your Sequence, Sevens of Clubs make the best people to seek out in time of need. Don't lean too heavily.

Seven of Clubs birthdates: March 29, April 27, May 25, June 23, July 21, August 19, September 17, October 15, November 13, December 11

FIVE OF DIAMONDS–SATURN CARD IN THE NEPTUNE LINE

You will not find much in common with this native, largely because you *do* have things in common, but neither of you is anxious to reveal them—even to yourselves. This could be an important friendship—something you have to work out. Don't be misled by what appears to be a materialistic trip for these natives. They, too, are in search of the meaning of *value*.

Five of Diamonds birthdates: January 22, February 20, March 18, April 16, May 14, June 12, July 10, August 8, September 6, October 4, November 2

QUEEN OF SPADES–URANUS CARD IN THE MERCURY LINE
(Uranus and Mercury Lines on the Diagonal)

If you can overlook the fact that this native (on the material plane) lives a somewhat disorderly life, this could be one of the people in your life who could help to make situations, thoughts, and circumstances a little easier for you. These Queens have a pretty good grasp on values—and are capable of explaining it, if you are ready to hear.

Queen of Spades birthdate: January 2

JACK OF CLUBS–NEPTUNE CARD IN THE VENUS LINE
(Uranus Line on the Vertical)

If you're a highly conservative "school-marm"—here is that exciting and daring motorcyclist who will whisk you off to Never-Never Land. The problem is that you'll have to hitch a ride back by yourself—and spend the next seven years of your life searching for an identity somewhere between Never-Never Land and the schoolyard. First rule: Don't go. Second Rule: Avoid meeting a Jack of Clubs. You may have a lot of fun for a short time—but the price will be more than substantial. If it's business, double-check all contracts and be personally available for all meetings.

Jack of Clubs birthdates: January 29, February 27, March 25, April 23, May 21, June 19, July 17, August 15, September 13, October 11, November 9, December 7

Vertical Line–Venus

FOUR OF SPADES–JUPITER LINE

A good combination that won't hurt you. You'll feel the differences of lifestyles—because you are two very different people, but if your search for values takes you into metaphysics, it's conceivable you'll have a common meeting ground. Romance is not foremost in these natives' minds, but they will be good to you in any kind of involvement.

Four of Spades birthdates: January 10, February 8, March 6, April 4, May 2

KING OF DIAMONDS—MARS LINE

These are not necessarily the values you seek, but you may think so for a certain period in your life. Don't avoid this relationship—even as fiery as it may get at times. You will find a certain amount of happiness here that you can't find in most places.

King of Diamonds birthdates: January 14, February 12, March 10, April 8, May 6, June 4, July 2

SEVEN OF DIAMONDS—VENUS LINE

A physical attraction is almost for certain here, but if you carry it through to matrimony, you are asking for trouble and probable divorce. These natives have their problems; you have yours; and they really don't blend. Have a good time—be friends, but look elsewhere for love.

Seven of Diamonds birthdates: January 20, February 18, March 16, April 14, May 12, June 10, July 8, August 6, September 4, October 2

ACE OF CLUBS—MERCURY LINE

Your restless nature will probably scare this native away—though this is an important person for you. You will never be satisfied until you realize some financial security which the Ace of Clubs can give you—but he is too frightened of being hurt emotionally to place his heart in your hands. At best, a good lesson can be learned by this relationship.

Ace of Clubs birthdates: May 31, June 29, July 27, August 25, September 23, October 21, November 19, December 17

FOUR OF DIAMONDS—NEPTUNE LINE
(Five of Hearts' Displacement Card)

You can't get away from this involvement, and this person will seem to be everything but what he really is. If you are in a personal relationship, he will be domineering—yet leaning very heavily on you. So forget letting these natives get too close. A difficult combination at best—but use it, learn from it—you can only profit in your searches.

Four of Diamonds birthdates: January 23, February 21, March 19, April 17, May 15, June 13, July 11, August 9, September 7, October 5, November 3, December 1

JACK OF CLUBS—URANUS LINE: SEE HORIZONTAL LINE

Diagonal Lines

QUEEN OF SPADES—MERCURY AND URANUS LINES:
SEE HORIZONTAL LINE

TEN OF HEARTS—JUPITER AND MARS LINES

You'll really like this person; you can talk to him about most anything, and when words are lacking, he'll still find a way to entertain you. Enjoy him—but forget business and romance. These natives make wonderful friends and can always give you that "lift" when you're down.

Ten of Hearts birthdates: July 31, August 29, September 27, October 25, November 23, December 21

FOUR OF CLUBS—MARS AND JUPITER LINES

This could be a great relationship from which neither of you will necessarily benefit greatly—but your lives will never be considered dull. These natives will travel everywhere with you and tell you all about everything. It could and should be an exciting involvement so don't miss it.

Four of Clubs birthdates: April 30, May 28, June 26, July 24, August 22, September 20, October 18, November 16, December 14

NINE OF CLUBS—VENUS AND SATURN LINES

You can have a good time with these natives also—but things will be more uptight. Their worrying ways and wandering eyes will not make your involvement the greatest thing that ever happened to you. Don't get closely involved, and you can really enjoy this native.

Nine of Clubs birthdates: January 31, February 29, March 27, April 25, May 23, June 21, July 19, August 17, September 15, October 13, November 11, December 9

THREE OF DIAMONDS—JUPITER CARD IN THE MERCURY AND URANUS LINES

A good relationship for friendship, with the possibility of romance. You'll love these natives' out-going ways and active lives. Pursue the involvement—it could be the excitement you've always known was "out there" somewhere, waiting for you.

Three of Diamonds birthdates: January 24, February 22, March 20, April 18, May 16, June 14, July 12, August 10, September 8, October 6, November 4, December 2

SIX OF DIAMONDS—MERCURY CARD IN THE JUPITER AND MERCURY LINES

This should not only be an immediate attraction, but the two of you could bring much solace to each other. Passionate, romantic love may not be the front runner of this relationship, but with maturity it will (also) cease to be the most important. And beneath it all is a person who has essentially the same viewpoints, goals, and ambitions that you possess. Give this relationship (on any level) a real try.

Six of Diamonds birthdates: January 21, February 19, March 17, April 15, May 13, June 11, July 9, August 7, September 5, October 3, November 1

NINE OF DIAMONDS—MERCURY CARD IN THE URANUS AND MARS LINES

This is not a good involvement for anything personal. You can work with these natives, but preferably not *for* them. They may misunderstand your intentions and become vindictive. However, your communication level should be good, so use it.

Nine of Diamonds birthdates: January 18, February 16, March 14, April 12, May 10, June 8, July 6, August 4, September 2

EIGHT OF HEARTS—VENUS CARD IN THE NEPTUNE AND JUPITER LINES

This could easily be the love of your life, and to pass it up on any level would be plain dumb. Here is romance, mysticism, home, family, fun, and probably everything you would search the world over to find. Of course, you will have to put up with a few of these natives' negative traits but it is still the best in the pack of cards for you. Enjoy!

Eight of Hearts birthdates: August 31, September 29, October 27, November 25, December 23

FIVE OF HEARTS FAMOUS BIRTHDATES

October 30	Ezra Pound
November 28	José Iturbi
December 26	Steve Allen
	Allan King
	Mao Tse-tung
	Henry Miller
	Richard Widmark

Five of Clubs

Clubs — Knowledge
Five of Clubs — Mental Curiosity
Five in Clubs — Changes in Mental Attitudes

The Saturn Card in the Mercury Line. Displaces the **Five of Hearts** in the Natural Spread.

There is a close tie-up with the Five of Hearts (through the Displacement), and there may be many similar problems. Since the Five of Clubs is less dependent upon affection than the Five of Hearts, the difficulties will be less of the heart than of the mind. Nevertheless, there is emotional imbalance and a sense of insecurity in relationships.

By rulership, although Saturn is most strongly emphasized in the mental reactions, the True Place offers a measure of protection by its Jupiter position in the Mars Line. In the Five of Hearts, this is lacking.

The Five of Clubs is a young soul at cross purposes with itself. Restless, inquiring, seeking, these natives are never satisfied with the "answers" they find in the life experience. They are constantly meeting with obstacles, never knowing quite what to do with them. They want constant movement and wide travel—they're eager to go anywhere rather than remain where they are. The mistake they make is dashing off on impulse, refusing to plan in advance or count the cost. If they would but engrave on their minds the familiar railroad sign—"Stop, Look and Listen," they would come closer to peace of mind.

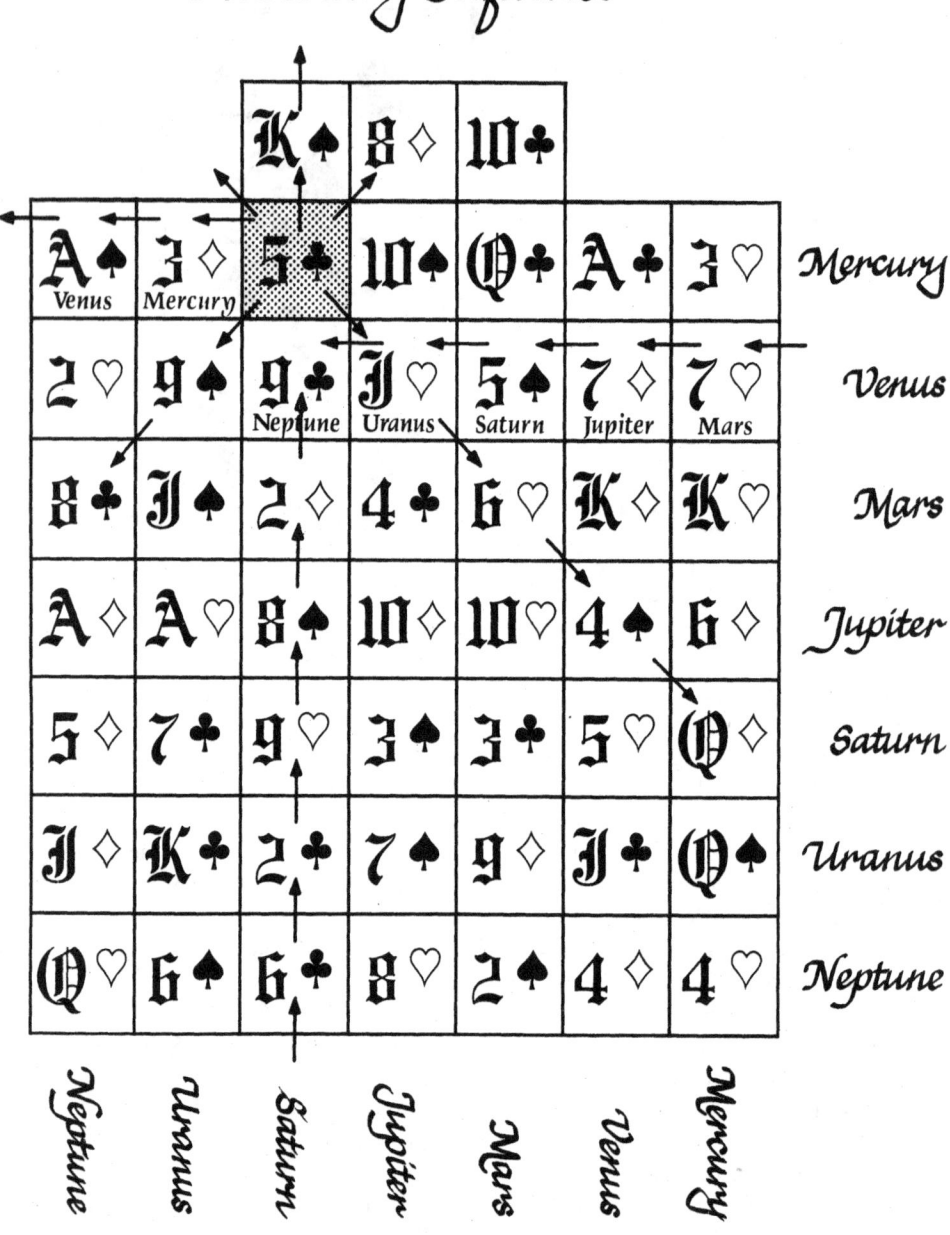

They have the equipment for acquiring a rounded-out knowledge; they have the natural inclination toward a sound education, but they usually lack the faculty for applying what they learn, having a conviction that all that is general and usual and useful does not apply in their case. The sense of ego is strong; they feel themselves to be special people, especially singled out for trouble.

The brilliant exceptions are those who educate themselves in some speciality that interests them and then pursue it to a successful outcome. They honestly try for a foundation and fight against the tangents that would lure them away from the necessity for building. They seek knowledge for the sake of its value and the enlightenment it will bring them rather than for satisfaction of idle curiosity. If they are willing to learn by experience and profit by information gained, success is assured.

Not often well suited for marriage, the secret wish is there and the experiment usually made. If married, there are apt to be secret jealousies and suspicions as well as a change in their own feelings.

Fives of Clubs never remain in the place of birth; they never stay long in the same school or finish the course they begin; they never adhere to the same line of business—or if they do, they make such radical changes in it that it becomes unrecognizable.

They must have an outlet for their natural mental keenness and the expression of their opinions. The better the educational background, the more likelihood there is for success. They have no set creed or religion, and what they devise for themselves is never satisfying.

Peace of mind comes from the willingness to accept life as it must be lived—constructively.

BIRTHDATES RULED BY THE FIVE OF CLUBS

MARCH 31–ARIES–RULED BY MARS

Very mental birthdate. Impulsive and progressive. Often pioneers in literature or philosophy. Have artistic talent and could make a great success by cultivating it. Are often careless about keeping agreements. Subject to injustice from others. Are not well adapted to law or politics. Should have an occupation that assures a living; no speculation. Should avoid jealousy in personal relationships. If they remain impersonal can train young people and become good leaders.

APRIL 29–TAURUS–RULED BY VENUS

Artists, sculptors, financiers and philanthropists belong here. May become very popular as leaders of groups or projects. Have a greater sense of protection and responsibility than many Fives of Clubs. Secretive regarding their affections and personal life. Want to live well. If not talented in some line, should have an artistic outlet for interest. Need harmony in surroundings. Apt to be absorbed and absentminded.

MAY 27–GEMINI–RULED BY MERCURY

Keenly interested in finance and may become financiers themselves. Regard the making of money as a fascinating (and profitable) game, so willing to stay with it. Penetrating minds and interested in people—but impersonally. Hate and fear insecurity. Writers, journalists, correspondents.

JUNE 25–CANCER–RULED BY THE MOON

Home very important. Like all Fives of Clubs, restless and eager for changes, but always want roots and have home on their minds while traveling. Ally themselves with groups but remain somewhat aloof. Interested in social problems and religion; often engage in institutional work and remain behind the scenes. Insistent upon comfort and like to be waited on. Should follow an intellectual pursuit rather than mechanical or commercial although many are bankers and merchants. More traditional than other Fives of Clubs.

JULY 23–CANCER OR LEO–RULED BY THE MOON OR THE SUN

More drive for power and prestige than June 25. Want recognition and leadership. Not satisfied with small returns for their efforts. Much depressed by temporary failure. Must cultivate patience; can then overcome obstacles. Often give up when on the brink of success. Are capable of making big money if persistent. Brokers, lawyers, merchants, writers. Can also succeed in the theater but will abandon it if fail to reach the top.

AUGUST 21–LEO–RULED BY THE SUN

Must be at the head of job or profession and want to be considered an authority in their field. Are creative and original—also careful and skeptical, but keep on investigating. Easily upset; worry; borrow trouble. Valuable in the educational field. May lack self-discipline but are strict with others. Can teach, publish, write. Have a sense of duty and are protective toward those weaker. Eager for truth and wisdom.

SEPTEMBER 19–VIRGO–RULED BY MERCURY

A Karmic date. Must pay for everything they get. Fearful and worried about insecurity. Must learn to overcome handicaps by loyalty, awareness of obligations, and sense of duty or will remain in a subordinate position. Are good investigators, scientists, chemists, accountants. Often interested in diets and may become faddists. Must guard against jealousy. Good lawyers and sometimes good actors but too shy and inexpressive to be outstanding.

OCTOBER 17–LIBRA–RULED BY VENUS

Love art and beauty. Usually attractive and personally magnetic. Money very important for appearance and satisfaction. Subject to misunderstandings and misinterpretations. Must be careful to have all agreements understood on both sides. Should not engage in equal partnership or become involved in legal matters. Better card for a man than a woman. Can commercialize art. Good for dealing in furniture, antiques, or art objects. Can succeed at real estate, interior decorating, designing. Good theater personalities.

NOVEMBER 15–SCORPIO–RULED BY MARS

Uncertain and discontented within, but fixed and stubborn on the outside. Absorb and imitate; do not learn by rule or books. Should guard against selfishness—which crops out even in spells of generosity. Can make money but do not save it. A marriage number as birthdate but demand complete personal freedom and do not always make good marriage partners. Resistant to change unless self-made. Adhere to principles—regardless of others, but the principles are not always sound. Have fine capabilities and potentialities; fixity is their great pitfall and the cause of their self-undoing. Can become fine philanthropists, statesmen, ambassadors, public servants of great value. Good physicians and diagnosticians.

DECEMBER 13–SAGITTARIUS–RULED BY JUPITER

Another Karmic date. For those who are working solely on the material plane, finances are very hard to accumulate and very hard to keep. There is always some unexpected need for outlay. Subject to unusual limitation which is inescapable. This is a great hardship, for they have a passion for freedom. Possessions assume too much importance. Need an outlet in art or music but cannot commercialize either. Those who are able to make money are seldom satisfied in their emotional life. Nervous—may be cranky. Spiritual understanding is the only safeguard. Can become preachers, writers, philosophers, or poets.

FIVE OF CLUBS–PLANETARY SEQUENCE OF PERSONAL RELATIONSHIPS

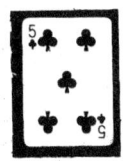

Horizontal Lines—Mercury and Venus

THREE OF DIAMONDS—MERCURY CARD IN THE URANUS LINE

These people usually have uncertain financial conditions most of their lives, but you will find them stimulating with things happening quickly. Caution that they do not become too dependent on you.

Three of Diamonds birthdates: January 24, February 22, March 20, April 18, May 16, June 14, July 12, August 10, September 8, October 6, November 4, December 2

ACE OF SPADES—VENUS CARD IN THE NEPTUNE LINE

You will like this person right away, and everything may seem really great—but give yourself time. This native will probably turn out to seem dull to you and far too secretive about inconsequential things.

Ace of Spades birthdates: January 13, February 11, March 9, April 7, May 5, June 3, July 1

SEVEN OF HEARTS—MARS CARD IN THE MERCURY LINE

You will not be attracted to these people and, immediately upon meeting them, may feel the impulse to disagree with them. Disagreements can run the gamut from ideas, lifestyles, to life in general. Not a good bet for a close involvement.

Seven of Hearts birthdates: September 20, October 28, November 26, December 24

SEVEN OF DIAMONDS—JUPITER CARD IN THE VENUS LINE

This is an immediate attraction and can be a long-lasting one. If you can find a common meeting ground on the metaphysical plane, this could be the one great relationship you want. Try to keep everything sound and secure or you might find your Seven of Diamonds wandering in one direction while you are off in another. In any event, it's a great love affair, whether for years or days and is exceptionally protective and good for you.

Seven of Diamonds birthdates: January 20, February 18, March 16, April 14, May 12, June 10, July 8, August 6, September 4, October 2

FIVE OF SPADES—SATURN CARD IN THE MARS LINE

These people want change for the sake of improvement and will want to take you along on the trip, without realizing that you are already on your own trip. They mean well, and much can be learned if there is an awareness that the two of you can be, and probably will be, argumentative throughout your relationship. Not good for a personal involvement.

Five of Spades birthdates: January 9, February 7, March 5, April 3, May 1

JACK OF HEARTS—URANUS CARD IN THE JUPITER LINE

These people will do the unexpected and certainly keep your home life jumping, but not necessarily in a positive manner. They will tend to bring in stray cats, dogs, and even people, and you will be expected to go along with it. If they seem self-centered, it might be wise to steer clear of a close entanglement as eventually your interest will probably wane.

Jack of Hearts birthdates: July 30, August 28, September 26, October 24, November 22, December 20

NINE OF CLUBS—NEPTUNE CARD IN THE SATURN LINE

These will be warm and friendly people who pay their debts, but in your keen eyes, they may seem to waste time and emotional energy on unimportant things. If you are a man and your Nine of Clubs is a woman, the relationship will probably be temporary—as it probably should.

Nine of Clubs birthdates: January 31, February 29, March 27, April 25, May 23, June 21, July 19, August 17, September 15, October 13, November 11, December 9

Vertical Line—Saturn

KING OF SPADES—CROWN LINE

This person can teach you rapidly, and you will have the ability to learn rapidly under his influence, but he must be evolved for you to feel you have learned something worthwhile. Press on. These natives all have something of value.

King of Spades birthdates: January 1

SIX OF CLUBS—NEPTUNE LINE

This is a love affair but probably not what it may seem to be at first. These natives have a lot to give so you can expect a lot from them. But chances of a long-term relationship's surviving are not too good—mainly because two worrywarts in the same house seldom find peace, and this native might be more of a worrier than you.

Six of Clubs birthdates: March 30, April 28, May 26, June 24, July 22, August 20, September 18, October 16, November 14, December 12

TWO OF CLUBS—URANUS LINE

These people would probably be difficult, uncooperative, and irritating to you. They will try to change you—and you've already got enough changes going for yourself. These natives will seem to lack tact and may try to push you in a completely different direction than what you have in mind for yourself, once you find out about yourself. Try to stay out of a real involvement.

Two of Clubs birthdates: May 30, June 28, July 26, August 24, September 22, October 20, November 18, December 16

NINE OF HEARTS—SATURN LINE

This person always undergoes tests, and one of them could turn out to be you if you are ever personally involved. They will probably never find the love you give them quite fulfilling or quite sufficient. You might do well in business together providing there is no personal friendship.

Nine of Hearts birthdates: August 30, September 28, October 26, November 24, December 22

EIGHT OF SPADES—SATURN LINE

These natives ride a conflict between idealism and confusion which would not create harmony in your head or in your home. On an impersonal level, they could help to take care of some of your "ills" with sound advice. A good friendship is possible.

Eight of Spades birthdates: January 6, February 4, March 2

TWO OF DIAMONDS—MARS LINE

A good business relationship. These people will always try a new venture with you and probably succeed, but they will need to discuss each and every move with you so be prepared for what may seem to be interminably long discussions about irrelevancies. Try patience and remember that these discussions are most important to you.

Two of Diamonds birthdates: January 25, February 23, March 21, April 19, May 17, June 15, July 13, August 11, September 9, October 7, November 5, December 3

NINE OF CLUBS—VENUS LINE: SEE HORIZONTAL LINE

Diagonal Lines

EIGHT OF DIAMONDS—CROWN AND JUPITER LINES

A probably short-lived relationship as these natives' drive for power will turn you off. Can be a dynamic influence on your life but not without problems in a personal relationship. Their values are on a different plane, and what you seek could be radically different from what they seek—and need.

Eight of Diamonds birthdates: January 19, February 17, March 15, April 13, May 11, June 9, July 7, August 5, September 3, October 1

NINE OF SPADES—VENUS AND URANUS LINES

Another short-lived relationship—or brief contacts over a long period. These natives are constantly having interruptions in their work—or so it seems—to the point where it may affect their nerves, thus causing your restless nature to lose interest. It's not a fantastic association, but don't take a pass.

Nine of Spades birthdates: January 5, February 3, March 1

EIGHT OF CLUBS—MARS AND NEPTUNE LINES

You will be naturally attracted to these people; they have good minds which you will admire if they show any signs of discipline whatsoever. You may find that the two of you have a great many differences in opinion, but overall, the relationship can be a lesson well-learned.

Eight of Clubs birthdates: March 28, April 26, May 24, June 22, July 20, August 18, September 16, October 14, November 12, December 10

JACK OF HEARTS—VENUS AND JUPITER LINES:
SEE HORIZONTAL LINE

SIX OF HEARTS—DOUBLE MARS LINES

You will like these people; they are affectionate and emotional but will hold you at arm's length at first. The problems arise when your changing nature is pitted against their nature of hating changes. Stay at arm's length and have a happy, comfortable friendship.

Six of Hearts birthdates: October 29, November 27, December 25

FOUR OF SPADES—JUPITER AND VENUS LINES

This person will seem to be a pusher, and you will feel his disappointment when he tries to push you and you don't move. These natives have knowledge but are not too flexible within it for your thoughts.

Four of Spades birthdates: January 10, February 8, March 6, April 4, May 2

QUEEN OF DIAMONDS—SATURN AND MERCURY LINES

This native will want financial security, both in your home and in your work, and may try to help you get it in all the ways that you don't want help. It's unlikely that he will be able to gain much through you as it will seem difficult to teach him anything—and it probably is.

Queen of Diamonds birthdates: January 15, February 13, March 11, April 9, May 7, June 5, July 3, August 1

Your Place in the Cards

FIVE OF CLUBS FAMOUS BIRTHDATES

March 31	Richard Chamberlain
April 29	Duke Ellington Emperor Hirohito of Japan Rod McKuen
May 27	Vincent Price Sam Snead
July 23	Don Drysdale Emperor Haile Selassie Simon Bolivar
August 21	Count Basie Wilt Chamberlain Princess Margaret Rose
October 17	Rita Hayworth
November 15	Petula Clark
December 13	Nostradamus

Five of Diamonds

Planetary Sequence

			K♠	8♦	10♣			
A♠	3♦	5♣	10♠	Q♣	A♣	3♥		Mercury
2♥	9♠	9♣	J♥	5♠	7♦	7♥		Venus
8♣	J♠	2♦	4♣	6♥	K♦	K♥		Mars
A♦	A♥	8♠	10♦	10♥	4♠	6♦		Jupiter
5♦	7♣	9♥	3♠	3♣	5♥	Q♦		Saturn
J♦	K♣	2♣	7♠	9♦	J♣	Q♠		Uranus
Q♥	6♠	6♣	8♥	2♠	4♦	4♥		Neptune

Neptune · Uranus · Saturn · Jupiter · Mars · Venus · Mercury

Mundane Spread

Diamonds — Values
Five of Diamonds — Fluctuation in Finances
Five in Diamonds — Values Clarified by Contracts and Spiritual Understanding

The Neptune Card in the Saturn Line. Displaces the **Nine of Diamonds** in the Natural Spread.

This Saturn-Neptune conjunction appears, on first thought, to be an irreconcilable combination. The idealistic, spiritual yearnings of Neptune are apparently brought to a short stop by the relentless materialism of Saturn. This is, indeed, the outcome in the lives of many of these natives. We must bear in mind, however, that Neptune is a gas (or a fog), and that while it does not penetrate through or break down a mass of rock, it can go under, around, over, and above it—and completely obscure it.

The solution is given by the True Place. This, too, is in the Saturn Line, but its position is Mars. *Work* yourself out of your difficulties; keep your initiatives on the Neptune level; fight for the principles and ideals that are your birthright, and Saturn himself will give you the reward for your efforts.

This does not imply that it is wise to try to escape reality; that can never be done with success. It simply means overcoming the restraints, frustrations, and material pressure of Saturn by substituting a determined self-development and spiritual awareness, which are in the gift of Neptune. There is the same type of conflict in all cards in this position; with the Five of Diamonds we have the uncertain financial security to contend with and the constant temptation to yield to expediency.

The Cross of this Five is the burden imposed by decision about values. Not all of these natives are lacking in financial security—although at some period in life there will be limitations; the restrictions may come through health or a hampering physical affliction, through uncongenial or troublesome children, through a loved one who is faced with trials that cannot be shared, or through an environment that is inharmonious to efforts for self-improvement.

Fives of Diamonds must choose their course and stick to it. They must seek a location where they can forget themselves and make a contribution. They must abolish fear, worry, and uncertainty. They must guard against a tendency to dominate. They must teach, preach, and *live* the true values they intuitively know.

More than the other Fives, Fives of Diamonds have a sense of obligation toward family and dependents. They are also less selfish and more considerate. The life is not an easy one, but victory is assured through the development of their own soul-power.

Money-consciousness is strong. When it is regarded as a means, not an end, it is usually at their disposal when needed. Changes are many; these natives seldom live near the place of birth. Health problems are difficult to diagnose—and seldom solved by orthodox, medical means. Personalities are important and contacts necessary. If a woman, there is usually help from a sympathetic husband, brother, or father.

BIRTHDATES RULED BY THE FIVE OF DIAMONDS

JANUARY 22—AQUARIUS—RULED BY URANUS

This is a constructive and powerful birthdate—especially if the work engaged in has a wide appeal, backed by a concept of universality. Many are attracted to the entertainment field but are not at their best there. If success is gained, their inner longings remain unsatisfied. Twenty-two is the number of the Master Builder; any work that taxes this Five of Diamonds' full capacity must be both practical and idealistic. Dislike changes that interfere with their determination to build for permanence. Their knowledge is used intuitively—often "dictated" from higher sources. Are hard workers but dislike routine. Musicians, poets, and dramatists may become famous. Usually have some form of bondage to contend with—illness or affliction of self or family, financial limitation or a type of service that keeps them overworked. Can succeed in international affairs.

FEBRUARY 20—PISCES—NEPTUNE

Mystical, poetic, and musical. Should avoid laziness and getting into a rut. If interested along spiritual lines, make good healers and practitioners. Can succeed in nursing, medicine, or hotel management. May reach a high place as musicians (especially with stringed instruments), dancers, or singers. The women have a strong sense of service unless too self-centered and operating under the Queen of Diamonds.

MARCH 18—PISCES—RULED BY NEPTUNE

More positive and universally minded than February 20. Have a gift for writing which they don't always recognize. The most unselfish of the Fives of Diamonds; apt to submerge themselves in service. Should develop self-sufficiency and less self-sacrifice. Good travelers, composers, artists, philosophers. Good foreign correspondents, public servants. If they have any planets in Fire signs, may become famous as leaders for causes. Should not narrow their field of activity to home interests. Need to cultivate impersonality.

APRIL 16—ARIES—RULED BY MARS

Ambitious and self-determined. Nervous and impulsive; self-protective. Always worried about money. Mentally alert. Make good lawyers—but not successful at law for their own interests. If the card belongs to a woman, may be mercenary through fear of lack of money and financial liabilities at the hands of men. May become interested in the occult for the sake of demonstrations. Self-confident, proud and courageous. Eager for self-development.

Want to shine. Any occupation must pay well or is abandoned. Some good artists and singers, but literary field more productive. May achieve popularity in the theater, but usually superficial. Like travel.

MAY 14—TAURUS—RULED BY VENUS

Want money for security but will work for a cause or principle. More mental than many Taureans. Profound thinkers, educators, researchers. If in business rather than professional field, make successful merchants. Want to be at the head of own business or in full command of own work. Demand personal freedom. Will be protective and generous toward loved ones. Not usually universally minded but are capable of making a contribution of universal importance. Secretive and reserved.

JUNE 12—GEMINI—RULED BY MERCURY

Mentally keen and inquiring. Socially inclined and usually popular. Like the excitement and stimulation of public life but do not want to make sacrifices for it. Fluent talkers and prolific writers. Like to make speeches and engage in debates. If a woman, industrious, interested in people, and clever at sizing them up. If a man, will be attracted to positive and intelligent women. Can succeed in real estate, salesmanship, any occupation that involves travel. Are attracted to the theater from the business or producing angle. Like to investigate phenomena.

JULY 10—CANCER—RULED BY THE MOON

Orthodox and traditional. Not fond of travel but may be engaged in it. Want to establish a home and will work to acquire one. Often lack a sense of humor but quick to detect human foibles and weaknesses. Want comfort and independence. Apt to be dominated by women—especially in business. Succeed best in a business that deals with people. Family relationships important; like to have family share their work. Interested in their own town and own neighbors. Subject to changes but prefer the known and familiar. Inclined to be fearful.

AUGUST 8—LEO—RULED BY THE SUN

Have much to contend with but will work hard for success. Like the spotlight and therefore the stage—but will not pursue it if they think their talent is insufficient for recognition. Will try production or business management. Can succeed in merchandising. Usually have loyal associates in work and strong family ties. May be held back by family obligations. Should keep control of own business and interests.

SEPTEMBER 6—VIRGO—RULED BY MERCURY

Experts at research. Attracted to work that deals with health measures and improvements in living conditions. Investigating minds. Interested in mental processes and make good psychological theorists—better than counselors. Nervous and impatient; not good teachers except for adult or fellow-investigators. Will accept responsibility from a sense of duty but are easily bored by it. Hate to be distracted from their work. If a woman, will give up work when she marries. Both sexes approach everything from a mental angle—art, literature, or the theater.

OCTOBER 4—LIBRA—RULED BY VENUS

Most self-indulgent of the Fives of Diamonds. Want diversion and escape from responsibility. Will make no effort to succeed unless interested or greatly benefited. Should guard against triviality and inconsequentiality. Are easily influenced by their associates, so should choose them with great care. Need a good example in youth and a training that will instill stability. Are good company and good (temporary) companions. The men often marry for money or security. The more constructive ones are aware of the power and advantage of the Four as their birthdate number. Can succeed in music, writing, art, or the theater. Make good traveling salesmen.

NOVEMBER 2—SCORPIO—RULED BY MARS

Success through concentration. Good sense of values, good sportsmanship, careful about obligations and dutiful toward loved ones. May inherit money but if dependent upon own efforts, are seldom adequately paid. Highly intuitive. Usually attracted to metaphysics and occultism. Want to know reasons and causes. Are good inventors, physicians—often surgeons. Can succeed in the theater or in business. If negative, become selfish and inconsiderate. "Talent" for sarcasm.

FIVE OF DIAMONDS—PLANETARY SEQUENCE OF PERSONAL RELATIONSHIPS

Horizontal Line—Uranus

QUEEN OF SPADES—MERCURY CARD IN THE MERCURY LINE

This would be a fast, kind of in-and-out relationship. The best you can probably expect would be a stalemate—without either of you realizing the value of the other.

Queen of Spades birthdate: January 2

JACK OF CLUBS—VENUS CARD IN THE VENUS LINE

You will find an immediate attraction for these people. If they are operating on the positive side, there is a possibility of a lasting relationship. They are capable of alleviating some of your own fears and uncertainties.

Jack of Clubs birthdates: January 29, February 27, March 25, April 23, May 21, June 19, July 17, August 15, September 13, October 11, November 9, December 7.

NINE OF DIAMONDS—MARS CARD IN THE MARS LINE

This relationship probably cannot work for you positively. You would be at each other's throats over money, and even in the "good times," there would be a certain amount of domineering and vindictiveness coming from both sides. Not recommended for much other than a casual acquaintance.

Nine of Diamonds birthdates: January 18, February 16, March 14, April 12, May 10, June 8, July 6, August 4, September 2

SEVEN OF SPADES—JUPITER CARD IN THE JUPITER LINE

This is a native you might find yourself pursuing as opposed to being pursued. His head is in another direction and he knows it. Cultivate your metaphysical side and you might find this person seeking you. The relationship could be extremely good if you can get it together.

Seven of Spades birthdates: January 7, February 5, March 3, April 1

TWO OF CLUBS—SATURN CARD IN THE SATURN LINE

Don't even bother to shake hands with this native because if you do become involved in any way, this relationship will eventually turn out to be a burden to you, in some way. It's the old "orange juice and castor oil" problem. Nice people, but not for you.

Two of Clubs birthdates: May 30, June 28, July 26, August 24, September 22, October 20, November 18, December 16

KING OF CLUBS—URANUS CARD IN THE URANUS LINE
(Double Uranus Lines on the Diagonal)

You will undoubtedly be drawn to this native. He will probably represent many new ideas that you may be able to see commercially executed, which results in a good, positive relationship for you both. When these people seem to be a bit lazy, push them a little. Sometimes they need it.

King of Clubs birthdates: January 27, February 25, March 23, April 21, May 19, June 17, July 15, August 13, September 11, October 9, November 7 December 5

JACK OF DIAMONDS—NEPTUNE CARD IN THE NEPTUNE LINE

You will be attracted to these people for business. You will tend to look up to them and appreciate them but be careful—the feet may be clay. And you may also find that you don't especially like their tactics—but because these natives are so financially successful for you, you may decide to live with it. A possible personal relationship can be had here, as well, but you may have to work on it much more so than they.

Jack of Diamonds birthdates: January 16, February 14, March 12, April 10, May 8, June 6, July 4, August 2

Vertical Line—Neptune

ACE OF DIAMONDS—JUPITER LINE

This could be a possible quick romance, and it may not be lasting. If there is a great love, however, it may interfere with your business (or the Ace's business), and this could lead to failure of the relationship. Sustain it at an even keel, and it could be a most rewarding experience—for a day or eternity.

Ace of Diamonds birthdates: January 26, February 24, March 22, April 20, May 18, June 16, July 14, August 12, September 10, October 8, November 6, December 4

EIGHT OF CLUBS—MARS LINE

You will be attracted to this person, but you may not be able to really understand him. Your goals and his goals may be extreme opposites. However, a relationship of some kind is inevitable and can only ultimately be good for you.

Eight of Clubs birthdates: March 28, April 26, May 24, June 22, July 20, August 18, September 16, October 14, November 12, December 10

TWO OF HEARTS—VENUS LINE

This, too, will be an attraction except that you may feel that this person's values seem to be misplaced. The result may be an irritation to you. Again, relationship of some sort is inevitable.

Two of Hearts birthdate: December 29

ACE OF SPADES—MERCURY LINE

These people will appeal to you immediately, but probably not romantically. They would make great friends but may tend to be a little too secretive and skeptical to get the love potion brewing within you.

Ace of Spades birthdates: January 13, February 11, March 9, April 7, May 5, June 3, July 1

QUEEN OF HEARTS—NEPTUNE LINE

This person would probably not only create a hardship for you, but turn out to be someone other than whom you thought him to be. You will like to be around him most of the time, but this is not a good bet for a close involvement.

Queen of Hearts birthdates: July 29, August 27, September 25, October 23, November 21, December 19

JACK OF DIAMONDS—URANUS LINE: SEE HORIZONTAL LINE

Diagonal Lines

ACE OF HEARTS—JUPITER AND URANUS LINES

As long as you're doing well, this relationship is fine but will probably begin to crumble when your finances do the same. Don't pass it up—it could work out very well for you.

Ace of Hearts birthdate: December 30

TWO OF DIAMONDS—MARS AND SATURN LINES

This is good for both your personal and business life with the exception that this person may get on your nerves occasionally. In the final analysis, the relationship could be fulfilling, so put up with the minor irritations if you can.

Two of Diamonds birthdates: January 25, February 23, March 21, April 19, May 17, June 15, July 13, August 11, September 9, October 7, November 5, December 3

JACK OF HEARTS—VENUS AND JUPITER LINES

These people, though you will instinctively like them, will give away too much of themselves and their possessions to suit you. They simply don't yearn for the same things as you; however, a relationship of small proportions can be very rewarding.

Jack of Hearts birthdates: July 30, August 28, September 26, October 24, November 22, December 20

QUEEN OF CLUBS—MERCURY AND MARS LINES

This person could be a good and valuable friend, on a personal basis, but not necessarily for romantic involvement. You will appreciate this native but will probably not see eye to eye when close to one another. You don't necessarily have to live with a good friend in order to be one—this is especially true in this case.

Queen of Clubs birthdates: January 28, February 26, March 24, April 22, May 20, June 18, July 16, August 14, September 12, October 10, November 8, December 6

KING OF CLUBS—DOUBLE URANUS LINES: SEE HORIZONTAL LINE

SIX OF CLUBS—NEPTUNE AND SATURN LINES
This could be love, especially if the Six of Clubs is a woman and you are a man, but the caution is to examine the relationship carefully to make sure your senses of values are not in heavy conflict.

Six of Clubs birthdates: March 30, April 28, May 26, June 24, July 22, August 20, September 18, October 16, November 14, December 12

FIVE OF DIAMONDS FAMOUS BIRTHDATES

January 22	U Thant
	Francis Bacon
February 20	Sidney Poitier
March 18	Edgar Cayce
	Grover Cleveland
April 16	Charlie Chaplin
	Peter Ustinov
	Edie Adams
May 14	Bobby Darin
	Wilbur Wright
June 12	Anthony Eden
July 10	David Brinkley
	Christopher Columbus
August 8	Andy Warhol
	Esther Williams
	Clara Bow
November 2	Burt Lancaster
	Marie Antoinette

209

Five of Spades

Spades — Labor; Service
Five of Spades — Crosses in Labors of Love
Five in Spades — Opportunity through Change

The Mars Card in the Venus Line. Displaces the **Ten of Hearts** in the Natural Spread.

The restlessness inherent in all fives assumes a different quality in spades. Here it is not so much a question of dissatisfaction, a personal urge for freedom, or a disaffection with the environment or with the people who belong to them. Five of Spades primarily want change for the sake of improvement—not only for themselves, but for their loved ones.

The Cross of the Five of Spades comes through the affections. These natives are seldom fickle or disloyal; they usually love deeply and permanently. It is those they love who bring the anxiety and heartache. No sacrifice is too great in the loved ones' behalf, no service too arduous—but Fives of Spades are usually called upon to bear separation or to witness suffering or hardship which they can do little to mitigate—except through love and service. This, of course, relates to the positive and constructive Five of Spades. There are many outstanding examples among the negative, and we do not always find devotion and sacrifice, even when it is logically due. These qualities generally are found, however, and from that angle we may list spades as the "best" of the fives.

If a woman, a Five of Spades' personality can be overpowered by her

husband. If the card belongs to a man, the mother can take over. There may be opposition to marriage, causing it either to be delayed or denied. Or the marriage may be brought about suddenly and entered into as an adventure. Both sexes meet opposition or criticism through friends. There is usually some form of grief through the affections, either through separation or death. And once these people get out of marriage by whatever means, it is questionable whether they will ever remarry.

When there is personal restlessness, it is mainly spiritual and these people take it without rebellion. They are on their way to Initiation; they want soul growth. It may be only an unrealized inner drive, but it is there, even among the lowliest. The underdeveloped Five of Spades wrestles with his problems through the emotions.

This is a traveler's card. Travel is enjoyed—especially in association with, and often required in the interests of—health or business. Being Spades, these people have a close connection with business and labor; there are few idlers among them. They are usually obliged to keep busy, but it is no hardship—although they are very averse to routine and limitation. Many in the lower walks of life allow themselves to get into a rut—sometimes through being beaten down by circumstances. In that event, their lot is dull and unhappy, and they become the drones and drudges who have no hope at all of improvement.

The True Place is Venus in the Neptune Line. Aspiration, impersonal love, and the determined quest for divine wisdom bring peace and security. All Fives of Spades should work for enlightenment, the training of the "higher mind."

BIRTHDATES RULED BY THE FIVE OF SPADES

JANUARY 9–CAPRICORN–RULED BY SATURN

Merchandising the most profitable. Well adapted for public life or a governmental position. More ambitious for place and power than other Fives of Spades. Interested in economics, government finances, and management of civic and community projects. Believe in controls and regimentation. Personally ambitious but will make sacrifices in private life for a worthy cause.

FEBRUARY 7–AQUARIUS–RULED BY URANUS

Averse to routine. Nervous, but have broad and tolerant viewpoint. Have talent for music which should be cultivated; can develop great skill in stringed instruments. Interested in human problems and progress. Can succeed in real estate. Apt to take many journeys for business. Want personal freedom. Fine writers.

MARCH 5—PISCES—RULED BY NEPTUNE

Artistic and poetic. Prefer art, music, and literature to business; but can succeed in oils, perfumes, shipping, and distant commerce. Restless but less energetic and determined than other Fives of Spades. Are often philanthropic and universally minded. Sponsor educational projects, movements for the improvement of hospitals, jails, etc.

APRIL 3—ARIES—RULED BY MARS

Make excellent promoters and salesmen—if they have faith in the product. If inclined to metaphysics, will go far. Sense of drama; are good speakers and convincing in arguments. Latent talent for art—especially decoration, furniture, architecture. Good taste, good judgment. Can write or teach.

MAY 1—TAURUS—RULED BY VENUS

Home important and necessary for happiness—but want to rule at home. Set in opinions. Fine writers—usually in serious vein (essays, philosophy). Women often have fine voices, dramatic personality. Meet with many changes but dislike them. Can succeed in any artistic profession.

FIVE OF SPADES—PLANETARY SEQUENCE OF PERSONAL RELATIONSHIPS

Horizontal Lines—Venus and Mars

JACK OF HEARTS—MERCURY CARD IN THE JUPITER LINE

A close relationship with this person can bring you much happiness—and almost as much pain. Your loyalty cannot be returned in the way you want and need it. These natives will satisfy some of the restlessness that lives inside of you, and if you keep everything on a friendship basis, there is much good to be given to each other. Romantic love would become difficult eventually.

Jack of Hearts birthdates: July 30, August 28, September 26, October 24, November 22, December 20

NINE OF CLUBS—VENUS CARD IN THE SATURN LINE

A definite romantic involvement that can leave your head spinning and your pockets emptier. This person can be disruptive to your way of life, and you may have contributed to making him that way. Not an impossible love relationship, but certainly one of the most difficult.

Nine of Clubs birthdates: January 31, February 29, March 27, April 25, May 23, June 21, July 19, August 17, September 15, October 13, November 11, December 9

NINE OF SPADES—MARS CARD IN THE URANUS LINE

This person will try to enlighten you in some way, and you will find yourself resisting what he may have to offer. It's a natural reaction, but it's also negative. Work on the positive plane; listen and communicate. These natives *do* have something to say which is, or eventually will be, of importance to you. A romantic relationship is not suggested, but if you can become friends, the experience will be most rewarding for you both—and important in your individual development.

Nine of Spades birthdates: January 5, February 3, March 1

TWO OF HEARTS—JUPITER CARD IN THE NEPTUNE LINE

You might feel that this native is the ideal person for you, and your hunch might be right. It's certainly worth pursuing. Your loyalty may finally convince him that his conviction of finding a "soul-mate" *is* possible. Don't jump into this relationship; he won't appreciate it, and the situation may be illusory. Besides, if it isn't *this* Two of Hearts—there may be another one right around the corner.

Two of Hearts birthdate: December 29

KING OF HEARTS—SATURN CARD IN THE MERCURY LINE

What can you do to help this person? This might be your first reaction. Other than healthy, positive conversation, the answer is probably nothing. This native is an immovable object for you. (And if you can't move something or someone around just a little, you'll probably lose interest.) You will not find stubbornness, but more of a contentment; these people are pretty satisfied with the way things are—even if they have some inner turmoil, they'll work that out. Accept and enjoy the King of Hearts as he is—there's no other way for you.

King of Hearts birthdates: June 30, July 28, August 26, September 24, October 22, November 20, December 18

KING OF DIAMONDS—URANUS CARD IN THE VENUS LINE
(Mars and Venus Lines on the Diagonal)

The only successful relationship you can possibly have here is romantic—and then only if you are female and your King of Diamonds, male. The price to pay for this combination may seem heavy to some. Ideally, this is the business tycoon (King of Diamonds) who has very little time for his family, so his wife (Five of Spades), who lacks for nothing on the materialistic plane, turns to humanitarian services and charity organizations. Many people operate successfully in this lifetime on this plane. Any other combination is likely to be a hardship on both people.

King of Diamonds birthdates: January 14, February 12, March 10, April 8, May 6, June 4, July 2

SIX OF HEARTS—NEPTUNE CARD IN THE MARS LINE
(Mars Line on the Vertical)

There is a double emphasis on everything about the relationship between this native and you. He will love you—but you will probably find him dull. Your nature will prod and poke away and probably drive the Six of Hearts frantic. These natives want peace; you want change—feeling that the peace they seek can come about as a result of the change. This is not necessarily true for you so don't force anything. They can be fun to be around, and they pretty much know what makes them tick. Another relationship to just enjoy.

Six of Hearts birthdates: October 29, November 27, December 25

Vertical Line—Mars

QUEEN OF CLUBS—MERCURY LINE

This is your lawyer, your friend, your confidant. Not necessarily a close relationship but certainly high on communications. You can discuss anything with these natives and know that in return you'll receive a fair understanding and a definite "sizing up" of the situation.

Queen of Clubs birthdates: January 28, February 26, March 24, April 22, May 20, June 18, July 16, August 14, September 12, October 10, November 8, December 6

TEN OF CLUBS—CROWN LINE

This person will be dynamic to you—he'll intrigue you, and you will certainly want to get to know him better. Don't try to push these natives either. They won't balk; they'll simply walk away, and you may lose the opportunity of having a good experience in your lifetime. Love can be just as rewarding and certainly possible, if you just remember—*don't* try to change these people. They know what they want and who they are.

Ten of Clubs birthdates: January 30, February 28, March 26, April 24, May 22, June 20, July 18, August 16, September 14, October 12, November 10, December 8

TWO OF SPADES—NEPTUNE LINE

These people may look good to you "on paper." They may seem to be just what you need in whatever situation you may happen to be involved. But it's probably not so. They have a struggle that can only add to your difficulties.

Make sure that all the ingredients are in the package before you plunge into anything and, last but not least, avoid marriage. It probably will be a short one.

Two of Spades birthdates: January 12, February 10, March 8, April 6, May 4, June 2

NINE OF DIAMONDS—URANUS LINE

You will like, and be attracted to, these people, but it may be difficult to have anything besides a negative relationship with them. On a positive plane, your interest in each other may wane due to your both trying to take care of each other—at the same time. This sounds ideal, but it can be frustrating and dull. A negative relationship would throw you into a role of subservience. If that turns you on, then maybe this native is for you, but it will not add to the enlightenment of your soul—which is the basic reason for your existence.

Nine of Diamonds birthdates: January 18, February 16, March 14, April 12, May 10, June 8, July 6, August 4, September 2

THREE OF CLUBS—SATURN LINE

The Displacement Card of the King of Diamonds is the Three of Clubs, which will possess some of the same qualities that can make life difficult for you. This particular native will create an impossible situation for you. Your life would be one of sacrifices and illnesses to the point that you may feel they are your lot in life. This feeling is partially accurate inasmuch as this is a Karmic relationship for you. But when you meet a Three of Clubs, don't permit romantic pangs even to enter into the situation. This is not for you.

Three of Clubs birthdates: May 29, June 27, July 25, August 23, September 21, October 19, November 17, December 15

TEN OF HEARTS—JUPITER LINE

In whatever areas you may be involved with this native, you will always find something good coming from the most unexpected situations. This is good for romance and friendship and perhaps in certain fields of business. Your restless nature will not threaten this native, and you could have a happy, fulfilling life together. The one big caution is: If you are both operating negatively, you are liable to find yourself in the role of doing all the work while the Ten of Hearts takes all the credit. And if you love this native or are intricately locked into a business relationship, it will be very hard to break it off without your appearing as the "heavy"—so you'll probably stick with it. When you see these first signs, squelch the relationship right away before it gets out of control and you find yourself miserable with the so-called love of your life.

Ten of Hearts birthdates: July 31, August 29, September 27, October 25, November 23, December 21

SIX OF HEARTS—MARS LINE: SEE HORIZONTAL LINE

Diagonal Lines

TEN OF SPADES—MERCURY AND JUPITER LINES
 The best relationship with this native might come through business, providing the Ten of Spades is not too engrossed in his personal activities. You will like this person—get along with him and find a great many things easy to talk about. There's even an element of romance, but it would be a quick meeting and perhaps quickly over with. This would be a shame because you could have a much more lasting involvement. From a feminine point of view, you may find an older Ten of Spades more attractive than a younger, more unsettled one. From the male standpoint, encourage your Ten of Spades to have her hair done, even if only occasionally. Don't let her get into a rut, or you won't like her—and it will be partially your fault.
 Ten of Spades birthdates: January 4, February 2

KING OF SPADES—CROWN AND SATURN LINES
 This is an unavoidable relationship that will eventually be harder on you than on this native. You can love and respect them and literally stand in awe of their capabilities—but nudge them a little and you've got a battle on your hands. Take it easy; they have many things to say and do and the whole thing can be most rewarding for you if you just don't press—let it happen.
 King of Spades birthdate: January 1

KING OF DIAMONDS—MARS AND VENUS LINES:
SEE HORIZONTAL LINE

SIX OF DIAMONDS—JUPITER AND MERCURY LINES
 You could really find your niche with this native. Though the love would not be the wild, throw-your-cares-away style, it could be more fulfilling overall. These natives will present a real challenge to you—besides the fact that you are magnetically drawn to them anyway. You can stand behind them, support them, and help them understand the values you inherently know. You could really enjoy this relationship.
 Six of Diamonds birthdates: January 21, February 19, March 17, April 15, May 13, June 11, July 9, August 7, September 5, October 3, November 1

ACE OF CLUBS—MERCURY AND VENUS LINES

Romance aspects are extremely good, but you will feel stronger affections for these natives than they will for you. You might even be irritating to them on occasion. Don't push them toward spiritual development—for the most of them, they are simply curious, not really interested. Communications are great, and the two of you could do some real mental exploring together.

Ace of Clubs birthdates: May 31, June 29, July 27, August 25, September 23, October 21, November 19, December 17

FOUR OF CLUBS—MARS AND JUPITER LINES

You and the Four of Clubs will be so active together—like clubwomen serving on the same committees of four major charity organizations or traveling salesmen who have the same territories and spend time together—it can be romance or friendship. Try to have a little patience if these natives seem to talk your arm off.

Four of Clubs birthdates: April 30, May 28, June 26, July 24, August 22, September 20, October 18, November 16, December 14

EIGHT OF SPADES—JUPITER AND SATURN LINES

There is great happiness here—in almost any kind of relationship, but be careful not to be a thorn in this native's side. You both are capable of falling into routines, and you should strive to avoid this—but there's not too much you can say to an Eight of Spades. He knows a lot and welcomes any form of new ideas, but he is much more sure-footed than you . . . so again . . . for a healthy relationship, make it a point to enjoy—and not try to change—this native.

Eight of Spades birthdates: January 6, February 4, March 2

SEVEN OF CLUBS—SATURN AND URANUS LINES

This is a lost cause for you. No matter what you do, what you say, this native will say, "Prove it." You will become frustrated and angry and may seek relief by climbing into your shell of day-to-day existence, silence, and drudgery. Avoid the relationship.

Seven of Clubs birthdates: March 29, April 27, May 25, June 23, July 21, August 19, September 17, October 15, November 13, December 11

JACK OF DIAMONDS—URANUS AND NEPTUNE LINES

The older these natives get, the more you will probably have in common with them, although you could easily be friends in your early years as well. Even though they appear to be far removed from your thinking, give the relationship a break—you might find a whole other person under the veneer.

Jack of Diamonds birthdates: January 16, February 14, March 12, April 10, May 8, June 6, July 4, August 2

FIVE OF SPADES FAMOUS BIRTHDATES

January 9   Joan Baez
                 George Balanchine
                 Rudolf Bing
                 Gracie Fields
                 Richard M. Nixon

February 7   Charles Dickens

March 5   Rex Harrison

April 3   Marlon Brando
                 Doris Day
                 George Jessel

May 1   Judy Collins
                 Glenn Ford
                 Jack Paar
                 Kate Smith
                 Claudette Colbert

Sixes

SIXES have a special significance. They are symbols of the Law—each from a different aspect. They are therefore Karmic in operation, Universal in application. Those who have Six as a Birth Card have a mission in life rather than a vocation; they are examples rather than independent operators.

The emblem of Six is the Double Trinity—as Above, so Below—the divine reflected in the human. It was called by the Pythagoreans the perfect number, symmetrical in all its parts, the "form of form," the number of the soul. It stands for beauty, harmony, order and completion, and the human family—father, mother, child—and therefore the home with its burdens and responsibilities. Numerologically, Six is the cosmic parent, the guardian and comforter, the educator and director, the shelterer and protector. It is union and cooperation, adjustment and responsibility.

From the negative aspect, Six is delay and monotony, an enemy of growth and progress, a barrier to action. There are many lazy and static Sixes; those who are living by themselves are invariably so. Many drop into a rut and stay there, but many break all the laws of the number, fleeing all responsibility, refusing all adjustments, disturbing the harmony and peace of all in their environment. They prefer action to protection, freedom to responsibility, selfishness to love—and thus wreck their own security. They are a law unto themselves instead of messengers of Divine Law.

There are a few however, who lack an inner realization that they have come into this world for a definite purpose, armed with a definite message. Their lives are not always beds of roses—although the Spreads present fewer indications of trouble and frustration than is the case with many—for responsibility toward others often interferes with personal aims and desires, and adjustment to situations and environments that may be inactive and limited are not easy for the restless and progressive birthdates. But as a rule, they are responsible and dependable, bearers of burdens for others, comforters and harmonizers.

Six of Hearts

Hearts represent the Christ Principle, which in itself entails sacrifice and selflessness.

Clubs are the "Heralds of Light." Their responsibility is a mental one. They *have* the knowledge and they are commissioned to send it forth and let it "shine."

Diamonds have come to exemplify the Law of Karma, the settlement of all debts, the planting of causes and the reaping of effects.

Spades proclaim "The Lord is risen." Theirs is the most important mission of them all—the abolishing of death. They know that to die is but to be born again, and this they must preach to a blind and incredulous world.

Hearts – Love
Six of Hearts – Sacrifice for Loved Ones
Six in Hearts – Cosmic Love

The Mars Card in the Mars Line. Displaces the **Four of Clubs** in the Natural Spread.

The Six of Hearts rules the Law of Love. This is the Christmas Card—a peaceful, kindly card. These natives are stable and dependable, affectionate and seldom swept off their feet by their feelings. The displacement of the Four of Clubs assures them of a certain amount of mental balance and good judgment—if they choose to exercise it. If not, they can get very smug; if they follow any line of study, this one line will be their only interest, and there is no way to change them.

Planetary Sequence

		K♠	8♦	10♣			
A♠	3♦	5♣	10♠	Q♣	A♣	3♥	Mercury
2♥	9♠	9♣	J♥	5♠	7♦	7♥	Venus
8♣ (Jupiter)	J♠ (Mars)	2♦ (Venus)	4♣ (Mercury)	6♥	K♦	K♥	Mars
A♦	A♥	8♠	10♦	10♥ (Neptune)	4♠ (Uranus)	6♦ (Saturn)	Jupiter
5♦	7♣	9♥	3♠	3♣	5♥	Q♦	Saturn
J♦	K♣	2♣	7♠	9♦	J♣	Q♠	Uranus
Q♥	6♠	6♣	8♥	2♠	4♦	4♥	Neptune

Neptune · Uranus · Saturn · Jupiter · Mars · Venus · Mercury

Mundane Spread

There is a tendency to be rather easy-going, and the love of ease, comfort and harmony often interferes with making any mark in life that involves a struggle. They are humanitarian and self-sacrificing, but they sometimes disregard their Mars position and their Club displacement and stay by the fireside instead of braving a cold world. The men are inclined to be rather more active than the women.

All Sixes of Hearts have come to express and to teach the Law of Love. They know that "love is fulfilling of the law" (Rom. 10:13) and they also know that they must love in order to be loved—an important truth for all Hearts.

Through the power of their affections they can overcome all difficulties; when they depart from their law, they are unhappy. There can be no "eye for an eye, tooth for a tooth" for these natives. They must forgive all injuries, cancel all debts and still "love the sinner." They are trustees—not owners—of their money. They are bearers of gifts, and as a rule they enjoy being lords and ladies bountiful.

While always protected, they like to make money themselves and usually have little difficulty in so doing. They are frequently found, however, in some charitable or institutional work where their services are contributed or their salaries negligible. The work they are doing or the projects in which they are interested are more important than the returns. They like to live well, and they want money at their disposal, but usually for the sake of freedom in giving and sharing.

They should strive for a good education. They have no difficulties in learning, but they do not always retain or profit by what they learn.

They dislike changes. Home is important, and once the surroundings are established, they want to keep them as they are. If called upon to travel, they set up a temporary home as they go—often loaded down with paraphernalia and familiar gadgets which make them feel at home. Family pictures are always in their pockets, family love in their hearts.

Unless loving negatively—that is, selfishly—they are comfortable, delightful people to know. The faults to overcome are criticism, domination and a tendency to take charge of the affairs of others and run them in their own way. They are good managers, but should wait to see if their management is wanted.

Sixes of Hearts are associated with people of wealth, usually inheriting through the father. They have keen minds and can be satisfied with what they are doing. And, in an ordinary sense, they can take life very much as it comes—sometimes not accomplishing too much one way or the other. It is important that they marry. The women are usually attracted to "club men" and the men are attracted to "club women" who have money.

These natives are drawn to inspirational writings and satisfaction in metaphysics and a contentment with what they do. They do what they want to do and like it.

BIRTHDATES RULED BY THE SIX OF HEARTS

OCTOBER 29–SCORPIO–RULED BY MARS
An easier card for a woman than a man. The women may be less concerned with "the world, the flesh, and the devil" and often become cosmic mothers. Both sexes are usually drawn to the occult, ancient mysteries, and metaphysical teaching. The feelings are intense, the critical faculty strong. They should strive for gentleness and tolerance. Apt to follow healing lines and can succeed in them as a profession. Astronomy, astrology, aeronautics, archeology—all that deal with the partially known are means to success. Thorough investigators.

NOVEMBER 27–SAGITTARIUS–RULED BY JUPITER
More self-interested than the other Six of Hearts birthdates; more willing to compromise. Have psychic power. May be interested in two things at once—and work at both. If the job is commercial, will turn to metaphysical interests at night. Less dependent upon home and family. Should follow inclination to teach or may become extroverted and neurotic. Can succeed as writers, publishers, or exporters.

DECEMBER 25–CAPRICORN–RULED BY SATURN
Scientists, writers, and statesmen belong to this card. Are natural philanthropists. Much concerned with questions of public interest, principles of government, justice, and the laws that deal with it. Great sticklers for principle and law. Become pillars of the church, model citizens. More tolerant and broad minded than many Capricornians. Sponsor established causes. Faithful and dependable.

SIX OF HEARTS — PLANETARY SEQUENCE OF PERSONAL RELATIONSHIPS

Horizontal Lines—Mars and Jupiter

FOUR OF CLUBS—MERCURY CARD IN THE JUPITER LINE
(Six of Hearts' Displacement Card)

A fast rapport you will enjoy; an attractive person who seems to have something to say. Best for friendship–business would be secondary, and personal involvements on a romantic level could prove to be difficult, unstable, and temporary.

Four of Clubs birthdates: April 30, May 28, June 26, July 24, August 22, September 20, October 18, November 16, December 14

TWO OF DIAMONDS–VENUS CARD IN THE SATURN LINE

A natural attraction, but a relationship that could prove to be too practical and in need of the material things that don't seem to matter to you. A good doctor for you—or someone who will take care of you physically. But you may not feel the energy to keep up with him on any other level. Don't press the relationship.

Two of Diamonds birthdates: January 25, February 23, March 21, April 19, May 17, June 15, July 13, August 11, September 9, October 7, November 5, December 3

JACK OF SPADES–MARS CARD IN THE URANUS LINE

This native will always keep you guessing as to what he'll come up with next—and you'll enjoy it. He will bring a form of excitement into your life that might not otherwise be there—even though he will also be irritating and inconsiderate at times. You will still put up with it, for the reward is worth the price. Don't get involved romantically, or you'll have a partner who will constantly harp at you for one thing or another. Keep the relationship strictly as friendship, and enjoy the things these natives can bring into your life.

Jack of Spades birthdates: January 3, February 1

EIGHT OF CLUBS–JUPITER CARD IN THE NEPTUNE LINE

A definite romantic attraction that will keep you guessing as to where you stand. A good involvement if you give these natives their heads—let them scoop in as much knowledge (reading books, going to school, etc.) as they can possibly handle, and you could have a lasting personal relationship. Friendship is best—business might be a little rough if you work for them; you will never be able to question their authority, even if you feel they are not correct.

Eight of Clubs birthdates: March 28, April 26, May 24, June 22, July 20, August 18, September 16, October 14, November 12, December 10

SIX OF DIAMONDS–SATURN CARD IN THE MERCURY LINE

An inevitable meeting on some level—hopefully a casual friend. Any other type of relationship may be too difficult to sustain (even with your outgoing, understanding ways). Be careful and don't let these natives "use" you—it could be an expensive lesson.

Six of Diamonds birthdates: January 21, February 19, March 17, April 15, May 13, June 11, July 9, August 7, September 5, October 3, Novemeber 1

FOUR OF SPADES–URANUS CARD IN THE VENUS LINE
(Jupiter and Venus Lines on Diagonal)

You cannot help but like this individual. For opposite sexes a romantic situation could develop. These natives will keep you interested but sometimes doubtful as to whether a one-to-one involvement can work for the two of you. You are much more adaptable than they—so if the problems aren't too severe, try to work out the relationship. Business, friendship, or romance are good—but don't expect the butterflies and bells. It will still work out well.

Four of Spades birthdates: January 10, February 8, March 6, April 4, May 2

TEN OF HEARTS—NEPTUNE CARD IN THE MARS LINE
(Jupiter Line on the Vertical)

One of the worst possible combinations for you in the romantic department, and yet you will probably persevere until you drop to make the relationship work. Don't even bother. It's never going to be what you are projecting—you will have fabulous times together, but that is probably all it will ever be. Accept what you get and don't press for more. Business is worse—friendship good if kept on a strictly impersonal level.

Ten of Hearts birthdates: July 31, August 29, September 27, October 25, November 23, December 21

Vertical Line—Mars

FIVE OF SPADES—VENUS LINE

Ideally, the two of you could work in public service together and be extremely effective. Friendship should work well because not only will you like this person, but you'll find him easy to talk to. A good rapport can exist as long as you don't let him take over your life. Preferably no romance, though you could be tempted, and business is only a possibility that you shouldn't pursue too much.

Five of Spades birthdates: January 9, February 7, March 5, April 3, May 1

QUEEN OF CLUBS—MERCURY LINE

An immediate attraction on any level. You'll appreciate these natives' ability to size up situations, have opinions that are positive, and, in general, relate to you as an individual. You can drop your smile and they'll understand. Don't neglect the relationship because you're "too tired."

Queen of Clubs birthdates: January 28, February 26, March 24, April 22, May 20, June 18, July 16, August 14, September 12, October 10, November 8, December 6

TEN OF CLUBS—CROWN LINE

This could be the proverbial irresistible force meeting the immovable object. Try not to react negatively to this native; he has a lot to say and can be a great friend—prodding you when you need it and complimenting you as well. Sometimes an irritating association, but try to overcome those feelings. Business might be a problem because you'll probably work for him. Romance is out—but work on the friendship.

Ten of Clubs birthdates: January 30, February 28, March 26, April 24, May 22, June 20, July 18, August 16, September 14, October 12, November 10, December 8

TWO OF SPADES—NEPTUNE LINE

A good relationship that can definitely work for you in either friendship or romance. Someone who is able to keep up with you socially—and rest with you at home. Try to guide these natives in a pleasant way when you think they are getting "off the beaten path" too much—your advice is sounder.

Two of Spades birthdates: January 12, February 10, March 8, April 6, May 4, June 2

NINE OF DIAMONDS—URANUS LINE

A difficult relationship that will probably leave you poorer but wiser. It's best not to get involved on any level—but you probably will. Keep the association light and impersonal, if possible.

Nine of Diamonds birthdates: January 18, February 16, March 14, April 12, May 10, June 8, July 6, August 4, September 2

THREE OF CLUBS—SATURN LINE

Another difficult relationship; every time you think you have given these natives the courage to do what they want to do (or have to do), they will probably disappoint you by running off in an entirely different direction. Don't get involved and save yourself the burden of this relationship.

Three of Clubs birthdates: May 29, June 27, July 25, August 23, September 21, October 19, November 17, December 15

TEN OF HEARTS—JUPITER LINE: SEE HORIZONTAL LINE

Diagonal Lines

SEVEN OF DIAMONDS—DOUBLE VENUS LINES

A strong love affair with good communications but probably short and sweet. Don't look for anything to sustain on a day-to-day basis; keep the relationship impersonal and sporadic. Business is excellent; these natives have the ideas, and you know how to execute them. Don't lose this friendship.

Seven of Diamonds birthdates: January 20, February 18, March 16, April 14, May 12, June 10, July 8, August 6, September 4, October 2

Sixes

THREE OF HEARTS–DOUBLE MERCURY LINES
An interesting friendship or love involvement that will probably be too demanding for you to maintain. Be occasional friends and don't seriously consider anything else.
Three of Hearts birthdates: November 30, December 28

TEN OF DIAMONDS–DOUBLE JUPITER LINES
Another fast love affair that you should avoid. Keep strictly to business. Excellent natives to make money with; good friends–but keep all involvements impersonal for best results.
Ten of Diamonds birthdates: January 17, February 15, March 13, April 11, May 9, June 7, July 5, August 3, September 1

NINE OF HEARTS–DOUBLE SATURN LINES
"If you don't want to get crucified, don't hang around crosses" is, of course, a facetious way of saying, don't get involved here. A difficult relationship on any level and best avoided–a possible friendship if kept impersonal.
Nine of Hearts birthdates: August 30, September 28, October 26, November 24, December 22

KING OF CLUBS–DOUBLE URANUS LINES
A knowledgeable person who, in your opinion, is not working to his full capacity. Best for friendship; you'll hear new and stimulating ideas. Business a possibility–romance should not be considered.
King of Clubs birthdates: January 27, February 25, March 23, April 21, May 19, June 17, July 15, August 13, September 11, October 9, November 7, December 5

QUEEN OF HEARTS–DOUBLE NEPTUNE LINES
A good buddy, always hospitable, happy, and smiling–someone you really enjoy being around. Romance is a definite possibility, but make sure you know the person, especially when the Queen of Hearts is a man and you, a woman. A good relationship in any event.
Queen of Hearts birthdates: July 29, August 27, September 25, October 23, November 21, December 19

JACK OF HEARTS–VENUS AND JUPITER LINES
A close friend whom you may not see too often, but when you do, it can be a most happy occasion; good communications–and you have a great deal

to talk about (mostly philosophical). Don't get into business with this individual and don't attempt a personal, romantic relationship unless you fully understand the person and the sacrifices.

Jack of Hearts birthdates: July 30, August 28, September 26, October 24, November 22, December 20

FIVE OF CLUBS—MERCURY AND SATURN LINES

An immediate romantic and/or friendship attraction; good rapport—but too trying a relationship to pursue on a personal level. These natives are too restless for your stay-at-home ways and probably too immature in their love lives to sustain your interest. Friendship is good on an impersonal level—don't get involved in other aspects.

Five of Club birthdates: March 31, April 29, May 27, June 25, July 23, August 21, September 19, October 17, November 15, December 13

FOUR OF SPADES—VENUS AND JUPITER LINES: SEE HORIZONTAL LINE

QUEEN OF DIAMONDS—SATURN AND MERCURY LINES

Another romantic involvement that you shouldn't press when it seems not to be working out well. Leave it alone and you'll be happier. These natives have too rough a lifestyle for your simple ways—too many problems to cope with—and it's not necessary for you to take them on. Friendship and business are workable but not advisable.

Queen of Diamonds birthdates: January 15, February 13, March 11, April 9, May 7, June 5, July 3, August 1

SIX OF HEARTS FAMOUS BIRTHDATES

November 27	Alexander Dubcek
	David Merrick
December 25	Tony Martin
	Rod Serling
	Clara Barton
	Humphrey Bogart
	Sir Isaak Newton
	Robert L. Ripley

Clubs – Mind
Six of Clubs – Intuition
Six in Clubs – Mental Responsibility

The Saturn Card in the Neptune Line. Displaces the **Eight of Spades** in the Natural Spread.

This is a messenger's card—a John the Baptist who has come to prepare the way for salvation. There are many Six of Clubs who are unaware of their important mission, unwilling to take the time or trouble to develop intuition —which is their greatest gift—and unable to separate their personal lives from their cosmic task. They are the true heralds of the Aquarian Age, the bearers of Light to those who are still at the threshold.

The strong drive of the Six toward duty and responsibility sets them apart as forerunners, or the easygoing lethargy of the Six makes them sluggards and lazybones. There seem to be no halfway measures. All have mental power and all have the gift of intuition, but their use is wholly in the hands of the individual and they can amount to a great deal or to practically nothing.

These people have long gaps of things going a certain way and then another long gap of the reverse. And with the Displacement Card as the Eight of Spades, the Six of Clubs needs and does take responsibility. When this card works on this kind of pattern, they stand a better chance of developing all the potential that they have.

Planetary Sequence

		K♠ Saturn	8♦ Jupiter	10♣ Mars			
A♠	3♦	5♣	10♠	Q♣	A♣ Neptune	3♥ Uranus	Mercury
2♥	9♠	9♣	J♥	5♠	7♦	7♥	Venus
8♣	J♠	2♦	4♣	6♥	K♦	K♥	Mars
A♦	A♥	8♠	10♦	10♥	4♠	6♦	Jupiter
5♦	7♣	9♥	3♠	3♣	5♥	Q♦	Saturn
J♦	K♣	2♣	7♠	9♦	J♣	Q♠	Uranus
Q♥ Venus	6♠ Mercury	6♣	8♥	2♠	4♦	4♥	Neptune
Neptune	Uranus	Saturn	Jupiter	Mars	Venus	Mercury	

Mundane Spread

Peace of mind is very precious to them and many sacrifices are made to attain it. They would rather yield to the requirements of environment or associations than to promote their own interests to the possible detriment of others. They have the power to overcome all obstacles; they know the "answers"; they bear the brand of destiny and the inner self urges them to its fulfillment. When they fail they are invariable unhappy, for they feel they have compromised with their Plan and nullified the greater part of their power.

All Sixes are worriers and the Six of Clubs is no exception. They worry about doing less than is expected of them; they worry about not being able to sufficiently commercialize their talents, and, most of all, they worry about the happiness, health, and progress of their loved ones.

The professional field is more in tune with them than the commercial; theirs is the path of light, not of labor. They should never overwork or allow themselves to become mentally tired; the mind must be keen, active, and aware at all times. They perform their tasks quietly and diligently and have little desire for the spotlight—as a rule. Their temper is even, their patience inexhaustible. They know that "ever by balance do the wise attain" (*Book of Tokens*).

They are good executives and know that they must work to attain the place they should hold. If they find themselves in a lowly, unproductive occupation it is because of their own lack of awareness. They can always have reliable guidance if they seek it. The displacement of the Eight of Spades also tells these natives that many of their problems have already been solved, but the True Place of their own card—the Saturn position in the Mars Line—tells them that work and self-discipline are in their pattern—and will bring their reward.

BIRTHDATES RULED BY THE SIX OF CLUBS

MARCH 30—ARIES—RULED BY MARS

There is great driving power in this birthdate but less enlightenment than in some of the others. If the education has been neglected, their contribution is not likely to be of lasting value. Six is hospitable and entertaining, and this quality is enhanced by the three in their birthdate. If not attracted to the educational field, they are likely to drift to the stage as light entertainers. The best success lies in the professions, especially along pioneering and progressive lines. They like to start things and leave the finishing to others. May become excellent teachers of adults, as college professors, philosophers, and lecturers. Because they move too fast and impulsively, they must guard against accidents.

APRIL 28—TAURUS—RULED BY VENUS

Talented and creative, but may be too absorbed in the needs of others to develop their own abilities. Sacrifice themselves from a sense of duty. Emotions and affections strong and can be turned to good account when not too personally applied. Often have good singing voices, good dramatic ability. Have inspirational ideas which should be heeded and set to work. Must cultivate emotional balance and face reality. Inclined to be lazy; work only by fits and starts. On the other hand, may overdo activity in discharge of real or fancied responsibilities. Must discover their ability and use it productively. Good decorators; fine color sense.

MAY 26—GEMINI—RULED BY MERCURY

Clever brains but often content with surface knowledge. Should strive for application and thoroughness. Can write, teach, or sell. Skillful with their hands and may become sculptors, wood-carvers, engravers, etc. Often attracted to commercial occupations but not well adapted to them. Accused, often unjustly, of being trivial and irresponsible (sometimes the accusation is well founded). When fully evolved, they are excellent teachers, serious writers. More interested in people than in causes, but are not generally understood and have few friends.

JUNE 24—CANCER—RULED BY THE MOON

Strongly attached to home and may allow it or a dominating woman to interfere with their career; when they do, life becomes drab and stagnant. When a sense of cosmic parenthood is developed, they become valuable guides and counselors. Attracted to religion, usually metaphysics. Have great psychic power. Dislike personal responsibility but realize they must take it or lose their power. Magnify joys and sorrows. Are sensitive and dramatic. Want to be comfortable but desire money, mainly for charity. Are always protected; even if not well paid for their services, receive many gifts and benefits. Can always raise money for causes. Good executors, managers, trustees. Can write, preach, teach, or lecture.

JULY 22—CANCER—RULED BY THE MOON

A Master Card. Closely allied to the King of Spades as one of the set principles. Have some *set* talent, which is usually used for the benefit of others rather than themselves. Have no desire for the limelight but may be forced into it because of their gifts. Like the other Cancer birthdate, home conditions may interfere with their freedom, but not their mission. Absorb their surroundings, so live under great tension, often affecting the nerves. Should have periods of aloneness to recuperate. A card of inheritance—either by marriage or from their own families. May have periods of financial limitation but should never have to look for money. Are loyal, devoted, and self-sacrificing. Great awareness of karmic conditions and never resent them. Are perfectionists in their work. Talents are diversified but music predominates; remarkable technicians.

AUGUST 20–LEO–RULED BY THE SUN

In conflict with themselves over a desire to serve without recompense on the one hand, and a realization of the necessity for money as a means of discharging obligations on the other. Sense of values uncertain, and they may be lacking in them to a greater extent than the other Sixes of Clubs. If they become materialistic they are bound to lose. Must be servers or philanthropists. Should be at the head of own business. Less mental and can succeed in commercial lines better than others. Good lawyers, manufacturers, bankers, real estate operators. Can organize charities, welfare movements, etc. Valuable group members.

SEPTEMBER 18–VIRGO–RULED BY MERCURY

Nervous, aloof, critical. Want a reason for everything they do and want to know exactly what they're dealing with. Inclined to live within themselves. Resent intrusion and criticism from others. Not usually well adapted for marriage; work best alone. Perfectionists in their work and exacting with others. Good statisticians, chartists, detail workers. Too impatient for teaching. Should cultivate faith and their intuition; otherwise may become selfish and penurious. Give too much power to money. Often seek seclusion through a fear complex.

OCTOBER 16–LIBRA–RULED BY VENUS

Both sexes are often dominated by some woman. To function happily, must be appreciated. Highly emotional, lovers of peace; will make many compromises and sacrifices to obtain it. May get into a rut through failure to use their mental gifts. Faithful and affectionate; messengers of peace. Must strive to live positively and not fear to express themselves. Too modest. Usually high minded and interested in humanitarian projects. Religiously inclined.

NOVEMBER 14–SCORPIO–RULED BY MARS

Strong in will and emotions. Intense and dramatic. Fixed ideas often interfere with influence and progress. Can commercialize their talents and want success. Demand action–no ruts. As leaders, can work well with groups. Lawyers, actors, writers, inventors. The women want positions of authority.

DECEMBER 12–SAGITTARIUS–RULED BY JUPITER

Want to make things work–and play. Must remain active and productive. Public spirited, progressive. Best in a mental occupation–writing, teaching, lecturing. Philosophical and broadminded. Should develop any talent for an emotional outlet; may commercialize it.

SIX OF CLUBS–PLANETARY SEQUENCE OF PERSONAL RELATIONSHIPS

Horizontal Line

SIX OF SPADES–MERCURY CARD IN THE URANUS LINE

This is a natural relationship. Easy to get to know each other, with the probability that you met rather rapidly and unexpectedly. It's doubtful you permit a close involvement; you will probably feel that "things are getting a little monotonous," thus crushing any possible romance. You will have the best opportunities for friendly relationships with once-a-week lunch companions or in metaphysical discussions.

Six of Spades birthdates: January 8, February 6, March 4, April 2.

QUEEN OF HEARTS–VENUS CARD IN THE NEPTUNE LINE

Here is real love. But don't be too sure that you really want it without close examination. A male Six of Clubs would find a female Queen of Hearts physically attractive–but make sure that she's mentally on the same plane, or there's trouble ahead. A female Six of Clubs with a male Queen of Hearts has a tougher pattern. He may be a little too fun-loving for your nature. They are warm, wonderful people and can bring both sexes a great deal, but *know* the individual before you plunge into romance.

Queen of Hearts birthdates: July 29, August 27, September 25, October 23, November 21, December 19.

TEN OF CLUBS–MARS CARD IN THE MARS LINE

You will enjoy being around this native because it will keep you mentally sharpened. You *have* to think just to be around them. And that forces you into a discipline that you sometimes wish you could enforce yourself. This is a vital card for you. If you're feeling down, this person will bring you up–even if they make you angry in the process. Don't think romantically, but don't ever turn your back on a Ten of Clubs, either. They are important for you to know and experience.

Ten of Clubs birthdates: January 30, February 28, March 26, April 24, May 22, June 20, July 18, August 16, September 14, October 12, November 10, December 8.

EIGHT OF DIAMONDS—JUPITER CARD IN THE JUPITER LINE

If you have any inclination to "marry for money," this is the card that can do it for you—whether they earn it for you or are indirectly responsible in *your* earnings. Romantic aspects are good too if you are willing to work a little at it. When your intuition tells you that this native is becoming a little extreme in the accumulation of money and the things it buys, help set their course more in line with yours. It won't always be an easy task—perhaps seemingly impossible—but the benefits are boundless.

Eight of Diamonds birthdates: January 19, February 17, March 15, April 13, May 11, June 9, July 7, August 5, September 3, October 1.

KING OF SPADES—SATURN CARD IN THE SATURN LINE
(Saturn Line on the Vertical Line)

Your first inclination will be to steer clear of this card. They will seem almost fanatical to you (and in some instances, they may be). But there is no way to avoid them. It's Karma, and not only important for your soul but for your earth growth as well. These people have the answers that you seek. You may not always understand by the way in which they inform you, because they, too, sometimes do not fully understand what comes out of their own mouths. But listen carefully—and also carefully put the puzzle (as it may seem to be) together. It could be a real awakening in you, if you want it to be. Romance, of course, should not be considered. It could make you old before your time.

King of Spades birthdates: January 1.

THREE OF HEARTS—URANUS CARD IN THE MERCURY LINE

This native could come and go in your life, leaving some confusion as to whether you really had something going with them or not. Chances are you didn't (which is one of the reasons why they're not around), but don't bemoan the situation. You'll like this person—and even more if it does not become a close personal involvement.

Three of Hearts birthdates: November 30, December 28.

ACE OF CLUBS—NEPTUNE CARD IN THE VENUS LINE

An immediate rapport could develop here. You will be drawn to this person. And here is a chance for you to learn a little more about your own intuition. Involved in their own mental search, an Ace of Clubs can enlighten you somewhat (without necessarily enlightening themselves)—or certainly create some desire in you to know more about yourself, and about them. Love is fine; you'll find each other not the "run of the mill." But again, make sure the situation is one you want and can cope with.

Ace of Clubs birthdates: May 31, June 29, July 27, August 25, September 23, October 21, November 19, December 17.

Vertical Line

TWO OF CLUBS—URANUS LINE

This card would be an unusual first meeting for you. Conversation would be good and the sudden flashes of impulse might titillate you. But it won't take long for you to see that this friendship, romance—or whatever—cannot really go anywhere. If it does, the crosses that you will bear as a result will be heavy.

Two of Clubs birthdates: May 30, June 28, July 26, August 24, September 22, October 20, November 18, December 16.

NINE OF HEARTS—SATURN LINE

One look and you're going to be attracted—there's no doubt. Your intuition will turn you off this native, and as usual, you should follow it. They will seem to be completely concerned with themselves. This is not really the case, but it shouldn't make any difference to you. The reality behind the self-indulgence would create just as great a hardship for you in any relationship.

Nine of Hearts birthdates: August 30, September 28, October 26, November 24, December 22.

EIGHT OF SPADES—JUPITER LINE
(Six of Clubs Displacement Card)

Friendship, or perhaps even more importantly, a business relationship, could do well for you here. They are as responsible as you and will work as hard as you to obtain results. You'll like them and feel a certain amount of protection in their company. Complications can arise on a romantic level because of similar hang-ups, so try to avoid this kind of involvement.

Eight of Spades birthdates: January 6, February 4, March 2.

TWO OF DIAMONDS—MARS LINE

In the Natural Spread, this card displaces the Six of Clubs, so here again is an unavoidable relationship. And here, too, it would be wise not to create a romantic situation. Although the relationship is protected through Jupiter, a hostility can develop to the point where you may never become involved enough to find out what may or may not have been. Try to work with it. You will naturally like these people, and it could be an interesting challenge to be their friend.

Two of Diamonds birthdates: January 25, February 23, March 21, April 19, May 17, June 15, July 13, August 11, September 9, October 7, November 5, December 3.

NINE OF CLUBS—VENUS LINE

You could wake up one morning and find yourself married to a Nine of Clubs and not quite know why you did it. It's love—but not without many problems. (It's also Karmic for you to have some kind of relationship with this native). And the problems could eventually consume the love. Keep the involvement to business (but make sure they're not involving you in some harebrained scheme to get rich quick) or to friendship, and enjoy life with this native more.

Nine of Clubs birthdates: January 31, February 29, March 27, April 25, May 23, June 21, July 19, August 17, September 15, October 13, November 11, December 9.

FIVE OF CLUBS—MERCURY LINE

This card is full of surprises for you—mostly on a mental plane and perhaps in the form of provocative statements, questions, etc. It is not a good personal involvement card inasmuch as this native's restlessness and your quest for peace of mind could meet in a head-on collision.

Five of Clubs birthdates: March 31, April 29, May 27, June 25, July 23, August 21, September 19, October 17, November 15, December 13.

KING OF SPADES—SATURN LINE: SEE HORIZONTAL LINE

Diagonal Lines

KING OF CLUBS—DOUBLE URANUS LINES

You cannot help but find mental stimulation with a King of Clubs. Communication between the two of you can be an all-time high for you, and you have many avenues of information to explore, many things to give and receive from each other. Enjoy this relationship—it will be most rewarding once the surface has been penetrated. Don't try to teach them; they will feel that that is *their* job for you. You know better, so relax.

King of Clubs birthdates: January 27, February 25, March 23, April 21, May 19, June 17, July 15, August 13, September 11, October 9, November 7, December 5.

FIVE OF DIAMONDS—VENUS CARD IN THE SATURN AND NEPTUNE LINES

A romantic involvement, not without its share of problems, but also not impossible. You will have to give more of yourself to this native, and there will be times when it will seem they are taking advantage of you and may try to dominate you. But you can overcome these things through your own understanding if you want to.

Five of Diamonds birthdates: January 22, February 20, March 18, April 16, May 14, June 12, July 10, August 8, September 6, October 4, November 2.

SEVEN OF SPADES—MERCURY CARD IN THE URANUS AND JUPITER LINES

This is a good relationship for you, especially in business. You will have no difficulty understanding each other and you each have the ability and power to do well financially—separately as well as together. An automatic, natural attraction that can be fulfilling for many years. If you're looking for romantic love, you probably won't find it here, but you would find another form of love that might eventually be more important to you.

Seven of Spades birthdates: January 7, February 5, March 3, April 1.

THREE OF CLUBS—VENUS CARD IN THE MARS AND SATURN LINES

Your sense of balance will never allow a long-term relationship with this card, even though you may find a love attraction in the beginning. Metaphysics could bring you together, but the chances of you both being at the same place at the same time are slim. Enjoy what you find with this native—and don't worry about what *could* or *might* have happened.

Three of Clubs birthdates: May 29, June 27, July 25, August 23, September 21, October 19, November 17, December 15.

FOUR OF SPADES—MARS CARD IN THE JUPITER AND VENUS LINES

This card cannot be called your soul mate, though it certainly may seem to be. And, you may not be able to resist this native. It is best if you don't try marriage; the inherent beauty in this card will only become laborious to you, and any marriage will probably end in divorce. A dynamic, stimulating love affair is probably more in its rightful place for you—but the best results of all will be in friendship. Use it and use it well. This can be a beautiful involvement.

Four of Spades birthdates: January 10, February 8, March 6, April 4, May 2.

KING OF HEARTS—JUPITER CARD IN THE MARS AND MERCURY LINES

Warmth, friendship, conversation, and sometimes minor irritations are essentially what you will find with this native. This relationship can be almost anything you want it to be. Their strength will help you with those worries that you tend to carry around with you, and your understanding (if you allow it to come through) will handle their occasional need to boss you around. This is a nice person for you to know.

King of Hearts birthdates: June 30, July 28, August 26, September 24, October 22, November 20, December 18.

SIX OF CLUBS FAMOUS BIRTHDATES

March 30	Warren Beatty Frankie Laine Vincent Van Gogh
April 28	Ann-Margret Lionel Barrymore
May 26	James Arness Peggy Lee John Wayne
June 24	Jack Dempsey Phil Harris
July 22	Alexander the Great
August 20	Edgar Guest
September 18	Frankie Avalon Rossano Brazzi Greta Garbo Rochester (Eddie Anderson)
October 16	David Ben-Gurion Eugene O'Neill
November 14	Claude Monet Nehru Prince Charles of England
December 12	Connie Francis Edward G. Robinson Frank Sinatra

Six of Diamonds

Diamonds — Values
Six of Diamonds — Settlement of Karma
Six in Diamonds — Adjustment to Values; Completion of Obligations

The Mercury Card in the Jupiter Line. Displaces the **Nine of Clubs** in the Natural Spread.

Values being the most important of all things for man to learn and Six being a number of settlement and completion, it is evident that the Six of Diamonds is the symbol of all others for the balancing of Karmic debts. That this can be done in the lifetime of these individuals is shown by the True Place of the card—the Jupiter position in the Saturn Line. Saturn represents the obligation, Jupiter the blessing and reward. The mundane position of the Birth Card is at the head of the Jupiter Line—Mercury, and the natives have only to establish the right attitude of mind (Mercury) to accept the justice and necessity of the Six of Diamonds' mission.

The acquisition of knowledge is not easy for these people; the displaced Nine of Clubs testifies to obstacles and frustrations along mental lines. There may be difficulty in acquiring an education in early life—or there may be unwillingness to bother with it on the part of these natives. Money is vital, and they want to begin earning before they know where their abilities lie or what sort of a foundation they need to be a success.

This is actually a very strong card, and there is a great deal of privilege that comes through the Six of Diamonds if the person is working on his natural

Planetary Sequence

			K♠	8♢	10♣		
A♠	3♢	5♣	10♠	Q♣	A♣	3♡	Mercury
2♡	9♠	9♣	J♡	5♠	7♢	7♡	Venus
8♣	J♠	2♢	4♣	6♡	K♢	K♡	Mars
A♢	A♡	8♠	10♢	10♡	4♠	6♢	Jupiter
Uranus	Saturn	Jupiter	Mars	Venus	Mercury		
5♢	7♣	9♡	3♠	3♣	5♡	Q♢ Neptune	Saturn
J♢	K♣	2♣	7♠	9♢	J♣	Q♠	Uranus
Q♡	6♠	6♣	8♡	2♠	4♢	4♡	Neptune

Neptune · Uranus · Saturn · Jupiter · Mars · Venus · Mercury

Mundane Spread

plane, which is Jupiter, signifying expansion, religion, and philosophy. When the Six of Diamonds abuses this privilege, he becomes financially disturbed and his hopes and wishes are not well integrated.

Saturn represents obedience; these natives' first step in development is to learn obedience to their own Law—the Law of Karma. Early training is vital, and those who are handicapped by parents unable to administer it must learn the hard way—by bitter experience and rigid self-discipline. They must learn what justice means; that every debt demands payment and every obligation must be discharged; that strict and fearless honesty is their portion and that nothing less ever "pays off."

Sixes of Diamonds are continually being tested. Those who have a good mental start pass the tests easily. They are natural mystics and aspirants; they gravitate toward religion and philosophy and know which values are eternal and which are not. They know that their situation in life is exactly what it should be—for it has been earned, for good or ill. They recognize their mission and mean to fulfill it.

Some may learn late in life—but they do learn at last, even though long-established habit interferes with application.

Finances may go to extremes and remain in one state for a long time—up or down. In a long period of "down," the unaware natives may succumb to discouragement and seek escape in drink or drugs or dissipation. In these cases, the fight must be waged against fear and for faith. Six of Diamonds people marry often, and they have secret love affairs. This is the Saturn aspect again; their love life is not often what they want as there are burdens with it. They actually must have a very understanding person around them, or they can be thrown for a loop, emotionally.

A very successful and satisfactory life can be built when money is not made the main objective. The women should strive not to depend upon their personalities for their success; the men not to seek a wealthy marriage for the sake of promoting their own objectives. Both sexes have a knowledge of true values and must share and distribute it—or lose it. Cause and Effect is also their Law.

BIRTHDATES RULED BY THE SIX OF DIAMONDS

JANUARY 21—CAPRICORN OR AQUARIUS—RULED BY SATURN OR URANUS

This is one of the dates on the threshold, and the natives may partake of both signs. Which one is the actual sign of birth can be determined by the birth hour. With either rulership there is domination by two desires—money and prestige. The true Capricornian always desires a high place and the respect of the community; the Aquarian wants leadership of a different kind, popularity and good fellowship. Life may be both pleasant and successful if the emotions are not too much involved; here there is apt to be disappointment or limitation. Any business engaged in should be well established. Can succeed as scientists, engineers, public officials or army officers. Often associated with banking or merchandising on a large scale. Must always work hard for results.

FEBRUARY 19–AQUARIUS OR PISCES–RULED BY URANUS OR NEPTUNE

Prefer an independent business to a sure thing in partnership; also succeed better when working alone. Are helped (especially Pisces) by those who have traveled and are internationally minded. Are attracted to theatrical people and become good agents for them. Are often excellent actors themselves. Interested in welfare and reform. May have outstanding talent for art or music; could commercialize it. Women of this date are often dominated by some woman who encourages them to follow a line for which they are not fit.

MARCH 17–PISCES–RULED BY NEPTUNE

There is definite psychic power in this date. Less fear than in most Pisceans; will take a gambler's chance and are good losers—which they usually have a chance to prove. Are kindly and humanitarian; often attracted to preaching or lecturing along religious lines. Make good judges and counselors; are both fair and merciful. Should guard against being dominated by money interests but can usually commercialize their talents or business abilities. If the women trade on their personalities, they are sure to regret it; must follow their own pattern—not the Queen of Diamonds. Great interest in health.

APRIL 15–ARIES–RULED BY MARS

Money comes easily and goes rapidly. Self-willed and independent. These children resent correction and coercion; can be led but not forced. Can succeed as lawyers, agents, or promoters. Like to explore and pioneer in their chosen field. As bankers, theologians, or writers employ novel and original methods in their work. Very progressive and influential.

MAY 13–TAURUS–RULED BY VENUS

Attract friends and are helped by them. Are loyal and generous, protective and dependable. Stubborn and hard to convince but can be won over through affections. Will work hard for results and for money—which is usually shared. The birthdate number often brings unforeseen trials—especially emotional. Fighters for principle. Not personally ambitious but will not spare themselves in working for a cause or an idea. Are children of nature; can succeed in products of the earth or dealing in commodities.

Your Place in the Cards

JUNE 11—GEMINI—RULED BY MERCURY

Versatile and clever. Are skilled musical technicians—skilled in any occupation that requires nimble fingers. Diversified interests. Choose occupations connected with travel or speaking. Can sell by talking. Authorities on data and statistics but seldom have time or patience for deep study. Can succeed in commercial lines but want a quick turnover.

JULY 9—CANCER—RULED BY THE MOON

Much concerned with questions affecting social conditions, political economy, and international problems. Usually traditional or reactionary, but may be progressive through the birthday number. Very humanitarian. Want Universal peace and harmony. Not fighters as a rule but have strong feelings, and many of the writers use a strong pen. Interested in commodities for general use, household helps. May be lazy.

AUGUST 7—LEO—RULED BY THE SUN

Attracted to big enterprises and well-advertised ventures; never satisfied with small returns. Large-minded and big-hearted. Want power and publicity. Are good actors, directors, and playwrights. Will not stay in any business that does not expand rapidly and pay well.

SEPTEMBER 5—VIRGO—RULED BY MERCURY

Intellectual and studious. Feel they can never learn enough so are never satisfied with their knowledge. Want spiritual contentment but are skeptical and demand proof. Apt to change type of work through restlessness or a sense of unfulfillment. Can succeed in real estate or as property managers. Composers—technical rather than inspirational. Statesmen of the intellectual type. Teachers of science; writers, critics.

OCTOBER 3—LIBRA—RULED BY VENUS

Expressive and emotional. Fluent speakers and writers. Not always stable in affections; apt to make experiments in love—usually because they are perfectionists. Dramatic in their approach to art, business, or individuals. Lovers of line, beauty, and color. May become very religious in later life. Can succeed in artistic or dramatic lines, but love is always more important than money or their material interests. Are successful in advertising or radio.

NOVEMBER 1—SCORPIO—RULED BY MARS

Want to probe the mysteries. Many occult and metaphysical students—or merely interested in phenomena. Superstitious if undeveloped. Good lawyers, metaphysicians, or medical doctors. Intense and dynamic; never lazy. Want money.

SIX OF DIAMONDS PLANETARY SEQUENCE OF PERSONAL RELATIONSHIPS

Horizontal Lines—Jupiter and Saturn

FOUR OF SPADES—MERCURY CARD IN THE VENUS LINE

A fast love affair—maybe someone you met at a party and found highly conversational. A good relationship for friendship, romance, or business but not necessarily a genuine close involvement.

Four of Spades birthdates: January 10, February 8, March 6, April 4, May 2

TEN OF HEARTS—VENUS CARD IN THE MARS LINE

A strong sexual attraction that can lead to love. Be careful—these natives' values are in a different place—and most of the time they will be too. Stimulating friendship.

Ten of Hearts birthdates: July 31, August 29, September 27, October 25, November 23, December 21

TEN OF DIAMONDS—MARS CARD IN THE JUPITER LINE

A good working relationship that can cause you problems only if you permit it to. These natives have strong money-making abilities that you may envy—use the involvement to help, not hinder.

Ten of Diamonds birthdates: January 17, February 15, March 13, April 11, May 9, June 7, July 5, August 3, September 1

EIGHT OF SPADES—JUPITER CARD IN THE SATURN LINE

Excellent person to be your doctor or nurse—any involvement concerning health would be beneficial. Good relationship for you, but use some caution in close attachments so that this person doesn't become wearisome.

Eight of Spades birthdates: January 6, February 4, March 2

ACE OF HEARTS—SATURN CARD IN THE URANUS LINE

A difficult relationship for you on any level; these natives' needs and desires will hold you down from your own responsibilities. Inevitable involvement in some way—but keep it impersonal.

Ace of Hearts birthdate: December 30

ACE OF DIAMONDS—URANUS CARD IN THE NEPTUNE LINE

Another difficult personal relationship, but it won't seem as blatantly impossible as one with the Ace of Hearts. Interesting friends and perhaps a good business associate—but keep everything light.

Ace of Diamonds birthdates: January 26, February 24, March 22, April 20, May 18, June 16, July 14, August 12, September 10, October 8, November 6, December 4

QUEEN OF DIAMONDS—NEPTUNE CARD IN THE MERCURY LINE
(Saturn Line on the Vertical)

From all outward appearances, it may seem that the two of you have a great deal in common, but you are asking for unnecessary problems (similar to your own in some ways) if you become involved on any level with this native. Know the person before you do anything.

Queen of Diamonds birthdates: January 15, February 13, March 11, April 9, May 7, June 5, July 3, August 1

Vertical Line—Mercury

KING OF HEARTS—MARS LINE

You will have an ability to converse with this native, but topics may be trivial and irksome to you. Try to overlook the minor irritations. Overall, this native can be quite stimulating. Keep relationship on an impersonal level.

King of Hearts birthdates: June 30, July 28, August 26, September 24, October 22, November 20, December 18

SEVEN OF HEARTS—VENUS LINE

Love and romance with a strong temptation toward marriage. If not operating independently of one another, this native can become jealous—to the point of causing your eyes to wander. Be careful of the involvement—but know there is a lot of love waiting here.

Seven of Hearts birthdates: September 30, October 28, November 26, December 24

THREE OF HEARTS—MERCURY LINE

This native's learning mechanisms are too insecure and faulty, which compounds your own problems. An irritation on any level—no matter which way you look at the relationship.

Three of Hearts birthdates: November 30, December 28

FOUR OF HEARTS—NEPTUNE LINE

This could be your secret love affair—where you run to escape from society's pressures, it's a good relationship—as long as you see it as it really is. Friendship, business, and romance are all available and possible here. Enjoy it.

Four of Hearts birthdates: October 31, November 29, December 27

QUEEN OF SPADES—URANUS LINE

Problems that can hang onto your coattails and slow you down by at least fifty percent of your potential if the association is on a personal basis. A poor romantic situation—possible friendship or business. Remote chance of relating in-depth on a metaphysical level, but not probable.

Queen of Spades birthdate: January 2

QUEEN OF DIAMONDS—SATURN LINE: SEE HORIZONTAL LINE

Diagonal Lines

KING OF DIAMONDS—MARS AND VENUS LINES

One of the best money-making situations you have, providing you both work at it. Slight chance for romance with opposite sexes—not the best way to go. Friendship fine but business better.

King of Diamonds birthdates: January 14, February 12, March 10, April 8, May 6, June 4, July 2

FIVE OF SPADES—VENUS AND MARS LINES

Total love and sexual drive. Someone who will really push you to your potential—or at least try. Good for friendship—not for business unless in public service.

Five of Spades birthdates: January 9, February 7, March 5, April 3, May 1

TEN OF SPADES—MERCURY AND JUPITER LINES

A stimulating friend but could prove irritating on a close basis for either romance or business. Actually looking in a different direction than you. Don't press any relationship.

Ten of Spades birthdates: January 4, February 2

KING OF SPADES—CROWN SATURN LINES

A relationship that can only leave you better off than before it happened. These natives will try to force their philosophies on you—listen; use and apply all positive knowledge. Don't get involved except impersonally.

King of Spades birthdate: January 1

FIVE OF HEARTS—SATURN AND URANUS LINES

Too restless for your way of life except on an impersonal level in business only. Don't get personally involved in any way.

Five of Hearts birthdates: October 30, November 28, December 26

NINE OF DIAMONDS—URANUS AND MARS LINES

A romantic attraction with a sexual drive on a personal level. Business possible especially in humanitarian fields. Friendship could be refreshing and stimulating—but sometimes irritating. Pursue all levels of the relationship.

Nine of Diamonds birthdates: January 18, February 16, March 14, April 12, May 10, June 8, July 6, August 4, September 2

EIGHT OF HEARTS—NEPTUNE AND JUPITER LINES

Heavy physical attraction, but folly to become personally involved. These natives lead too active a life—they'll be too confusing for you to enjoy fully. A protected relationship that you should handle on a straight-on, practical basis. Appreciate this native; he can bring another way of living into your life.

Eight of Hearts birthdates: August 31, September 29, October 27, November 25, December 23

SIX OF DIAMONDS FAMOUS BIRTHDATES

February 19	Eddie Arcaro
	Lee Marvin
	Merle Oberon
March 17	Rudolf Nureyev
	Frank Buck
April 15	Leonardo da Vinci
May 13	Daphne Du Maurier
	Joe Louis
June 11	William Styron
July 9	O. J. Simpson
September 5	Carol Lawrence
	Bob Newhart
	Raquel Welch
	Darrel F. Zanuck

Six of Spades

Spades — Labor, Wisdom
Six of Spades — Awakening to the Law
Six in Spades — Responsibility as Heralds of Awakening

The Uranus Card in the Neptune Line. Displaces the **Nine of Spades** in the Natural Spread.

This card represents Fate and Destiny. It represents the will of God, and it is a card that belongs not to the neophyte, but to the acolyte. It is the card of Resurrection, and because of this spiritual significance, it is often associated with Easter Day. The card rules the first four months of the year and very often rules the Easter date. The potential is Universal awareness. Six of Spades birthdates prior to April are "hibernating" and germinating. The Resurrection month brings the Heralds of Awakening. Divine Will begins to operate in man and to activate him to a manifestation of his spiritual awareness. Sacrifice for this end belongs in the pattern of all Sixes of Spades, for the Displacement Card is the Nine of Spades—a number that is the symbol of selflessness and Universality. So a Six of Spades may not find much satisfaction in a life lived on personal levels. The True Place is also in the Neptune Line, but its position is Mars, so there will be a conflict—either for or against the fulfillment of the mission.

As in the case of all Sixes, there will be monotony, delay, and boredom or harmony, adjustment, and peace. It is the individual who must make the decision and direct his mental attitude toward one course or the other.

The Mars-Neptune conjunction in the True Place is a call to action in the realm of idealism; if the Six of Spades chooses to turn it into action for

Planetary Sequence

			K♠ Jupiter	8♦ Mars	10♣ Venus		
A♠	3♦	5♣	10♠	Q♣ Neptune	A♣ Uranus	3♥ Saturn	Mercury
2♥	9♠	9♣	J♥	5♠	7♦	7♥	Venus
8♣	J♠	2♦	4♣	6♥	K♦	K♥	Mars
A♦	A♥	8♠	10♦	10♥	4♠	6♦	Jupiter
5♦	7♣	9♥	3♠	3♣	5♥	Q♦	Saturn
J♦	K♣	2♣	7♠	9♦	J♣	Q♠	Uranus
Q♥ Mercury	6♠	6♣	8♥	2♠	4♦	4♥	Neptune

Neptune · Uranus · Saturn · Jupiter · Mars · Venus · Mercury

Mundane Spread

self-interest, bubble-chasing, and schemes to get rich quick, he has no one to blame but himself for his inevitable descent into confusion and final disaster. The number Nine is one of the most beautiful and protected numbers in the cycle. Because the world has chosen the distorted plan, Nine always means disappointment or futility when it appears in the Mundane Spread. But in God's Plan it is fulfillment. For the Six of Spades the displaced Nine of Spades means fulfillment of the purpose and the mission—Universal love, brotherhood and unfailing good will. In these there can be no disappointment.

For those unaware of the tremendous potentialities in this card there is a drift toward discouragement, monotony in work, and lack of initiative. These people have no vision and no hope; they are aware only of material benefits—which they fail to acquire. The laziness of the six takes hold and helps them to drift; the "let Providence provide for me" philosophy fails them—as it must, and they make no contribution whatever to the lives of others or their own.

Influence of the mother is strong for Six of Spades people. The card is also rather protective. These natives are easily affected by kindliness and affection. A Six of Spades mother is willing to sacrifice for education. Both sexes are attracted to very mental women.

By propinquity, the Six of Spades is allied to the Six of Clubs, for two cards of like number invariably affect each other, whether they stand ahead or behind. The Saturn position of the Six of Clubs directs mental discipline to the Sixes of Spades as a valuable foundation for their activities. The better the education, the less likelihood there is for them to remain in the rut of manual labor. Through their mental attitude, Sixes of Spades can always turn any disappointment into success; it is a card of overcoming. Growth comes through impersonality.

These natives are strictly just—and may seem hard and unfeeling. They are tried and tested; if they are beaten down, it is only to rise again and try harder. They are strong of will and determined, often fixed and stubborn. They know there is no death, only Eternal Life; this they came to prove. They belong to the Initiates.

BIRTHDATES RULED BY THE SIX OF SPADES

JANUARY 8—CAPRICORN—RULED BY SATURN
Usually there is less awareness and more difficulty in spiritual development with this native than with the other Sixes of Spades. Learning comes through overcoming obstacles. They have a strong bent toward commerciality. A tendency to bigotry. Practical and "down to earth." Are writers, lecturers, or public servants when not engaged in business. Are ambitious for leadership and prominence.

Your Place in the Cards

FEBRUARY 6–AQUARIUS–RULED BY URANUS
Progressive, inventive, and inspirational. Intuition highly developed. Interested in politics and the humanities. Want to change existing laws. Enthusiastic. May be preachers or exhorters—of the evangelical type. Want equal rights and justice for all. If engaged in business, believe in profit-sharing, fine working conditions. May be attracted to the stage.

MARCH 4–PISCES–RULED BY NEPTUNE
Idealistic and uplifting. Want to improve everything they deal with. High ideals—not always practical, but sincere. If obstructed, many become nuns or priests. Can succeed in art or music, playwriting, or acting. Strong religious streak. Often have a sacrificial and submissive attitude toward life; not convinced of their own power.

APRIL 2–ARIES–RULED BY MARS
Pioneering and progressive. Want to make the world over. Personally restless; want to travel and explore. Are creative and original. Cooperative. Less independent than many Arians. Must not be tied to routine. Writers, educators, explorers. Usually working for a cause. Not overly ambitious.

SIX OF SPADES — PLANETARY SEQUENCE OF PERSONAL RELATIONSHIPS

Horizontal Lines–Neptune, Crown, and Mercury

QUEEN OF HEARTS–MERCURY CARD IN THE NEPTUNE LINE
You may seek this person to add some zest to your life. Hopefully, it will be a friendship situation, and you will not get involved romantically or businesswise, except where this individual is your salesman, or in a people-oriented type of position. This relationship could be profitable for you.

Queen of Hearts birthdates: July 29, August 27, September 25, October 23, November 21, December 19

TEN OF CLUBS–VENUS CARD IN THE MARS LINE
A sexually attractive person that will turn out to be impressive in many other areas. Someone you could "take home to mother." Only probable problem is that you have knowledge that you won't necessarily be able to "prove," whereas this native will have knowledge backed up by books and statements. Don't get involved in word games—you are seeking different paths but can enjoy each other simultaneously.

Ten of Clubs birthdates: January 30, February 28, March 26, April 24, May 22, June 20, July 18, August 14, September 12, October 10, November 8, December 6

EIGHT OF DIAMONDS–MARS CARD IN THE JUPITER LINE

A seemingly difficult relationship for you on any level—but not necessarily so. For opposite sexes, sexually stimulating and attractive, but don't consider a long-term involvement with marriage in mind; it's too rough for a day-to-day association. Listen to these natives—they can help you "back *up*"; don't be closed-minded. They only want good for you.

Eight of Diamonds birthdates: January 19, February 17, March 15, April 13, May 11, June 9, July 7, August 5, September 3, October 1

KING OF SPADES–JUPITER CARD IN THE SATURN LINE

Another good relationship that may trouble you—but possibly predestined. Regardless of what kind of involvement, you will eventually receive more than is given—and be much the wiser for the encounter. If romance is considered, it may be better if you are female and the King of Spades, male—but the involvement is important in any way it occurs. Listen, most of all—even if it sounds negative; you both can overcome any negative aspects that may have a tendency to creep into your lives.

King of Spades birthdate: January 1

THREE OF HEARTS–SATURN CARD IN THE MERCURY LINE

An encounter that may remind you of some of the things you neither need nor want in this lifetime. These natives will demand too much of your personal time and probably not look into themselves enough to suit you. Conversation is possible but most likely difficult. Take a pass if you can.

Three of Hearts birthdates: November 30, December 28

ACE OF CLUBS–URANUS CARD IN THE VENUS LINE

A surprising glimpse into another type of living that may interest you for a time—but probably not sufficiently to make you go out of your way to create any kind of romanticism. Too trying and energy-draining a relationship to sustain, but certainly interesting and should be pursued (somewhat).

Ace of Clubs birthdates: May 31, June 29, July 27, August 25, September 23, October 21, November 19, December 17

QUEEN OF CLUBS–NEPTUNE CARD IN THE MARS LINE

You might feel a negative reaction on first meeting this native, but don't let that keep you from getting to know him better. Don't get personally involved, and you'll find a fine friend, business associate, or neighbor who will always have good advice to give (without some kind of axe to grind).

Queen of Clubs birthdates: January 28, February 26, March 24, April 22, May 20, June 18, July 16, August 14, September 12, October 10, November 8, December 6

Vertical Line—Uranus

KING OF CLUBS—URANUS LINE

Great communication—if you'll listen. New ideas, new thoughts—all of which can enhance your own way of life. Great for friendship and business; doubtful in the romantic areas and probably temporary if you try to get too close to each other.

King of Clubs birthdates: January 27, February 25, March 23, April 21, May 19, June 17, July 15, August 13, September 11, October 9, November 7, December 5

SEVEN OF CLUBS—SATURN LINE

A crazy romance that will leave you with your head spinning—if you permit it to happen. Best for friendship if you don't try to take on these natives' problems. Business is possible but not necessary to enjoy what this native has to offer.

Seven of Clubs birthdates: March 29, April 27, May 25, June 23, July 21, August 19, September 17, October 15, November 13, December 11

ACE OF HEARTS—JUPITER LINE

Don't get involved in a romantic situation, or you will be disappointed. Your idea of romance and this native's could be worlds apart, and probably are. Friendship and business are both possible, but nothing extraordinary. Watch your temper—the relationship is not worth the negativity.

Ace of Hearts birthdate: December 30

JACK OF SPADES—MARS LINE

An interesting, if not powerful, relationship for both romance and friendship, with the latter being more important from this native's point of view. Be careful that you don't lapse into a rut with each other—especially if you are male and this individual is female. Business is possible if you are in allied fields requiring humanitarian abilities as opposed to money-making abilities. Enjoy the involvement fully.

Jack of Spades birthdates: January 3, February 1

NINE OF SPADES—VENUS LINE
(Six of Spades' Displacement Card)

A true Karmic relationship—it will be unavoidable from the first time you meet. More difficult for you to maintain than for this native. Not an easy involvement—but probably the most important of your life. An absolute necessity for friendship, a definite possibility for romance, but not workable for business if either of you is operating on any level of the material plane. Stick with this relationship.

Nine of Spades birthdates: January 5, February 3, March 1

THREE OF DIAMONDS—MERCURY LINE

These natives will probably be too progressive in their thinking and too outgoing for your own taste. You may even feel that they're not trustworthy—but this is erroneous; use your own good feelings to understand them better. You will probably not have any inclination to get involved on any level, and this would be a pity; these natives have much to offer and can show you a little more about an easier way of thinking—and of living.

Three of Diamonds birthdates: January 24, February 22, March 20, April 18, May 16, June 14, July 12, August 10, September 8, October 6, November 4, December 2

Diagonal Lines

JACK OF DIAMONDS—URANUS AND NEPTUNE LINES

A temporary person as far as you are concerned—someone in whom you have no personal interest. You will probably not agree with his philosophy, his way of life, or the people he associates with. Don't be too quick to judge. This native has a great deal to offer—especially if he is older. Listen—and learn.

Jack of Diamonds birthdates: January 16, February 14, March 12, April 10, May 8, June 6, July 4, August 2

TWO OF CLUBS—URANUS AND SATURN LINES

A totally confusing individual to you; he may seem to be one way one day and another the next. You'll feel these natives can't be trusted, that they ask too many questions. Don't consider any kind of involvement, and you'll be right—the relationship is too difficult for you both.

Two of Clubs birthdates: May 30, June 28, July 26, August 24, September 22, October 20, November 18, December 16

THREE OF SPADES—SATURN AND JUPITER LINES

A romantic involvement that, if either or both of you are living negatively, could leave you both following a path of obstacle after obstacle. You are both probably too difficult to convince to be together romantically. Be very careful that this doesn't become an extremely negative involvement—on any level.

Three of Spades birthdates: January 11, February 9, March 7, April 5, May 3, June 1

TEN OF HEARTS—JUPITER AND MARS LINES

This could easily turn into a masochistic relationship if you are involved romantically; as friends, it won't always be good—but never bad. Business associations could suffer unless this native is the salesman side of a partnership and you are the accountant. Don't carry the torch on any level—it will hurt you far more than them.

Ten of Hearts birthdates: July 31, August 29, September 27, October 25, November 23, December 21

KING OF DIAMONDS—MARS AND VENUS LINES

Romance, friendship, and business can all be highly successful with this person. Probably the best combination in the pack for you. Use it positively— don't let it get into a rut whatever you do—and enjoy it, most of all.

King of Diamonds birthdates: January 14, February 12, March 10, April 8, May 6, June 4, July 2

SEVEN OF HEARTS—VENUS AND MERCURY LINES

This native will bring too many problems that will seem to interfere with your way of life to be of any interest to you personally. They are talkative but seemingly too self-indulgent and disinterested in the things that make up your life. Best not to get involved—and if you do, keep it on an impersonal level.

Seven of Hearts birthdates: September 30, October 28, November 26, December 24

SIX OF SPADES FAMOUS BIRTHDATES

January 8	José Ferrer
	Elvis Presley
	Soupy Sales
February 6	Fabian Forte
	Zsa Zsa Gabor
	Ronald Reagan
	Babe Ruth

Sixes

March 4   Miriam Makeba
               Knute Rockne

April 2   Buddy Ebsen
               Sir Alec Guinness
               Jack Webb
               Casanova

Sevens

SEVEN is the most mystical of all numbers, the hardest to understand (and to live with), or the most beautiful and rewarding influence in anyone's life.

We have seen that it is the center and foundation of the two plans, or Spreads, in the "Little Book"—under the rulership of the seven planets, built on the plan of seven rows down, seven cards across—and set in the center of each suit.

The Seventh Card is the Neptune Card, the Seventh Row, the Neptune Row, which may account, in part, for the confusion that arises in our attempts to understand it. Neptune is "extrasensory"—and so is Seven. As soon as we use it on the level of cold facts, mundane interests, and physical responsibilities, we deprive ourselves of a good half of its power—if, in thus using it, we lose sight of its spiritual significance.

Seven is called the dominical or "holy" number, the Sabbath of rest and pause to "see that all is good" or perfect. It is this requirement of perfection that we can't quite live up to—the rest and pause-for-examination to which we refuse to give the time. We must therefore encounter the confusions, obstacles, and possible defeat that Neptune invariably bestows upon those who lack vision and have no concern for the gifts of the spirit. The key is found in the Seventh Statement in the Pattern on the Trestleboard: "Living from that Will, supported by its unfailing Wisdom and Understanding, mine is the Victorious Life." As soon as we have learned to *live* by that Will, Wisdom, and Understanding, Seven will bring us to victory. On the Tree of Life the Seventh *is* the Sphere of Victory.

For a better understanding of the Divine Plan for the four Sevens, note the True Place of each:

Hearts is the Neptune Card in the Mercury Line. The *ideal* love is the right mental attitude.
Clubs is the Uranus Card in the Mars Line. In the acquisition of knowledge intuition is to be developed and the channel opened for inspiration.
Diamonds is the Saturn Card in the Saturn Line—a warning to use strict self-discipline in estimating true values.
Spades is the Jupiter Card in the Neptune Line. There is thus a sure reward for the seeker after the wisdom of the "higher realm."

Seven is the number of the soul. In silence, peace and self-examination, we go toward "perfection." In criticism of others, suspicion, judgment on face value, and sharp practice, we create our own obstacles and invite our own difficulties. There are no "young souls" with a Seven Birth Card. All *know* that theirs is the quest for truth.

Seven of Hearts

Hearts — Love
Seven of Hearts — Obstacles in the Fulfillment of the Heart's Desire
Seven in Hearts — Love of Truth and Beauty

The Mercury Card in the Venus Line. Displaces the **Eight of Hearts** in the Natural Spread.

The Seven of Hearts is a card that has a lot of problems. It displaces the Eight of Hearts, and of all the cards in the deck, it is the one card that wants to work things out through love and affection. Sevens of Hearts have a deep capacity for love, but they draw unreliable people to them. There is a secret wish for the power of love to work all things out, but if they are not jealous themselves, they draw jealousy to them. If they are not unreliable or unstable themselves, they draw this type of person to them. The card is one of sacrifice, but it is not a weak card. Sevens of Hearts might be very strong on the evil or on the good side, but in either case, it is a card of strength. They will also wallow in emotional disturbances. Spiritually, this is a card of service rendered. It is a willingness to take on the responsibility of people; therefore these people are involved with monasteries, convents, or simply a desire for seclusion. Their need is for spiritual values, and they have the ability to handle spiritual things.

The Displaced Card also shows that there is plenty of power at the disposal of these natives. The test comes in its use. The gift of power imposes certain obligations and responsibilities, and Seven does not take kindly to them. The tendency is to force things and break down obstacles and human wills when

Planetary Sequence

			K♠	8♦	10♣		
A♠	3♦	5♣	10♠	Q♣	A♣	3♥	Mercury
2♥	9♠	9♣	J♥	5♠	7♦	7♥	Venus
Uranus	Saturn	Jupiter	Mars	Venus	Mercury		
8♣	J♠	2♦	4♣	6♥	K♦	K♥ Neptune	Mars
A♦	A♥	8♠	10♦	10♥	4♠	6♦	Jupiter
5♦	7♣	9♥	3♠	3♣	5♥	Q♦	Saturn
J♦	K♣	2♣	7♠	9♦	J♣	Q♠	Uranus
Q♥	6♠	6♣	8♥	2♠	4♦	4♥	Neptune

Neptune · Uranus · Saturn · Jupiter · Mars · Venus · Mercury

Mundane Spread

they stand in the way. The interests are apt to be personal rather than humanitarian—and humanitarian concern is a requirement for Hearts. When responsibility in this direction is accepted, defeat is turned into victory.

Suspicion is apt to enter into personal relationships, and jealousy often results. They may also give just cause for jealousy themselves, for fidelity in love is not one of their strong points—unless they hold the right mental attitude toward love itself.

There is a close connection between this card and the Seven of Spades, for the position of the Eight of Hearts in the Mundane Spread displaces the Seven of Spades in the Natural Spread. This connection offsets much of the unreliability of the Seven of Hearts, and we thus find many lovers, husbands, and wives true to their vows and devoted until death.

The best that is in them is encouraged by mingling with large groups having some humanitarian objective. These people are great talkers and fine propagandists, and through the charm and magnetism of their personality (if cultivated), they are able to sway opinions and exert important influence over the ignorant or doubting.

The women of this card need approval and encouragement. There is an inclination to cater to the opposite sex, and they usually prefer working with men who are likely to be intrigued by their appearance and approach. The men can always improve their situations by working under the Jack or the King, but it takes self-development and application (together with a considerable amount of sacrifice). Too often they waste much of their own power, and they may become wanderers or triflers—sailors who sail the seven seas (with a girl in every port), or travelers who leave home because its responsibilities are irksome.

Among the more developed Sevens of Hearts, this is a martyr's card; personal benefits are sacrificed for the good of a cause, a group, or an individual. They are sensitive and emotional, subject to disappointment and heartache in their personal lives—until suspicion and jealousy are uprooted and destroyed.

Union is very important, but union with groups is safest. When people of this card are in a situation where they can serve others and have recognition and appreciation, they are at their best and happiest. They like to be of consequence in whatever they do.

BIRTHDATES RULED BY THE SEVEN OF HEARTS

SEPTEMBER 30—LIBRA—RULED BY VENUS

Must guard against self-indulgence, laziness, and selfishness. Want to shine in their chosen work—as star and benefactor. Like to live in ease and comfort, but often have to work hard for success. Love affairs are intense while they last. There is much talent in this birthdate and much ability to succeed independently—if the talent is cultivated and an artistic or dramatic line chosen. If they go into business, they need cooperation and guidance. Are good talkers and make excellent trial lawyers. Can also engage in advertising, publishing, and, in some cases, banking.

OCTOBER 28–SCORPIO–RULED BY MARS

Have fixed ideas—and devotion to them. Cannot be talked out of an opinion once it is formed. Subject to accidents that may interfere with their work. May have sudden breaks or climaxes in their lives, long-lasting illnesses or a chronic condition, inherited or acquired. More dutiful and self-sacrificing than the other Seven of Hearts birthdates (often needlessly), but their acts seldom are appreciated. Given to unconventional unions. Must guard against escape from discouragement through drink or drugs. May be strongly attracted to occultism, which can change the whole course of their lives. If so, they become active in secret orders. Are seekers for truth. Succeed as teachers, lecturers, or writers. If not interested in the mysteries, are apt to follow engineering, mechanics—or undertaking.

NOVEMBER 26–SAGITTARIUS–RULED BY JUPITER

Intellectual and practical, but also endowed with imagination and a sense of poetry. Nervous and restless—actually seeking peace and poise. Should seek an occupation in the field of education, literature, or philosophy—anything that taxes their fine mental capacity. Clever (often gifted) at working in bronze, tin, or marble. Money doesn't come easily and should be budgeted. Should have frequent sojourns in the country—alone.

DECEMBER 24–CAPRICORN–RULED BY SATURN

Highly ambitious. More self-sufficient than the rest. Dignified and self-important. Critical and easily offended. Serious-minded and responsible. Should never retire; need constant activity. Should avoid connection with hospitals, institutions of confinement. Can succeed in business or as trustees, government officials, or public administrators.

SEVEN OF HEARTS–PLANETARY SEQUENCE OF PERSONAL RELATIONSHIPS

Horizontal Line

SEVEN OF DIAMONDS–MERCURY CARD IN THE VENUS LINE

Communications always good. Love possible, friendship better, because this is an in-and-out kind of involvement. You are aware of too many of each other's problems to spend lengthy amounts of time together discussing them. Business okay but not advisable. Your heads are looking in different directions, but both trying to solve the same question.

Seven of Diamonds birthdates: January 20, February 18, March 16, April 14, May 12, June 10, July 8, August 6, September 4, October 2.

FIVE OF SPADES—VENUS CARD IN THE MARS LINE

A love affair, but not the one you're really looking for—too many changes to make you happy, and you will probably not agree with their politics. Enjoy it for what it is, but don't look for an easy relationship. This isn't it.

Five of Spades birthdates: January 9, February 7, March 5, April 3, May 1.

JACK OF HEARTS—MARS CARD IN THE JUPITER LINE

Admiration, respect, but hopefully you'll pass them by in a personal involvement. A good friend who can be open-minded in your time of need. No close relationships, including business relationships. They won't work hard enough to suit you, because it simply isn't what they want to do.

Jack of Hearts birthdates: July 30, August 28, September 26, October 24, November 22, December 20.

NINE OF CLUBS—JUPITER CARD IN THE SATURN LINE

A Karmic relationship that will bring good things to you—probably a gambler type who can tune you into the stock market and urge you to take those chances you are so usually elusive about. A definite change for the better through this relationship, but be careful of romance. It could have great compensations, but at great prices.

Nine of Clubs birthdates: January 31, February 29, March 27, April 25, May 23, June 21, July 19, August 17, September 15, October 13, November 11, December 9.

NINE OF SPADES—SATURN CARD IN THE URANUS LINE

Another card of Karma—this one definitely not romantic. If romance is tried, you are setting your negative side up to rule you through jealousies and suspicions. Avoid the relationship as much as possible.

Nine of Spades birthdates: January 5, February 3, March 1.

TWO OF HEARTS—URANUS CARD IN THE NEPTUNE LINE

You'll like this native, but no chords in you will be struck. Even if you took the time, which you won't, you won't understand them. Consider it a new experience.

Two of Hearts birthdate: December 29.

KING OF HEARTS—NEPTUNE CARD IN THE MERCURY LINE
(Mars Line on the Vertical Line)

Another trouble card for you. You'll always feel that the King of Hearts is flirting or showing off or whatever—creating an uncomfortable atmosphere for you. Good as a salesman for you, but make sure the King can back up the verbal orders with written contracts. A nice person—whom you'll like—and forgive—a lot.

King of Hearts birthdates: June 30, July 28, August 26, September 24, October 22, November 20, December 18.

Vertical Line

THREE OF HEARTS—MERCURY LINE

A sociable and attractive person with whom you will find many things to talk about—most of all your individual love lives. This relationship could be short-lived, because you are interested in expanding yourself beyond this native and will not want to be as socially active.

Three of Hearts birthdates: November 30, December 28.

FOUR OF HEARTS—NEPTUNE LINE

Definite romantic attraction that probably won't work for you because of this native's profession or avocation. Since they are always interested in being in the public eye somewhat, you will never feel that you can truly trust them and therefore will look elsewhere. But a good friend—if you permit them to be.

Four of Hearts birthdates: October 31, November 29, December 27.

QUEEN OF SPADES—URANUS LINE

An immediate dislike can result here it you judge the periphery instead of the person. This native is exceptionally bright and can give you a new form of illumination, if you can wade through the piles of data around them like so many stacks of old newspapers; they definitely have a disorganized aura surrounding them. Chances are it will be too irritating to bother. But try: There may be a new way of life that would be happier—not with the Queen of Spades personally, but with their particular life-style.

Queen of Spades birthdate: January 2.

QUEEN OF DIAMONDS—SATURN LINE

A give-and-take friendship that can never run smooth. Their needs for daily living will be imposing to you, and your problems an irritation to them—but the friendship will survive on a see-you-occasionally basis. Difficult for love—you're in different spaces. Business aspects good, but not great.

Queen of Diamonds birthdates: January 15, February 13, March 11, April 9, May 7, June 5, July 3, August 1.

SIX OF DIAMONDS–JUPITER LINE

Karmic tie which will more likely be a spiritual enlightenment–in retrospect. You'll admire and respect their abilities, but try to avoid personal contacts.

Six of Diamonds birthdates: January 21, February 19, March 17, April 15, May 13, June 11, July 9, August 7, September 5, October 3, November 1.

KING OF HEARTS–MARS LINE: SEE HORIZONTAL LINE

Diagonal Lines

ACE OF CLUBS–MERCURY AND VENUS LINES

You can be turned on by this native, but not for long. Their insecure love life will be a blow to your own desires, and you'll run like a rabbit out of this situation. Friendship, even though it's probably short-term, is fine.

Ace of Clubs birthdates: May 31, June 29, July 27, August 25, September 23, October 21, November 19, December 17.

KING OF DIAMONDS–MARS AND VENUS LINES

Definite mental attraction that can lead to sex and love (with any "Diamond man" who might be operating under the King). Romance is short-lived, so enjoy it while you have it. Good for business; they can help you make money if you let them and don't let your emotions rule you.

King of Diamonds birthdates: January 14, February 12, March 10, April 8, May 6, June 4, July 2.

TEN OF HEARTS–MARS AND JUPITER LINES

If you fall for this native romantically–and you probably will–you could wind up on a psychiatrist's couch. Dynamite love affair; it may never seem better–until the Ten of Hearts is gone on his/her merry way, and you're red-eyed and locking yourself up for weeks at a time. If you love this native, make them chase you. That's the only way you'll get them,–if you can continue playing the game for as long as twenty years or so. Great for friendship, and that's where the relationship should rightfully stay. This card will cause your eyes and hands to roam, and then you'll have no relationship at all. Be friends only.

Ten of Hearts birthdates: July 31, August 29, September 27, October 25, November 23, December 21.

THREE OF SPADES—SATURN AND JUPITER LINES

An immediate dislike, because you will be forever trying to convince them of something, and sooner or later it won't seem worth it. Don't attempt romance, though through loneliness you might be tempted. Best to avoid the relationship if you can.

Three of Spades birthdates: January 11, February 9, March 7, April 5, May 3, June 1.

TWO OF CLUBS—URANUS AND SATURN LINES

Your dreams for happiness can be found here, providing you take special care to guard against being suspicious of some of this person's secret activities. All good things will come to you as a result of this association, and you (on the positive side) will never cease to be amazed and surprised throughout the relationship. A Karmic tie and an inevitable involvement on some level.

Two of Clubs birthdates: May 30, June 28, July 26, August 24, September 22, October 20, November 18, December 16.

SIX OF SPADES—NEPTUNE AND URANUS LINES

A necessary relationship for your own growth, though certainly not among the more pleasant situations with people in general. You'll feel they don't pull their weight and are too harsh and critical in their evaluations of people, places, and things. If you're involved, try to keep it to a minimum—for maximum happiness.

Six of Spades birthdates: January 8, February 6, March 4, April 2.

SEVEN OF HEARTS FAMOUS BIRTHDATES

September 30	Truman Capote
	Johnny Mathis
October 28	Elsa Lanchester
	Jonas Salk
	Joan Plowright
November 26	Robert Goulet
	Charles M. Schulz
December 24	Ava Gardner
	Kit Carson
	Howard Hughes

Seven of Clubs

Clubs — Knowledge
Seven of Clubs — Worry About Accomplishment
Seven in Clubs — Spiritual Power in Revelation

The Uranus Card in the Saturn Line. Displaces the **Eight of Diamonds** in the Natural Spread.

This card never lacks the inspiration of Uranus, as its True Place is also in the Uranus position (Mars Line). There are three rulerships to consider: Saturn for the Line, Uranus for the position and Mars for the True Place. Saturn will always make trouble if his laws are disregarded, and thus it is with the Seven of Clubs. Instead of cultivating their great gift of intuition and *listening* for their instructions, people of this card too often succumb to the Saturn pressure, accept discouragement, or rail against the obstacles in their path, while worrying over a multitude of things that never happen.

The displaced Eight of Diamonds assures them of the power behind them, a power that not only gives them an opportunity to exercise right judgments concerning values, but also secures their protection when discrimination is exercised. The Mars rulership of the True Place says: Work for it, fight for it if necessary, but *use* it at all costs. These people can always make money, which is their chief worry, if they will work for it. Many of them do work, but periodically they get into a panic and plunge into some unwise investment or get-rich-quick scheme that leaves them poorer than ever.

Planetary Sequence

			K♠	8♢	10♣			
A♠	3♢	5♣	10♠	Q♣	A♣	3♡		Mercury
2♡	9♠	9♣	J♡	5♠	7♢	7♡		Venus
8♣	J♠	2♢	4♣	6♡	K♢	K♡		Mars
A♢	A♡	8♠	10♢	10♡	4♠	6♢		Jupiter
5♢ *Mercury*	7♣	9♡	3♠	3♣	5♡	Q♢		Saturn
J♢	K♣ *Neptune*	2♣ *Uranus*	7♠ *Saturn*	9♢ *Jupiter*	J♣ *Mars*	Q♠ *Venus*		Uranus
Q♡	6♠	6♣	8♡	2♠	4♢	4♡		Neptune

Neptune *Uranus* *Saturn* *Jupiter* *Mars* *Venus* *Mercury*

Mundane Spread

Much of the troubles that come with the Seven of Clubs lie in a lack of preparation. Being in the realm of Clubs, a thorough education is the prime essential. When this is neglected, they get off to a bad start, as far as accomplishment is concerned. Some periods of financial limitation are bound to come, and they need trained minds and well-stocked brains to combat them.

The number Seven is the Number of the Soul. They are interested in soul development and understanding, but they should shun any psychic experiences that are on the lower Astral plane. They are too vulnerable for this. Sevens of Clubs also want proof and tangibility, and when that is not forthcoming, they abandon the particular creed or code they have been experimenting with and try another. If their state of mind about religion is sufficiently troubled, they will keep on seeking until they find some kind of faith to cling to.

The men of this card should strive to work under the King of Clubs; in that sequence the answers to their problems will come more readily.

There is sometimes scandal and backbiting connected with this card—especially for those who waste their time and substance and scatter their energies. Trouble in their work usually comes through labor disputes and unreliable employees. This often works unfavorably on their health, increasing their natural nervousness and mental confusion. They must realize that they can succeed—and splendidly—through work and application. They must shun petty and frivolous associates, gambling, drink, and careless, thoughtless living.

Because of the Displacement Card, a good many Sevens of Clubs are born to wealth, or acquire wealth in certain periods of their lives. The negative Seven of Clubs will lie about his money—he may say he has more than he actually has or he may deny having what he does have.

Sevens of Clubs are also people who require seclusion. The turmoil of the world affects them, and periodically they should have time for themselves.

Those who are "right side up" (and there are many) have provided themselves with a fine educational foundation, have developed their intuitional power, and have crowned their lives with splendid achievement and success.

BIRTHDATES RULED BY THE SEVEN OF CLUBS

MARCH 29—ARIES—RULED BY MARS

The mental attitude must be kept clear and strong—no negativity. These people often suffer from the machinations of others and become embittered and easily discouraged. Should stick to a course and not give up. Clever and inventive. Good draftsmen, mechanical engineers, architects, surveyors. May be connected with law or politics. If in a commercial line, succeed best with metals, machinery, sharp instruments. The women often make good nurses, laboratory technicians, or experts in home economics.

APRIL 27–TAURUS–RULED BY VENUS

Helped by women, but not romantically involved with them. However, the men are more apt to become attached to those women who are less helpful and more glamorous. Are naturally intuitive. Love music and should cultivate some artistic line as an outlet for their emotions. May be dominated by conditions at home or by the mother. Are more at peace when living close to the earth. Should strive to eliminate fear of insecurity. May gain a position of authority, which dispels their fears. May be interested in social, political, or prison reform. Have a more universal viewpoint than many Sevens of Clubs and are usually well educated and well balanced. Are studious and philosophical. May attain a high place in government service. Good writers, usually along serious lines: history, philosophy, etc.

MAY 25–GEMINI–RULED BY MERCURY

The majority of these people are doubting Thomases. Very talkative and self-expressive by nature, but seldom reveal their true sentiments on any subject. This subtlety may give them an occasional advantage in business, but it does not help their personal relationships. They like to sound people out and agree to whatever is popular or expedient. Will never commit themselves without keeping an ace in reserve. Are interested in the races, in business involving transportation, or anything that moves rapidly and frequently changes. The more developed and educated often go to the other extreme and become deep thinkers, philosophers, or psychologists. For them, writing is the most important field of influence. Those who are less exceptional can succeed as lawyers, agents, salesmen, or auctioneers.

JUNE 23–CANCER–RULED BY THE MOON

(This birthdate may fall in the last degree of Gemini but it is rare.)

Restless and ambitious but not always sure of themselves. They need encouragement and affection. In certain directions, however, they have strong opinions and firm convictions, and these they will go to any lengths to uphold. Of all the Sevens of Clubs, they are the most dependent upon affections and the most devoted to those they love. They want to shine as sponsors of the underprivileged, but their timidity keeps them in the background. They are disturbed about lack of money and are always charitable with what they have. They are idealistic, poetical, and musical but cannot commercialize the arts. They make good managers of apartment houses and hotels, good caterers and successful dealers in household commodities. They often like to follow the sea or live close to it. Can deal in liquids—especially perfumes.

JULY 21—CANCER—RULED BY THE MOON

Much more self-assertive and self-promotive than the other Cancer birthdate. Like the limelight and are attracted to the stage or platform, whether talented or not. Many playwrights and actors are found in this date; also singers, musicians, and lecturers. The women are especially gifted in clothes designing, running dress shops, or executing orders for interior decorations. Like display and are clever in creating it. Work best when they have an appreciative audience. Influenced by home and family. Usually have a home that is artistic and in good taste. Want cooperation but are unusually independent—for Cancer. Must avoid selfishness and a critical tendency. Like to have others dependent upon them. Are generous and protective.

AUGUST 19—LEO—RULED BY THE SUN

Self-confident and highly ambitious. Aspire to a position of authority in whatever line they follow. When they have learned tolerance and developed a humanitarian spirit, become valuable leaders—but this usually is delayed until they are advanced in years. Must have prominence and excitement, so many are attracted to the theater; often make a success of it. Better for the stage then the movies, for they prefer to be their own directors. If in a commercial line, should be at the head of the business. Strong supporters of law and order. Reactionary. Original and creative. Good merchandisers, customs house brokers, or government officials. Always dramatic.

SEPTEMBER 17—VIRGO—RULED BY MERCURY

Can drive hard bargains. Should cultivate breadth of viewpoint in money matters and avoid pettiness and penuriousness. Good tax experts, accountants, technicians. Efficient and thorough in drawing up documents, legal papers (briefs), and trust deeds; never miss a point. Dislike limitation but do not exert themselves to eliminate it. Have periods of generosity and extravagance. Should try to eliminate ulterior motives.

OCTOBER 15—LIBRA—RULED BY VENUS

Love art, music, poetry—and beauty. Strong religious inclinations; not usually orthodox. Like ceremony and "setting" with their religion. Usually endowed with a strong humanitarian urge and will use their talents to promote culture, education, and general welfare. Will become actors to "elevate the stage," or marry to reform the mate. Work better when married—and loved. Eager for popularity. Want to live up to what is expected of them. Better suited to a literary or professional career than a commercial. Good agents, diplomats, and go-betweens. Often have talent for art; always have ability for writing.

NOVEMBER 13—SCORPIO—RULED BY MARS

There are saints and sinners in this birthdate; it all depends upon the understanding of this karmic number and the use of the great power in the Sign. There is an inclination to bewail the hard lot and rail against the obstacles. They are seekers of knowledge, but often they are too skeptical and critical to recognize the truth when they find it. They feel underpaid and unappreciated, which makes them bitter and resentful. If they don't know any better, they try to wreak their vengeance on society, with lamentable results for themselves. When willing to accept their crosses as logical results of their own causes, and when they set about discharging their karmic debts willingly, they become truly great people—and the crosses miraculously disappear. They are gifted as writers, healers, teachers, metaphysicians, and philosophers. They can succeed in any business connected with mines or metals.

DECEMBER 11—SAGITTARIUS—RULED BY JUPITER

Tense and nervous but dynamic and determined. Can achieve good mental balance only through wisdom and understanding. Inclined to be dictatorial. If working for own ends, not likely to go far. With larger interests and a sincere concern for universal good, they can become valuable and respected leaders. Should avoid temperamentalism; should seek inspiration. They belong on the higher levels. Good government officials, national representatives, economists, writers.

SEVEN OF CLUBS—PLANETARY SEQUENCE OF PERSONAL RELATIONSHIPS

Horizontal Line

FIVE OF DIAMONDS—MERCURY CARD IN THE NEPTUNE LINE

The financial problems of each of you may seem to be too much of a burden to sustain a relationship, but don't be misled. It may not be as difficult as you think. Conversation is easy with this native, so talk it out before you make a radical decision on anything.

Five of Diamonds birthdates: January 22, February 20, March 18, April 16, May 14, June 12, July 10, August 8, September 6, October 4, November 2.

Your Place in the Cards

QUEEN OF SPADES—VENUS CARD IN THE MERCURY LINE

You'll love this native—until you start talking. That will probably turn you off. You won't want to waste your time with a lady or a man who doesn't *seek*—and who seems to be resigned to a pattern that no longer (or never did) fit you. You're probably right, but the experience will be worth the effort, so don't miss it.

Queen of Spades birthdate: January 2.

JACK OF CLUBS—MARS CARD IN THE VENUS LINE

If you are male and you find a close relationship with a male Jack of Clubs, you are probably involved in an immature relationship. You will probably relate to this native in some way, but for your own material and spiritual growth, you would be better off if you did not become involved. would be better off if you did not become involved with this native.

Jack of Clubs birthdates: January 29, February 27, March 25, April 23, May 21, June 19, July 17, August 15, September 13, October 11, November 9, December 7.

NINE OF DIAMONDS—JUPITER CARD IN THE MARS LINE

On a positive plane, this native could represent a good friend who can give you a shot in the arm when you need to pick yourself up and begin *doing* something about your finances. Negatively, it could be disastrous. You could both wallow in self-pity, constantly moaning about your dissatisfactions with life. Be careful of this involvement. There is no middle ground, and the last thing you need is to have someone pulling you down.

Nine of Diamonds birthdates: January 18, February 16, March 14, April 12, May 10, June 8, July 6, August 4, September 2.

SEVEN OF SPADES—SATURN CARD IN THE JUPITER LINE

A Karmic tie. Although they may not be able to do it themselves, they are able to show *you* the Way. The relationship is not easy, but compensates by the good things that can come of it. Not on the romantic wire for you.

Seven of Spades birthdates: January 7, February 5, March 3, April 1.

TWO OF CLUBS—URANUS CARD IN THE SATURN LINE

This relationship is definitely one you don't need. Your own problems will be doubly emphasized, and it could turn into one of the most difficult associations you've ever known. These natives are "downers" to you—don't get involved.

Two of Clubs birthdates: May 30, June 28, July 26, August 24, September 22, October 20, November 18, December 16.

Sevens

KING OF CLUBS—NEPTUNE CARD IN THE URANUS LINE
(Uranus Line on the Vertical Line)

If you are a man and the King of Clubs is a male friend, here is your magic carpet ride. With the King as your Personality Card, you would feel a closer attachment and perhaps would be a little more open to him. For both sexes, this is the person who can set your sights back in their proper perspective. They will understand you, perhaps better than you understand yourself. They'll help you shake old bugaboos and arrange a new meaning. Don't scoff or challenge them—they are the holders of some of your truths that lie behind the veil.

King of Clubs birthdates: January 27, February 25, March 23, April 21, May 19, June 17, July 15, August 13, September 11, October 9, November 7, December 5.

Vertical Line

ACE OF HEARTS—JUPITER LINE

This could be romance. You would certainly find things in common and things to talk about. You are both realists, and any kind of relationship could prove to be interesting and good for you. It's not a wild love affair, and you might be better friends than lovers. The combination is doubtful.

Ace of Hearts birthdate: December 30.

JACK OF SPADES—MARS LINE

You will be physically attracted to this person, but don't expect them to work at sustaining the relationship. It might be more than they can handle right now. If there's to be an involvement of any kind it will be up to you. Don't expect much. They probably don't want to lose the space in their spiritual growth that they feel you may not have attained as yet.

Jack of Spades birthdates: January 3, February 1.

NINE OF SPADES—VENUS LINE

You will never be able to get things working in this relationship. Marriage with a Nine of Spades is almost a sure divorce, or as close as you can get without actually getting one. Both of you have obstacles in your life patterns—and the ones *you* don't have, *they* do. Try to steer clear of the whole thing.

Nine of Spades birthdates: January 5, February 3, March 1.

THREE OF DIAMONDS—MERCURY LINE

A good relationship, providing you don't get too close. This should be someone that you're able to talk to, but in a personal involvement, their uncertainty about life is liable to reinforce the negative in yours.

Three of Diamonds birthdates: January 24, February 22, March 20, April 18, May 16, June 14, July 12, August 10, September 8, October 6, November 4, December 2.

SIX OF SPADES—NEPTUNE LINE

This native will probably bore you beyond belief. And when they're not doing that, it will seem as if they're laying a heavy hand on your shoulder to explain to you why you shouldn't have gotten involved in your last wild adventure. It's Karma, so there's not much you can do to escape the relationship, but you won't like it on a day-to-day basis.

Six of Spades birthdates: January 8, February 6, March 4, April 2.

KING OF CLUBS—URANUS LINE: SEE HORIZONTAL LINE

Diagonal Lines

ACE OF DIAMONDS—JUPITER AND NEPTUNE LINES

Your business life can be greatly enhanced by the friendship of this native. That is, if romance doesn't get in the way. Don't try both—at least not at the same time. Be careful that one of you is practical *at all times*. You cannot be successful together otherwise. Chances are you won't feel a strong romantic attraction, so don't worry about it.

Ace of Diamonds birthdates: January 26, February 24, March 22, April 20, May 18, June 16, July 14, August 12, September 10, October 8, November 6, December 4.

TWO OF CLUBS—URANUS AND SATURN LINES: SEE HORIZONTAL LINE

EIGHT OF HEARTS—NEPTUNE AND JUPITER LINES

It's all over with if you meet an Eight of Hearts of the opposite sex. You will feel as if you've found the perfect one. And chances are you have—for you. What about them? If you want to keep your Eight of Hearts around for a while (and you will want to), you will overlook any fits of childishness they may have and concentrate on being the real, positive you. *Use* the power of your Displacement Card: catch up on your reading, take some new educational classes, etc., and always behave in a mature fashion (even when they seems as if they are not). Your love life will never be better, and you may never be happier.

Eight of Hearts birthdates: August 31, September 29, October 27, November 25, December 23.

JACK OF DIAMONDS—URANUS AND NEPTUNE LINES

Business deals with this native could turn sour even when they look 100 percent sure. You're right in your judgment about their ability to make money—but don't think that this is necessarily applicable to you. The unexpected can happen, and it may just not turn out to be the deal you thought it was. This doesn't mean don't get involved; just check it out thoroughly and make sure everything's on top of the table. A female Seven of Clubs might be attracted to a male Jack of Diamonds, but chances are that a romantic relationship will never really pan out.

Jack of Diamonds birthdates: January 16, February 14, March 12, April 10, May 8, June 6, July 4, August 2.

EIGHT OF SPADES—JUPITER AND SATURN LINES

If you and your Eight of Spades are both well educated, you stand a good chance of having a romantic involvement. In any event, it is a relationship you shouldn't miss. They have most of the right things to put you together—and they have the spirit and the tenacity to follow it through. An earned compliment given to them now and then makes for a better relationship.

Eight of Spades birthdates: January 6, February 4, March 2.

FOUR OF CLUBS—MARS AND JUPITER LINES

This is an immediate attraction romantically and sexually; it will probably even make you think about home fires burning. They are basically content with themselves and quite talkative—both of which may make you nervous. But this kind of nervousness would be petty on your part, so be aware. Above all, enjoy a full, and perhaps beautiful, relationship.

Four of Clubs birthdates: April 30, May 28, June 26, July 24, August 22, September 20, October 18, November 16, December 14.

FIVE OF SPADES—VENUS AND MARS LINES

This is *not* romance for you, although you will feel a magnetic draw towards this native. Beyond an evening's entertainment, it could be disastrous for you. You will feel manipulated by this native and the relationship will not add to your own development. Pass it right on by.

Five of Spades birthdates: January 9, February 7, March 5, April 3, May 1.

ACE OF CLUBS—MERCURY AND VENUS LINES

This is one of those relationships that must be tried. A true friend, companion, or lover, this native will always be there—most of the time with those things you need. And they will love you in return. You can present many more problems to them than they to you. They can help to keep you

Your Place in the Cards

going when you think that hope is almost gone. Try to be more positive and give this native the love and affection that you are capable of—and that they need from you.

Ace of Clubs birthdates: May 31, June 29, July 27, August 25, September 23, October 21, November 19, December 17.

SEVEN OF CLUBS FAMOUS BIRTHDATES

March 29	Pearl Bailey
	Cardinal Mindzenty
April 27	Ulysses S. Grant
May 25	Gene Tunney
	Ralph Waldo Emerson
	Bennett Cerf
June 23	Duke of Windsor
July 21	Isaac Stern
	Ernest Hemingway
August 19	Alfred Lunt
	Jill St. John
	Ogden Nash
	Willie Shoemaker
	Orville Wright
	Bernard Baruch
September 17	Ann Bancroft
	Roddy McDowall
	James Kavanaugh
October 15	Friedrich Nietzsche
	Oscar Wilde
November 13	Robert Louis Stevenson

Seven of Diamonds

Diamonds – Values
Seven of Diamonds – Conflict between Spirit and Matter
Seven in Diamonds – Peace through Victory

The Venus Card in the Venus Line—Displaces the **Nine of Hearts** in the Natural Spread.

The Seven of Diamonds and the Nine of Hearts are inextricably linked together. Sevens represent material *or* spiritual victory; Nines represent personal disappointment and frustration, or peace and fulfillment through universal love. Under whichever aspect of this card the life is lived, there is always a double emphasis. For the majority, there is always one problem or the other—money or love. When the love life is smooth, the finances are upset; when there is wealth, love is a problem, a burden, or a heartache. This card is necessarily associated with money, for good or ill, little or much, but wealth seldom brings its natives happiness unless they are working with the "top side" or positive side, of the Nine of Hearts.

Emotional problems are keenly felt and often result in illness. The double Venus position makes love a vital factor in life, while the Saturn insistence strips off the glamor and puts on the pressure. With these people, there is a great love of home, but they have to wait for it. Early life doesn't seem to provide it without many changes and vicissitudes. But it is always in the back of their minds, and they save and sacrifice, if necessary, or finally manage to locate in one place and use the funds for it that may have been at their disposal from the start.

Money is often spent carelessly and futilely; besides being a Card of Power and Accomplishment, it is also productive of the "wine, women, and song"

Planetary Sequence

			K♠	8♦	10♣			
A♠	3♦	5♣	10♠	Q♣	A♣	3♥	Mercury
2♥ Saturn	9♠ Jupiter	9♣ Mars	J♥ Venus	5♦ Mercury	7♦	7♥	Venus
8♣	J♠	2♦	4♣	6♥	K♥ Neptune	K♥ Uranus	Mars
A♦	A♥	8♠	10♦	10♥	4♠	6♦	Jupiter
5♦	7♣	9♥	3♠	3♣	5♥	Q♦	Saturn
J♦	K♣	2♣	7♠	9♦	J♣	Q♠	Uranus
Q♥	6♠	6♣	8♥	2♠	4♦	4♥	Neptune

Neptune · Uranus · Saturn · Jupiter · Mars · Venus · Mercury

Mundane Spread

people who have not acquired a sense of values. Inheritance is frequent, as well as marriage into money. Money is always important as a goal to be attained. This card is not happy without it and will work very hard for it if it has not come through gift or inheritance. This is not a card of idleness.

The life seems to follow cycles of five or seven years; changes are often violent, always sudden. Persons of this card are always discontented until the desire to live well is satisfied—unless they have dedicated themselves to service and forgotten self-interest.

BIRTHDATES RULED BY THE SEVEN OF DIAMONDS

JANUARY 20—CAPRICORN—RULED BY SATURN

Money may be accumulated but rarely is, except by hard work. There is a certain sternness and rigidity in these people that does not deny friendliness but seldom evinces any sympathy. Make good, hardheaded physicians, courteous but unbending ambassadors or diplomats. The other side of the picture is selfish, overambitious, and a climber. Influenced by the personalities of others but seldom show it. Can succeed as labor leaders or property managers. If aware of the inspiration in the birthday number, can successfully cultivate some latent talent and commercialize it.

FEBRUARY 18—AQUARIUS—RULED BY URANUS

Demand personal freedom but have a desire for service. If a man, eager for movement and travel. Do not want responsibility but will not shirk it if affectional ties are involved. Want recompense for any service. Make good doctors, experimenters in cures. Are attracted to the stage and may become very popular—seldom famous. Are better suited for business and may become large-scale financiers. There may be a talent for technical music, but there is seldom success in any other art form.

MARCH 16—PISCES—RULED BY NEPTUNE

Are fearful of lack of protection in old age. Want to accumulate and set aside for the rainy day. More independent than many Pisceans. Want power and believe that money is the key to it. Not attracted to partnerships; prefer to work alone and be at the head of own business. Can succeed in hotel work and transportation. If they reach a high point of success, they are inclined to become dictatorial. Have an attraction for the arts but are better suited for their business aspects than as artists or performers. Inclined to a religion that demonstrates what they want—notably Christian Science or certain types of new thought. Could become good mental healers.

APRIL 14—ARIES—RULED BY MARS

Must learn to check impulses and cultivate accuracy. Enjoy promotion and speculation but not always successful at either. Good starters, poor finishers; too scattered in their interests, too restless to see things through. Should work in the open—road engineering, surveying, bus driving, etc. Have a tendency to scatter their energies and waste their time. Should avoid the law as a profession as well as any legal entanglements in their own affairs. If willing to take themselves seriously, can succeed as writers, financiers, or theologians. They must guard against carelessness and thoughtlessness. Must realize that neither money nor love are playthings.

MAY 12—TAURUS—RULED BY VENUS

Responsible and solid. Understand divine laws intuitively. Have a paternal and protective attitude toward the world in general and a strong desire for service. May be mistaken in beliefs but are sincere in them and cannot be changed. Want to be comforters and providers. The women are fine mothers and nurses. Men are good employers and generous contributors to charity. Love the earth. Can succeed as horticulturists, landscape architects, etc. Great sense of beauty and color. Interior decorators, artists, poets, musicians, teachers, and philosophers. The undeveloped will stubbornly espouse an unpopular or questionable cause for the excitement of it—or pure devilishness.

JUNE 10—GEMINI—RULED BY MERCURY

Restless, nervous, changeable. Easily bored. Must cultivate dependability and unselfishness. Want a profession connected with people, variety, and excitement. Are good court reporters, journalists, travel guides, explorers. Demand freedom and independence. Not always good marriage partners, as they are too exacting and self-insistent. Wither under monotony, because it has a bad mental effect on them. Learn readily and forget easily. Are subject to nervous ailments.

JULY 8—CANCER—RULED BY THE MOON

Acquisitive and self-protective—through fear of lack. Want money badly but cannot always keep it; self-indulgent spenders. Like to be prominent in the community and appear well-to-do. Will contribute to projects but want their names at the top of the list. Apt to be lazy but will work if there is a chance to accumulate. Are often gifted along artistic lines and should cultivate any latent talent; this brings out the best in them. If they make a career of business, may become ruthless and penurious. Those who are less money-conscious become active in community, church, or general welfare projects.

AUGUST 6–LEO–RULED BY THE SUN

A difficult birthdate unless dedicated to service. In this case, money is apt to be a problem, but sacrifice is cheerfully accepted. The usual August 6 people are the most monied of all the Sevens of Diamonds; they are either born to money, inherit it, or marry it. In the last case, the personal life leaves much to be desired. Have many opportunities but seldom embrace them. Will spend lavishly on home and personal comfort. Need to be loved for themselves but are usually sought for their money. When these people become truly philanthropic and eager to share their wealth, they stand a fine chance of personal peace and happiness. The usual picture is one of boredom, loneliness, and an accumulation of ailments. Succeed best in a large business—banking, brokerage, or manufacturing. May be good lawyers, actors, or directors.

SEPTEMBER 6–VIRGO–RULED BY MERCURY

Must work hard to attain a key position. Apt to be meticulous and fussy, swamped with detail. The mind is keen but critical; their very mentality may become a burden. Must avoid worry and fretfulness. Very successful at research and technical details. Also well adapted for real estate, commodities—especially groceries—merchandising and selling small articles. Can teach or write if other factors in the chart are supporting.

OCTOBER 2–LIBRA–RULED BY VENUS

This is the most artistic and gifted of all the Sevens of Diamonds. Great painters belong to this birthdate, as well as actors and composers. To the majority, art and beauty come first. Interested in foreign countries and foreign travel. Good foreign agents, diplomats, and ambassadors. If not artistically inclined, should study law. May become strongly religious and universal-minded. Have high ideals and great influence over others. May become too self-effacing and sacrificial for their own good. If not well balanced mentally, may have a martyr complex.

SEVEN OF DIAMONDS— PLANETARY SEQUENCE OF PERSONAL RELATIONSHIPS

Horizontal Line

FIVE OF SPADES–MERCURY CARD IN THE MARS LINE

Good for a working relationship; short bursts of temper possible when they try to force their own ideas on you. Good mental association, if you can live with the situation. Forget romance—they won't think of you or be with you nearly as much as you want and need.

Five of Spades birthdates: January 9, February 7, March 5, April 3, May 1.

JACK OF HEARTS—VENUS CARD IN THE JUPITER LINE

Love at first sight—but don't do anything radical or you'll regret it. The kind of love you need is not possible from a Jack of Hearts. Their love goes to many, and what will be left will be wafer-thin for you. They are probably too fixed in their emotions and ideas for you to try to do anything about it, so accept it as it is given to you—and nothing more.

Jack of Hearts birthdates: July 30, August 28, September 26, October 24, November 22, December 20.

NINE OF CLUBS—MARS CARD IN THE SATURN LINE

Stimulation will be prevalent, but it will be an irritating kind—almost as if you cannot hurdle the mountain of effort it would take to get through to this native. Your own busy life cannot give the approving nods and sympathetic words that they want and need—stay out of any kind of legal affairs or entanglements—you won't come out the winner. Studiously avoid marriage—it can only end in divorce.

Nine of Clubs birthdates: January 31, February 29, March 27, April 25, May 23, June 21, July 19, August 17, September 15, October 13, November 11, December 9.

NINE OF SPADES—JUPITER CARD IN THE URANUS LINE

A good father for you but not a good husband. You probably don't fit into the romantic life of this native, so don't press in trying to force it to happen. They are on a different wavelength from yours and you have much better associations available.

Nine of Spades birthdates: January 5, February 3, March 1.

TWO OF HEARTS—SATURN CARD IN THE NEPTUNE LINE

You won't feel an attraction here at all, because you'll innately know this person is someone who will cross your path from time to time, but never be a part of your life. It's just as well; their pessimistic attitudes and their detachment towards most things would leave you cold anyway.

Two of Hearts birthdate: December 29.

KING OF HEARTS—URANUS CARD IN THE MERCURY LINE

An immediate friendship. They are kindly, sometimes a little temperamental, but it's over quickly. You can learn how to *feel* positive love through this native, even though at times they will seem to be repetitious and grate on your nerves.

King of Hearts birthdates: June 30, July 28, August 26, September 24, October 22, November 20, December 18.

KING OF DIAMONDS–NEPTUNE CARD IN THE VENUS LINE
(Mars Line on the Vertical Line)

You won't always believe that they're really doing what they say they're doing. They will protect you and take care of you financially, if necessary. In business, this is a great combination for making a great deal of money. In love, there probably won't be the romantic love you think you want, but the compensations are well worth the effort.

King of Diamonds birthdates: January 14, February 12, March 10, April 8, May 6, June 4, July 2.

Vertical Line

ACE OF CLUBS–MERCURY LINE

Depending on what you're looking for, this native has some of the answers. This is a high communication card for you, but also a quick relationship—one that could last for years; an on-again-off-again involvement. The problem here is that communication can go in one way or the other, but seldom more than one way at any particular time. So you must choose intellect, money, or love. This may not be enough to satisfy you.

Ace of Clubs birthdates: May 31, June 29, July 27, August 25, September 23, October 21, November 19, December 17.

FOUR OF DIAMONDS–NEPTUNE LINE

This is love, but you had better make sure that the person you think you're getting is really in the package. These natives have a lot to offer, and any kind of involvement should be considered. But don't fool yourself. See it as it really is.

Four of Diamonds birthdate: January 23, February 21, March 19, April 17, May 15, June 13, July 11, August 9, September 7, October 5, November 3, December 1.

JACK OF CLUBS–URANUS LINE

They'll be charming, likable, and you'll feel sexually attracted, but a close relationship will bring quarrels, accidents, and a total case of indifference on their part. Don't even consider romance. It won't work even if you become totally subservient—which you won't.

Jack of Clubs birthdates: January 29, February 27, March 25, April 23, May 21, June 19, July 17, August 15, September 13, October 11, November 9, December 7.

FIVE OF HEARTS–SATURN LINES

This friendship (don't consider love because they're too fickle for you) will always have one problem or another connected to it. They will attempt to lay every little problem that upsets their lives right at your feet. The problems vary, but all are emotionally oriented. Either too active a love life or too little. Someone at work is not cooperative, or someone is overly friendly and (maybe) therefore can't be trusted. You'll give a lot more in this relationship than you'll get.

Five of Hearts birthdates: October 30, November 28, December 26.

FOUR OF SPADES–JUPITER LINE

If you meet these cards, and they are of the opposite sex, you might find one of the most beautiful romantic relationships of your life. It's Karma and unavoidable, but you must permit them to be their own persons. Chances are that you won't—but try. It has excellent aspects for succeeding. Success is entirely possible in business and friendship as well—just don't try to run them. They know where they're going, even if it sometimes seems otherwise.

Four of Spades birthdates: January 10, February 8, March 6, April 4, May 2.

KING OF DIAMONDS–MARS LINE: SEE HORIZONTAL LINE

Diagonal Lines

THREE OF HEARTS–DOUBLE MERCURY LINES

A real mentally active involvement that can create a constant exchange of ideas about people, feelings, etc. Fun acquaintances, but keep them at a distance. Any romantic involvement will probably be short-lived.

Three of Hearts birthdates: November 30, December 28.

SIX OF HEARTS–DOUBLE MARS LINES

While you'll like these natives a lot, there will always be an underlying feeling that they can't give you the things that you need emotionally (which, of course, includes romance). You'll like their popularity but, as with the Three of Hearts, be friends—from a distance. You'll like each other more.

Six of Hearts birthdates: October 29, November 27, December 25.

TEN OF DIAMONDS–DOUBLE JUPITER LINES

You can only profit by an association with this native. Romantically, this relationship could be the all-time love of your life—on the material plane. You won't find the spiritual side that you seek in this involvement, and you might find eventually that this one-dimensional love—although it has great compensations—may not be fulfilling enough. Remember, businesswise, nothing can stop the two of you from making a great deal of money.

Ten of Diamonds birthdates: January 17, February 15, March 13, April 11, May 9, June 7, July 5, August 3, September 1.

NINE OF HEARTS—DOUBLE SATURN LINES
(Seven of Diamonds Displacement Card)

You can't get it together with this native no matter how hard you try. They will dump their problems on you, expect you to come up with answers, and argue down any answers that you may have to give. A karmic tie that you can't escape, but keep it on an impersonal level.

Nine of Hearts birthdates: August 30, September 28, October 26, November 24, December 22.

KING OF CLUBS—DOUBLE URANUS LINES

This card will always appeal to you. If a woman, be careful the King is not operating under the Jack (immaturely) or you'll have problems. If a man, the female King of Clubs is quite another story. She has a keen mind and will probably let you know. She'll try to master you as well, but in either case, the relationship is good and can grow.

King of Clubs birthdates: January 27, February 25, March 23, April 21, May 19, June 17, July 15, August 13, September 11, October 9, November 7, December 5.

QUEEN OF HEARTS—DOUBLE NEPTUNE LINES

As a man, here is a card that will mother you—not necessarily take care of you, but love you a lot. With dirty dishes in the sink and broom sweepings under the rug. As a female, you should know immediately that a male Queen of Hearts is too weak and lazy for you. Much wiser to be friends than lovers—you're too complicated for this card.

Queen of Hearts birthdates: July 29, August 27, September 25, October 23, November 21, December 19.

QUEEN OF CLUBS—MERCURY AND MARS LINES

This can start out as a fast-moving kind of attachment, an intellectual-sexual relationship that could turn out to be enduring and profitable. There's mutual respect and admiration, and only highly evolved natives should attempt a romantic involvement. Romanticism will always include a great deal of mental companionship—for you both.

Queen of Clubs birthdates: January 28, February 26, March 24, April 22, May 20, June 18, July 16, August 14, September 12, October 10, November 8, December 6.

Your Place in the Cards

EIGHT OF DIAMONDS—CROWN AND JUPITER LINES

A successful relationship on any level. You may be a little turned off by their more hard-nosed attitude in business, but know that these natives can help you hang onto all of the money you are capable of making. A definite involvement on some level which should be pursued for the happiness outcome of both of you.

Eight of Diamonds birthdates: January 19, February 17, March 15, April 13, May 11, June 9, July 7, August 5, September 3, October 1.

KING OF HEARTS—MERCURY AND MARS LINES:
SEE HORIZONTAL LINE

SEVEN OF DIAMONDS FAMOUS BIRTHDATES

January 20	George Burns
	Patricia Neal
February 18	Andrés Segovia
	Wendell Willkie
March 16	Jerry Lewis
	James Madison
April 14	Julie Christie
	John Gielgud
	Rod Steiger
May 12	Yogi Berra
	Krishnamurti
	Florence Nightingale
June 10	Judy Garland
July 8	Billy Eckstine
	Nelson Rockefeller
	George W. Romney
	J. D. Rockefeller, Sr.
	Donalie Fitzgerald
August 6	Lucille Ball
	Robert Mitchum
	Alfred Tennyson
September 4	Mitzi Gaynor
	Jesse James
October 2	Bud Abbott
	Maury Wills

Seven of Spades

Spades — Labor, Wisdom
Seven of Spades — Victory over Materiality
Seven in Spades — Peace in the Higher Self

The Jupiter Card in the Uranus Line. Displaces the **King of Diamonds** in the Natural Spread.

This is the "resurrection" card, the first of the Sevens that comes "out of the night" at the beginning of the resurrection month. The Seven of Spades is an entirely different card to deal with; this is a Master's Card. Actually, like all these Master Cards they can either reach the heights or sink to low levels—particularly true of the men.

There is material trouble, physical and financial, for all Sevens of Spades—but here the Displaced Card is a King, a card of overcoming, and the task allotted to the Seven of Spades is less arduous than the others'. Naturally, the first prerequisite is awareness of the power behind this pattern; the next step is to learn to use it. The Uranus Line provides the intuition; the Jupiter position bestows the blessing—redoubled in this case, for the True Place is also Jupiter—in the Line of the idealistic Neptune.

Despite this "higher plane" material, there are many Sevens of Spades living very close to the ground, grubbing for money that is never enough to meet their needs and subservient to those who are far beneath them in the ranks of God's elect. One thing only keeps them there: their faulty judgment of values. The King of Diamonds is proof that substance is not denied them, but command over it is not assured unless it is to be applied to the fulfillment of their mission. They are diggers for truth, contenders for the growth of the

Planetary Sequence

			K♠	8♦	10♣		
A♠	3♦	5♣	10♠	Q♣	A♣	3♥	Mercury
2♥	9♠	9♣	J♥	5♠	7♦	7♥	Venus
8♣	J♠	2♦	4♣	6♥	K♦	K♥	Mars
A♦	A♥	8♠	10♦	10♥	4♠	6♦	Jupiter
5♦	7♣	9♥	3♠	3♣	5♥	Q♦	Saturn
J♦ (Mars)	K♣ (Venus)	2♣ (Mercury)	7♠	9♦	J♣	Q♠	Uranus
Q♥	6♠	6♣	8♥ (Neptune)	2♠ (Uranus)	4♦ (Saturn)	4♥ (Jupiter)	Neptune

Neptune · Uranus · Saturn · Jupiter · Mars · Venus · Mercury

Mundane Spread

soul, heralds of the doctrine of eternal life—as is the case with all spades. Seven is the dominical number and there is no escaping the divine appointment.

There is additional power drawn from the Eight of Hearts—the card that displaces its own True Place—so enduring and idealistic love is not more denied them is money. These people do not have to be afraid where money is concerned. If they would realize this there would be no need for fear. They are powerful people by endowment and if they do not become leaders and examples it is because sickness stands in the way, or their own Karma is too heavy.

However, no Seven of Spades should be interested in becoming a financial wizard or accumulating great amounts of money. When not living up to the Seven of Spades, one may resort to heavy drinking, taking sleeping pills to get to sleep at night because of running away from the True Self, and not living up to the high calling within the Self. These people know when they are not living right; those who do not wish responsibility are working under the personality card of the Jack of Spades and, since the Jack can be a wayward card, they work on the negative side, causing the individual to drink.

There are few of these natives who have not been through many initiations. They have learned in the past that money is not always value nor display always beauty. They must never act from ulterior motives, for within themselves they know that each voluntary act of theirs must be accounted for and balanced. They know, too, that whatever sorrow they encounter in this life is a just debt, payment for which is justly demanded.

Illness may come through worry over business, or a frustrating desire to live beyond their means. Their heritage of power is sometimes misdirected to a longing for magnificence, and disappointment is their lot until they awaken to greater wisdom.

The real keynote of this card is its spiritual ability. Part of the Sequence is under Uranus and part under Neptune; so unless this person reaches out and gets interested in something beyond just ordinary living, he can become neurotic and end up institutionalized.

They destroy themselves the minute they use their power on the material plane. The card was never intended for anything except a teacher. When they are ruled by the Jack of Spades, their superconsciousness knows they are denying their own birthright. These people are very difficult to convince—both men and women. All Sevens of Spades should marry over the average intelligence so they have some aspirations. They are attracted to people who are intelligent.

They work quietly—often secretly—and are usually willing to remain behind the scenes. For that reason, they are valuable in secret service and are greatly aided by their instinctive discernment of truth or falsehood. They have many friends but few loves. Generosity is a strong point as is willingness to serve. Of all cards, they represent the best teachers and wisest counselors. In business, they are honest and reliable. In love, they are faithful.

BIRTHDATES RULED BY THE SEVEN OF SPADES

JANUARY 7–CAPRICORN–RULED BY SATURN

Can commercialize any of their natural abilities. Are mental and analytical. Less personally ambitious than many Capricornians but want leadership because they feel they are good leaders. Willing to work as silent partners but want the control in their own hands. They believe they know what is best for the people they are dealing with. Would like to be president—for the good of the nation. Can successfully run a business for others as well as themselves. Often attracted to medicine and more apt to be specialists than general practitioners. Good psychologists. Always patient and not too sympathetic. Will wait for others to reveal their hand before expressing an opinion. Can smooth over difficult situations with diplomacy.

FEBRUARY 5–AQUARIUS–RULED BY URANUS

Strongly attracted to religion and usually have a brand of their own in which they firmly believe. Are magnetic and influential. Make good exhorters and evangelists. If they follow an established creed, it must be one of love and tolerance. Very spiritually minded but not interested in psychic phenomena. Believe that God is the Supreme Ruler and that the aspirant must deal directly with Him—without intermediaries. Good writers, usually for propaganda. Interested in causes of disease, or of mental or emotional distress. Believe that faith and spiritual development can cure all ills.

MARCH 3–PISCES–RULED BY NEPTUNE

This is the weakest of the Sevens of Spades and the most likely to scatter forces. Gifted in art and poetry, and often attracted to the theater. Creative and original; good designers and decorators. Grow stronger if they choose a practical career and, even though interested in making a business pay, are always mindful of its general usefulness and the good it may do. Can become very successful—even famous—in the business world. Often gifted with inventive power and may devise or create something that is of universal benefit. Can be very valuable in connection with hospitals, sanitariums, and institutions for the afflicted and underprivileged. Interested in prison reform.

APRIL 1–ARIES–RULED BY MARS

This is the most active and dynamic of the Sevens of Spades. There seem to be two distinct types of people belonging to this birthdate: the busy, bustling, down-to-earth financiers or merchandisers—ambitious, restless, and self-promotive—and the strongly religious who want to go into all the world and preach the gospel to every creature. Here is either spirit or matter, but seldom a combination of the two, as in the other birthdates. This is the Resurrection Card and the spiritually minded predominate. These people are born into the new light, the forward march and they want others to share their firm conviction that life is everlasting and redemption is for all. They are powerful and convincing light-bearers.

SEVEN OF SPADES—PLANETARY SEQUENCE OF PERSONAL RELATIONSHIPS

Horizontal Line

TWO OF CLUBS—MERCURY CARD IN THE SATURN LINE
Can work well in secretive activities; you probably won't like their methods—try to guide and teach them to be more on the up and up. No personal involvements are best.
Two of Clubs birthdates: May 30, June 28, July 26, August 24, September 22, October 20, November 18, December 16.

KING OF CLUBS—VENUS CARD IN THE URANUS LINE
Love, admiration, and a delight in how they handle themselves. A definite must-try relationship that would surprise no one if it became a marriage. A close friendship card and good for business.
King of Clubs birthdates: January 27, February 15, March 23, April 21, May 19, June 17, July 15, August 13, September 11, October 9, November 7, December 5.

JACK OF DIAMONDS—MARS CARD IN THE NEPTUNE LINE
A driving, forceful person who could give you reason to reexamine your own goals and ambitions. Not especially well-liked by you, but probably misunderstood. Always give them a second chance—but don't get personally involved. Too irritating for a close relationship.
Jack of Diamonds birthdates: January 16, February 14, March 12, April 10, May 8, June 6, July 4, August 2.

FOUR OF HEARTS—JUPITER CARD IN THE MERCURY LINE
Fun-loving people who will attract you physically as well as mentally. A good friend, possible lover/mate. Enjoy this relationship.
Four of Hearts birthdates: October 31, November 29, December 27.

FOUR OF DIAMONDS—SATURN CARD IN THE VENUS LINE

A Karmic love relationship that could conceivably interfere with your own calling. An involvement you would be better off without over a period of time. To thine own self be true. If you are intricately associated with this native, remember to keep pursuing your own objectives—all the time.

Four of Diamonds birthdates: January 23, February 21, March 19, April 17, May 15, June 13, July 11, August 9, September 7, October 5, November 3, December 1.

TWO OF SPADES—URANUS CARD IN THE MARS LINE
(Neptune and Mars Lines on the Diagonal Line)

Too fearful of your thoughts and ideas to permit a close association—but your influence will definitely affect them, in some way. Don't argue—you know the truth. It's up to them to hear.

Two of Spades birthdates: January 12, February 10, March 8, April 6, May 4, June 2.

EIGHT OF HEARTS—NEPTUNE CARD IN THE JUPITER LINE
(Neptune Line on the Vertical Line)

Someone to run off on a fishing trip with—they'll help you to forget some of the mundane problems that seem to drag you down at times. A good friendship to escape to in time of need, but don't party too much or neither of you will accomplish anything. Romantic relationship possible as long as you know the individual extremely well.

Eight of Hearts birthdates: August 31, September 29, October 27, November 25, December 23.

Vertical Line

THREE OF SPADES—SATURN LINE

They'll listen to you but probably never believe you. Don't spend an overabundance of time here or the association will become extremely wearisome.

Three of Spades birthdates: January 11, February 9, March 7, April 5, May 3, June 1.

TEN OF DIAMONDS—JUPITER LINE

Romance, love, marriage. This native will definitely take care of you financially; easier situation for a male Ten of Diamonds. He can operate under the Jack of Diamonds and probably relate to you spiritually while giving you the comforts on the material plane. Any other combination might leave a lack of spiritual contact. In any event, a warm, loving relationship that you shouldn't miss.

Ten of Diamonds birthdates: January 17, February 15, March 13, April 11, May 9, June 7, July 5, August 3, September 1.

FOUR OF CLUBS–MARS LINE

Someone who has a great deal to say without it necessarily applying to you or your interests. Male relationships can be stimulating. Anything else can be irritating. Don't get personally involved.

Four of Clubs birthdates: April 30, May 28, June 26, July 24, August 22, September 20, October 18, November 16, December 14.

JACK OF HEARTS–VENUS LINE

A kind, loving friend—you could be in the clergy together, or in similar circumstances dealing with humanities. Romantic aspects extremely good; you are both on similar wave lengths.

Jack of Hearts birthdates: July 30, August 28, September 26, October 24, November 22, December 20.

TEN OF SPADES–MERCURY LINE

If you're close friends with this native, be careful you aren't spending most of your time barhopping. On the positive side, a co-worker—a compliment to your efforts—but a problem to you much of the time. For best results, don't get involved personally.

Ten of Spades birthdates: January 4, February 2.

EIGHT OF DIAMONDS–JUPITER AND CROWN LINES

A good mind that can mesh with yours for a successful combination in almost anything you undertake. A romantic involvement may be too demanding on you, however—but not impossible.

Eight of Diamonds birthdates: January 19, February 17, March 15, April 13, May 11, June 9, July 7, August 5, September 3, October 1.

EIGHT OF HEARTS–NEPTUNE LINE: SEE VERTICAL LINE

Diagonal Line

SIX OF CLUBS–NEPTUNE AND SATURN LINES

Great communication at first that could leave you exhausted in the end. Work with their intuitive side for best results. Romance and close friendship could prove disappointing.

Six of Clubs birthdates: March 30, April 28, May 26, June 24, July 22, August 20, September 18, October 16, November 14, December 12.

TWO OF SPADES—NEPTUNE AND MARS LINES: SEE HORIZONTAL LINE

NINE OF HEARTS—DOUBLE SATURN LINES

You may feel it's your duty to enlighten these natives—and you may very well be the only one who can. A difficult involvement on any level but rewarding in another time and another place. Pursue a friendship—but only until it becomes a hardship. And don't get involved in any other way.

Nine of Hearts birthdates: August 30, September 28, October 26, November 24, December 22.

ACE OF HEARTS—JUPITER AND URANUS LINES

A love life full of surprises; this native can bring much love to you and even help you in the making of money—but don't expect intellectual discussions of any depth. Good for friendship and business.

Ace of Hearts birthdate: December 30.

EIGHT OF CLUBS—MARS AND NEPTUNE LINES

Run out and accomplish is how you'll feel after meeting this native. You could also feel highly irritated over their know-it-all attitude, but don't let that be a guideline for ending the relationship. They have knowledge and are willing to part with it—so use it.

Eight of Clubs birthdates: March 28, April 26, May 24, June 22, July 20, August 18, September 16, October 14, November 12, December 10.

THREE OF CLUBS—SATURN AND MARS LINES

Talking to this native may seem the same as talking to a wall. Don't spend yourself and your time if it seems futile—and stay away from personal involvements.

Three of Clubs birthdates: May 29, June 27, July 25, August 23, September 21, October 19, November 17, December 15.

FOUR OF SPADES—JUPITER AND VENUS LINES

Undoubtedly the best romantic affiliation for you in the entire pack. Total love and understanding, and an ensured life of comparative comfort. A good match—don't ruin it by being negative—on any level.

Four of Spades birthdates: January 10, February 8, March 6, April 4, May 2.

KING OF HEARTS—MARS AND MERCURY LINES

You could get into a lot of trouble with this native if you are operating on the negative side and good times with very little thought for tomorrow. Positively, this native can get your thoughts back on a loving, spiritual plane, resulting in good feelings and impersonal love towards your fellow man. A difficult but worthwhile relationship on a sporadic basis. Too volatile for anything else.

King of Hearts birthdates: June 30, July 28, August 26, September 24, October 22, November 20, December 18.

SEVEN OF SPADES FAMOUS BIRTHDATES

January 7	Millard Fillmore
	Charles Addams
February 5	Red Buttons
	Adlai Stevenson
March 3	Alexander Graham Bell
	Jean Harlow
April 1	Debbie Reynolds
	Prince Otto von Bismarck

Eights

EIGHTS are the Power Cards. Some of the early mystery schools taught that Eight was the number of God and that its use by man would bring him evil. From this superstition, the practice arose among many of the old-school numerologists of assigning to Eight the rulership of Saturn as the embodiment of evil. Today we know—both from experience and from the Higher Teaching—that Eight is the number of the Sun (and therefore of God) and that Saturn is *not* the embodiment of evil.

Our mathematical symbol for infinite measure or "infinity" is the horizontal Eight, and this same symbol, as "all power" is over the head of the Magician in the Tarot and of the woman in the *Eighth* card—Strength—who is opening the lion's jaws with her hands.

When we come to look upon wealth as the symbol of power and write our numeral Eights with a very small loop at the top and a very large one below then, of course, Eight may bring us evil, and money may be justly be called its root. It is actually a picture of God's circle of power above reflected in man's below.

In the cards, we find several geometrical figures of repeated fours—two squares, eight triangles, two tetrads, two right angles, etc., the security of four doubled, or the intimation that upon a firm foundation may be built another of greater power and expansion. Eight is the first *free* number, for it comes at the "turn" of the sevens. It is the "Eternal Splendor of the Limitless Light" (Pattern on the Trestleboard).

The natives of these cards can expand in any direction according to their will and the outlines of their pattern. The *power* is always with them. They may turn the power to evil uses if they choose (and there are many Eights who operate very negatively indeed) but they are *free*; they reflect God's plan but they are not bound by it.

Your Place in the Cards

Hearts have the power to harmonize their lives, increase their resources and expand their field of service through Love—personal, universal and divine.

Clubs have the power to acquire knowledge—and the obligation to disseminate it. If they will not learn and *teach* they cannot fulfill their mission. They must follow the admonition of Saint Peter to "add knowledge to your faith."

Diamonds have the power to acquire wealth—and the obligation to share it. The "Limitless Substance" is at their disposal, twice over. They are "Crowned," therefore custodians and trustees. They represent the bank of spiritual and material security.

Spades have the power to acquire true wisdom and to live under God's Laws. Symbols of death, they are free to disprove its reality.

Eight of Hearts

Planetary Sequence

		K♠ Uranus	8♦ Saturn	10♣ Jupiter			
A♠	3♦	5♣	10♠	Q♣	A♣	3♥ Neptune	Mercury
2♥	9♠	9♣	J♥	5♠	7♦	7♥	Venus
8♣	J♠	2♦	4♣	6♥	K♦	K♥	Mars
A♦	A♥	8♠	10♦	10♥	4♠	6♦	Jupiter
5♦	7♣	9♥	3♠	3♣	5♥	Q♦	Saturn
J♦	K♣	2♣	7♠	9♦	J♣	Q♠	Uranus
Q♥ Mars	6♠ Venus	6♣ Mercury	8♥	2♠	4♦	4♥	Neptune
Neptune	Uranus	Saturn	Jupiter	Mars	Venus	Mercury	

Mundane Spread

Your Place in the Cards

Hearts — Love
Eight of Hearts — Power in Love
Eight in Hearts — Success in Relationships

The Jupiter Card in the Neptune Line. Displaces the **Seven of Spades** in the Natural Spread

To the natural power of this card is added the spiritual power of the displaced Seven of Spades—but the latter, while it may be latent, is not at their disposal for use unless there is spiritual aspiration in their hearts and spiritual application in their deeds. There is a natural conflict, as well, because the Displacement Card being a Spade represents one thing and the Birth Card being a Heart, represents another. There is an inborn compatability between Spades and Diamonds; there is none between Hearts and Spades.

This card likes a good time and a lot of people. An Eight of Hearts likes groups and has enough intuition through the mental power to overcome many situations. It has to be done mentally, not physically. This card is also Neptune, which can get a little far-out. It can become *too* involved. They can also become too involved in things that deal with psychic knowledge. If controlled, the power gives the ability to touch this life, or this world.

Eight of Hearts people feel they can overcome all problems through the power of love, dealing through their emotions, as a Heart card. But they can also get into ruts at various times in the life, almost to the point of seeming to go through a plowed field; yet still thrashing it after the fact. Sometimes events transpire that bring an awakening, but it is through the mental side, and not through the physical. They have a profound approach to insight, and are usually attracted to psychology. Victory on the higher plane is assured if they work for it—and happiness in the emotional life follows as a natural consequence.

Principal difficulties are emotional. Finances may be fluctuating and not always sufficient to meet the desire for having and giving; the work may be underpaid or wholly unrewarded, but there is always ample provision for security. They have no valid excuse for worrying about lack—although they often do.

It is the love life that brings them periodical heights or depths, and the depths cause them to suffer intensely. Their ideals are so high and exacting that they are rarely met, and when they are they are of brief duration. Disillusion steps in and breaks the relationship or, as is the case more frequently, separation is caused by death. This is the link with the Displacement Card—the Seven of Spades.

Eight of Hearts people must learn that there is no death and, therefore, no separation other than what is caused by a long journey. This is a direct call to the development of spiritual perception and the extrasensory potential that exists in all of us. The Seven of Spades exacts upon the Eight of Hearts that through wisdom, there is overcoming. And the Eight of Hearts has the power to overcome. True wisdom, however, is elusive and, although the majority of the Eight of Hearts natives want it and strive for it, their interests and relationships are so many and so varied, they allow themselves to be distracted from its pursuit.

The women, being more emotional and less inclined to compromise, are the greatest sufferers. All Eights of Hearts must love and be loved—and while they are often the objects of jealousy and contention, they never lack friends and admirers. They can transmute their love and find happiness in their work and their friends.

There are also obstacles in their work. They always undertake more than they can accomplish easily and wear themselves out trying to meet their often self-imposed obligations. They are very unhappy unless in the right field of expression and should never be forced into a career that is distasteful to them. If working mainly on the material plane, they are attracted to business that deals with large organizations or foreign interests. They usually do considerable foreign traveling themselves. In either field, material or spiritual, they have the power of leadership.

They are broadminded and sympathetic, friendly and generous—or negative, selfish and self-indulgent, spoiled and childish. They will fight for a principle.

BIRTHDATES RULED BY THE EIGHT OF HEARTS

AUGUST 31—VIRGO—RULED BY MERCURY

Hard-working. Set in one line of activity and not interested elsewhere. Their own circle of prime importance. Strive to keep conditions unchanging. Development very important to success. Plodders but willing to serve. State of health chronic, for good or ill. Succeed in institutional work, teaching, accounting, or real estate operations. Secretaries.

SEPTEMBER 29—LIBRA—RULED BY VENUS

Art, merchandising, and politics (law) are the main fields of success. Are nervous and tense. Work better if married or in partnership. For happiness, should forget self, and work for others; apt to brood over own misfortunes. Hate any form of menial work and are unhappy if forced into it. May need a good psychoanalyst to help them achieve impersonality. Stimulated by appreciation and congenial surroundings. Have inspirational power but do not always know how to use it.

OCTOBER 27—SCORPIO—RULED BY MARS

A universal card; carries the burdens of the world. May be attracted to the medical profession but too sympathetic to be efficient. Set and forceful but very loyal. Will not be coerced or called to account. Very religious but never orthodox. Good counselors, metaphysicians, writers, teachers, musicians. May become great financiers but use a large part of their money for philanthropy. Personal life seldom smooth except for brief periods. Suffer intensely through their emotions.

NOVEMBER 25–SAGITTARIUS–RULED BY JUPITER

Public-spirited and philanthropic. May espouse a mistaken cause, but blindly devote themselves to it. Understand common needs; universal minded. Become successful through their own efforts. Want full justice. Interested in large enterprises and want to improve methods. Too blunt for diplomacy, but like politics. Teachers, psychologists, lawyers, architects, lecturers. Reformers.

DECEMBER 23–CAPRICORN–RULED BY SATURN

Ambitious for leadership. Often stern and impersonal. Interested in money and personal success. The women can make money through friendly relations and the power of their personality. Apt to marry those with good financial background. Can commercialize their own abilities. Interested in large organizations and want big returns. Jealous. Hysterical when emotionally aroused. Love art and beauty as collectors but must employ others to judge it. Too possessive.

EIGHT OF HEARTS–PLANETARY SEQUENCE OF PERSONAL RELATIONSHIPS

Horizontal Line

SIX OF CLUBS–MERCURY CARD IN THE SATURN LINE

For the best results, this is a working relationship—good communications; therefore, preferably a mental or professional field. It may seem, at times, that you are always encouraging them—emotionally carrying them—but this is not necessarily true. You could be more of a burden to them than they to you. Enjoy the relationship and don't expect them to be so perfect. They're very bright people and you will recognize and appreciate if you try.

Six of Clubs birthdates: March 30, April 28, May 26, June 24, July 22, August 20, September 18, October 16, November 14, December 12.

SIX OF SPADES–VENUS CARD IN THE URANUS LINE

You will be more attracted to this Six card but these natives will give you more problems in the long run. You lead much too active a life to bring them real happiness. It may seem great to you both at first but a closer look will reveal two very different life-styles. Tread easy in this relationship before serious thoughts of spending any length of time together; for whatever purpose, get to know the person behind the card.

Six of Spades birthdates: January 8, February 6, March 4, April 2.

QUEEN OF HEARTS–MARS CARD IN THE NEPTUNE LINE

This is a highly physical involvement and you will always feel something emotional about this native. If you are a woman and this card is a man, you will be too powerful and sometimes too scatterbrained for him to cope with. If you are a man and this card is a woman, you have a better chance. However, your Queen of Hearts will fall from her pedestal (where you have put her), and it still won't work out like the storybook ending you might have projected. In both sexes, this card will stimulate you, get some energy working—probably in an area such as psychic phenomena, metaphysics, etc., among others. In any event, you should have a good time together.

Queen of Hearts birthdates: July 29, August 27, September 25, October 23, November 21, December 19.

TEN OF CLUBS–JUPITER CARD IN THE MARS LINE

These natives can be of great benefit to you as colleagues, teachers, close, personal friends. Knowledge that you seek can be acquired directly or indirectly through these people. Good mental rapport, conversations, etc. If you are truly fair with a Ten of Clubs, this could be the romantic relationship that has seemed always to escape you. Put your best foot forward and keep it there. Only good can come from this involvement.

Ten of Clubs birthdates: January 30, February 28, March 26, April 24, May 22, June 20, July 18, August 16, September 14, October 12, November 10, December 8.

EIGHT OF DIAMONDS–SATURN CARD IN THE JUPITER LINE
(Crown Line on the Vertical Line)

There will always be a double emphasis in your relationship with this person. Hopefully, romance will not be one of them. But since there is the karmic tie, don't bet that it won't be romance. It's better for you both if it isn't. In one way or another, you are dealing with two things with this card. Responsibility to this person or learning something from him. Or both. Meet them on equal ground—remember, you are both Eights.

Eight of Diamonds birthdates: January 19, February 17, March 15, April 13, May 11, June 9, July 7, August 5, September 3, October 1.

KING OF SPADES–URANUS CARD IN THE SATURN LINE

This card can affect you in two ways, also, but two entirely different ways. With your own interest (whether slight or driving) in the realm of spiritualism, this native could become a guru or a flag-waving fanatic in your life. In either case, you will learn and be able to disseminate the information for your own use. Listen to these natives, they always have something to say.

King of Spades birthdate: January 1.

THREE OF HEARTS—NEPTUNE CARD IN THE MERCURY LINE

A friend. (Perhaps even a quick romance, but not recommended.) As a friend, be prepared to listen to their romantic problems that can change with the weather. The best advice you can give them when they are emotionally involved with someone (at any level) is that they should try not to pick the other person apart so much. This is the basic root problem of their romantic quests. If the relationship of the Three of Hearts (and someone else) seems to work, encourage them to try it out, overlooking the minor irritations that may turn out to be unimportant after all.

Three of Hearts birthdates: November 30, December 28.

Vertical Line

SEVEN OF SPADES—URANUS LINE
(Eight of Hearts Displacement Card)

The lack of compatibility between Spades and Hearts (mentioned earlier) could lead from a level of good communication to a spiritual conflict that may seem to you to be a burden. They are friendly, but not as much of a party person as you. Use the understanding you inherently have and you could find this relationship extremely fulfilling. Try to avoid romantic tendencies, if they exist, as it may seem as if you are in competition with each other.

Seven of Spades birthdates: January 7, February 5, March 3, April 1.

THREE OF SPADES—SATURN LINE

You cannot help but feel an attraction for this native, almost as if you've met them someplace before. However, don't get too excited. If it's romance, you're apt to have a mate who will tend to be on the sickly side, which you will be able to cope with; however, you may not be able to cope with the pessimistic attitude that may have created the illness in the first place. On first meeting, you will both feel a tendency to do something together—immediately—whether it's planning to go to an event, to simply meet again, or even to fall in love. Resist the latter and take a little more time. Give yourselves a chance. And the chance is that the relationship will probably not work out.

Three of Spades birthdates: January 11, February 9, March 7, April 5, May 3, June 1.

Eights

TEN OF DIAMONDS—JUPITER LINE

If you've ever met a businessman you like and respect for his ability but are sometimes irritated by his methods, he may turn out to be this card. At least, this is how you may react to him. This native can stimulate you and aggravate you at the same time, but the end results in retrospect will always be good. Marriage might be too difficult with a Ten of Diamonds for you, but don't overlook the possibility of any other kind of association, if for no other reason than it could be highly profitable.

Ten of Diamonds birthdates: January 17, February 15, March 13, April 11, May 9, June 7, July 5, August 3, September 1.

FOUR OF CLUBS—MARS LINE

The two of you should really be able to get it together. Watch out for those little explosions that may happen with this combination and remember the good things while you're thinking of the bad. When you're fighting for that principle, ask yourself if you are behaving maturely. You may not have to, on the other hand. A true Four of Clubs will have told you so already (which, incidentally, may create even more immaturity on your part). Approach this relationship straight on—it could really happen for you.

Four of Clubs birthdates: April 30, May 28, June 26, July 24, August 22, September 20, October 18, November 16, December 14.

JACK OF HEARTS—VENUS LINE

Don't try to have romance here—no matter how important you feel the vibrations may be. This person could also be a drain on your natural juices in a straight friendship relationship. You may not be able to escape some kind of involvement—but the lighter you keep it, the better it'll be for you. And, the more you can truly enjoy a Jack of Hearts.

Jack of Hearts birthdates: July 30, August 28, September 26, October 24, November 22, December 20.

TEN OF SPADES—MERCURY LINE

Your busy life will more than intrigue these natives. They will grab onto you like a dog on a bone, and the relationship can be excellent for love or friendship, especially if you are both interested in spiritual knowledge. Give them lots of love—you have it and they not only want it, but have the capacity to return it to you.

Ten of Spades birthdates: January 4, February 2.

EIGHT OF DIAMONDS—NEPTUNE CARD: SEE HORIZONTAL LINE

Diagonal Lines

NINE OF DIAMONDS—URANUS AND MARS LINES

If this person doesn't give to you so that you can take as well as give, take a pass on the relationship. You won't have the fun with the Nine of Diamonds that you can have with others, but your finances can be a little more stable and you will probably appreciate the different roles they can play with others.

Nine of Diamonds birthdates: January 18, February 16, March 14, April 12, May 10, June 8, July 6, August 4, September 2.

FIVE OF HEARTS—SATURN AND VENUS LINES

Yes, this is love. But you will never know where you stand with this individual. You will even enjoy this particular side of this native's personality and, probably without knowing it or understanding it. Look to the more positive side. This native is not for you. They tend to fluctuate in their personal feelings about romance, and you are really quite a homebody. Do your best to not get too involved—even when it is so tempting.

Five of Hearts birthdates: October 30, November 28, December 26.

SIX OF DIAMONDS—JUPITER AND MERCURY LINES

Your natural attitude will be to attempt to guide these natives so they are not leaping in and out of job situations or any other type of involvement where they have first not prepared themselves. Again, pass on the relationship, if possible.

Six of Diamonds birthdates: January 21, February 19, March 17, April 15, May 13, June 11, July 9, August 7, September 5, October 3, November 1.

TWO OF CLUBS—URANUS AND SATURN LINES

This is not a good relationship for you. They will tend to put down the things you are most interested in and attempt to turn your good nature into a subservient role. And you both will probably be very childish towards each other. Obviously not a recommended involvement.

Two of Clubs birthdates: May 30, June 28, July 26, August 24, September 22, October 20, November 18, December 16.

SEVEN OF CLUBS—SATURN AND URANUS LINES

Another poor relationship, unless the two people involved are highly evolved, and then, at best, it can be difficult. You may find inspiration to accomplish things through this native but you are already so involved with projects and people, don't take on something new too readily.

Seven of Clubs birthdates: March 29, April 27, May 25, June 23, July 21, August 19, September 17, October 15, November 13, December 11.

ACE OF DIAMONDS—JUPITER AND NEPTUNE LINES

You will find an attraction here but ultimately you will know that this native is probably where you were—five years ago. This won't always be the case, so take the time to check the person out. But don't think in terms of marriage.

Ace of Diamonds birthdates: January 26, February 24, March 22, April 20, May 18, June 16, July 14, August 12, September 10, October 8, November 6, December 4.

EIGHT OF HEARTS FAMOUS BIRTHDATES

August 31	James Coburn
	Arthur Godfrey
	Buddy Hackett
	Fredric March
	William Saroyan
September 29	Michelangelo
	Gene Autry
	Stanley Kramer
October 27	Theodore Roosevelt
	Dylan Thomas
November 25	Joe DiMaggio
	Ricardo Montalban
	Andrew Carnegie
December 23	José Greco
	Paul Hornung
	J. Arthur Rank

Eight of Clubs

Clubs — Knowledge
Eight of Clubs — Power in Knowledge
Eight in Clubs — Material Mastery through the Power of the Mind

The Neptune Card in the Mars Line. **No Displacement.** This is one of the Fixed Cards and remains in the same position in both the Mundane and the Natural Spreads.

Neptune holds the key to this card and the Mars conjunction either sharpens its power value or destroys it.

The mixture of mental strength, spiritual awareness, psychic power, and powerful emotions is sometimes too much for these people to handle and dire confusion is the result. When the psychic power is extreme (as in some cases), unless great care is taken for protection, they become fields for possible invasion. They should strive at all times for mental balance and not allow their emotions, their fixed ideas or tendencies to temperament to dominate them. The charts (astrological and numerological) of the children of these dates should be carefully studied for any mental support along practical lines, and these points strengthened in the early years. There is no finer material to be found anywhere than in the Eight of Clubs equipment, but it must be guarded and guided.

If the Eight of Clubs doesn't use its ability to acquire knowledge and fulfill its mission with this, it becomes a scattering card—someone who goes through life and doesn't accomplish much. A Sagittarian Eight of Clubs should use this knowledge, because the Jupiter involvement is more pronounced than it

Planetary Sequence

			K♠	8♦	10♣			
A♠	3♦	5♣	10♠	Q♣	A♣	3♥		Mercury
2♥	9♠	9♣	J♥	5♠	7♦	7♥		Venus
8♣	J♠	2♦	4♣	6♥	K♦	K♥		Mars
A♦	A♥	8♠	10♦	10♥	4♠	6♦		Jupiter
Neptune	Uranus	Saturn	Jupiter	Mars	Venus	Mercury		
5♦	7♣	9♥	3♠	3♣	5♥	Q♦		Saturn
J♦	K♣	2♣	7♠	9♦	J♣	Q♠		Uranus
Q♥	6♠	6♣	8♥	2♠	4♦	4♥		Neptune
Neptune	Uranus	Saturn	Jupiter	Mars	Venus	Mercury		

Mundane Spread

would be with a Scorpio Eight of Clubs. Both would have a different approach and the drive would be of a different type. However, the Sagittarian Eight of Clubs can do a great deal of work, and can be one of the highest paid in their field of work.

Set principles and fixed mental attitudes have been brought over and from these they cannot be swerved. When they are able to clarify their objectives, they always go straight toward them—and attain them. Through the power of knowledge, which is their heritage, they can overcome any obstacle and attain any desire. Their entire Planetary Sequence is in the Jupiter Line and protection surrounds them in all departments of life.

Being a member of the Trinity of Fixed Cards, they are allied with the wisdom of the King of Spades and the sacrifice of the Jack of Hearts. They, too, are on the cross—as is often verified in their emotional lives.

The majority have an avid desire for knowledge and allow nothing to interfere with its pursuit. They have come to teach and they intend to equip themselves for it. They work better with large groups than with individuals or small circles. The greater numbers seem to generate additional power.

If they form any alliance with the Jack of Hearts or the King of Spades, or become attached to any natives of these birthdates, an expansive force is produced that is far-reaching and cannot be broken.

They should adhere strictly to their own Birth Card and never attempt to operate under the personality; if they do, they lose much of their power.

On the negative side, these people may not only amount to nothing whatsoever, but they may have no awareness of the extent of their influence or the power invested in them. On the destructive side, they can, if they choose, reverse this power and become black magicians.

Eights of Clubs have power in the overcoming of things. These people have healing ability. If they are sick, it can be emotional, due to overwork or overactivity. They have an excellent recuperative ability. There is no reason for any Eight of Clubs not to overcome any situation he is wrestling with. This is a spiritual card; this is a power card, and it can work physically on the material plane, as well.

Unless very strong and sure of themselves, they should avoid psychic phenomena. They are actually in close touch with the higher planes and have no concern with the astral. Danger lies there—with the possibility of invasion. They have been given an important commission and must adhere to it.

BIRTHDATES RULED BY THE EIGHT OF CLUBS

MARCH 28—ARIES—RULED BY MARS

Impulsive and dynamic. Lack vision and seldom stop to consider the final results of their actions. Argumentative—often quarrelsome. Have capacity for deep affection—and need it—but are undiplomatic and unintentionally inconsiderate. Impatient with stupidity. Always disturbed emotionally. Succeed best with men—in politics, law, partnerships, that involve questions of judgment. Very restless and "Martian." May be gifted in art or music, but better suited for business.

APRIL 26—TAURUS—RULED BY VENUS

Build constructively for the future. Desire a home and will work for it. Want to stand well with others and are disturbed by inharmony. Often marry for money for the sake of security. Generous if they have the means. Prefer connection with large enterprises: manufacturing, banking, produce merchandising. Are often artists or musicians and if they lack talent for success, still want the outlet and take it up as a hobby. Can succeed also in the educational field and welfare projects.

MAY 24—GEMINI—RULED BY MERCURY

Interested in people and curious about them. Experimental and brilliant, sometimes erratic and wholly irresponsible. Natural gamblers because interested in results but seldom win. If willing to cultivate a sense of responsibility and conquer the tendency to scatter their forces, can become great teachers, leaders, preachers, and arbitrators. The women like to establish "salons" and bring noted people together.

JUNE 22—GEMINI OR CANCER—RULED BY MERCURY OR THE MOON

This birthdate usually falls in Cancer, but may occur in the last degree of Gemini. Seldom find themselves until middle life. In the early years are undecided and vacillating. When settled in a career are eager to impart their knowledge to others. Must exercise self-discipline and cultivate emotional stability. Can succeed in medicine, nursing or any line that improves the physical condition. Keenly mental and intuitive. Women succeed well with home economics, dress shops (or dressmaking), or teaching. In both sexes, the gift for writing may be outstanding.

JULY 20—CANCER—RULED BY THE MOON

Successful in public life and humanitarian works. May get into a rut through laziness. Can become leaders in politics or religion. Are patient and make successful teachers of children, especially in domestic relations. Interested in child welfare and reform. If musically talented, can commercialize it. Give good advice but don't follow it themselves.

AUGUST 18—LEO—RULED BY THE SUN

Have a great drive for power and the limelight. Must be at the head of own business; cannot work for others. May become famous in their chosen line.

Successful in connection with banking, administration of wills and trusts, management of others' money, etc. Good executives and also good agents and solicitors. Should strive to be less materialistic and acquisitive. Move rapidly. Should guard against accidents, especially of the head and back. Have good recuperative powers.

SEPTEMBER 16—VIRGO—RULED BY MERCURY

A teacher's card. Must be sure of their objectives; otherwise become confused or aimless. A Karmic birth number; must be willing to give service. Often drawn to some form of religion. May have real talent but seldom get due recognition during their lifetime. Marriage may be a limitation; often have an unsympathetic partner who shakes their self-confidence, perhaps unconsciously. Are too easily suppressed. If not able to express themselves, may develop chronic illnesses, psychological or physical. Should cultivate faith in themselves. When positive, are excellent writers, investigators, scientists, statesmen.

OCTOBER 14—LIBRA—RULED BY VENUS

Good disposition and adaptable; will compromise for peace—often at the expense of their own power. Very self-indulgent and self-protective. Interested in the home more than in their own mental development. Too apt to live on the lower plane and take the easiest way. If developed, are good promoters, writers, actors, and directors. Clever at designing small articles for decoration or adornment. Always present a good appearance and like to be admired. Are affectionate and persuasive; can always extricate themselves from a difficult situation. Like to take a chance but too timid for any heavy gambling. Money is very important but they can manage with little.

NOVEMBER 12—SCORPIO—RULED BY MARS

A detective's card. Can ferret out secrets and discover the trouble at the roots. Always know when people are lying. Work best in groups but must be given a free rein in their own department. Active in achieving their own ends and must avoid working from motives of expediency. Good advertisers, soap-box orators. Feel strongly on all subjects. Are determined and persistent. Are critical within but have a friendly manner and are highly magnetic. Often have a healing gift. Interested in metaphysics, science, medicine, drugs, etc. Not good enemies but are loyal friends.

DECEMBER 10—SAGITTARIUS—RULED BY JUPITER

Interested in business on a large scale; not adapted for small enterprises. Must have authority, and will not be questioned. Should guard against self-importance. Are closely connected with money and have a good earning capacity; will make money or inherit it. Can commercialize any talent. Are sensitive and intuitional—often psychic. Highly nervous. Inclined to religion and philosophy. Usually are aware of their destiny—to give out the knowledge they have acquired. Good lawyers and teachers. Too blunt and opinionated for diplomacy.

EIGHT OF CLUBS–PLANETARY SEQUENCE OF PERSONAL RELATIONSHIPS

Horizontal Line–Jupiter

SIX OF DIAMONDS–MERCURY CARD IN THE MERCURY LINE
Good communications. Take care in how you phrase your words—the Six of Diamonds can learn a great deal from you; it's up to you to help him understand. Too mercurial for an intense relationship of any kind.
Six of Diamonds birthdates: January 21, February 19, March 17, April 15, May 13, June 11, July 9, August 7, September 5, October 3, November 1

FOUR OF SPADES–VENUS CARD IN THE VENUS LINE
Love, romance, friendship, business. All are good with this Card. Respect his opinions as much as you do your own and you'll always find happiness with the Four of Spades.
Four of Spades birthdates: January 10, February 8, March 6, April 4, May 2

TEN OF HEARTS–MARS CARD IN THE MARS LINE
A personal romantic involvement with this native is a definite probability but don't be too disappointed when the party's over. He can be a stimulating friend but not necessarily a good husband or wife. Enjoy the Ten of Hearts for the moment, and don't think about the future.
Ten of Hearts birthdates: July 31, August 29, September 27, October 25, November 23, December 21

TEN OF DIAMONDS–JUPITER CARD IN THE JUPITER LINE
Good business relationship; all other involvements possible and probable. You'll appreciate and enjoy knowing a Ten of Diamonds. Not dynamic in love.
Ten of Diamonds birthdates: January 17, February 15, March 13, April 11, May 9, June 7, July 5, August 3, September 1

EIGHT OF SPADES—SATURN CARD IN THE SATURN LINE

Any relationship with this Card could be a Karmic responsibility. Excellent as your doctor or in other areas of healing. A good friend who will feel equally good about you. Probably too difficult for a close involvement.

Eight of Spades birthdates: January 6, February 4, March 2

ACE OF HEARTS—URANUS CARD IN THE URANUS LINE
(Jupiter and Uranus Lines on the Diagonal)

You'll understand this native but not necessarily want to spend a lot of time around him. His personal desires won't seem to be too important to you, even though you'll enjoy the little surprises he is capable of creating.

Ace of Hearts birthdate: December 30

ACE OF DIAMONDS—NEPTUNE CARD IN THE NEPTUNE LINE
(Jupiter Line on the Vertical)

You may never completely understand the motivations of this Card. When it seems to be one thing, it could be another. A frustrating relationship if on a day-to-day basis.

Ace of Diamonds birthdates: January 26, February 24, March 22, April 20, May 18, June 16, July 14, August 12, September 10, October 8, November 6, December 4

Vertical Line—Neptune

TWO OF HEARTS—VENUS LINE

A quick involvement that will not turn out to be what you may have thought it was. Not an impossible relationship, but improbable.

Two of Hearts birthdate: December 29

ACE OF SPADES—MERCURY LINE

You'll be forever trying to convince this native of everything but don't stop answering their questions; they need information and you have some of it. Romance could bring problems; you may feel worlds apart.

Ace of Spades birthdates: January 13, February 11, March 9, April 7, May 5, June 3, July 1

QUEEN OF HEARTS—NEPTUNE LINE

A happy person who can bring a great deal of love into your life. If on a daily basis, it may require a lot of understanding on both sides. Outcome can be most beneficial on all levels.

Queen of Hearts birthdates: July 29, August 27, September 25, October 23, November 21, December 19

JACK OF DIAMONDS—URANUS LINE

A good business relationship but try to prepare for the unexpected ups and downs. Love possible but confusing; business best.

Jack of Diamonds birthdates: January 16, February 14, March 12, April 10, May 8, June 6, July 4, August 2

FIVE OF DIAMONDS—SATURN LINE

Goals are too different to keep you interested for long. Don't get romantically involved. A good employee for you.

Five of Diamonds birthdates: January 22, February 20, March 18, April 16, May 14, June 12, July 10, August 8, September 6, October 4, November 2

ACE OF DIAMONDS—JUPITER LINE: SEE HORIZONTAL LINE

Diagonal Lines

NINE OF SPADES—VENUS AND URANUS LINES

The more you get to know about this native, the more you will like him. Help keep him on a positive plane and any kind of relationship can work to the advantage of you both.

Nine of Spades birthdates: January 5, February 3, March 1

FIVE OF CLUBS—MERCURY AND SATURN LINES

A difficult involvement but Karmic. High in conversation but too changeable for your own knowledge. Don't make too great an effort or you could find a handful of problems as your reward.

Five of Clubs birthdates: March 31, April 29, May 27, June 25, July 23, August 21, September 19, October 17, November 15, December 13

EIGHT OF DIAMONDS—CROWN AND JUPITER LINES

A beneficial relationship if you don't lock horns. You have the power to understand this native so the degree of the involvement is up to you.

Eight of Diamonds birthdates: January 19, February 17, March 15, April 13, May 11, June 9, July 7, August 5, September 3, October 1

ACE OF HEARTS—JUPITER AND URANUS LINES: SEE HORIZONTAL LINE

Your Place in the Cards

NINE OF HEARTS—DOUBLE SATURN LINES

Extremely difficult personal involvement and should be avoided. Business and friendship are not recommended on a close basis; a burden to you if you permit him to be.

Nine of Hearts birthdates: August 30, September 28, October 26, November 24, December 22

SEVEN OF SPADES—URANUS AND JUPITER LINES

A stimulating friendship; good on metaphysical plane. You'll find good rapport—someone whom you'll respect. Enjoy the relationship.

Seven of Spades birthdates: January 7, February 5, March 3, April 1

TWO OF SPADES—NEPTUNE AND MARS LINES

Too fearful and irritating. Not a good relationship for anything other than friendship and then probably too frustrating. Better avoided.

Two of Spades birthdates: January 12, February 10, March 8, April 6, May 4, June 2

EIGHT OF CLUBS FAMOUS BIRTHDATES

March 28	Edward Anhalt
	Raphael
April 26	Carol Burnett
May 24	Bob Dylan
	Queen Victoria
July 20	Natalie Wood
August 18	Roberto Clemente
	Shelley Winters
September 16	Lauren Bacall
	Peter Falk
October 14	Dwight D. Eisenhower
November 12	Kim Hunter
	Grace Kelly
December 10	Chet Huntley
	Edith L. Randall

Eight of Diamonds

Diamonds — Values
Eight of Diamonds — Substantial Success
Eight in Diamonds — Material Control

The Central Card in the Crown Line. Displaces the **Queen of Spades** in the Natural Spread.

All Eights are power, but it is the Eight of Diamonds that surpasses the others in *material* power. Its position in the Crown Line not only denotes its high calling but endows it with greater freedom of choice than is possessed by any of the cards below that line. All the Crown Cards are granted Movable Choice and can operate in any position that best suits their requirements. This freedom makes the Eight of Diamonds people very independent—at times domineering and exacting. The displacement of the Queen of Spades only increases this tendency, for the Queen of Spades natives, while willing to work and to serve, are always conscious of their position of rulership.

The face arrangement of all Eights denotes balance; again the Eight of Diamonds surpasses the rest by being in the exact center at the top. The sense of balance is naturally directed to values and they usually know when and what to buy and what it is worth, exactly.

The Eight of Diamonds has a responsibility in any field that the native works in. On the material level, the card has a terrific drive for power in its own particular field, that furthers its own interests. Spiritually, they are concerned with groups, gatherings. As in all cases, their power is used or misused. They can be philanthropic or mercenary, benefactors or misers, universal minded or self-servers. When they choose to operate negatively, the

Planetary Sequence

		K♠ Mercury	8♦	10♣			
A♠	3♦ Neptune	5♣ Uranus	10♠ Saturn	Q♣ Jupiter	A♣ Mars	3♥ Venus	Mercury
2♥	9♠	9♣	J♥	5♠	7♦	7♥	Venus
8♣	J♠	2♦	4♣	6♥	K♠	K♥	Mars
A♦	A♥	8♠	10♦	10♥	4♠	6♦	Jupiter
5♦	7♣	9♥	3♠	3♣	5♥	Q♦	Saturn
J♦	K♣	2♠	7♠	9♦	J♣	Q♠	Uranus
Q♥	6♠	6♣	8♥	2♠	4♦	4♥	Neptune
Neptune	Uranus	Saturn	Jupiter	Mars	Venus	Mercury	

Mundane Spread

inevitable result is suffering and tragedy. For many, the requirement is too exacting—or it may be unrecognized. They may not know that their Birth Card is the Sun Card and that they are direct emissaries of the Central Sun. But the soul knows, and if they take the time and trouble to become acquainted with their own souls, they will be told.

They are the manifestation of the creative principle, closely associated with the Resurrection and the certainty of rebirth. Theirs is the gift of sublimation; theirs the ability to overcome all obstacles and conquer all enemies. The majority is well aware of the heavy responsibilities and is willing to discharge them. If this is not realized in youth, recognition comes after thirty-six. As a rule, trust and confidence may be freely given them. They are wise guardians of the goods of the dead, and wise conservers of the interests of the living. They will serve honestly and faithfully, often at their own expense.

Any person who is the Eight of Diamonds must realize that the potential is strictly on the spiritual level. Crown Cards have a responsibility to the Universe and anyone who has these cards in their Spreads as well as being born here, have to accept this responsibility. They can't compromise with anything short of Divine Protection. They cannot compromise with anything short of service rendered, through the Queen of Spades in the Natural Spread. Not as pettiness, selfishness, but as the Universal Mother.

All Eights of Diamonds aspire to attain a certain place in life. If it is all materialistic, then it is going to be wrought with turmoil. Eight of Diamonds men marry women who have money. They are attracted to women who have a certain type of mentality. Women Eights of Diamonds are affected differently. If they go into business for themselves, they usually wind up with a manager who is technically smarter than they are. They can specialize in some specific field and use this knowledge to good advantage. An Eight of Diamonds man who marries a Queen of Clubs woman, could be dominated by his wife. He might not be sure of this relationship, but the tendency would be that the woman would be just as powerful in her activities as the man. And, if the man marries a woman who was smarter than he, then it could create uncertainty. Invariably, both sexes of Eight of Diamonds marry more than once.

The main pitfalls are love of power and a certain ruthlessness in exercising it, and love of the money that enhances it. The Eight of Diamonds can be very materialistic; money can be very important; they want the comforts of living and they want to be looked up to. They may be thrown completely off balance by worshiping the Golden Calf, forget their obligations, spend the inheritance entrusted to them and swiftly accomplish their own downfall and disgrace. "Those who rise high, fall hard." Their place is already high—and they have the strength in their wings to keep them there.

To fulfill their destiny, they need not be financial magnates or kings in industry. They may be the mother who sacrifices, the teacher who opens doors of understanding, or the professional man who helps the client in need—without pay.

BIRTHDATES RULED BY THE EIGHT OF DIAMONDS

JANUARY 19–CAPRICORN–RULED BY SATURN
The women are successful managers of home and family; can always make both ends meet. In any occupation, efficiency is stressed. Ambitious to be the best of their kind. Men succeed as heads of their own business. Often choose merchandising that furnishes supplies for scientists or professionals. A karmic number. Must be strictly just and fair. Not always satisfied in the personal life. Unusual streak of poetry and mysticism for Capricorn. Have high ideals.

FEBRUARY 17–AQUARIUS–RULED BY URANUS
Original methods in business or profession. Full of unusual ideas. Intuitive and inventive. Always mental in attitude. Usually have a strong inclination to religion—their own brand. Believe in universal good will. If operating negatively, can be cruel and vindictive. Succeed as writers, scientists, managers of large enterprises. Want an unlimited field to work in.

MARCH 15–PISCES–RULED BY NEPTUNE
Mystical, idealistic. Are devoted and self-sacrificing. Should avoid being too secretive. Make good confidants, investigators, executives in institutions for the sick, afflicted, or criminal. Can develop psychic gifts to a marked extent. Have a protective attitude toward humanity. Good writers, producers, government officials.

APRIL 13–ARIES–RULED BY MARS
Eager to express views and opinions. Want to be out in front as leaders of the people. Should avoid blustering and riding roughshod over those of divergent beliefs. Very curious about public reactions. Self-promotive and not always able to properly evaluate their mission. Work hard for a while, then give up. If the interests are universal, can become great. Succeed as merchants, public leaders, surgeons, publishers.

MAY 11–TAURUS–RULED BY VENUS
Not always sure of their objectives so should have them clearly defined and work toward them. Naturally skeptical. Home harmony essential; need support. Must cultivate faith in others. Attracted to stage—music or acting. Have real religious inclination, of which they are often unaware. Apt to be influenced by personalities in their environment. Should have the courage to pursue and adhere to own principles. Self-indulgence and desire for protection makes them weak and useless.

JUNE 9–GEMINI–RULED BY MERCURY

Undecided and vacillating before thirty-six. Ability for success, but must be allowed to express their ideals or they will go along with the easiest way. Personal responsibilities should not be assumed before they have found themselves. Naturally idealistic and philanthropic but are blocked by an eye for expediency. Fine legal minds. Need people, variety, some travel, and enough cooperation to boost their self-confidence. Make good lawyers, journalists, public officials, counselors. May be too procrastinating for own good. Must stress truth in all dealings.

JULY 7–CANCER–RULED BY THE MOON

Concerned with public welfare and will work for conservation of civic and national interests. Propaganda writers, philosophers, producers. Make good government officials if not too involved in politics. Self-protective materially but have a strong streak of spirituality. The emotions are influenced and happiness determined by home harmony. Should cultivate people of strength and determination. Too irresolute.

AUGUST 5–LEO–RULED BY THE SUN

This is the most positive of the Eight of Diamonds and the most successful in the eyes of the public. Can always make money and manage to keep it better than the others. May be mercenary. On the alert for a favorable deal. Need contacts and are strongly attracted to the stage or films. Successful writers, salesmen, attorneys, and "top" diplomats. Count much on appearance.

SEPTEMBER 3–VIRGO–RULED BY MERCURY

Willing to help others and are helped by them. Uncertain in own beliefs but apparently fixed and stubborn. Good brief writers, technicians, scientists —especially botany and zoology. May not rise above a clerical position unless very well educated. Good accountants, telegraph operators, analysts. Often attracted to law but need special training in effectiveness and public speaking.

OCTOBER 1–LIBRA–RULED BY VENUS

Strong religious tendencies, with a metaphysical trend. Often psychic. Like to dramatize their abilities. Need an appreciative audience. Confused by home problems. Nervous. Skeptical of others' motives. Inclined to independence, but work best with cooperation. Like to lead groups, conduct classes, appear on platforms. Have pleasing personalities and make good ambassadors. May have musical talent but better conductors than performers.

Your Place in the Cards

EIGHT OF DIAMONDS—PLANETARY SEQUENCE OF PERSONAL RELATIONSHIPS

Horizontal Line

KING OF SPADES—MERCURY CARD IN THE SATURN LINE

A problem for you if you are involved in any kind of personal association: business, romance, and even friendship. Too stubborn and unwilling to bend to your way of thinking (and sometimes to anyone else's as well). Communications are good, but burdensome. You probably have very little in common other than the ability to control (or be in control of) groups of people. This would be a collision if you are in the same group. Avoid the relationship except as a listener. They have much to say and you can only profit by their words.

King of Spades birthdate: January 1.

THREE OF HEARTS—VENUS CARD IN THE MERCURY LINE

An attraction and understanding, but a short-termed involvement if romantic. Friendship can be more profitable for you both—business should not be considered unless this native works for you in a public contact situation. Don't always take what they have to say as gospel, but do always understand the make-up of the person—from an impersonal association.

Three of Hearts birthdates: November 30, December 28.

ACE OF CLUBS—MARS CARD IN THE VENUS LINE

If you meet this native at a party you'll be hoping that you see each other again. A strong physical attraction; good communications and a glimmer of the potentiality of romance. The native will not measure up to what you think you are looking for, but enjoy the relationship—just don't get married. Good for friendship, business—but not marriage.

Ace of Clubs birthdates: May 31, June 29, July 27, August 25, September 23, October 21, November 19, December 17.

QUEEN OF CLUBS—JUPITER CARD IN THE MARS LINE

(Mercury and Mars Lines on the Vertical Line)

A good friendship, a good rapport (most of the time). Irritating at times because of an imaginary brick wall that seems to keep the two of you from thinking similarly. Don't dwell on this. A good overall relationship with overtones of romance, which shouldn't be overlooked.

Queen of Clubs birthdates: January 28, February 26, March 24, April 22, May 20, June 18, July 16, August 14, September 12, October 10, November 8, December 6.

TEN OF SPADES—SATURN CARD IN THE JUPITER LINE
(Mercury Line on the Vertical Line)

An unavoidable relationship on some level—probably work. Not always to your liking, but you'll feel as if you have the upper hand. This card is good for you, listen to what they have to say and use it in a positive fashion. Try not to get personally involved on any level—it could prove to be a trying situation for you.

Ten of Spades birthdates: January 4, February 2.

FIVE OF CLUBS—URANUS CARD IN THE SATURN LINE
(Mercury and Saturn Lines on the Diagonal Line)

A relationship that will intrigue you; someone you will find interesting and conversational—but unattractive because they seemingly cannot add anything to your way of life. Too restless and unpredictable for your ambitions. Keep the involvement on an impersonal level and you will enjoy it more.

Five of Clubs birthdates: March 31, April 29, May 27, June 25, July 23, August 21, September 19, October 17, November 15, December 13.

THREE OF DIAMONDS—NEPTUNE CARD IN THE URANUS LINE

A very positive and outgoing person. You may have difficulty in understanding their motivations, and it may not be necessary to understand. These people do things for people not only out of monetary gain, but for personal pleasure as well—so enjoy the involvement at whatever level. A native to surely keep you guessing, but not probable for a close, personal or romantic involvement.

Three of Diamonds birthdates: January 24, February 22, March 20, April 18, May 16, June 14, July 12, August 10, September 8, October 6, November 4, December 2.

Vertical Line

EIGHT OF HEARTS—NEPTUNE LINE

Good communications—the ability to keep up with you intellectually. You'll never quite know where they are mentally, and, depending on your own frame of mind, whether they are illusion or disillusion. A lively companion who will keep things and people moving; action in many different areas but don't look for the "growing old together"—it's doubtful with this native, unless you can maintain the intellectual side.

Eight of Hearts birthdates: August 31, September 29, October 27, November 25, December 23.

SEVEN OF SPADES—URANUS LINE

An unusual kind of romantic relationship if you both work at it. In the beginning, you may have to have more understanding than this native because of material problems, but most rewarding in later years. Not only love but spiritual development and expression will become a part of your lives together, if developed. Good for friendship and business, if you can help them to overcome their worries about things that may never happen.

Seven of Spades birthdates: January 7, February 5, March 3, April 1.

THREE OF SPADES–SATURN LINE

A difficult relationship on any level—too negative and too anxious for your way of thinking. A possible sexual attraction for opposite sexes but very short-lived. Don't put any time or effort into an involvement; it will probably prove not to be worth it.

Three of Spades birthdates: January 11, February 9, March 7, April 5, May 3, June 1.

TEN OF DIAMONDS–JUPITER LINE

The best possible business relationship that you will ever find. Definitely on the material plane, and successful in almost everything they do. They can match your ability in the business world and enhance it. Don't miss the opportunity. A possible romance, and probable friendship as well. Pursue the involvement on any level.

Ten of Diamonds birthdates: January 17 February 15, March 13, April 11, May 9, June 7, July 5, August 3, September 1.

FOUR OF CLUBS–MARS LINE

An involvement that will affect your life in some way; a nice person but too verbal about unnecessary things as far as you're concerned. A close involvement will not make you happy and probably will be too irritating to cope with.

Four of Clubs birthdates: April 30, May 28, June 26, July 24, August 22, September 20, October 18, November 16, December 14.

JACK OF HEARTS–VENUS LINE

An attraction, but more admiration than sexual or personal; you'll like their ideas but not want to be a part of them. You'll understand and appreciate their goals but not want to be involved. Friendship is best—anything else could be a waste of your time.

Jack of Hearts birthdates: July 30, August 28, September 26, October 24, November 22, December 20.

TEN OF SPADES–MERCURY LINE: SEE HORIZONTAL LINE

Diagonal Lines

FIVE OF CLUBS–MERCURY AND SATURN LINES:
SEE HORIZONTAL LINE

NINE OF SPADES–VENUS AND URANUS LINES
You could love this native deeply, yet wonder how much longer you will have to hold them up mentally, spiritually, and maybe even physically and financially. When operating positively, you will find this to be one of the best possible romantic situations for you, but be careful about giving in–or letting them give in to some of the day-to-day problems that confront them. Give them courage; the relationship could be extremely rewarding for you both.
Nine of Spades birthdates: January 5, February 3, March 1.

EIGHT OF CLUBS–MARS AND NEPTUNE LINES
An equal relationship–someone you may feel capable of conversing with on a seldom-found level of awareness and knowledge. Great, energizing vibrations; keep them all positive. Watch your testy tongue if you feel the native "too knowing" and trying to push off their knowledge on you. You have much to learn from each other and should keep all involvements on a higher level of thinking, and only in a mature fashion. You may not quite understand them and it may not be important–just listen. Business is fine, romance is better forgotten.
Eight of Clubs birthdates: March 28, April 26, May 24, June 22, July 20, August 18, September 16, October 14, November 12, December 10.

QUEEN OF CLUBS–MERCURY AND MARS LINES:
SEE HORIZONTAL LINE

SEVEN OF DIAMONDS–DOUBLE VENUS LINES
Love at first sight could be best described here. This native can do little wrong and the feeling is probably vice versa. A good match, romantically; your needs and wants are very similar. Good for friendship and excellent for business. A don't-miss involvement in any way.
Seven of Diamonds birthdates: January 20, February 18, March 16, April 14, May 12, June 10, July 8, August 6, September 4, October 2.

Your Place in the Cards

KING OF HEARTS—MARS AND MERCURY LINES

There is probably very little that this native can say without irritating you. You have completely different perspectives on life, goals, and desires. A stimulating friend if you both choose to see the good side of things—but not good for business unless this native works for you (and under your jurisdiction). Romance should not be considered; even an eye contact from across the room could prove to be aggravating to you.

King of Hearts birthdates: June 30, July 28, August 26, September 24, October 22, November 20, December 18.

EIGHT OF DIAMONDS FAMOUS BIRTHDATES

January 19	Edgar Allan Poe
	Robert E. Lee
February 17	Marian Anderson
	Harry S. Truman
March 15	Andrew Jackson
April 13	Thomas Jefferson
May 11	Mort Sahl
	Irving Berlin
	Salvador Dali
	Phil Silvers
	Henry Morgenthau
June 9	Robert Cummings
July 7	Marc Chagall
	Vincent Edwards
	Satchel Paige
	Ringo Starr
August 5	Guy de Maupassant
	Isaak Walton
September 3	Allan Ladd
October 1	Julie Andrews
	Richard Harris
	Laurence Harvey

Eight of Spades

Spades — Wisdom, Labor
Eight of Spades — Power in Healing
Eight in Spades — Control in Health and Labor Problems

The Saturn Card in the Jupiter Line. Displaces the **King of Clubs** in the Natural Spread.

Like all Eights, this is a very powerful card, but part of its life spread is under Saturn. The Eight of Spades has the capacity to acquire true wisdom. This is a card of healing and actually the keynote for this card is the overcoming of all problems—through spiritual attainment. The fact that it is the Saturn Card in the Jupiter Line is important because here is an astrological trine of Jupiter and Saturn, which are the two planets of the soul in good aspects to each other.

This is a Card of Overcoming—also a healing card. The tests for these people are many and varied. Never relieved of the pressure from Saturn; duty and responsibility are their daily portion. They keenly sense the obligation to work, and they all work hard, whether or not they know the reason why. When they do know, much of the burden is lightened; when they are unenlightened, they tax health and strength in the drive to get things done. And still another class of these natives, realizing little or nothing besides their innate power, work for the money they can amass and the joy of being big shots on their own level.

The True Place is in the Neptune Line—again in the Saturn position. There is often a conflict between idealism and confusion, with no way out but a sound education and a cultivated understanding.

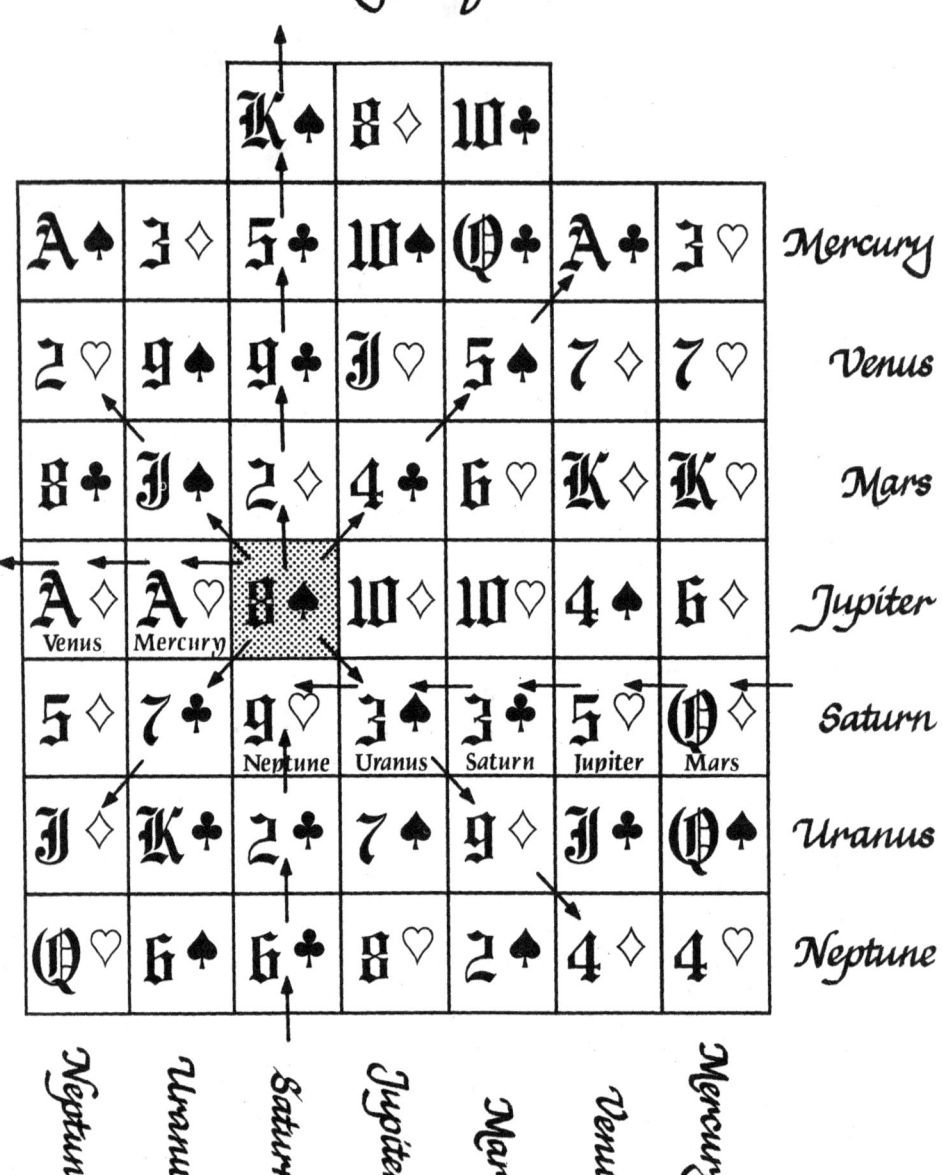

Among the lesser lights, there is a tendency to work under the Personality Card—which invariably detracts from their power. The women especially drift into menial work as the easiest way to provide for their comfort. But they usually do their job efficiently, unless too distracted by various interests outside of it.

There is a constant unrest because no Eights of Spades are ever satisfied with the material things they want. After they get what they want, they always want something else. They never feel contented. Men and women who marry, immediately want to buy a piece of property; they feel that the security they get with the real estate is important to them.

Backed by the Ten of Diamonds (the preceding card), there is often an inheritance from the parents or substantial help from members of the family. But the mother is usually an irritating source to these people. They are excellent "receivers." The women, especially, but both sexes are attracted to those in the professional field. They welcome anything that supports their prestige. Money is the great obstacle to their spiritual growth and, therefore, the source of many of their tests. Through grief, loss, or illness, at some period in their lives—usually late—they are forced to learn values.

The displacement of the King of Clubs affirms that power is increased by the search for knowledge. If early education has been neglected or ignored, these people should make every effort to make up for it by joining study groups, going to night school, or taking correspondence courses—no matter at what age. It is their knowledge and not their money that will enable them to take their place among the high ones.

There is assured success for them in choosing a career that deals with health: nursing, medicine, or the healing arts in the drugless field. Many are attracted to the stage, to education, or to government positions. Among a few, religion is a mania. Spades, in themselves, are cards whereby there is a great deal of mystery. In dealing with an Eight of Spades, this could be especially true. You may spend a great deal of time with an Eight of Spades without actually realizing what type of person he or she really is.

BIRTHDATES RULED BY THE EIGHT OF SPADES

JANUARY 6—CAPRICORN—RULED BY SATURN

Ambitious and materialistic. Must avoid narrow-mindedness and penuriousness. Love of "shining" and importance of place take many into the theater. Better adapted for business, however, and can handle one that is extensive. Successful in dealing with the soil—especially products of the earth after they have become salable. Very patriotic and will work hard for law and principle. Are good government officials—especially if they can give orders.

FEBRUARY 4—AQUARIUS—RULED BY URANUS

Are enthusiastic about progress and advanced methods. Educators and playwrights, full of original and startling ideas. Inventive and intuitive. Discover new techniques and methods. Natural experts in machinery and electricity. Fine aviators.

MARCH 2—PISCES—RULED BY NEPTUNE

Natural benefactors—especially the financiers. The most religious of the Eight of Spades may become fanatics on the subject. Are true seekers of wisdom if at all developed. Willing to serve and sacrifice for humanity. Writers—with a message. Idealistic and poetic. Preachers of the true and the beautiful.

EIGHT OF SPADES—PLANETARY SEQUENCE OF PERSONAL RELATIONSHIPS

Horizontal Line

ACE OF HEARTS—MERCURY CARD IN THE URANUS LINE

Friendship and business only here. This native can initiate new ideas and create an easier atmosphere in your business; good rapport; interested in many of the same things you are, but not on the personal level. An occasional friend or a working companion is best.

Ace of Hearts birthdate: December 30.

ACE OF DIAMONDS—VENUS CARD IN THE NEPTUNE LINE

A possible romance—but not without the problem of communication. Better for friendship if you're not intricately involved and best for business. These natives have the drive to accomplish some of the things you wish you had time to do, providing there is monetary remuneration involved.

Ace of Diamonds birthdates: January 26, February 24, March 22, April 20, May 18, June 16, July 14, August 12, September 10, October 8, November 6, December 4.

QUEEN OF DIAMONDS—MARS CARD IN THE MERCURY LINE

A definite dislike—you probably won't agree with much of anything they say, although you'll understand the whys and wherefores of what they're saying. You may even put up with it for a short time, but this native will not turn you on. Avoid the relationship.

Queen of Diamonds birthdates: January 15, February 13, March 11, April 9, May 7, June 5, July 3, August 1.

FIVE OF HEARTS—JUPITER CARD IN THE VENUS LINE

A romantic or strong friendship attraction that you will undoubtedly pursue, and ultimately will be disappointed. It doesn't have to end that way if you're careful about understanding this native. They want love as much as you, but need a certain amount of freedom with it. Work it out if possible—friendship is good and business is possible if they will put forth the work that is necessary.

Five of Hearts birthdates: October 30, November 28, December 26.

THREE OF CLUBS—SATURN CARD IN THE MARS LINE

Great difficulties in convincing this native of anything, and it may be obligatory that you do. Work it out as easily as possible and then take a pass on any other forms of involvements. Too problematical for a long-term association.

Three of Clubs birthdates: May 29, June 27, July 25, August 23, September 21, October 19, November 17, December 15.

THREE OF SPADES—URANUS CARD IN THE JUPITER LINE

Another Doubting Thomas for you, but not necessarily as unsuccessful. These people could surprise you with unexpected understanding, favors, ideas, all of which could feel rewarding to your gift of time and effort to them. Keep all involvements impersonal for best results.

Three of Spades birthdates: January 11, February 9, March 7, April 5, May 3, June 1.

NINE OF HEARTS—NEPTUNE CARD IN THE SATURN LINE
(Saturn Line on the Vertical Line)

Double emphasis of Neptune and Saturn will create confusing situations in any kind of involvement with this native. You may think they have it together—and then suddenly, without warning, they may appear to be something altogether different. Don't get involved on any level or you may be setting yourself up for disillusionment like you've never experienced before.

Nine of Hearts birthdates: August 30, September 28, October 26, November 24, December 22.

Vertical Line

TWO OF DIAMONDS—MARS LINE

Stimulating conversation is about all you can expect from this native, unless you are both working in the health field as doctors, nurses, etc. You could be a dynamic team and have a working association along these lines. Don't consider anything personal in any case, as it will cause sparks to fly between the two of you and it would be a waste to throw away a perfectly good friendship.

Two of Diamonds birthdates: January 25, February 23, March 21, April 19, May 17, June 15, July 13, August 11, September 9, October 7, November 5, December 3.

NINE OF CLUBS—VENUS LINE

An unavoidable love affair that could prove to be long lasting. This native will give you more love than you've ever anticipated. And, in turn, you will keep him or her happy and protected and always surprised by your thoughts and abilities. A good relationship for romance; fine for friendship; possible for business but personal emotions are apt to interfere, so business is best avoided.

Nine of Clubs birthdates: January 31, February 29, March 27, April 25, May 23, June 21, July 19, August 17, September 15, October 13, November 11, December 9.

FIVE OF CLUBS—MERCURY LINE

You'll love listening to their stories—whether true or false—and their tales of their travels, etc. But don't try to get too close, even if this native is of the opposite sex and it's enticing. It's not worth the effort. Too aggravating for you on a one-to-one basis. Impersonal friendship on an occasional level is best.

Five of Clubs birthdates: March 31, April 29, May 27, June 25, July 23, August 21, September 19, October 17, November 15, December 13.

KING OF SPADES—CROWN LINE

A good working relationship, especially if you are both men. Be careful if the King of Spades is a female—she may not be able to produce as much as she thinks she can. Don't let them try to run you; you have more understanding of your power than they. Listen when they talk—their ideas are not only good but useful to you in many areas. A personal relationship will probably be next to impossible, but don't avoid it if it comes your way. It could be the experience of your life.

King of Spades birthdate: January 1.

SIX OF CLUBS—NEPTUNE LINE

An unavoidable meeting that will leave you in a cloud as to what it was all about. Don't pursue anything on a personal level; friendship is all right but it could be a problem for you if you try to help them to be enlightened (which you might feel compelled to do). Business could be a problem and romance should be out.

Six of Clubs birthdates: March 30, April 28, May 26, June 24, July 22, August 20, September 18, October 16, November 14, December 12.

TWO OF CLUBS—URANUS LINE

If you need a private detective, this is the person to hire. Any other type of relationship might be foolish, especially if you attempt to confide in this native. Take a pass and be happier.

Two of Clubs birthdates: May 30, June 28, July 26, August 24, September 22, October 20, November 18, December 16.

NINE OF HEARTS—SATURN LINE: SEE HORIZONTAL LINE

Diagonal Lines

FOUR OF CLUBS—MARS AND JUPITER LINES

A friend who will tell you irritating things "for your own good." Romance could be sexually stimulating and an advantage, but probably temporary. Business is good if this native is a spokesman, or lecturer on behalf of your company, etc. Try to keep the relationship impersonal.

Four of Clubs birthdates: April 30, May 28, June 26, July 24, August 22, September 20, October 18, November 16, December 14.

FIVE OF SPADES—VENUS AND MARS LINES

Sexually stimulating—an eye contact from across the room, an immediate love affair, that could leave you working your fingers to the bone while they're traveling around the world. And when they're not traveling, they'll be figuring out ways to change you, your home, your friends, etc., all for your own good. Be careful of this one. Know the individual before you make a commitment. Good for friendship, and business is possible, especially if you are both involved in public affairs.

Five of Spades birthdates: January 9, February 7, March 5, April 3, May 1.

ACE OF CLUBS—MERCURY AND VENUS LINES

Another possible romantic attraction, but more mentally or sexually stimulating than actual love. Use the relationship positively and don't get yourself into trouble in other areas. It's not worth the price you may have to pay. Good for friendship if you need someone shoving you with curiosity; possible for business providing they work for you. If this is the case, don't become aggravated when they insist on doing things a certain way—they may have found a better way.

Ace of Clubs birthdates: May 31, June 29, July 27, August 25, September 23, October 21, November 19, December 17.

SEVEN OF CLUBS—SATURN AND URANUS LINES

An irritating person with odd ideas as far as you're concerned. Don't get too involved; it's a temporary involvement at best.

Seven of Clubs birthdates: March 29, April 27, May 25, June 23, July 21, August 19, September 17, October 15, November 13, December 11.

JACK OF DIAMONDS—URANUS AND NEPTUNE LINES

A great working relationship; although you may not be willing to understand their tactics, you will appreciate them and probably resort to .the "ostrich theory" in order to cope with them. Good money-makers for you, and you'll like them as well. Don't get personally involved from a romantic standpoint or you'll be disappointed—with the exception that the later years could bring happiness on a one-to-one basis. Stick to business first, if possible.

Jack of Diamonds birthdates: January 16, February 14, March 12, April 10, May 8, June 6, July 4, August 2.

JACK OF SPADES—MARS AND URANUS LINES

An unusual kind of relationship that will be mostly mentally stimulating; someone you enjoy being with but not live with. Enjoy the involvement for what it is.

Jack of Spades birthdates: January 3, February 1.

TWO OF HEARTS—VENUS AND NEPTUNE LINES

When you meet this native you'll really think you're in love, and it's conceivable that you're right. The problem lies in a one-to-one relationship. You may not have the time, energy, and desire to reassure and reaffirm your love for them as much as they insist and demand. Work on the positive side of both cards for any kind of happiness. Don't speculate in business.

Two of Hearts birthdate: December 29.

EIGHT OF SPADES FAMOUS BIRTHDATES

January 6	Joan of Arc
	Carl Sandburg
	Danny Thomas
	Loretta Young
	Tom Mix
February 4	Charles A. Lindbergh
	Ida Lupino
March 2	Desi Arnaz, Sr.
	Pope Pius·XII
	Pope Leo XII
	Jennifer Jones

Nines

NINES include all numbers and all planets; Nine is a universal, all-containing symbol.

As a Birth Card, we may emphasize the Cross of Five (the number of man) in the center; we may remain within the security of the two protective (and often limiting) squares at the top and bottom, or we may leave the lower triad behind us, cross the central path, and operate in the higher.

Nine is the finisher, for here we reach the end of the single digits; it is also the beginning, for we at once proceed to another cycle of nine, which always *ends* in Nine. (18, 27, 36, 45, etc.) It tears down, sweeps away, and terminates—but is never lost because it always reproduces itself. It destroys and it fulfills; it is the end and the beginning.

Because of its destructive and expelling force, the Ancients allotted it to the planet Mars; because of its Allness as opposed to Oneness, it is called the Card of Disappointment. It is actually a Number—and a Card—of complete fulfillment when we grasp its meaning and live its law.

The true Nine is dedicated to service—anywhere, everywhere, to anyone or to everyone. It demands the relinquishment of self. But because of its size, extension, and inclusion—an overall outpouring—it is the most emotional influence we have to deal with. Nines love more than the rest because they have more territory to cover. And they suffer more; they give more than the rest because they have a greater store, which leaves them more bereft. They are more idealistic than the rest because they have been sent to establish Universal Love and the Brotherhood of Man, and they become more disillusioned.

A Card of Disappointment? Assuredly it is when we chart our lives by personal loves and personal desires. A certain portion of personal love is not denied, but it always brings trouble. Nine represents the Great Desire, but the desire must conform to the inexorable law or result in frustration, sorrow, and loss. There is no easy *personal* pattern for any of the nines.

Hearts have the hardest problem of them all for they live by their emotions, and Saturn lays a heavy hand on them; in God's plan it is the Venus Card in the Venus Line—but God's plan is Universal.

Clubs must seek knowledge for Universal good, never for their sole advantage. When they develop intellectual snobbishness they are doomed to failure, and isolation.

Diamonds must acquire—then sell all and give to the poor.

Spades must labor in his neighbor's vineyard before he may gather his own grapes.

For all, there is sacrifice—and there is no reward without it. Nines do not sign their names or label their gifts; they are people of magnificent obsession. Like the number of their card, they must lose their identity in order to find their rightful place.

Nine of Hearts

Hearts — Love
Nine of Hearts — Disappointment in Love
Nine in Hearts — Universal Love

The Saturn Card in the Saturn Line—Displaces the **Seven of Diamonds** in the Natural Spread.

This has been called the Wish Card—and the displaced Seven of Diamonds shows us very clearly the close connection between the wish for love and the wish for money. For this combination money is not easy to acquire for purely personal use. Money may come but the two never seem to work together for any length of time. It is well not to expect too much from personal relationships; they will be disappointing when the requirements are set too high. It is well, too, not to long for extreme wealth; it is not in the pattern except in a few isolated cases where money must take the place of everything else. Happiness most of all.

The Saturn-Saturn position brings tests in all departments of life. The great reminder of debts—but no more to be feared than the taxes imposed by a just government or the bills we have voluntarily contracted. He merely tells us that *now* is the time to pay them, and it may be highly inconvenient. For the

Nine of Hearts, it usually is. Ability to judge values must be cultivated; it doesn't come naturally to these people. Once acquired, disappointments will be less frequent. Money is usually spent in considerable quantity for illness— either for themselves or for those dear to them. It seems to be on hand when needed, however, and is always available for any good purpose in which self is not too involved.

There is usually a good understanding of the higher laws. The Nine of Hearts people are never weak; if they were, they could not handle the pattern they have. They have tolerance and they want understanding and are willing to make sacrifices for it. The life is never an easy one and it may actually be too burdensome for some of them to meet efficiently. In that case, it is not an act of cowardice to work under the Personality Card and it often serves to smooth the pathway and bring more accomplishment than might be possible under the Birth Card. It is not the best procedure as a general rule, but if there is some uncontrollable handicap, it is folly not to try to mitigate its effect. When it is done, however, it must be done consciously and deliberately. The women will find the Queen of Hearts pleasanter and more powerful than their own Nine of Hearts. The men should strive to live up to the strength of the King of Hearts. If they choose the Jack instead, they must be wary of making more sacrifices and self-subordinations than are consistent with their original Nine.

We can alter our lives and make our own worlds if we choose. We can *not*, however, depart from the *laws* that govern the Birth Cards, the numbers or the horoscopes. If you are a Nine of Hearts, you must love your neighbor as yourself, and don't forget that he lives all over the world.

BIRTHDATES RULED BY THE NINE OF HEARTS

AUGUST 30—VIRGO—RULED BY MERCURY

The Birthday Number gives an inclination to the development of talent, but the approach and expression of any ability are always mental. Should cultivate self-confidence by making a definite choice and working on its technical foundation. The stage attracts many of this date and some reach a high place through perfection of *form*. In writing, facts are more productive than fiction. Can also succeed as nurses, chemical researchers, geologists, and horticulturists.

SEPTEMBER 28—LIBRA—RULED BY VENUS

Playwrights and politicians may attain fame in this date. Many are found in industry, but not usually from choice. Big business may be selected from necessity or inheritance but art, literature, or government connections are more favored. Art in some form should be followed as a hobby. Usually very effective speakers.

OCTOBER 26—SCORPIO—RULED BY MARS

Money very important and *big* operations are thought to be the best way to obtain it in large quantities. Many magnates of industry are found here, and are usually able to hold their wealth. Should guard against a tendency to penuriousness. Will sponsor philanthropic projects, but will want full credit. Good physicians and surgeons. Interested in art and music, but not as performers. Need a practical woman as co-worker. Can commercialize any ability.

NOVEMBER 24—SAGITTARIUS—RULED BY JUPITER

Writers, philosophers, counselors, and preachers are well-suited to this date. Highly nervous—often erratic—but will work hard and make sacrifices. Best of all the Nines of Hearts for partnerships. Mental attitudes receptive and amenable. Not attracted to orthodox medicine and should not attempt it. Are easily influenced, so should be careful in choice of associations. Have strong sense of responsiblity. Should watch inflation of their ego.

DECEMBER 22—CAPRICORN—RULED BY SATURN

Should fight against depression, nervousness, and worry. Have high ideals but want them productive. Must guard health—often affected by fits of temperament. Producers, promoters, government officials, critics. If not developed, are avaricious and neurotic.

NINE OF HEARTS—PLANETARY SEQUENCE OF PERSONAL RELATIONSHIPS

Horizontal Line

SEVEN OF CLUBS—MERCURY CARD IN THE URANUS LINE

A fast relationship, and if you never see them again you really won't be disturbed about it. They're too negative and too scattered for you, and you know you have your own problems. You'll appreciate their interest in metaphysics but you will think they can never quite catch up to where you are (or want to be).

Seven of Clubs birthdates: March 29, April 27, May 25, June 23, July 21, August 19, September 17, October 15, November 13, December 11.

FIVE OF DIAMONDS—VENUS CARD IN THE NEPTUNE LINE

Definite romantic attraction that is up to you. If you want it, you'll have to go after it. Take your time or the book may not fit the cover. Good for friendship—poor for business.

Five of Diamonds birthdates: August 30, September 28, October 26, November 24, December 22.

QUEEN OF SPADES—MARS CARD IN THE MERCURY LINE

Difficult to find a common meeting ground—sloppy, boring people as far as you're concerned. Relationship could start out with a fast love affair—don't press this involvement, it won't be worth it to you unless you have a metaphysical bond on the intellectual level.

Queen of Spades birthdate: January 2.

JACK OF CLUBS—JUPITER CARD IN THE VENUS LINE

Don't look for that fantastic love life here—love, yes, but they'll never be as involved with you as you are with them. Same for friendship. Be careful, you could be setting yourself up for another disappointment. In any case, you will still gain.

Jack of Clubs birthdates: January 29, February 27, March 25, April 23, May 21, June 19, July 17, August 15, September 13, October 11, November 9, December 7.

NINE OF DIAMONDS—SATURN CARD IN THE MARS LINE

Head-on collision. You won't like the material space they occupy and they'll never understand you. Avoid this relationship; you can be very destructive to each other.

Nine of Diamonds birthdates: January 18, February 16, March 14, April 12, May 10, June 8, July 6, August 4, September 2.

SEVEN OF SPADES—URANUS CARD IN THE JUPITER LINE

Admiration, respect, and friendship. A natural bond and a great deal to talk about regarding feelings. You can learn a great deal from each other if you cultivate discussions on the spiritual level.

Seven of Spades birthdates: January 7, February 5, March 3, April 1.

TWO OF CLUBS—NEPTUNE CARD IN THE SATURN LINE

Probable strong Karmic tie, but should be kept as occasional friend. These natives will try to depreciate any spiritual aspirations you may have. Don't waste your breath until you have the spiritual strength as well as the desire. Chances are it still won't help.

Two of Clubs birthdates: May 30, June 28, July 26, August 24, September 22, October 20, November 18, December 16.

Vertical Line

EIGHT OF SPADES—JUPITER LINE

You can be yourself more openly and honestly with this card than any

Nines

other. They will understand you and help you to understand yourself. A good mental and spiritual relationship with give-and-take from both sides.

Eight of Spades birthdates: January 6, February 4, March 2.

TWO OF DIAMONDS—MARS LINE

Love—with problems. Busy people who can't and won't cater to you in any way, creating frustration and disenchantment. Good for business partnerships but you will have to make the relationship work.

Two of Diamonds birthdates: January 25, February 23, March 21, April 19, May 17, June 15, July 13, August 11, September 9, October 7, November 5, December 3.

NINE OF CLUBS—VENUS LINE

Sexual attraction that you know out in front is not really what you want. They'll seem silly and sometimes too odd. They will gamble with you and leap into a personal relationship, but you cannot afford the price.

Nine of Clubs birthdates: January 31, February 29, March 27, April 25, May 23, June 21, July 19, August 17, September 15, October 13, November 11, December 9.

FIVE OF CLUBS—MERCURY LINE

Magnetism, warmth—communications and good vibrations; yet you'll find you're worlds apart in every way you act, react, and feel. Native can drive you in circles with their ever changing minds. May come and go quickly in your life. A difficult relationship that will require effort on your part more so than theirs. They are not as aware as you.

Five of Clubs birthdates: March 31, April 29, May 27, June 25, July 23, August 21, September 19, October 17, November 15, December 13.

KING OF SPADES—CROWN LINE

A taxing relationship with very strong Karma ties. Don't neglect this relationship, whatever the price. Much to be learned—try to avoid romanticism.

King of Spades birthdate: January 1.

SIX OF CLUBS—NEPTUNE LINE

You'll know the intuitive powers of this native and spend the rest of your life trying to convince them. Don't get too closely involved. Relationship good for psychical research and intellectual discussions.

Six of Clubs birthdates: March 30, April 28, May 26, June 24, July 22, August 20, September 18, October 16, November 14, December 12.

TWO OF CLUBS—URANUS LINE: SEE HORIZONTAL LINE

Diagonal Lines

TEN OF DIAMONDS—DOUBLE JUPITER LINES

You'll be more attracted to these natives then they to you. You'll especially appreciate their life-style and ability to make money. If you are involved on any of your metaphysical trips, they aren't interested and that's not why you're together.

Ten of Diamonds birthdates: January 17, February 15, March 13, April 11, May 9, June 7, July 5, August 3, September 1.

SIX OF HEARTS—DOUBLE MARS LINES

A loving, mature relationship that you will never have as your own unless you are willing to be somewhat dominated (which you aren't). The love they give you will not seem as passionate as you would like perhaps. Relationship best on an impersonal love basis—perhaps in working together for the good of others.

Six of Hearts birthdates: October 29, November 27, December 25.

SEVEN OF DIAMONDS—DOUBLE VENUS LINES
(Nine of Hearts Displacement Card)

Irksome at times—and they won't be as conscious of it as you. Inextricably tied as Displacement Card so, therefore, inescapable relationship. Must work it out as part of Karma. Stay out of personal involvements—you know too much about each other.

Seven of Diamonds birthdates: January 20, February 18, March 16, April 14, May 12, June 10, July 8, August 6, September 4, October 2.

THREE OF HEARTS—DOUBLE MERCURY LINES

An immediate attraction will always have a barrier between the two of you. Too much uncertainty will rule the relationship. They'll never feel you love them—and you'll never feel they love you enough. Stay friends—at arm's length.

Three of Hearts birthdates: November 30, December 28.

KING OF CLUBS—DOUBLE URANUS LINES

You'll never know where you are with this native; always unpredictable, doing unexpected things. They'll know right where you are and won't hesitate to tell you so. Good communications.

King of Clubs birthdates: January 27, February 25, March 23, April 21, May 19, June 17, July 15, August 13, September 11, October 9, November 7 December 5.

QUEEN OF HEARTS—VENUS CARD IN THE DOUBLE NEPTUNE LINES

Take a good look before you fall in love. It won't be as expected, but still could be good—especially romantic, tender, and gentle. Don't drive this happy person, just know them—and love them—for exactly who and what they are.

Queen of Hearts birthdates: July 29, August 27, September 25, October 23, November 21, December 19.

SEVEN OF SPADES—MERCURY CARD IN THE URANUS AND JUPITER LINES: SEE VERTICAL LINE.

TWO OF SPADES—VENUS CARD IN THE NEPTUNE AND MARS LINES

A strong physical attraction that won't turn out to be as it seems. Asking for trouble through a close involvement. Problems through this native's fear may delay your own spiritual development. Weigh all aspects carefully before you make this committment.

Two of Spades birthdates: January 12, February 10, March 8, April 6, May 4, June 2.

ACE OF HEARTS—MERCURY CARD IN THE JUPITER AND URANUS LINES

Your need and this desire could be an answer for you (on the love level) but probably only temporarily. Good communication level—good relationship. Handle firmly but be kind, they don't have their finger on the world as you do.

Ace of Hearts birthdate: December 30.

EIGHT OF CLUBS—VENUS CARD IN THE MARS AND NEPTUNE LINES

Love—stimulation. They will force their opinions on you and it's even more irritating when most of the time they're right. A battle if closely involved—but highly sexual. A truly exciting friendship and necessary for you.

Eight of Clubs birthdates: March 28, April 26, May 24, June 22, July 20, August 18, September 16, October 14, November 12, December 10.

Your Place in the Cards

NINE OF HEARTS FAMOUS BIRTHDATES

August 30	Fred MacMurray
	Joan Blondell
September 28	Al Capp
	Barry Sullivan
October 26	Jackie Coogan
	Mahalia Jackson
November 24	William F. Buckley
	John Vliet Lindsay
	Toulouse-Lautrec
December 22	Andre Kostelanetz

Planetary Sequence

		K♠	8♢	10♣		
A♠	3♢	5♣	10♠	Q♣	A♣	3♡
2♡	9♠	9♣	J♡	5♠	7♢	7♡
	Venus	Mercury				
8♣	J♠	2♢	4♣	6♡	K♢	K♡
		Neptune	Uranus	Saturn	Jupiter	Mars
A♢	A♡	8♠	10♢	10♡	4♠	6♢
5♢	7♣	9♡	3♠	3♣	5♡	Q♢
J♢	K♣	2♣	7♠	9♢	J♣	Q♠
Q♡	6♠	6♣	8♡	2♠	4♢	4♡

Mercury / Venus / Mars / Jupiter / Saturn / Uranus / Neptune (rows, top to bottom from row 2)

Neptune / Uranus / Saturn / Jupiter / Mars / Venus / Mercury (columns, left to right)

Mundane Spread

Clubs — Knowledge
Nine of Clubs — Obstacles to Mental Control
Nine in Clubs — Knowledge Universally Applied

The Saturn Card in the Venus Line. Displaces the **Queen of Hearts** in the Natural Spread.

The Nine of Clubs is a Card of a speculative nature. There is a certain vacillation—as a Saturn Card in the Venus Line. Vacillation isn't so much the word as that it wonders as well as wanders. This is a card that takes a chance. This is also a card that gets confused when the emotions of family matters are not going too clearly.

This is an excellent example of the workings of the Law of Nine. As in the case of the Nine of Hearts, the position is Saturn, indicating a struggle in relation to any mental development. The difficulty could be due to finances, but since it is the Venus Line and the Displacement Card is the Queen of Hearts, it is much more apt to be due to the native's proclivity for wasting time and emotional energy on frivolity and self-indulgence. (The Queen of Hearts can be a distracting and demoralizing influence.)

The answer as well as safe guidance is in the True Place. Here the Nine of Clubs is the Mercury Card in the Jupiter Line, fortified by the proximity of the Ten of Clubs. Expansion for mental development; forget the Venusian satisfactions and hew to the line of duty to eliminate the disappointments that are sure to follow the negative operation of this Birth Card. God's plan for the Nine of Clubs is ruled by Mercury and Jupiter; by following it, all loss will turn into fulfillment.

As a rule, these people have warm and friendly personalities and a keen sense of obligation. They keep promises and pay debts. Note that the True Place of the Nine of Clubs is displaced by the Six of Diamonds, establishing still another connection with the Birth Card. All Sixes are working with Karmic Law, and know it, so there is no desire to escape responsibility.

Without getting too far out of line as far as duty is concerned, the Nine of Clubs is an adventurer's card. They like to gamble and are always willing to take a chance for the satisfaction of curiosity or interest. When the adventurous spirit extends to the field of knowledge, they often become extremists, but at least they are seeking. They are capable of making some discovery that is of wide benefit.

When not influenced by the wrong kind of women, association with one of kindliness and humanitarian qualities increases their own. They worry too much, and are too dependent upon approval and sympathy. Many of their early difficulties and gropings disappear in middle life, or as soon as they are ready to settle down and lay aside the objectives that are strictly personal and emotional.

The men are attracted to Heart women, or very wealthy women. They will go from one extreme to another. They are best in business for themselves and they want power. This is their objective. And with it there is no uncertainty. They can do as they please and they don't have to have any responsibility.

The women of this card want men who can support them; they might work a little after marriage, but actually this is not what the Nine of Clubs really wants. The Nine of Clubs women would prefer being the Queen of Hearts, which can be gay; a mother who is frivolous. The women, especially, must watch the tendency to flirtatiousness and triviality. The satisfaction (if any) is always transitory and the chances for a dependable and harmonious association may be spoiled.

Drinking comes through the close association to the Jack of Spades. The challenge is to be the elder brother and to take responsiblity and not be shiftless, irresponsible, or vague in any way. After a period of irresolution, incompatability, etc., the Nine of Clubs can overcome problems through the power of the mind—through groups, teaching, large organizations; this is using knowledge acquired and giving power over a situation, if the challenge is met.

Any close association formed with a Six of Diamonds or a Queen of Hearts is an indication that there is a Karmic element in the experience gained. All Nines have come to pay off old obligations *now* and in the case of the Nine of Clubs; these people (the Six of Diamonds and the Queen of Hearts) constitute some of the agents or "collectors." The less they express through the personality, the surer their fulfillment.

BIRTHDATES RULED BY THE NINE OF CLUBS

JANUARY 31–AQUARIUS–RULED BY URANUS

If homelife provides a good anchorage, work goes well. Interested in labor and politics, but not in holding any office. Best success in mental lines: newspapers, interviews, personnel managers, etc. Dramatic in manner. Can often succeed in the theater; showmanship carries them far. Gift for writing—seriously. Unorthodox; defy established customs.

FEBRUARY 29–PISCES–RULED BY NEPTUNE

A rare birthdate. Should cultivate balance and guard against erraticism. Very intuitive, on the psychic side; temperamental. May become soft and lazy. Should choose work that allows them to serve, unless there is some outstanding talent. Make fine dancers if willing to work on technique. Lean to poetry or poetic prose in writing. Must avoid psychic experiments and be sure of their ground.

MARCH 27–ARIES–RULED BY MARS

Very self-determined; inclined to egotism. Make friends easily but are Good starters. Must avoid becoming mercenary. Are successful as lawyers (prosecutors), politicians, scientists. Many are universally minded, progressive, and militant for reforms.

APRIL 25–TAURUS–RULED BY VENUS

Creative and inventive. Work best if there is a heart interest. Want to live well and have security for the whole family; often have to create it themselves and cannot depend upon the mate. May write but are best adapted for artistic work: painting, singing, dramatics, modeling, composing. Excellent designers and decorators.

MAY 23–GEMINI–RULED BY MERCURY

Dissatisfied with results. Impatient, changeable. Give up too easily. Always have a mental approach. Good draftsmen, architects, critics, journalists. Opinionated. Skillful with hands and with words. Speakers, reporters, translators. Good linguists. Attracted to theather, radio, television, electricity. Always make themselves heard and felt in any crowd.

JUNE 21–GEMINI–RULED BY MERCURY

Less touch-and-go than the other Gemini birthdate; more public-spirited. If they remain impersonal, can make considerable money. Want a home but not always happily married. Good guides or travel agents, canvassers, stewards, demonstrators, etc. Good entertainers, hosts, and companions. More optimistic than many Nines of Clubs but may have long fits of depression.

JULY 19–CANCER–RULED BY THE MOON

A life of destiny. Must pay in full. Inclined to laziness, but must work hard for accomplishment. Like business that brings them before the public. Deal well in small articles, sold on credit. Can sell whatever they believe in. Love home but will not be restricted by it. Fond of eating and drinking, which oftens affects the health. Self-protective; hate to face facts. Merchants, writers, public servants. Make good family physicians. Can become outstanding in a profession.

AUGUST 17–LEO–RULED BY THE SUN

Public-spirited and humanitarian. If not in the theater (and many are), are always dramatic and dynamic in approach. Associated with money and can make it independently. Prefer to leave business details to others. Leaders in their own field. Very successful as writers and publishers. Want an occupation that is capable of expansion. May be subject to hampering home conditions but never fail in duty and devotion.

SEPTEMBER 15—VIRGO—RULED BY MERCURY

Childhood apt to be overburdened with responsibility, which they assume and often overdo. Stubborn and skeptical. Not too sure of their ground but won't yield a point once taken. Given to worry, especially about their health; may become hypochondriacs. Careful to preserve their reputations and keep up appearances. Seldom in want but always fear it. Not happy alone; need some one to care for, and worry about. Should avoid narrowness and fretfulness. Services not always appreciated. Technicians, architects, accountants, critics.

OCTOBER 13—LIBRA—RULED BY VENUS

Hate limitation and direction but are sometimes dictatorial themselves. Work best in association and remain harmonious when others are friendly. Like to have their own way. Orthodox but skeptical. Have one dominating influence in life. Proud of family tradition and background. May be gifted in writing, acting, or singing but business is most productive. Should not marry young. Devoted to home and family, but they may be a deterrent influence. Should guard against being critical and nagging. Have good memories. Often called the Old Maid and Old Bachelor birthdate.

NOVEMBER 11—SCORPIO—RULED BY MARS

Educators, actors, and financiers can succeed with this birthdate. Nervous and highstrung, forceful and emotional. Should have an outlet in a congenial occupation or may become neurotic. If there is any talent for art or music it may develop into something important, but will not be along regulated lines. Work from inspiration and imagination, and put their own stamp on it. Safeguard lies in service—and metaphysics. Good diagnosticians, magnetic healers; must cultivate balance.

DECEMBER 9—SAGITTARIUS—RULED BY JUPITER

Must have freedom of action. Unhappy if bound by home or burdensome ties. Like to travel in early and middle life. Good itinerant preachers, lecturers, teachers—but not for the young. Have a scientific trend of mind and make good chemists, researchers, and discoverers. Nervous, or jittery; self-determined. Will escape responsibility through drink if not developed.

Your Place in the Cards

NINE OF CLUBS—PLANETARY SEQUENCE OF PERSONAL RELATIONSHIPS

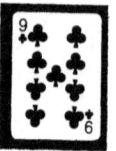

Horizontal Line—Venus and Mars

NINE OF SPADES—MERCURY CARD IN THE URANUS LINE

A personal attraction that you might never be able to fully understand. Good for mental stimulation, especially new ideas. Don't look for any permanence.

Nine of Spades birthdates: January 5, February 3, March 1.

TWO OF HEARTS—VENUS CARD IN THE NEPTUNE LINE

An enchanting love affair that can never be as you first saw it. Your behaviorial pattern will send them scurrying—if you pursue it, learn more about the person before making any commitments. It's possible, if you're willing to really work at it.

Two of Hearts birthdate: December 29.

KING OF HEARTS—MARS CARD IN THE MERCURY LINE

A driving force and influence for you if you operate totally on the positive plane with this native. Negatively, they would be irritating people who try to (or seem to) force their opinions and philosophies on you. Listen—in either case you'll feel drawn to them. Don't get personally involved on any level.

King of Hearts birthdates: June 30, July 28, August 26, September 24, October 22, November 20, December 18.

KING OF DIAMONDS—JUPITER CARD IN THE VENUS LINE

Friendship, love, and business are all good for you with this native. With men, appeal to his younger side occasionally—to drag him away from business. A good provider on the material plane, and a good friend for you.

King of Diamonds birthdates: January 14, February 12, March 10, April 8, May 6, June 4, July 2.

SIX OF HEARTS—SATURN CARD IN THE MARS LINE

A difficult-to-understand relationship; someone you see occasionally and feel the warmth, but don't share the same viewpoints. Best left alone on anything other than an impersonal involvement.

Six of Hearts birthdates: October 29, November 27, December 25.

FOUR OF CLUBS—URANUS CARD IN THE JUPITER LINE

Surprising news that will always keep you guessing about the next time. A good relationship but not necessarily romantic. Friendship best; business could be a problem; romantic love should not be discounted.

Four of Clubs birthdates: April 30, May 28, June 26, July 24, August 22, September 20, October 18, November 16, December 14.

TWO OF DIAMONDS—NEPTUNE CARD IN THE SATURN LINE
(Mars Line on the Vertical Line)

A relationship that is more confusing than aggravating, but with plenty of both. You may never understand this native—and there may be no reason to try. Take a pass if possible.

Two of Diamonds birthdates: January 25, February 23, March 21, April 19, May 17, June 15, July 13, August 11, September 9, October 7, November 5, December 3.

Vertical Line—Saturn

FIVE OF CLUBS—MERCURY LINE

You'll find a hundred things of mutual interest to talk about but not a good relationship because this native will tend to bring out your negative side—an African safari or a midnight swim in the canal is not going to aid you in the discovery of your True Self.

Five of Clubs birthdates: March 31, April 29, May 27, June 25, July 23, August 21, September 19, October 17, November 15, December 13.

KING OF SPADES—CROWN LINE

A loving friend who can set your house in order if you can see through all the gingerbread that accompanies the advice. Love possible but best if the King of Spades is a man—preferably older. The reverse romantic situation will bring a living-closer-to-the-ground lifestyle. Love comes to you through this native on any level.

King of Spades birthdate: January 1.

SIX OF CLUBS—NEPTUNE LINE

A boring relationship that will start off with a bang. Use their intuitive side—it will give you energy without knowing where it came from, but nonetheless a difficult involvement.

Six of Clubs birthdates: March 30, April 28, May 26, June 24, July 22, August 20, September 18, October 16, November 14, December 12.

Your Place in the Cards

TWO OF CLUBS—URANUS LINE

These natives can find out anything of a secretive nature that you want to know about. Revealing, surprising, but for your own good in almost all cases. A tough romantic involvement—he or she'd probably rifle your pants pockets or go through your purse, and never let you forget what they found.

Two of Clubs birthdates: May 30, June 28, July 26, August 24, September 22, October 20, November 18, December 16.

NINE OF HEARTS—SATURN LINE

This native will come and go in your life, probably over a period of years, and will usually leave you feel worse than before the visit. A karmic tie, but it's doubtful that you can add anything positive to their constant dilemmas. Put up with it, or take a pass, but don't let it bring you down.

Nine of Hearts birthdates: August 30, September 28, October 26, November 24, December 22.

EIGHT OF SPADES—JUPITER LINE

Someone who can perhaps discover a hidden talent you possess; a good affiliation for friendship and perhaps business. Don't expect romance, it probably won't be there.

Eight of Spades birthdates: January 6, February 4, March 2.

TWO OF DIAMONDS—MARS LINE: SEE HORIZONTAL LINE

Diagonal Lines

TEN OF SPADES—MERCURY AND JUPITER LINES

A good relationship if you listen to what they have to say. Common bonds and usually philosophical, although may not practice what they preach. Business might be difficult—love a possibility but probably not long lasting.

Ten of Spades birthdates: January 4, February 2.

TEN OF CLUBS—CROWN AND MARS LINES

An automatic attraction and yet an irritation—perhaps over envy for this native. Don't let those negative vibes in. Listen and learn—they show good examples. Romance could be exceptional if you permit it.

Ten of Clubs birthdates: January 30, February 28, March 26, April 24, May 22, June 20, July 18, August 16, September 14, October 12, November 10, December 8.

JACK OF SPADES—MARS AND URANUS LINES

A quick involvement that could place the two of you in unusual situations together. Highly energetic, watch your temper. No involvements of any duration—especially romantic.

Jack of Spades birthdates: January 3, February 1.

ACE OF DIAMONDS—JUPITER AND NEPTUNE LINES

One of the best romantic involvements you can have, although you may never fully understand them. Love, protection. Possibility of disillusionment in the beginning; you may think they have more money than they do, etc. But not enough to stand in the way of pursuing someone who is good to you and who loves you. A reciprocal involvement but you may give them many more problems than they give you. Enjoy it.

Ace of Diamonds birthdates: January 26, February 24, March 22, April 20, May 18, June 16, July 14, August 12, September 10, October 8, November 6, December 4.

THREE OF DIAMONDS—MERCURY AND URANUS LINES

Highly conversational and interesting, but a close involvement would reveal as many problems as you. Their insecurities will send you running. Sporadic kind of friendship or a one-time-only meeting. Don't look for more.

Three of Diamonds birthdates: January 24, February 22, March 20, April 18, May 16, June 14, July 12, August 10, September 8, October 6, November 4, December 2.

FOUR OF CLUBS—MARS AND JUPITER LINES

A talkative relationship that will start off great and disintegrate into a once-a-year thing, if that. You know that they're talking "at" you for your own good, but you cannot help but resent it. On the positive side, listen and wear the shoes if they fit—which they probably will. A possible sexual involvement but nothing permanent.

Four of Clubs birthdates: April 30, May 28, June 26, July 24, August 22, September 20, October 18, November 16, December 14.

TEN OF HEARTS—JUPITER AND MARS LINES

One look and you'll grab onto this native as if they're the last person on earth. It's Mr. Right as far as you're concerned, but you're asking for a bag of problems. Love life high for both of you, but the temperamental outbursts of these natives will leave you alone a good deal of the time—and set your eyes to wandering. A volatile relationship—for good or ill—depending on how you both handle it.

Ten of Hearts birthdates: July 31, August 29, September 27, October 25, November 23, December 21.

FIVE OF HEARTS—SATURN AND VENUS LINES

An eye contact across the room and suddenly you're in emotional turmoil. Romance, but sex comes first here. Doubtful if it can be sustained and, if so, a burden to you both. Marriage would bring divorce. Do yourself a favor and don't bother in the beginning.

Five of Hearts birthdates: October 30, November 28, December 26.

QUEEN OF SPADES—URANUS AND MERCURY LINES

A good relationship—both personal and business. Romance may be routine and take a back seat even if you are romantically involved. Be careful you don't have problems over the lack of money; it would be natural (but negative) in this association.

Queen of Spades birthdate: January 2.

NINE OF CLUBS FAMOUS BIRTHDATES

January 11	Carol Channing
	Norman Mailer
	Jackie Robinson
	Jersey Joe Walcott
	Franz Schubert
March 27	Gloria Swanson
	Sarah Vaughn
April 25	Ella Fitzgerald
May 23	Douglas Fairbanks, Sr.
June 21	Jane Russell
August 17	Mae West
September 15	Jackie Cooper
	Genghis Khan
	William Howard Taft
October 13	Yves Montand

November 11	Jonathan Winters
	Alger Hiss
December 9	Lee J. Cobb
	Kirk Douglas
	Douglas Fairbanks, Jr.
	William Hartack
	John Milton

Nine of Diamonds

Diamonds – Values
Nine of Diamonds – Dissatisfaction in Money
Nine in Diamonds – Generosity or Selfishness

The Mars Card in the Uranus Line. Displaces the **Queen of Diamonds** in the Natural Spread.

There seems to be no middle ground for these people; they are either philanthropic, generous, and protective toward others, or live for themselves alone—unable to acquire the money they want and dissatisfied with life. This is a card that can be found with millionaires and it is "accumulative money." The two distinct types of Nine of Diamonds are either the person who is constantly struggling because he doesn't have any money, or the other person who is constantly struggling because he has too much. A real struggle. They can have a completeness of finances and have all the things that money can buy, or be someone who is always broke and wondering where the next penny is coming from.

Planetary Sequence

			K♠	8♦	10♣			
A♠	3♦	5♣	10♠	Q♣	A♣	3♥		Mercury
2♥	9♠	9♣	J♥	5♠	7♦	7♥		Venus
8♣	J♠	2♦	4♣	6♥	K♦	K♥		Mars
A♦	A♥	8♠	10♦	10♥	4♠	6♦		Jupiter
5♦	7♣	9♥	3♠	3♣	5♥	Q♦		Saturn
J♦	K♣	2♣	7♠	9♦	J♣	Q♠		Uranus
Jupiter	Mars	Venus	Mercury					
Q♥	6♠	6♣	8♥	2♠	4♦	4♥		Neptune
				Neptune	Uranus	Saturn		

Neptune · Uranus · Saturn · Jupiter · Mars · Venus · Mercury

Mundane Spread

The circumstances of a Nine of Diamonds will determine whether he is operating on the positive side or the negative side of this card. There can be extreme losses of money even though they are wealthy. But again, the money is made and spent in various directions. This is negative. The one who has a philanthrophic approach to life will understand the laws of accumulation (which the Nine of Diamonds does understand), and by keeping it in reasonable circulation, he himself can profit by it.

For all Nines of Diamonds, there is no escaping obstacles and disappointment if they are selfish. The True Place is the Neptune Card in the Saturn Line—which is but another way of saying that duty, responsibility, and full payment constitute the goal in life and should be idealized and sought eagerly. When it is, it is attained happily.

There are no weaklings in the birthdates of this card, but in early life or in the case of some strong attachment, there is a tendency to be dominated. When this occurs, once the tie is broken, they may become domineering themselves—to get even. Marriage is a problem and Nine of Diamonds people run away and get married or run away secretly and get divorced. It may not always mean divorce, but there is some limitation to the marriage with this card. They should marry; it should be their experience and the Nine of Diamonds may not always wish to get married. The women might marry more than once, and marry men who drink—or they might wake up one day and find out that the husband is either highly immature or sexually indeterminate. The men are apt to marry women who cause them worry, cost them money, or fail to give satisfaction. Both sexes may stay in married life for convention's sake, even if it is a headache.

There is usually a goodly amount of self-insistence and aggressiveness. They want to think and act for themselves—and should—but they fear they may not be able to unless they demand it.

There is a close tie between the Nine of Diamonds and the Queen of Diamonds, a tie that surpasses the displacement influence. Those belonging to these dates have some Karmic debt to work out, and the association is not always an agreeable one. In the case of a woman, there is a double dose to be reckoned with and great care should be taken in handling these associations.

For the most part, these people are slated for success. They are inclined to materiality, and may be mercenary, but the natural tendency is toward generosity, even though they never forget to protect themselves.

If they are to avoid disappointment, they must clearly define their values. They should be helped to this end very early in life. "As the twig is bent" is very significant in their case and colors their entire life. Those whose inclinations are on the spiritual level and have acquired a working philosophy have few obstacles to overcome. Consciously or unconsciously, they follow the Law of Nine and *give* of themselves, their efforts and their goods. With any Nine, a certain degree of cosmic urge is a requirement. Those who deny it only defeat themselves.

The women have more to overcome than the men, for they are always struggling with their personality—and that Queen of Diamonds is difficult. Both sexes are apt to overestimate their abilities. Both are interested in things that move too fast and are, therefore, subject to accidents.

They often choose, and are well-adapted for, welfare work, Red Cross, Salvation Army, YMCA, or some allied branch of public service. The less they concentrate on their own security, the better.

BIRTHDATES RULED BY THE NINE OF DIAMONDS

JANUARY 18—CAPRICORN—RULED BY SATURN
Scholarly, thorough, industrious. Ambitious and studious. Approach everything from a mental angle. Orthodox and cautious; take no chances. For Capricorn, quite universally minded. No imagination. Can write if along solid and serious lines. Want to cover a large field: big business, big audiences, a big "place." Successful in manufacturing and merchandising.

FEBRUARY 16—AQUARIUS—RULED BY URANUS
These people are critical and controversial. Like to argue and often take the opposite side, not from conviction but because they enjoy it. Interested in people and the rights of the underdog. More biased than balanced; go all out for any cause they espouse. Imagination, enthusiasm, and emotionalism carry many into the theater—often to marked success. Can also succeed as correspondents, columnists, or government officials.

MARCH 14—PISCES—RULED BY NEPTUNE
Very talented in art or music (also dancing), or very scientific, capable of making a valuable contribution to a general knowledge and progress. Idealistic and humanitarian. In the less gifted and intellectual, there is a tendency to drift. Benefited by interests at a distance. Make good agents, managers of transportation, hospital or prison employees, secret service investigators. May gain through perfumes, oil, narcotics, or fishing.

APRIL 12—ARIES—RULED BY MARS
Promoters, politicians, members of armed forces, orators, and propagandists. May also succeed in publishing. The majority are not attracted to merchandising. Always self-promotive, often too aggressive and egotistic.

Good talkers, good salesmen, and like a good fight. Feel very sure of themselves.

MAY 10–TAURUS–RULED BY VENUS

Good leaders, directors, and initiators. Like to be associated with groups and clubs but want some official position near the top. Work well with others if allowed to keep their independence. Honest and reliable; affectionate and protective. Attracted to intelligent women. Can commercialize products for general use. Good cooks and gardeners.

JUNE 8–GEMINI–RULED BY MERCURY

Mental and inquiring. Are highly nervous, which affects the health. Usually want more power than they can handle or acquire. Apt to develop chronic conditions due to negative states of mind and a tendency to hypochrondria. Good traders, writers, talkers, extemporaneous speakers. Illnesses and obstacles often come unexpectedly; surprising changes. Should be careful of lungs.

JULY 6–CANCER RULED BY THE MOON

Patriots and sticklers for principle. Sincere devotees of worthy causes. Objectives often delayed until later years. Good government leaders and officials. When merchandising is chosen, usually deal in small articles, home products, foods. Not an easy birthdate; life full of effort and hard work.

AUGUST 4–LEO–RULED BY THE SUN

Positive and direct. Dramatic. Full of family pride. May have trouble with in-laws. Must be at the head of own business or shine in the limelight. Always good showmen. Stage producers, directors, performers, or backers. Good hosts; good entertainers. If business or investments chosen, may make big money. Inclined to be dictatorial–kings in their own right, but are kind at heart and protective of their dependents.

SEPTEMBER 2–VIRGO–RULED BY MERCURY

The most mentally disturbed and uncertain of the Nine of Diamonds. Want to do big things but fear to move far from their small radius. Too nervous for routine work but often choose it for safety. Bookbinders, accountants, researchers. The more fortunate have a gift in writing, and take refuge in it. Full of dreams and longings. May be poets. Should be guided early to an occupation that is varied and interesting.

Your Place in the Cards

NINE OF DIAMONDS—PLANETARY SEQUENCE OF PERSONAL RELATIONSHIPS

Horizontal Line—Uranus and Neptune

SEVEN OF SPADES—MERCURY CARD IN THE JUPITER LINE

One of the better positive relationships for you, especially in friendship and advisement capacities. They have good judgment and you can trust it. Don't look for anything to last a lifetime, but whatever kind of involvement occurs—it will only benefit you.

Seven of Spades birthdates: January 7, February 5, March 3, April 1.

TWO OF CLUBS—VENUS CARD IN THE SATURN LINE

Someone you will like—probably an employee—but also someone who is actually a burden to you. An employee who is constantly asking for advances; a gossipy neighbor; or a relative, etc. Romantically, good for you if you are materially inclined. Don't get involved if you are philanthropic.

Two of Clubs birthdates: May 30, June 28, July 26, August 24, September 22, October 20, November 18, December 16.

KING OF CLUBS—MARS CARD IN THE URANUS LINE

This native will advise you when you don't want to be advised and yet never seem able to take care of his or her own affairs. This could be a most rewarding relationship for you if you use it properly. First, don't get personally involved; second, take a second look at some of the things they have to say and use them to your advantage—whether mentally or financially.

King of Clubs birthdates: January 27, February 25, March 23, April 21, May 19, June 17, July 15, August 13, September 11, October 9, November 7, December 5.

JACK OF DIAMONDS—JUPITER CARD IN THE NEPTUNE LINE

A great business relationship as partner/advisor. This is where the money is. Although they may be somewhat devious about their tactics, the end results will work out well. Don't put total trust—check everything out. Your inner feelings about the native's ability to do the job are right. Romantically, this is the husband who calls and says he has to work and won't be coming home for dinner, which is probably not true but not necessarily destructive for you, either; or the wife who inwardly digs the lifeguard at the local country club, which is not destructive to you, either. Pursue any adventures and/or relationships; they should work out favorably.

Jack of Diamonds birthdates: January 16, February 14, March 12, April 10, May 8, June 6, July 4, August 2..

FOUR OF HEARTS—SATURN CARD IN THE MERCURY LINE

You may hear things from this native that you would rather be unaware of. A difficult relationship unless this native works for you in a type of sales capacity. Don't attempt any other kind of involvements, even though you are motivated to do so.

Four of Hearts birthdates: October 31, November 29, December 27.

FOUR OF DIAMONDS—URANUS CARD IN THE VENUS LINE
(Neptune and Venus Lines on the Diagonal Lines)

A great work relationship that could include romance. Not the best love situation inasmuch as this native will depend and demand to continue working in some capacity, even if you are worth a million dollars. And if you are on the opposite end of the money tree, this native will feel an obligation to work to support you and the family. Best for business; friendship would be inspirational; romance could be temporary.

Four of Diamonds birthdates: January 23, February 21, March 19, April 17, May 15, June 13, July 11, August 9, September 7, October 5, November 3, December 1.

TWO OF SPADES—NEPTUNE CARD IN THE MARS LINE
(Neptune Line on the Vertical Line)

A confusing relationship on any level that will probably irritate you. Too afraid to be in business with you; too stubborn to make money with you; and too dramatic to appeal to you. Take a pass, before you get involved without knowing it.

Two of Spades birthdates: January 12, February 10, March 8, April 6, May 4, June 2.

Vertical Line—Mars

THREE OF CLUBS—SATURN LINE

A negative person as far as you're concerned, but you'll have a feeling of concern over being able to help them. If words don't do it, don't waste your time further. Stay away from all involvements, if possible.

Three of Clubs birthdates: May 29, June 27, July 25, August 23, September 21, October 19, November 17, December 15.

TEN OF HEARTS—JUPITER LINE

A natural love affair that you will thoroughly enjoy—until it ends. The one possible saving factor might be that you'll be too busy to put up with their seemingly flirtatiousness and the relationship won't become negative to you. They are lovely people, and someone who can help you in every way. Enjoy what you have or will get, and if and when it's over, write it off as a deductible loss. Good for friendship; fair for business.

Ten of Hearts birthdates: July 31, August 29, September 27, October 25, November 23, December 21.

SIX OF HEARTS—MARS LINE

Sexual stimulation—for a short time. Not good for overall relationships unless you are willing to take criticism that may irritate you. Don't get involved unless you are prepared for a high exchange of ideas and emotions.

Six of Hearts birthdates: October 29, November 27, December 25.

FIVE OF SPADES—VENUS LINE

You'll agree and accept the in philosophy—and you should—but don't become personally involved unless you want to spend the rest of your life getting rearranged. A good relationship on any level and not destructive, although it may seem to be. Accept what you can and enjoy the rest.

Five of Spades birthdates: January 9, February 7, March 5, April 3, May 1.

QUEEN OF CLUBS—MERCURY LINE

An individual who will tell you things for your own good, although they are not to your liking. An unavoidable association at some time in your life, but best kept where it will probably be—impersonal.

Queen of Clubs birthdates: January 28, February 26, March 24, April 22, May 20, June 18, July 16, August 14, September 12, October 10, November 8, December 6.

TEN OF CLUBS—CROWN LINE

A knowledgeable person who can always liven up a discussion; negotiate a business deal, etc. Not advisable for romance; your lives are on a different wave length. Business and friendship good.

Ten of Clubs birthdates: January 30, February 28, March 26, April 24, May 22, June 20, July 18, August 16, September 14, October 12, November 10, December 8.

TWO OF SPADES—NEPTUNE LINE

What it may appear to be will not be what it will turn out to be, so be careful of any and all relationships. Know the person rather than the personality. Anything is possible, but nothing is probable. Don't invest too much time.

Two of Spades birthdates: January 12, February 10, March 8, April 6, May 4, June 2.

Diagonal Lines

FIVE OF HEARTS—SATURN AND VENUS LINES
Too scattered to relate to you for any length of time. A possible love interest but doubtful that it goes anywhere beyond interest. Difficult for friendship because their problems could be a drain on you. Business possible, but not recommended.
Five of Hearts birthdates: October 30, November 28, December 26.

SIX OF DIAMONDS—JUPITER AND MERCURY LINES
A romantic relationship that could be most disappointing if you permit it to be. Keep their spirits up when they falter; let them know you're "in their corner." A good involvement with a great deal of love and similar ways of life.
Six of Diamonds birthdates: January 21, February 19, March 17, April 15, May 13, June 11, July 9, August 7, September 5, October 3, November 1.

EIGHT OF HEARTS—NEPTUNE AND JUPITER LINES
A real go-getter; someone who has something to say and says it. A good relationship, but probably temporary if romance is attempted. Too scattered for your practical side, but nonetheless someone you will always enjoy being with on an impersonal, less involved level. Possible business affiliation, especially if this native is representing you in some way.
Eight of Hearts birthdates: August 31, September 29, October 27, November 25, December 23.

FOUR OF DIAMONDS—NEPTUNE AND VENUS LINES
A good co-worker partner, someone who will carry their own weight. Good friendship and possible romance, but temporary. Be cautious of misunderstanding this native; they are hard workers more than opportunists.
Four of Diamonds birthdates: January 23, February 21, March 19, April 17, May 15, June 13, July 11, August 9, September 7, October 5, November 3, December 1.

THREE OF SPADES—SATURN AND JUPITER LINES
Too uncertain and misdirected as far as you're concerned for a personal involvement, but certainly someone who can add to your own intellect. Friendship possible; all other involvements would be difficult.
Three of Spades birthdates: January 11, February 9, March 7, April 5, May 3, June 1.

EIGHT OF SPADES—JUPITER AND SATURN LINES

A romantic attraction that would be more advantageous for you than for this native, and yet difficult for either of you to maintain. Don't press—if it's not there, take a pass. Chances are you are on different roads. Friendship is good, as well as business, as long as you don't permit your personal feelings to dictate.

Eight of Spades birthdates: January 6, February 4, March 2.

JACK OF SPADES—MARS AND URANUS LINES

Absolute disagreement—you may even think this individual a little "far out" in his or her thinking. Don't pursue the involvement; they have a great deal to say, but if you don't hear it, it's time wasted.

Jack of Spades birthdates: January 3, February 1.

TWO OF HEARTS—VENUS AND NEPTUNE LINES

Romance—and you shouldn't miss it. A love affair that can keep both of your interests up. Show your love more; this native will enjoy knowing (and letting others know). Great for friendship, but mediocre for business. In any event, take a chance; the native and the experience will be rewarding.

Two of Hearts birthdate: December 29.

NINE OF DIAMONDS FAMOUS BIRTHDATES

January 18	Muhammed Ali (Cassius Clay)
	Cary Grant
	Danny Kaye
	Daniel Webster
February 16	Edgar Bergen
	Sonny Buono
March 14	Albert Einstein
May 10	Fred Astaire
June 8	Frank Lloyd Wright
July 6	Dorothy Kirsten
	Janet Leigh

Nine of Spades

Spades – Labor, Initiation
Nine of Spades – Accomplishment or Disappointment in Labor
Nine in Spades – Labor for Universal Good

The Uranus Card in the Venus Line. Displaces the **King of Hearts** in the Natural Spread

The keynote for success in this card is the sublimination of the emotions. The position bespeaks difficulties but the pattern itself is not a hard one.

The Nine of Spades contains all numbers. In analyzing the card, consideration of the power in back of the card is necessary. The Nine of Spades stands for Universal Love. He must not be concerned with himself alone, but must also be concerned with others as well. The minute this card becomes too personal, or too self-centered, the Nine of Spades becomes ill—could even go so far as to have a stroke and lie in bed for years, all because they are afraid of the future. The Nine of Spades can be very superstitious and dogmatic, which should not be the true nature of the card. The negative side of this card can come more easily through Capricorn, so these people must learn to be universal, or suffer the consequences.

As in the case of all Nines, impersonality must be developed or there is bound to be suffering. The great obligation imposed upon Spades is always latent, consciously or subconsciously, and is further augmented by the Nine. The Venus Line directs them to love as an objective but as soon as they become personally involved, their work is interfered with, obstacles to accomplishment arise, and an inner conflict is set up that disturbs their equilibrium and wrecks their nerves. They suffer when they become unfit to

Planetary Sequence

		K♠	8♦	10♣			
A♠	3♦	5♣	10♠	Q♣	A♣	3♥	Mercury
2♥ (Mercury)	9♠	9♣	J♥	5♠	7♦	7♥	Venus
8♣	J♦ (Neptune)	2♦ (Uranus)	4♣ (Saturn)	6♥ (Jupiter)	K♦ (Mars)	K♥ (Venus)	Mars
A♦	A♥	8♠	10♦	10♥	4♠	6♦	Jupiter
5♦	7♣	9♥	3♠	3♣	5♥	Q♦	Saturn
J♦	K♣	2♣	7♠	9♦	J♣	Q♠	Uranus
Q♥	6♠	6♣	8♥	2♠	4♦	4♥	Neptune
Neptune	Uranus	Saturn	Jupiter	Mars	Venus	Mercury	

Mundane Spread

serve. These people are closing one phase of their soul evolution and are being initiated into another. The majority of them are not undeveloped nor unaware, and it is that very awareness that disturbs them. Due to their emotional conflicts, "psychic" illnesses often develop and they may, for a time, be incapacitated for active work.

They are curious people. They are curious about associations. They are curious about what makes people click, and they are joiners. They are concerned with the movement of groups. If the card belongs to a woman, she could have more than one husband; her first husband might be considerably older. The second one would be concerned with money; or an attorney, a power in his own right. A man Nine of Spades might marry, but not for the same reason. Many of these natives don't marry at all. They want the association of people so much that they don't want to be tied down to any one person.

Nine of Spades like to go in partnership with those who have money, but must be careful not to get hooked. With the Six of Hearts as the Jupiter Card, there is love of humanity, the Law of Love, the Christ Principle. The Nine of Spades must function on this plane. Therefore, no matter how small the environment, a Nine of Spades might live where he could be asked to help in meeting the needs of others. This could be seating people at church dinners, or helping those who are sick. This all results from the gift of wanting to live a religious Law.

The Displacement Card gives evidence of the power to overcome their difficulties, and they often contact some wise, kindly and fatherly man who sets them back on their feet and instills in them the self-confidence that should never be lacking. These are truly great people and they must be made to realize it. Nervous, romantic, unconventional; they can turn all these qualities into working assets, and they do when they use their talents for service and concern themselves with the world at large. Their pens, their talents, and their executive ability give mighty account of themselves once they are set on the Universal Wire.

BIRTHDATES RULED BY THE NINE OF SPADES

JANUARY 5—CAPRICORN—RULED BY SATURN

Personally ambitious; Interested in politics as an avenue to prominence. Subject to disappointment if not working with humanitarian objectives. Often become discouraged and give up. Cannot work profitably with the soil, but can commercialize its products. Mental and restless. Eager for achievement but seldom realize that the only road to it lies in self-elimination. Capable of becoming leaders—even rulers. Should guard against being despotic when in a position of power. Can succeed at writing or lecturing.

FEBRUARY 3–AQUARIUS–RULED BY URANUS

Inventive, but not usually inspirational—too technical. Have a keen sense of what the public wants and can successfully cater to it. Interested in the theater as a commercial proposition. Make good impresarios, advance agents, managers, etc. May be gifted in art or music, but are inclined to burden their work with studied skill or elaborate detail. Journalists and authors, newspaper owners, and publishers. Always work for a popular appeal. Interesting and unusual personalities; always in demand at public functions. Good speakers, but prefer to prepare themselves well in advance.

MARCH 1–PISCES–RULED BY NEPTUNE

Writers, musicians, actors, and artists belong in this birthdate. Idealistic and emotional, but always mental. Work hard for results. Personal life and chosen occupation may be wholly satisfactory but there is always an inner, unsatisfied longing which they may not be able to define, even to themselves. This often results in nerves and high tension, and may act unfavorably on the health. Give willing service. Especially valuable in work for the sick and afflicted. With any musical ability, are especially adapted for music therapy. Have many abilities, but music and writing are the most outstanding. Should try to avoid fits of depression.

NINE OF SPADES–PLANETARY SEQUENCE OF PERSONAL RELATIONSHIPS

Horizontal Lines–Venus and Mars

TWO OF HEARTS–MERCURY CARD IN THE NEPTUNE LINE

This native may give the appearance of a possible romance interest to opposite sexes, but it's doubtful if the two of you will ever get together, and better if you don't. Good for communications—work. Not desirable for a business affiliation on an equal basis. Stay impersonal.

Two of Hearts birthdate: December 29.

KING OF HEARTS–VENUS CARD IN THE MERCURY LINE
(Nine of Spades Displacement Card)

A difficult romance or personal involvement due to the Displacement—one or the other will attempt to rule the other. Great for friendship, especially if this native is older (and seemingly wiser). Successful business is possible but not probable.

King of Hearts birthdates: June 30, July 28, August 26, September 24, October 22, November 20, December 18.

KING OF DIAMONDS—MARS CARD IN THE VENUS LINE

A dynamic business involvement—good for partnerships; you'll love 'em and you'll hate 'em, but they'll make money for you, and vice versa if you make the slightest effort. Don't get involved romantically; it would be destructive. Friendship is possible, but be aware that this native will probably attempt to dominate you, or give a feeling of superiority. A good involvement if you don't get too close.

King of Diamonds birthdates: January 14, February 12, March 10, April 8, May 6, June 4, July 2.

SIX OF HEARTS—JUPITER CARD IN THE MARS LINE

A friend whom you'll like and respect and who will always have something positive to say to you, although it may not always seem to be that way. Romance is possible and probable for opposite sexes, as long as you both love your neighbors as much as you do yourselves and each other. Don't attempt business involvements unless you are very careful and the affiliation is defined out in front.

Six of Hearts birthdates: October 29, November 27, December 25.

FOUR OF CLUBS—SATURN CARD IN THE JUPITER LINE

If you get involved in any way with this native, whatever the involvement, will turn out to be a problem or a burden for you. However, the end results are good, even though it may be difficult to see that at the time. No personal relationships are best. You'll be tempted, so know the person, the circumstances, and protect yourself as much as possible.

Four of Clubs birthdates: April 30, May 28, June 26, July 24, August 22, September 20, October 18, November 16, December 14.

TWO OF DIAMONDS—URANUS CARD IN THE SATURN LINE
(Mars and Saturn Lines on the Diagonal Line)

A problematical relationship that could create an "illness" for you. Too methodical and materialistic; too involved in situations and people that don't concern you. Don't get personally involved; but if you do, try to keep it impersonal on a business level.

Two of Diamonds birthdates: January 25, February 23, March 21, April 19, May 17, June 15, July 13, August 11, September 9, October 7, November 5, December 3.

JACK OF SPADES—NEPTUNE CARD IN THE URANUS LINE
(Mars Line on the Vertical Line)

This native will seem new and stimulating, with fresh ideas, theories, philosophies—all of which will interest you but probably not "convert" you. Don't be misled by their cover; they have some of the same goals that you have and you could find a delightful friend in this person.

Jack of Spades birthdates: January 3, February 1.

Vertical Line—Uranus

THREE OF DIAMONDS—MERCURY LINE

Great unexpected communications. You'll find that you have many things in common with this native. A good friend who is interested in business, having a good time in life whenever possible. A general concern for most people's welfare. Romance is probably well-intended, but too sporadic with this card to keep you involved for long. All other relationships should work well.

Three of Diamonds birthdates: January 24, February 22, March 20, April 18, May 16, June 14, July 12, August 10, September 8, October 6, November 4, December 2.

SIX OF SPADES—NEPTUNE LINE

The Displacement Card of this card is the Nine of Spades, and the Six of Spades represents Destiny. Therefore, this is probably a situation that is not only unavoidable, but also impossible to escape—should the two of you ever meet. Once you do, it's all over with. Opposite sexes will find love and friendship is inevitable. You don't have to go into business with this native; it's not the best situation, so stay away from that aspect. Stay completely on the spiritual side and the two of you can find a rare kind of love together, with many rewarding experiences. If you attempt to live on the material plane, you may meet with problems.

Six of Spades birthdates: January 8, February 6, March 4, April 2.

KING OF CLUBS—URANUS LINE

A teacher who has many new things to say to you. New things to learn about, always to your liking, and a definite "must" relationship. A fine friend or business associate.

King of Clubs birthdates: January 27, February 25, March 23, April 21, May 19, June 17, July 15, August 13, September 11, October 9, November 7, December 5.

SEVEN OF CLUBS—SATURN LINE

A possible romantic attraction that should not be considered because it could turn out to be totally destructive and an unreliable involvement. Especially stay away from any type of gossiping or scandalous situations. These natives are searching in similar directions as you, but for different reasons and for different end goals. You cannot have a good rapport in a close relationship; although you'll like them, stay impersonal for best results.

Seven of Clubs birthdates: March 29, April 27, May 25, June 23, July 21, August 19, September 17, October 15, November 13, December 11.

ACE OF HEARTS—JUPITER LINE

An attraction that you may feel is unexpected and destined. Difficult but still possible from many standpoints. Different goals, but similar objectives. Keep this native independent (which could be a problem), and you can have a happy relationship for both romance and friendship. Business is not advisable.

Ace of Hearts birthdate: December 30.

JACK OF SPADES—MARS LINE: SEE HORIZONTAL LINE

Diagonal Lines

ACE OF SPADES—MERCURY AND NEPTUNE LINES

You will think this native has heard every word you've said until they ask you a question or make a remark on the subject in question. It's almost impossible to converse on any level other than material, because they probably won't believe you. Don't make a big deal of it; meet them at a comfortable half-way mark and enjoy them on an impersonal basis only. Casual friendship is fine; don't attempt anything else unless you are both working in a type of charitable work, or in public service.

Ace of Spades birthdates: January 13, February 11, March 9, April 7, May 5, June 3, July 1.

TWO OF DIAMONDS—MARS AND SATURN LINES:
SEE HORIZONTAL LINE

TEN OF DIAMONDS—DOUBLE JUPITER LINES

Great business relationship; someone to make money with, but not steady; could come and go quickly, but can profit in any event. Religion and philosophy probably won't be shared on a one-to-one basis, but still a possible foundation for a good marriage, friendship, or involvement.

Ten of Diamonds birthdates: January 17, February 15, March 13, April 11, May 9, June 7, July 5, August 3, September 1.

THREE OF CLUBS—SATURN AND MARS LINES

An extremely difficult meeting, much less relationship. Someone who could seemingly agree, but go on their own pattern—which could be negative and obvious to you. Don't get involved unless it's necessary and, if so, keep the association strictly positive from your point of view. Not a constructive association.

Three of Clubs birthdates: May 29, June 27, July 25, August 23, September 21, October 19, November 17, December 15.

JACK OF CLUBS—URANUS AND VENUS LINES

A romantic attraction that could work out very well for you both. Don't feel insecure when they are not around; use the time for the many things you have wanted to accomplish. They will not make the demands on your time that many of your other associations will make, giving you the time you really want. Good for business and friendship if you don't try to get too wrapped up in each other to the point of mental and physical asphyxiation.

Jack of Clubs birthdates: January 29, February 27, March 25, April 23, May 21, June 19, July 17, August 15, September 13, October 11, November 9, December 7.

FOUR OF HEARTS—NEPTUNE AND MERCURY LINES

Too demanding for any kind of close physical involvement. Their needs will drain you with nothing left over for yourself. Good friend if on a casual basis; possible business acquaintance, but not a partner.

Four of Hearts birthdates: October 31, November 29, December 27.

EIGHT OF CLUBS—MARS AND NEPTUNE LINES

A good friend who has a great deal to say (both spiritually and educationally) that can keep you going when the going gets rough. Follow their advice; it's probably some of the best, even if you don't want to hear what they have to say. A good business relationship, but make sure all aspects of the business situation are specified. These people are most trustworthy, but very exacting.

Eight of Clubs birthdates: March 28, April 26, May 24, June 22, July 20, August 18, September 16, October 14, November 12, December 10.

FIVE OF CLUBS—MERCURY AND SATURN LINES

Highly conversational with many things to discuss and probe, but too changeable to make any real dent in your lifetime. Friendship could get boring after a while. Keep it impersonal and occasional, and you'll enjoy everything more.

Five of Clubs birthdates: March 31, April 29, May 27, June 25, July 23, August 21, September 19, October 17, November 15, December 13.

EIGHT OF DIAMONDS—CROWN AND JUPITER LINES

A love affair that could also be too demanding, unless you are prepared to accept it, and this native. Excellent financial aspects if you meet the obligations; they can only bring good fortune to you. Great for friendship and business. A definite must on any level.

Eight of Diamonds birthdates: January, February 17, March 15, April 13, May 11, June 9, July 7, August 5, September 3. October 1.

NINE OF SPADES FAMOUS BIRTHDATES

February 3	Shelley Berman
	Norman Rockwell
	James Michener
	Horace Greeley
	Felix Mendelssohn-Bartholdy
March 1	Harry Belafonte
	Dinah Shore
	Frédéric Chopin

Tens

"Fully Accomplished" or "all complete" is the translation of the Greek word panteleia—the Decad or the number Ten.

TENS are called Success Cards—a term that seems far too weak to apply to such a powerful symbol. To the Pythagoreans Ten represented Deity, Heaven, Eternity, and the Sun.* To ourselves Ten is Man and God Ahead. A heaven to reach for, although we may not grasp it.

Nine, with all the numbers behind it, is the completed cycle of man's experience; Ten begins the new cycle, on a higher spiral, the cycle of man's aspiration.

On the Tree of Life there are Ten spheres or Ten Emanations of the Divine Sephiroth and Malkuth, the Kingdom is the *Tenth*—our own world; in the Pattern on the Trestleboard there are Ten Statements; our laws of conduct were given in Ten Commandments and the decimal system is used all over the world. Unattainable as it may appear and mighty as it surely is, Ten is *our* number to use and to succeed with. If Ten is your Birth Card, you have the tools with which to fully accomplish.

In the Mundane Spread, we have placed one of the Ten's in the exact center (it would be Diamonds!); another stands behind it; a third is the center of the Mercury Line; and the fourth leads the Sun or Crown Line. In any position in which the card is held, we find the triangle—symbol of perfection in expression.

Here is success on all sides, as man stands in the center—two patterns of five (the number of man), carrying the protection of the Pentagram. Every

---

W. Wynn Westcott, Numbers.

Ten should consciously live in the realization that he is Man twice over—Man as himself and Man in the image of God. So are we all, but Ten is the only card that has that zero ever beside it. No forward step can be taken without meeting it, face to face.

Since what constitutes success is a purely individual question, we find every variety of expression in these Tens—a few of the very great, more of the very successful, and the vast majority who are utterly oblivious to the power in the equipment they have brought to earth as their kit of tools. None of them can be wholly devoid of elements of greatness, but many can and do live as though the purpose of life were to amass, attain, and control. But not even the atheist escapes his divine origin.

Hearts attain their success and overcome their obstacles through the Power of Love.

Clubs find their success in the mental field and secure it by sharing their knowledge.

Diamonds succeed as Masters of Matter. Their dominion is over all created *things.*

Spades success depends upon the degree of maturity they have reached. For them Ten is their initiation into a higher grade.

Ten of Hearts

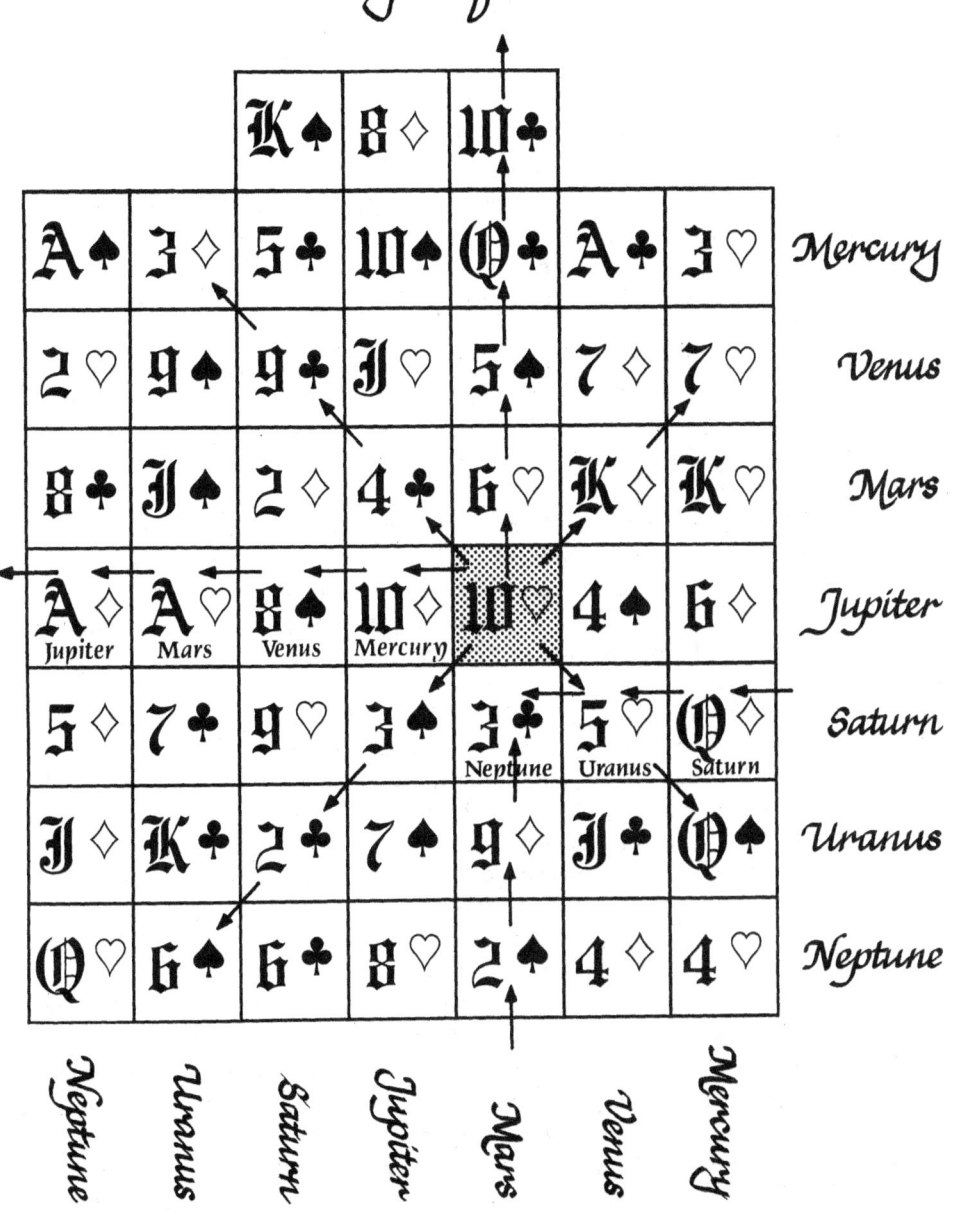

Hearts — Love
Ten of Hearts — Success in the Pursuit of Love
Ten in Hearts — Leadership and Idealism in Love

The Mars Card in the Jupiter Line. Displaces the **Jack of Clubs** in the Natural Spread

Through the initiatory steps of Eight and Nine—Power in Love and the achievement of Unselfishness—the Ten of Hearts people have reached a stage of independence and individuality in human relations. They know that all obstacles can be overcome through love, but they are (or should be) less personally involved than are those on the less developed levels. They have more chance for success in the pursuit of their objectives because they are not torn to pieces by their reactions to the threat they feel they receive from others.

For those who are living positively, there is no denial of warmth in relationships or of emotional satisfaction for themselves. They can love and be loved in security. On the negative side, there is such a drive for power and recognition that all personal love is lost in the conflict and the end result is a barrier of coldness and a lonely life. Like the Eight from which the power is derived, all people can operate on either plane—the mundane or the spiritual, or a balance can be struck between the two and release the initiative (Ten) for creation, progress, and pioneering in the fields that offer the best opportunities for individual growth. When that is attained, recognition and accomplishment follow as a natural consequence. Ten is the "higher octave" of One.

Because of the displacement of the Jack of Clubs, the first step for these people is the right direction of their mental attitudes. The Jack of Clubs is not always a clear thinker and may be quite indolent and sloppy. Reason and logic—the constructive qualities of the Jack of Clubs—should form the basis for all efforts for accomplishment.

The women are apt to be guided or dominated by their husbands; they are not always successful in marriage but will make a sincere effort for harmony. The men may operate under the Jack or the King (preferably the King) and find fewer obstacles and broader opportunities.

There is an element of so-called luck in the Ten of Hearts, augmented by the other Ten (Diamonds) in proximity. They are much affected by the Displacement Card. While they want to dispense love and kindliness, their natural approach is mental, and may be calculating, although the Mars-Jupiter conjunction usually inclines to impulsiveness.

Independence is highly prized and they will not submit to too much responsibility. Especially the men. When the women are stressing the Personality Card, they prefer easy and harmonious conditions to any assumption of personal power. Both emanate and respond to love and kindness, but there is seldom found any great tragedy connected with lost or misplaced love. They may miss the thrill and upliftment of the grand passion but they also escape the emotional devastation that often follows in its wake. To them, the attainment of the heights does not compensate for the fall to the depths. It is only in the uncertainty of the later years that they may mourn their lost dreams.

BIRTHDATES RULED BY THE TEN OF HEARTS

JULY 31–LEO–RULED BY THE SUN

Willing to work hard. Want business on a friendly basis and in a big way. Success comes through personal effort. If attracted to merchandising, like to handle small articles for general use and in large quantities; if to land, want a large acreage, cut into small lots for many people; if to politics, want to establish laws and principles for universal adoption. Have a strong cosmic attitude of mind. Writers, propagandists—always on important subjects. Can succeed as lawyers, artists, stage directors, managers.

AUGUST 29–VIRGO–RULED BY MERCURY

Money-minded. Want an occupation that brings quick results. Need an intelligent person to encourage them. Apt to be overcritical, nervous, and worrisome. Unlike many born in Virgo, are attracted to art, music, or drama. If in art, develop a careful technique. Can commercialize any talent. Writers, philosophers, essayists, preachers, teachers. Can succeed as manufacturers or engineers. Should develop their gift of intuition for release from narrow-mindedness and their overdeveloped critical faculty.

SEPTEMBER 27–LIBRA–RULED BY VENUS

Interests usually Venusian or literary, on the serious side. Many actors and composers in this date. May also be fine teachers of art or dramatics. Keen sense of beauty, high ideals. When writing is chosen, often direct their efforts to political reform. Are broad and universal in their thinking; believe that people are naturally right-minded and idealistic. Always give others the benefit of the doubt. Have a spirit of good will toward all.

OCTOBER 25–SCORPIO–RULED BY MARS

Great desire for affection; emotional life more disturbed than the majority of the Tens of Hearts. Keep problems bottled up and endure their suffering in silence. Will not be hampered in work or dictated to in private life. Never take orders. Anxious to succeed—in reputation as well as money. Demand perfection from employees. Good and just leaders. Capable in science, architecture, mining, and metal working. Seekers. Write history, philosophy, metaphysics. If seeking art—erratic, unusual.

NOVEMBER 23—SAGITTARIUS—RULED BY JUPITER

Highly nervous; should cultivate mental balance and avoid capricious excursions that may invite obsessions. Influenced by others but are a law unto themselves. Interested in a humanitarian cause and can teach it. May be unusually talented in music. Good government officials, lawyers, geologists, archeologists, chemists. Must work for humanity.

DECEMBER 21—SAGITTARIUS—RULED BY JUPITER

Unlike the other Sagittarius, have a fine mental balance and a strong sense of practicality, as well as a humanitarian spirit. Idealistic politicians or merchants. Work for the greatest good—and may become great themselves. Want all benefits on a universal scale. Successful writers with uplifting philosophy; political reformers, philanthropic business magnates. May seek art or theater but cannot go very far toward fame.

TEN OF HEARTS—PLANETARY SEQUENCE OF PERSONAL RELATIONSHIPS

Horizontal Line—Jupiter and Saturn

TEN OF DIAMONDS—MERCURY CARD IN THE JUPITER LINE

Great for business; communication and understanding. Excellent for friendship and love—except that all are probably short term. Use the relationship on a positive level, these natives are good for you no matter what you do with them.

Ten of Diamonds birthdates: January 17, February 15, March 13, April 11, May 9, June 7, July 5, August 3, September 1.

EIGHT OF SPADES—VENUS CARD IN THE SATURN LINE

If you ever fall in love with your doctor, he or she'll turn out to be this card. But forget the love other than on a friendship basis. This relationship will be a challenge that can turn into a burden, and you will walk away in the long run. Friendship is best.

Eight of Spades birthdates: January 6, February 4, March 2.

ACE OF HEARTS—MARS IN URANUS

You could knock yourself out fulfilling their need for love and only find aggravation as your reward. A stimulating friendship on an impersonal level—especially in the mutual discoveries of new ideas and ways to make money.

Ace of Hearts birthdate: December 30.

ACE OF DIAMONDS—JUPITER CARD IN THE NEPTUNE LINE

You might think that this is "the one" but you'll probably find someone with a completely different set of values than you. Extremely good for friendship and business, but don't get carried away emotionally on any level.

Ace of Diamonds birthdates: January 26, February 24, March 22, April 20, May 18, June 16, July 14, August 12, September 10, October 8, November 6, December 4.

QUEEN OF DIAMONDS—SATURN CARD IN THE MERCURY LINE

Great communication, except you'll find the realities they place before you too difficult to deal or cope with at times. Inevitable that you have this association, but try not to get closely involved.

Queen of Diamonds birthdates: January 15, February 13, March 11, April 9, May 7, June 5, July 3, August 1.

FIVE OF HEARTS—URANUS CARD IN THE VENUS LINE
(Saturn and Venus Lines on the Diagonal Lines)

An interesting relationship—but not fulfilling. They can be as fickle as you can be detached. A definite romantic attraction that's better forgotten. Unusual kind of friendship can form between the two of you. Business possible but other factors of the relationship may be too distracting for it to be successful.

Five of Hearts birthdates: October 30, November 28, December 26.

THREE OF CLUBS—NEPTUNE CARD IN THE MARS LINE
(Saturn Line on the Vertical Line)

A totally confusing and irritating relationship to which you may feel some sort of obligation. It's rare if you are able to pierce the shell, so don't create unnecessary problems for yourself. Step aside and call it quits if it obviously doesn't work.

Three of Clubs birthdates: May 29, June 27, July 25, August 23, September 21, October 19, November 17, December 15.

Vertical Line—Mars

SIX OF HEARTS—MARS LINE

Good rapport; strong mutual feelings about impersonal love. Admiration yet aggravating that they seem to be able to handle it. Why not you? Stay clear of personal attachments.

Six of Hearts birthdates: October 29, November 27, December 25.

FIVE OF SPADES—VENUS LINE

A true love association that you can't live with—nor they. Your winning ways with others will send them traveling anywhere rather than be with you. And from the very beginning you will become more winning as the Five of Spades subtly moves in to control you.

Five of Spades birthdates: January 9, February 7, March 5, April 3, May 1.

QUEEN OF CLUBS—MERCURY LINE

A stimulating argument can always be had between the two of you. Keep it on a positive level and you can both gain. Watch your immature side—don't let it take you over.

Queen of Clubs birthdates: January 28, February 26, March 24, April 22, May 20, June 18, July 16, August 14, September 12, October 10, November 8, December 6.

TEN OF CLUBS—CROWN LINE

A friend for life; romantic love possible but not as strong as man to man or woman to woman friendship. Any relationship a definite must.

Ten of Clubs birthdates: January 30, February 28, March 26, April 24, May 22, June 20, July 18, August 16, September 14, October 12, November 10, December 8.

TWO OF SPADES—NEPTUNE LINE

This may seem to be a great spree but wait twenty-four hours. This is probably not the person you thought he or she was and any committment could lead to problems. Difficult involvement on any level.

Two of Spades birthdates: January 12, February 10, March 8, April 6, May 4, June 2.

NINE OF DIAMONDS—URANUS LINE

Difficult to relate to unless both are involved in social welfare (volunteer) work. Not a good personal involvement on any level.

Nine of Diamonds birthdates: January 18, February 16, March 14, April 12, May 10, June 8, July 6, August 4, September 2.

THREE OF CLUBS—SATURN LINE: SEE HORIZONTAL LINE

Diagonal Lines

KING OF DIAMONDS—MARS AND VENUS LINES

Good person to be in business with; you do the selling and he does the signing. Minor temperamental explosions have nothing to do with you.

Possible romance, but not good if the King of Diamonds is female. Friendship not too probable.

King of Diamonds birthdates: January 14, February 12, March 10, April 8, May 6, June 4, July 2.

SEVEN OF HEARTS—VENUS AND MARS LINES

Dynamite sexual relationship that can lead to romance and marriage. Probable divorce due to your flirting and their jealousy. Good for friendship on an impersonal level—poor for business.

Seven of Hearts birthdates: September 30, October 28, November 26, December 24.

THREE OF SPADES—JUPITER AND SATURN LINES

A lot of talk and you might find something positive, but an overall poor relationship that is better left as a brief encounter.

Three of Spades birthdates: January 11, February 9, March 7, April 5, May 3, June 1.

TWO OF CLUBS—URANUS AND SATURN LINES

A romantic attraction that can turn you off one day—and on the next. Difficult to sustain an involvement on any level.

Two of Clubs birthdates: May 30, June 28, July 26, August 24, September 22, October 20, November 18, December 16.

SIX OF SPADES—NEPTUNE AND URANUS LINES

An important Karmic relationship; your opposite reflection. A discomforting involvement—probably argumentative, and probably unfounded. Don't permit a close association.

Six of Spades birthdates: January 8, February 6, March 4, April 2.

FIVE OF HEARTS—SATURN AND VENUS LINES; SEE HORIZONTAL LINE

QUEEN OF SPADES—URANUS AND MERCURY LINES

A romantic and/or friendship attraction that can be hard to cope with; their lifestyles could surprise you. A possible business relationship but probably of short duration.

Queen of Spades birthdate: January 2.

FOUR OF CLUBS—MARS AND JUPITER LINES

An intellectual friendship that could lead to a deep emotional feeling—brief encounters. Can be argumentative more than knowledgeable. Probably not a long-lasting involvement.

Four of Clubs birthdates: April 30, May 28, June 26, July 24, August 22, September 20, October 18, November 16, December 14.

NINE OF CLUBS—VENUS AND SATURN LINES

One look and you'll be in love, but you'll probably never have any money. A probable inescapable relationship and, depending on your own values, possible. A good friend but sometimes a little too much. A native who can really give you a run for your money—the question is whether or not it's really worth it to you. No business involvements.

Nine of Clubs birthdates: January 31, February 29, March 27, April 25, May 23, June 21, July 19, August 17, September 15, October 13, November 11, December 9.

THREE OF DIAMONDS—MERCURY AND URANUS LINES

Too worried about the future to hold your interest for long. Inconsistent in desires; an aggravation to you.

Three of Diamonds birthdates: January 24, February 22, March 20, April 18, May 16, June 14, July 12, August 10, September 8, October 6, November 4, December 2.

TEN OF HEARTS FAMOUS BIRTHDATES

August 29	Ingrid Bergman
	Elliot Gould
	Charles Boyer
October 25	Anthony Franciosa
	Pablo Picasso
	Admiral Richard Byrd
November 23	Boris Karloff
December 21	Jane Fonda
	John W. McCormack
	Joseph Stalin

Ten of Clubs

Clubs — Knowledge
Ten of Clubs — Mental Illumination
Ten in Clubs — The Will of Good plus the Science of Mind

The Mercury Card in the Crown Line. Displaces the **Jack of Spades** in the Natural Spread.

The Crown or the Sun Cards have the privilege of choosing their position—and their lives and relationships—but do not depart from the inherent qualities of suit or number.

The Ten of Clubs, being the first card in its line, is under the rulership of Mercury and is therefore conditioned by all that planet stands for: mental processes, approaches, and reactions; ideas and communications; education and mind-training.

Being Clubs, it symbolizes knowledge—its acquisition and dissemination. Regardless of the planetary influence—its basic ingredients remain.

The displacement of the Jack of Spades suggests the danger of fixation. The firmness in the Jack of Spades and adherence to principle are well worthy of emulation, but the Ten of Clubs can go astray through stubbornness.

Their greatest success invariably lies in the mental field. If their knowledge is applied from high motives, their needs are supplied from the Limitless Substance, there is seldom any real lack of supply, although they often fear limitation. They are looking toward the Eight of Diamonds in their own line and they should have no trouble in establishing a right sense of values. Again, looking forward, the King of Spades gives power through wisdom.

Planetary Sequence

		K♠ Venus	8♦ Mercury	10♣			
A♠	3♦	5♣ Neptune	10♠ Uranus	Q♣ Saturn	A♣ Jupiter	3♥ Mars	Mercury
2♥	9♠	9♣	J♥	5♠	7♦	7♥	Venus
8♣	J♠	2♦	4♣	6♥	K♦	K♥	Mars
A♦	A♥	8♠	10♦	10♥	4♠	6♦	Jupiter
5♦	7♣	9♥	3♠	3♣	5♥	Q♦	Saturn
J♦	K♣	2♣	7♠	9♦	J♣	Q♠	Uranus
Q♥	6♠	6♣	8♥	2♠	4♦	4♥	Neptune

Neptune　Uranus　Saturn　Jupiter　Mars　Venus　Mercury

Mundane Spread

There is always the power to make money, but the effort is sometimes lacking. The gift of choice may become a source of confusion, for they can't always tell just where they are or should be operating. They want to be productive and successful, but if they have not reached the stage in their development where they can depend upon intuitional guidance. They sometimes waste many valuable years in experimentation before they find the right vocation. "Make your calling and election sure," said St. Paul—and he might have been talking directly to the Ten of Clubs.

The True Place is the Venus Card in the Jupiter Line. The gift of knowledge is not the only star in their crown; in the Plan, love shines beside it with equal brilliance—love of their work and love for those with whom they have come to share their knowledge. Those who are working in that consciousness are Jupiter's own heirs.

BIRTHDATES RULED BY THE TEN OF CLUBS

JANUARY 30–AQUARIUS–RULED BY URANUS

Very ambitious people and fully equipped for leadership. Can excel in any line they choose and should not be hampered by equal partnerships or associates from whom they must take orders. Always willing for improvement. Art or science are the best fields, with government offices a close second. Exceptional qualities and unusual popularity may elevate them to high government positions.

FEBRUARY 28–PISCES–RULED BY NEPTUNE

Restless and changeable. May suffer from people who are changeable themselves—and unreliable. May become famous in music, drama, or art, but often lack application and persistence. Subject to accidents through carelessness or daydreaming. Like travel and a variety of interests, but should guard against a tendency to laziness. Should seek advice in making investments.

MARCH 26–ARIES–RULED BY MARS

Work well by fits and starts. Too apt to lose interest and abandon a project that gives promise of success through persistence. Like to lay out a progressive plan and leave it to others to execute. Want to make money quickly; not so good for the long pull. Work well with women as employees, not as partners. Good promoters. Good dealers or executives in artistic lines but seldom gifted as artists or performers. Cultivation of an attractive personality goes far toward success.

APRIL 24–TAURUS–RULED BY VENUS

Responsible and protective. May become leaders through willingness to respond to the demands made upon them. Must be kings in their own homes. Like to be entertained and waited upon. Attracted to the stage as actors. If business is chosen, want it big. Fair and honest in all dealings. Emotional and warmhearted. Can write fluently and dramatically. If in a government position, more fatherly than dictatorial.

MAY 22–TAURUS OR GEMINI–RULED BY VENUS OR MERCURY

Those who still carry the stamp of Taurus are inclined to acting, composing, and playwriting and can easily commercialize their talents. The Gemini-born are more mental than emotional or dramatic. These may succeed in the educational field, as critics or satirical writers, essayists, etc. All are affected by home conditions; inharmony interferes with ability to concentrate—and consequent success. Deep interest (Taurus) or curiosity (Gemini) in metaphysics.

JUNE 20–GEMINI–RULED BY MERCURY

Writers, lecturers, politicians. Should be before the public. Clever and versatile. Willing to give service if interested in the "cause." Like to deal with people and changing conditions. Always curious about what makes people (or things) tick. Have ups and downs in finances. Often undertake more than they can carry through. Want business that is quick-moving, bringing quick returns. Liable to become overextended. Not as sure of themselves as the Geminis of May 22nd.

JULY 18–CANCER–RULED BY THE MOON

Homelife uncertain; often disturbed. Self-protective. Want to make a good impression and shine in the community, on the platform, or in the classroom. Self becomes less important in the later years and gives way to the spirit of service. May become absorbed in metaphysics and undergo a complete change of viewpoint. Health affected by emotions; suffer through disillusionment. Must work for impersonality. May inherit from family estate or be aided by some woman. Want technical perfection in their work.

AUGUST 16–LEO–RULED BY THE SUN

If high-minded, may attain great heights along spiritual lines. If connected with business, should deal with large corporations, handle big money. The majority have the right mental attitude toward their assets and use them generously and philanthropically. Interested in humanity, often in lost causes. Good counselors; can give practical as well as spiritual guidance. On the less exalted levels are good entertainers and show people.

SEPTEMBER 14—VIRGO—RULED BY MERCURY

Restless, mental, curious. Often have inventive ability arising from research. Good school teachers, accountants, investment counselors. Values usually referred to money. Like a fast-moving business but become swamped with details. Good for publishing—if the distribution is left to others. Secretive about their private affairs. Better at developing an established business than initiating a new one.

OCTOBER 12—LIBRA—RULED BY VENUS

Emotionalism apt to interfere with good mental balance and strength of character. Should not work alone but should avoid becoming emotionally involved with associates in work. Must keep home and business separated. Are domestic, magnetic, and popular. May become well-loved figures in public life. Will not submit to limitation; will walk out if inharmony develops. Have a keen eye for beauty and line; make good architects. Can also succeed as artists, actors, lawyers, and judges. Must cultivate firmness and clear thinking.

NOVEMBER 10—SCORPIO—RULED BY MARS

If not developed, will be opinionated, egotistic, dominating—even ruthless. Apt to think they are infallible in judgment. Too exacting with associates. Are strictly honest but biased in opinions. Want to work for the good. Interested in intelligent people. May become absorbed in occultism; often psychic and impressionable to higher influences. Can diagnose intuitively. Make good public servants, reformers, writers, directors, scientific researchers. Protected financially.

DECEMBER 8—SAGITTARIUS—RULED BY JUPITER

Interested in the ground. Can succeed in real estate and should own a home in the country. Must guard against becoming mercenary. Usually connected with considerable money. Attracted to banking, large corporations. If drawn to metaphysics, can go far as writers, reformers, educators, and religious teachers. Always executive and clear-headed. May become of great value to the community.

TEN OF CLUBS—PLANETARY SEQUENCE OF PERSONAL RELATIONSHIPS

Horizontal Line—Crown and Mercury

EIGHT OF DIAMONDS—MERCURY CARD IN THE JUPITER LINE

Perfect association for business; cannot help but bring success. Temporary or sporadic for romance or friendship but, in any event, a valued association.

Eight of Diamonds birthdates: January 19, February 17, March 15, April 13, May 11, June 9, July 7, August 5, September 3, October 1.

KING OF SPADES—VENUS CARD IN THE SATURN LINE

A love and a responsibility; someone you care enough about to spend some of your precious time—to help them better understand themselves. In rare instances, a guru-type to you (and to all). Don't let the relationship weigh you down—especially if it leans on the negative side.

King of Spades birthdate: January 1.

THREE OF HEARTS—MARS CARD IN THE MERCURY LINE

Too much uncertainty about self-image to interest you. Conversations feel one-sided and negative. Don't let it get to you; pass on the relationship.

Three of Hearts birthdates: November 30, December 28.

ACE OF CLUBS—JUPITER CARD IN THE VENUS LINE
(Mercury and Venus Lines on the Diagonal Lines)

Immediate attraction for romance or friendship; you'll like their inquiring minds and can truly feel your strength through this native. Sex life may not be fantastic but you'll have a lot to talk about. Good involvement on any level.

Ace of Clubs birthdates: May 31, June 29, July 27, August 25, September 23, October 21, November 19, December 17.

QUEEN OF CLUBS—SATURN CARD IN THE MARS LINE
(Mercury Line on the Vertical Line)

A Karmic relationship, perhaps a male co-worker. Irritations and frustrations because you may feel they are not as articulate as you, which can be extremely erroneous. Use your awareness on the positive level—you both deserve to know each other. Don't attempt any close associations.

Queen of Clubs birthdates: January 28, February 26, March 24, April 22, May 20, June 18, July 16, August 14, September 12, October 10, November 8, December 6.

TEN OF SPADES—URANUS CARD IN THE JUPITER LINE
(Mercury and Jupiter Lines on the Diagonal Lines)

A good work affiliation—keep after them a little bit in order for them to work at their full potential. You'll find it's worth it. Personal involvements are possible but if you're choosing. Pick friendship over romance.

Ten of Spades birthdates: January 4, February 2.

FIVE OF CLUBS—NEPTUNE CARD IN THE SATURN LINE

Confusion and probable disillusionment will rule this relationship if you become involved in any way other than a total impersonal association. Don't bother, you may be projecting traits and qualities into this native that truly aren't there.

Five of Clubs birthdates: March 31, April 29, May 27, June 25, July 23, August 21, September 19, October 17, November 15, December 13.

Vertical Line—Mars

TWO OF SPADES—NEPTUNE LINE

Another relationship that you should think twice about. Difficult on any level because they won't understand you and you won't understand why. Take a pass.

Two of Spades birthdates: January 12, February 10, March 8, April 6, May 4, June 2.

NINE OF DIAMONDS—URANUS LINE

A friend—or lover—who may attempt to spar with you, probably in achievements. Take your time and really get to know this native before you get closely associated in anything.

Nine of Diamonds birthdates: January 18, February 16, March 14, April 12, May 10, June 8, July 6, August 4, September 2.

THREE OF CLUBS—SATURN LINE

Not a good combination on any level; very little rapport. You'll have difficulties in reaching them on almost any subject. Best left alone.

Three of Clubs birthdates: May 29, June 27, August 23, September 21, October 19, November 17, December 15.

TEN OF HEARTS—JUPITER LINE

This native can do no wrong—even when you recognize their follies, you'll understand, forgive, and start over. A good relationship for you on a friendship level. Romance would leave you in a fluctuating state and business is even worse, but not impossible. Don't miss this involvement—even their memory will leave you better off in the long run.

Ten of Hearts birthdates: July 31, August 29, September 27, October 25, November 23, December 21.

Your Place in the Cards

SIX OF HEARTS–MARS LINE

Stimulating and energizing attitudes to take life a little easier is what this native will bring to you. Don't attempt a close involvement of any kind or it could be destructive. Casual friendship is best.

Six of Hearts birthdates: October 29, November 27, December 25.

FIVE OF SPADES–VENUS LINE

Good feelings about this person that may surprise you. Perhaps a co-worker, or someone in a similar type of work. Not a close relationship as you won't put up with them on a one-to-one basis.

Five of Spades birthdates: January 9, February 7, March 5, April 13, May 1.

QUEEN OF CLUBS–MERCURY LINE: SEE HORIZONTAL LINE

Diagonal Lines

TEN OF SPADES–MERCURY AND JUPITER LINES: SEE HORIZONTAL LINE

NINE OF CLUBS–VENUS AND SATURN LINES

An immediate romantic attraction that could turn into a real burden on you if you are unable to control this native. A probable inescapable involvement so keep them on a leash from the beginning.

Nine of Clubs birthdates: January 31, February 29, March 27, April 25, May 23, June 21, July 19, August 17, September 15, October 13, November 11, December 9.

JACK OF SPADES–MARS AND URANUS LINES
(Ten of Clubs Displacement Card)

An absolute irritation you won't be that aware of in the beginning. Heavy sex drive for opposite sex and a challenging involvement until you realize that it isn't going anywhere. A probable attempt to dominate you–or master you–in some way, because of the Displacement Card. Walk on eggs with this native.

Jack of Spades birthdates: January 3, February 1.

ACE OF DIAMONDS–JUPITER AND NEPTUNE LINES

A good, close friend or romantic involvement where you will never really know everything about them. Your end goals are quite different, so be careful in the romance department. Good relationship on all levels.

Ace of Diamonds birthdates: January 26, February 24, March 22, April 20, May 18, June 16, July 14, August 12, September 10, October 8, November 6, December 4.

ACE OF CLUBS—MERCURY AND VENUS LINES:
SEE HORIZONTAL LINES

SEVEN OF HEARTS—VENUS AND MERCURY LINES

You'll be romantically turned on by this native but probably won't be able to reach them verbally. Even if you do, chances are the relationship is quite short-term. You two are living in two different worlds.

Seven of Hearts birthdates: September 30, October 28, November 26, December 24.

TEN OF CLUBS FAMOUS BIRTHDATES

January 30	Franklin Delano Roosevelt
February 28	Zero Mostel Svetlana Stalina
March 26	Tennessee Williams Robert Frost
May 22	Sir Laurence Olivier
June 20	Errol Flynn
July 18	Red Skelton
August 16	Robert Culp
November 10	Richard Burton Martin Luther
December 8	Sammy Davis, Jr. James Thurber

Ten of Diamonds

Diamonds — Values
Ten of Diamonds — A Master of Matter
Ten in Diamonds — A leader in Material Control

The Jupiter Card in the Jupiter Line. Displaces the **Queen of Clubs** in the Natural Spread

This is the most important of the money cards, for it is in the exact center of the Mundane Spread. Man chose to make money the pivotal point around which all else should swing and selected the most powerful of the money cards to guarantee "success." The Ten of Diamonds is one of the Master Cards.

In the Divine Plan, Receptivity and Intelligence are the focal points. And while these qualities are relegated to second place in the eyes of the world, the aware ones may "borrow" them by virtue of displacement.

The majority of these natives are money-conscious, but there are many who are, instead, Value conscious—a very different matter. They translate their full accomplishment into cosmic terms.

In general, there is a lack of true spirituality. The type of religion they profess is traditional and orthodox; the goal they prize is acquisition. They are in great danger of becoming mercenary.

This is a better card for a man than a woman. The men can avoid the Queen of Diamonds and its unfortunate sequence. For both sexes, there is usually the promise of inheritance. They can always succeed and are always protected where money is involved. They may get down to the last dollar, threatened with loss of business or property—and then, by clever manipulation or last-minute help, turn the threatened failure to success.

Planetary Sequence

			K♠	8♦	10♣			
A♠	3♦	5♣	10♠	Q♣	A♣	3♥		Mercury
2♥	9♠	9♣	J♥	5♠	7♦	7♥		Venus
8♣	J♠	2♦	4♣	6♥	K♦	K♥		Mars
A♦	A♥	8♠	10♦	10♥	4♠	6♦		Jupiter
Mars	Venus	Mercury						
5♦	7♣	9♥	3♠	3♣	5♥	Q♦		Saturn
			Neptune	Uranus	Saturn	Jupiter		
J♦	K♣	2♣	7♠	9♦	J♣	Q♠		Uranus
Q♥	6♠	6♣	8♥	2♠	4♦	4♥		Neptune

Neptune Uranus Saturn Jupiter Mars Venus Mercury

Mundane Spread

If a man, will benefit by association with a successful woman; if a woman, is likely to be in business for herself or in a key position of management. They all like to associate with people who have something to offer—if not actual money, then position, social standing, or family background. They are not necessarily snobs, but they want to stand well in the eyes of the world and they want their surroundings to give evidence of prosperity.

Commercializing their abilities comes easily. If they engage in business, they never fear size or extent; they know they can handle it, and make it pay.

The True Place is the Mercury Card in the Uranus Line. There are few who lack brains and sharp wits. While their education is sought primarily along business lines, they have great respect for knowledge and want to acquire enough of it to be able to take their place in any company.

There are many philanthropists and benefactors in these birthdates, many with a strong sense of universal obligation and a desire to put their money to constructive use. They are invariably generous with any surplus and some there are who will deprive themselves to help the less fortunate. Great buildings, enterprises, and monuments have been established in their name and many good deeds live after them. They are tested by their sense of values.

BIRTHDATES RULED BY THE TEN OF DIAMONDS

JANUARY 17—CAPRICORN—RULED BY SATURN

Very patriotic. Excellent government officials: ambassadors, representatives, diplomats. Interested in sociological questions, state or federal laws, government procedure. If in business, usually for themselves. Self-confident in the business world, not in their emotional lives; changeable in feelings. Want to be associated with things that are well established; no gamblers. Can succeed in oil, mining, and manufacturing.

FEBRUARY 15—AQUARIUS—RULED BY MARS

Famous actors, writers, and educators are found in this birthdate. Always have a large following; their works have a wide distribution. Personal lives disturbed by doubt and unrest. Make good salespeople, attorneys, and realtors. Interested in labor problems. Want spiritual security, but do not know how to cultivate it. Should make a determined study of metaphysics.

MARCH 13—PISCES—RULED BY NEPTUNE

Less self-confident than the other Ten of Diamonds. Full of fears and worries. Build their world around their own small circle. Give willing service, but always personal. Can succeed in transportation; like travel but seldom satisfied with journeys. Good musicians; may be good dancers. Dutiful and devoted nurses. Should serve in broad fields, impersonally. Lives often narrow and unproductive.

APRIL 11–ARIES–RULED BY MARS

Square-dealing; honest. Nervous and emotional. Ambitious; dominated by a desire to stand well. Willing to serve, but want full payment. Need plenty of action to be happy. Not content with small or inactive business. Can succeed at law but should not become judges; too emotional and biased. Swayed by personal opinions and fixed ideas. Very moral. Should avoid intolerance.

MAY 9–TAURUS–RULED BY VENUS

Want harmony at home and among friends. Want to stand well and put up a good front. Combine business with social activities. Ruled by emotions and ambition. Apply their efforts to accumulation.

Make good doctors; have good bedside manners. Can succeed in real estate, home furnishings, food. Not always as universally minded as their birthday number requires. Climbers.

JUNE 7–GEMINI–RULED BY MERCURY

Want quick turnovers. Will work only if interested. Can lecture, teach, and make money at it. Can overcome the tendency to superficiality by cultivating the mind. Have a variety of skills. Give the impression of instability but are often serious, even depressed. Uncertain of right place; will make many experiments before settling down. Can sell if they have a faith in the product. A mental occupation best for success.

JULY 5–CANCER–RULED BY THE MOON

Seek important and successful people as background. Self-indulgent. Dislike too much work or effort. Expect help from others. Can be public-spirited and philanthropic if they want to. Writers, philosophers, art patrons, bankers, merchants. Like a social type of business, with short hours.

AUGUST 3–LEO–RULED BY THE SUN

Perhaps the most ambitious, but surely the warmest-hearted of the Ten of Diamonds. Want top place; can fill it and give good service. Loved by their intimates; popular if in the public eye. Make good leaders and directors, top merchants, actors, and dramatists. Can commercialize drama; can always make a profit. Effective and dramatic writers. Appealing personalities.

SEPTEMBER 1–VIRGO–RULED BY MERCURY

Scientists and researchers. Can commercialize diet, health, beauty culture, and cults. Motives usually personal; want good returns for all efforts. Careful and thorough in work; can usually command high salaries. Particular about appearance, good dressers. Willing to work very hard for results. Hate to soil their hands. Inclined to be critical. Must guard against selfishness and narrow-mindedness. Are "choice" and precise.

TEN OF DIAMONDS–PLANETARY SEQUENCE OF PERSONAL RELATIONSHIPS

Horizontal Line–Jupiter and Saturn

EIGHT OF SPADES–MERCURY CARD IN THE SATURN LINE

An excellent choice to invest in real estate with, especially in medical buildings. However, explore other avenues of business with hesitation. Good for friendship; a close confidant-type; romantic associations are temporary and probably difficult, so try to avoid that area of involvement.

Eight of Spades birthdates: January 6, February 4, March 2.

ACE OF HEARTS–VENUS CARD IN THE URANUS LINE

A surprising love affair/marriage that will probably surprise you as well; someone you would not ordinarily pick. Good for friendship, but probably not too profitable for you on a straight business basis. Pursue the personal involvement first.

Ace of Hearts birthdate: December 30.

ACE OF DIAMONDS–MARS CARD IN THE NEPTUNE LINE

Sexual stimulation, but probably not (in your opinion) what you're really looking for in a mate. You're right. This association is much better in the friendship or business category, but don't always give them as much credit as they might demand of you. Spell out all impersonal relationships—as you probably will on the personal level.

Ace of Diamonds birthdates: January 26, February 24, March 22, April 20, May 18, June 16, July 14, August 12, September 10, October 8, November 6, December 4.

QUEEN OF DIAMONDS–JUPITER CARD IN THE MERCURY LINE

This native will probably lie verbally and lay down their life physically— for you. Sometimes a destructive force for themselves, they will only bring good things to you. A possible love interest that should be pursued; an interesting friend who always has something to say. Business might be a little more difficult than necessary, but you will still profit by the affiliation.

Queen of Diamonds birthdates: January 15, February 13, March 11, April 9, May 7, June 5, July 3, August 1.

FIVE OF HEARTS–SATURN CARD IN THE VENUS LINE

A love affair/marriage that could drain you dry. You will hardly ever know where you stand emotionally with this native, thus thrusting you farther into your work and depriving yourself of the warm feeling of love. Don't get involved if you can help it, on any level.

Five of Hearts birthdates: October 30, November 28, December 26.

THREE OF CLUBS–URANUS CARD IN THE MARS LINE

Many little surprises that seem to be a constant source of irritation to you; someone who seems to have sidestepped the normal path and whose form of progressiveness can become aggravating. Don't bother to get too involved. You are really not on the same path.

Three of Clubs birthdates: May 29, June 27, July 25, August 23, September 21, October 19, November 17, December 15.

THREE OF SPADES–NEPTUNE CARD IN THE JUPITER LINE

Someone whom you may never be able to understand but who will never do anything to hurt you; an ethereal type person who may seem "spaced" at times, believing, but always "writing endings" on situations and people. Friendship is fine but don't attempt anything else without close scrutiny.

Three of Spades birthdates: January 11, February 9, March 7, April 5, May 3, June 1.

Vertical Line–Jupiter

FOUR OF CLUBS–MARS LINE

Much too talkative to understand what you might be saying, too frustrating a relationship. Stimulating at times but not worth the overall effort involved to sustain any kind of involvement.

Four of Clubs birthdates: April 30, May 28, June 26, July 24, August 22, September 20, October 18, November 16, December 14.

JACK OF HEARTS–VENUS LINE

A definite romantic attraction that is at extreme opposite ends. Concessions that this native would have to make to make the relationship work from your point of view; a love affair that could work for you both if you are willing to give each other enough freedom to fulfill your individual tasks. This is more of a problem for you than for the Jack of Hearts.

Jack of Hearts birthdates: July 30, August 28, September 26, October 24, November 22, December 20.

TEN OF SPADES—MERCURY LINE

A good business affiliation, especially if you permit them to do as much work as is possible from home. A stimulating friend capable of great philosophical conversations. Neither a lover nor a husband or wife, so don't pursue it if you haven't already.

Ten of Spades birthdates: January 4, February 2.

EIGHT OF DIAMONDS—CROWN LINE

Excellent for any and all involvements. Business exceptional as are both friendship and romantic love. You will both live extremely well, and together, if you don't try to outdo each other. Good rapport on both material and spiritual planes, if you try.

Eight of Diamonds birthdates: January 19, February 17, March 15, April 13, May 11, June 9, July 7, August 5, September 3, October 1.

EIGHT OF HEARTS—NEPTUNE LINE

A salesman; you won't know how he does it, but he does it. Don't spread him too thin, some of his power could be lost. Don't get involved romantically; it may be inevitable but you may also regret it.

SEVEN OF SPADES—URANUS LINE

One of the more quiet members of your business relationships, but not without elements of surprise. Good for business in general; an excellent casual acquaintance; a teacher, etc. But may be too pushy and unsettled for a satisfactory romantic involvement.

Seven of Spades birthdates: January 7, February 5, March 3, April 1.

THREE OF SPADES—SATURN LINE: SEE HORIZONTAL LINE

Diagonal Lines

TWO OF DIAMONDS—MARS AND SATURN LINES

Good communications; a possible affiliation with an Eight of Spades, as well. Especially stimulating if in the field of medicine. Romantically, sexy and temporary; friendship could be irritating, and complaining.

Two of Diamonds birthdates: January 25, February 23, March 21, April 19, May 17, June 15, July 13, August 11, September 9, October 7, November 5, December 3.

NINE OF SPADES—VENUS AND URANUS LINES

A personable person who will attract you immediately; urge them to be involved with public service work or a type of philanthropic work and they'll keep you happier. A definite romance that should not be missed. Good for friendship and possible for business providing they work for you.

Nine of Spades birthdates: January 5, February 3, March 1.

ACE OF SPADES—MERCURY AND NEPTUNE LINES

As much as you try, you'll never be able to convince this person of anything; so stop trying. Enjoy them on the material plane, where you can both relate and stop getting aggravated; it's not really their fault. Friendship best; business not recommended; and romance should be completely out.

Ace of Spades birthdates: January 13, February 11, March 9, April 7, May 5, June 3, July 1.

THREE OF CLUBS—SATURN AND MARS LINES

A good verbal relationship on subjects you don't have to associate with business; friendship a probability; business and romance should not be considered.

Three of Clubs birthdates: May 29, June 27, July 25, August 23, September 21, October 19, November 17, December 15.

JACK OF CLUBS—URANUS AND VENUS LINES

You like them but you won't know what to think of them. A good business affiliation—successful and lucrative; poor for romance although you will undoubtedly wish or want or be involved; fair for friendship if you don't put too much faith in this native without a written contract.

Jack of Clubs birthdates: January 29, February 27, March 25, April 23, May 21, June 19, July 17, September 13, October 11, November 9, December 7.

FOUR OF HEARTS—MERCURY AND NEPTUNE LINES

A highly emotional individual who is always willing to tell you about his or her fantasies but rarely is capable of executing their heart's desire. An irritating and frustrating situation for you; best to avoid if possible, other than an impersonal friendship.

Four of Hearts birthdates: October 31, November 29, December 27.

Your Place in the Cards

SIX OF HEARTS—DOUBLE MARS LINES

A totally stimulating and sometimes offensive relationship. An excellent salesman for you. Although you may not approve of their methods, you would certainly approve of the final financial outcome. Don't get involved romantically, and only sporadically if a friendship.

Six of Hearts birthdates: October 29, November 27, December 25.

SEVEN OF DIAMONDS—DOUBLE VENUS LINES

A definite love of all kinds—possibility of the two of you going into business together; results could be sensational. Be more practical while they're emotional. Pursue any and all involvements.

Seven of Diamonds birthdates: January 20, February 18, March 16, April 14, May 12, June 10, July 8, August 6, September 4, October 2.

NINE OF HEARTS—DOUBLE SATURN LINES

An impossible relationship; you can never supply their needs nor they, yours. Casual friendship is best. Try to stay away from all other involvements.

Nine of Hearts birthdates: August 30, September 28, October 26, November 24, December 22.

KING OF CLUBS—DOUBLE URANUS LINES

They'll never cease to amaze you with their knowledge, and you'll never cease to help them apply it. Romance is a definite must; business good; and friendship excellent. Pursue them all.

King of Clubs birthdates: January 27, February 25, March 23, April 21, May 19, June 17, July 15, August 13, September 11, October 9, November 7, December 5.

QUEEN OF HEARTS—DOUBLE NEPTUNE LINES

You probably won't particularly like this person; won't trust them and will find them to be almost irritating. Trust your own emotions. These individuals have wonderful winning ways, but can also be negative. Know the person extremely well before any kind of committment whatsoever.

Queen of Hearts birthdates: July 29, August 27, September 25, October 23, November 21, December 19.

TEN OF DIAMONDS FAMOUS BIRTHDATES

January 17	Al Capone
	Benjamin Franklin

February 15	Galileo Cyrus McCormick	
May 9	Candice Bergen Albert Finney Pancho Gonzalez Mike Wallace	
June 7	Tom Jones Dean Martin	
July 5	Georges Pompidou P. T. Barnum George Sand Andrei Gromyko	
August 3	Tony Bennett Ernie Pyle	
September 1	Melvin Laird	

Ten of Spades

Planetary Sequence

			K♠	8♦	10♣			
A♠ Mars	3♦ Venus	5♣ Mercury	10♠	Q♣	A♣	3♥	Mercury
2♥	9♠	9♣	J♥ Neptune	5♠ Uranus	7♦ Saturn	7♥ Jupiter	Venus
8♣	J♠	2♦	4♣	6♥	K♦	K♥	Mars
A♦	A♥	8♠	10♦	10♥	4♠	6♦	Jupiter
5♦	7♣	9♥	3♠	3♣	5♥	Q♦	Saturn
J♦	K♣	2♣	7♠	9♦	J♣	Q♠	Uranus
Q♥	6♠	6♣	8♥	2♠	4♦	4♥	Neptune

Neptune | Uranus | Saturn | Jupiter | Mars | Venus | Mercury

Mundane Spread

Spades — Labor; The Path to Wisdom
Ten of Spades — Success in Work and Development
Ten in Spades — Glorification of Labor

The Jupiter Card in the Mercury Line. Displaces the **Four of Hearts** in the Natural Spread

For these people, home and business are closely associated, and the one may seriously interfere with the other. They are often found conducting their business at home, hampered by constant interruptions and lack of application.

While Tens are Success Cards, the natives are not always successful people, even though they are invariably protected up to a certain point. This is especially true of the Ten of Spades, for his achievement depends entirely upon the degree of maturity he has reached. Until thirty-six, he is usually operating (in the case of the men) under the Jack of Spades; thereafter, he may choose the King, if he has the spiritual ambition to seek a pattern of greater development. For the men of all cards up to the Court group, there are three planes of operation: the Birth Card, the mental card (the Jack), and the rulership card (the King). For the women, there are but two: the Birth Card and the Personality Card (the Queen); if the Queen is the Birth Card there is, of course, no alternate.

The position of the Ten of Spades is similar to a Mercury-Jupiter conjunction—a combination of good mind and good judgment. The card is crowned by the Eight of Diamonds, so these qualities may be especially operative in the realm of finance. That this is not always the case is due to the fact that we are not always aware of our "crowns," so we fail to wear them.

In the majority of cases, these people are successful in commercial lines. They are more stimulated when the turnover is speedy: mail order, telephone, messages.

Development, awareness, and especially the urge to seek the wisdom they have come to acquire—often delayed until middle life. Operating under the Jack can and often does result in shiftlessness and irresponsibility; if that persists, the birthright is lost and the Ten of Spades goes down to a defeat that is all the more ignominious because of his high calling.

Homelife may be neglected for business, or vice versa. The displacement of the Four of Hearts causes love and its security to be an important factor. Unnecessary sacrifices are made in its name and a resultant self-undoing defeats the main objectives.

The Ace of Spades (the Mars Force) is the Master Card for these Ten of Spades. When the desire for wisdom is paramount, they may become Kings in their own right and assume full command over their material affairs. For the women there is a greater problem; they may be weakened by negative operation under the Queen and may become household servants or drudges.

One is never sure of just what course these natives will take, nor are they always sure themselves. Their potential is great; their performance often below the level of mediocrity. Working toward the King of Spades, the highest of the Initiates, may seem too distant a goal to strive for.

Your Place in the Cards

BIRTHDATES RULED BY THE TEN OF SPADES

JANUARY 4–CAPRICORN–RULED BY SATURN

Can work well behind the scenes, as detectives, in secret service, or as confidential agents of the government. Can succeed in commerce and commercial projects on a large scale. Willing to work hard. Are dependable and strictly honest. Good managers of building and contracting projects. Are well fitted for a high government post, given the requisite educational foundation.

FEBRUARY 2–AQUARIUS–RULED BY URANUS

Interested in people—human nature as a study. Writers, psychologists, sociologists, economists. May have outstanding musical talent, especially for stringed instruments. Attracted to cults and theories—technocracy, isms and ologies. Can go farther if they will cultivate more frankness; are often charged with untruthfulness. Are constitutionally secretive.

TEN OF SPADES–PLANETARY SEQUENCE OF PERSONAL RELATIONSHIPS

Horizontal Line—Mercury and Venus

FIVE OF CLUBS–MERCURY CARD IN THE SATURN LINE

A temporary relationship that will probably blow through your life like a cool breeze but leave you somewhat worse off than you were before. Best not to attempt any kind of involvements at all.

Five of Clubs birthdates: March 31, April 29, May 27, June 25, July 23, August 21, September 19, October 17, November 15, December 13.

THREE OF DIAMONDS–VENUS CARD IN THE URANUS LINE

Someone you will definitely like; full of little pleasant surprises. A good person to work for you or to be in business with. Romance a definite possibility, as is friendship.

Three of Diamonds birthdates: January 24, February 22, March 20, April 18, May 16, June 14, July 12, August 10, September 8, October 6, November 4, December 2.

ACE OF SPADES–MARS CARD IN THE NEPTUNE LINE

A sexual attraction—or mental stimulation if in a business relationship. You don't feel them totally trustworthy. Take another look; it may be your own aggravations jading your mind. Friendship and business possible if you are the boss; don't attempt a personal relationship in any event.

Ace of Spades birthdates: January 13, February 11, March 9, April 7, May 5, June 3, July 1.

SEVEN OF HEARTS–JUPITER CARD IN THE MERCURY LINE

If romantically inclined, be prepared to work at home; this is where this native would want you. A good relationship for friendship and romance, especially verbal. Not bad for business, but not dynamic.

Seven of Hearts birthdates: September 30, October 28, November 26, December 24.

SEVEN OF DIAMONDS–SATURN CARD IN THE VENUS LINE

Possibly an inevitable love affair at some point in your life. Better not pursued in marriage, as could be difficult for you and for them. Friendship and business both probable. Listen; they do know how to make money.

Seven of Diamonds birthdates: January 20, February 18, March 16, April 14, May 12, June 10, July 8, August 6, September 4, October 2.

FIVE OF SPADES–URANUS CARD IN THE MARS LINE

Explosive problems over work; understand that these individuals mean well. Explore all possibilities, but an impersonal involvement is best.

Five of Spades birthdates: January 9, February 7, March 5, April 3, May 1.

JACK OF HEARTS–NEPTUNE CARD IN THE JUPITER LINE

These people will never hurt you and you know this. Somewhat strange and sometimes disillusioning; best to keep it strictly on an occasional, impersonal basis.

Jack of Hearts birthdates: July 30, August 28, September 26, October 24, November 22, December 20.

Vertical Line–Jupiter

EIGHT OF DIAMONDS–CROWN LINE

A good advisor in financial matters; a good friend; but not a lover. Stay with the business aspects and listen to their advice. They usually know what to do and how to do it.

Eight of Diamonds birthdates: January 19, February 17, March 15, April 13, May 11, June 9, July 7, August 5, September 3, October 1.

EIGHT OF HEARTS–NEPTUNE LINE

You could be completely enraptured with this native before you knew what was happening–relax and enjoy it. They are fun loving people who can bring much excitement and new things into your otherwise dull life. If closely involved, try to keep them from getting too involved in outside activities or you'll find yourself joining, or staying home alone.

Eight of Hearts birthdates: August 31, September 29, October 27, November 25, December 23.

SEVEN OF SPADES—URANUS LINE

You may think this native a little too "far-out" and progressive in their approach to situations and people, and it may be aggravating, but not so much so that you should overlook the opportunity to have a successful business as a result of some of their efforts. A good business association; friendship okay; but romantic love could have too much irritation.

Seven of Spades birthdates: January 7, February 5, March 3, April 1.

THREE OF SPADES—SATURN LINE

Not an easy relationship by any standards, but profitable to you in the long run—a lesson learned. Your seeming stability may cause them to seek you out, and you could be responsible in helping to rearrange their lives to a more positive plane. Don't enter into any involvements purposefully, but don't run away from any either.

Three of Spades birthdates: January 11, February 9, March 7, April 5, May 3, June 1.

TEN OF DIAMONDS—JUPITER LINE

An excellent business association even though you are worlds apart in your ideals and general thinking. More old-fashioned, with an eye for the more established ways as opposed to taking chances (which may seem to be established to you). Don't pass up a business involvement or a friendship situation, but think carefully before you fall in love.

Ten of Diamonds birthdates: January 17, February 15, March 13, April 11, May 9, June 7, July 5, August 3, September 1.

FOUR OF CLUBS—MARS LINE

A good salesman or spokesman for you, but don't get closely involved or you will find yourself surprised at how many times this native can irritate you.

Four of Clubs birthdates: April 30, May 28, June 26, July 24, August 22, September 20, October 18, November 16, December 14.

Tens

JACK OF HEARTS—VENUS LINE
Someone you will love and admire, but will probably never quite understand. Make life easy on yourself; be friends and leave it at that. Anything else could be a disappointment to you.
Jack of Hearts birthdates: July 30, August 28, September 26, October 24, November 22, December 20.

Diagonal Lines

KING OF SPADES—CROWN AND SATURN LINES
A teacher to you—in almost anything that you do; take advantage of both the material plane and the spiritual level; these natives can be highly successful at both (but not necessarily at the same time). Use the relationship well; it's very important to you. Romance should not be considered as it will probably be temporary.
King of Spades birthdate: January 1.

FIVE OF SPADES—VENUS AND MARS LINES
A temporary love affair that could make you feel pressured. Similar feelings in friendship but not as difficult on an impersonal basis. Business is fine, especially if you are both involved in government or public service work, but be careful that the whole involvement isn't here today and gone tomorrow.
Five of Spades birthdates: January 9, February 7, March 5, April 3, May 1.

KING OF DIAMONDS—VENUS AND MARS LINES
An excellent working relationship—someone to be in business with and do extremely well financially. An individual whom you will enjoy, admire, and shrug your shoulders at, all at the same time. But don't pass up the opportunity to be involved in any financial transactions, although they may be temporary or sporadic. Not good for your love life, so try not to get involved.
King of Diamonds birthdates: January 14, February 12, March 10, April 8, May 6, June 4, July 2.

SIX OF DIAMONDS—JUPITER AND MERCURY LINES
An irritating relationship because they will not listen to you as much as you feel is necessary to get the job done; this is true in any involvement whether it be business, friendship, or romance. Don't place too much faith in this individual on the material plane unless you are both older and wiser.
Six of Diamonds birthdates: January 21, February 19, March 17, April 15, May 13, June 11, July 9, August 7, September 5, October 3, November 1.

TEN OF CLUBS—CROWN AND MARS LINES

A highly stimulating involvement, especially in the fields of education. Ideas come quickly, and you are capable of executing them. A good working relationship, but not necessarily on a day-to-day basis, although this could work well also. Excellent for friendship, but possibly volatile on the romantic side.

Ten of Clubs birthdates: January 30, February 28, March 26, April 24, May 22, June 20, July 18, August 16, September 14, October 12, November 10, December 8.

NINE OF CLUBS—VENUS AND SATURN LINES

A love affair that keeps drawing you back to each other. Although life may be difficult with them, it seems to be just as difficult without them. Too open and flirtatious for your own lifestyle and you would do better to be just friends on an impersonal basis. Poor for business, as they will take chances against your advice.

Nine of Clubs birthdates: January 31, February 29, March 27, April 25, May 23, June 21, July 19, August 17, September 15, October 13, November 11, December 9.

JACK OF SPADES—MARS AND URANUS LINES

A boring relationship that could inwardly aggravate you. A little too know-it-all to your way of thinking, without seemingly deserving it. Don't get involved unless you are both in a humanitarian type of work on a strictly nonpersonal level.

Jack of Spades birthdates: January 3, February 1.

ACE OF DIAMONDS—JUPITER AND NEPTUNE LINES

A good relationship for both business and friendship, just don't try to figure out where "their head is." You may never find out and it may never be important. Keep it impersonal for best results.

Ace of Diamonds birthdates: January 26, February 24, March 22, April 20, May 18, June 16, July 14, August 12, September 10, October 8, November 6, December 4.

TEN OF SPADES FAMOUS BIRTHDATES

January 4	Jakob Grimm
	Louis Braille
February 2	Jascha Heifetz
	Tom Smothers

Jacks

JACKS represent mentality. Are willing to learn by experience and may become a power through training the mind. On the other hand, they may become tramps and wanderers.

They make their living through their individual efforts: writing, composing, selling their ideas, promoting, advertising, or the type of journalism that involves foreign countries. They are always in search of experience or adventure. They represent youth, and, from one angle, the neuter gender.

There are many superstitions connected with the number eleven—the correspondence with the eleventh card of the "Little Book". By some it was called the Number of Evil because it transcended the number of commandments and did not attain twelve, the number of grace and perfection. History and experience refute the stigma and the number Eleven has come to be regarded as a Number, one of the most priceless gifts of the gods. It is man beside God, eager to blaze the trail of return to Kother, the Crown.

Eleven is the direct recipient of inspiration from the One Source—the preacher, messenger, and Lightbearer from On High. Eleven is the number of the Path on the Tree of Life that is assigned to Aleph, the first Tarot card, the Magician, in the direct line from Kether to Chokmah, or Will to Wisdom. It is the spirit of Air, the Divine Breath. It was not by accident that Jacks—Eleven—were assigned as "ushers" of the Court Cards—the first inheritors of the Crown.

Your Place in the Cards

Jacks carry a great responsibility and because they are the symbol of two Ones, the disposal of their lives rests entirely on their own decision. They represent the mental attitudes of the Birth Cards of their individual suits. If the process of development has gone any distance at all, then mental attitudes are wholly within each individual's control. We may rule them and earn our "crowns" or we may consign them to every wind that blows "where it listeth" and bask or struggle in a state of immaturity as long as we live.

Jacks are the "divine androgynes"—the Christ-nature toward which the world is evolving—or the vacillating neuters who are neither one thing nor the other, incapable of decision or direction. In all of them, however, there is a certain fixity and stubbornness. When it is the result of maturity and applies to principle, it is a quality to be praised—but too often it is the expression of ingrained triviality, irresponsibility, shiftlessness, the youth who must have his own way because he knows no better.

Hearts — Win their Crown through sacrifice for love.
Clubs — Win their Crown through the spoken word.
Diamonds — Win their Crown through good guardianship of their birthright.
Spades — Win their Crown because they have chosen the path of Initiation.

All are our elder brothers. All are sons of the King.

Jack of Hearts

Planetary Sequence

			K♠	8♦	10♣			
A♠	3♦	5♣	10♠	Q♣	A♣	3♥		Mercury
2♥ Mars	9♠ Venus	9♣ Mercury	J♥	5♠	7♦	7♥		Venus
8♣	J♠	2♦	4♣ Neptune	6♥ Uranus	K♠ Saturn	K♥ Jupiter		Mars
A♦	A♥	8♠	10♦	10♥	4♠	6♦		Jupiter
5♦	7♣	9♥	3♠	3♣	5♥	Q♦		Saturn
J♦	K♣	2♣	7♠	9♦	J♣	Q♠		Uranus
Q♥	6♠	6♣	8♥	2♠	4♦	4♥		Neptune

Neptune · Uranus · Saturn · Jupiter · Mars · Venus · Mercury

Mundane Spread

Hearts — Love
Jack of Hearts — The Christ Principle
Eleven in Hearts — Examples in Love

The Jupiter Card in the Venus Line. **No Displacement**—a Fixed Card.

The Jack of Hearts is the most innocent of the Jacks, but not the most immature. This card is the symbol of the Christ Principle—Christ on the Cross, the one who sacrifices. Among all the cards, and especially among the Jacks, these are the Way-showers. They have come to show that Truth resides in all of us and makes us kin, and that forgiveness on the part of all toward all is the only way to universal love. This is a Master Card, placed at the center (Jupiter) of the Venus Line.

This card is a humanitarian messenger. The negative side of this is fixations, martyrdom; these people feel sorry for themselves.

But the Jacks of Hearts are essentially teachers. Their power lies in the Law of Love, and their commission is to preach its gospel. To do this effectively, they must live it, and the path they have to follow is not made for easy going.

It is natural for these people to develop a martyr complex—for good or ill. When they have learned the folly and weakness of this attitude of mind, they abandon it; but martyrs they actually are—especially in youth.

Up to age eighteen, there are many sacrifices demanded of them: in love, in education, or in cherished objectives. If they are sufficiently developed to learn, grown, and profit by them, the personal disappointment is mitigated. Between eighteen and thirty-six, the plan is for training in dedication. To "leave all and follow Me" is an exacting command for the young in heart, whose lives are attuned to the principle of love.

Many there are who cannot go through this period in strict obedience, even though they may be well aware of their destiny. If they can and do, after thirty-six they may operate under the King and encounter fewer obstacles and frustrations in their personal lives. If the dedication is delayed, it does not mean it must be abandoned for all time but that the intervening period will bring heartache and disappointment. The hardest lesson for those children of love to learn is impersonality. If they cannot choose it in early life, they must learn its value the hard way.

This is not a happy card. It isn't a card that takes life easily. This is the person who takes on all the cares of the world and supports his family, his father and mother and all of the rest. There is usually some estrangement with the family, and it usually comes through the father or through an older son. Or, it can be a card of a woman, who can be separated from her husband many years without a divorce. The fixation through the Jack of Hearts is a fixed mind. Fixed ideas, opinions. It is almost impossible to talk them out of something. Try, and see how far you get. This is also true of the Jack of Spades.

These people are teachers and are symbolic of Christ in the Temple. There aren't many who measure up to their example, but even though it may require many earth experiences to bring them to full awareness of their pattern, they are all *on the way*. There are no Jack of Heart natives who do not have qualities that are worthy of emulation or who have not endured sacrifices in the name of an unselfish love. They may not be published—or even apparent—but they exist, and by their hidden beauty they help raise mankind to a higher level of development.

There are negatives, of course, among these birthdates: careless, thoughtless, or indifferent escapists who seem to contribute nothing except the problem of themselves. They are invariably friendly, kindly, and cooperative. They never bear grudges and never leave you worse off than they find you. At their worst, they have something to commend them.

BIRTHDATES RULED BY THE JACK OF HEARTS

JULY 30—LEO—RULED BY THE SUN

Loyal and high-minded. Become stubborn when opposed. Have a universal attitude of mind, and do spectacular and dramatic things. Good promoters, scout leaders, heads of youth movements. Interested in improvements and advancement, both in business and in bettering the conditions of workers. Must be the center of authority. Seek prestige through large gestures and projects. Go to extremes. Attracted to manufacturing on a large scale, to law and journalism. Can succeed on the stage but prefer a career that is more practical and productive.

AUGUST 28—VIRGO—RULED BY MERCURY

Neither the Leo nor the Virgo natives of the Jack of Hearts are as much influenced by their sign of birth as by their card. Leo chooses business more often than the stage; Virgo chooses poetry, writing, and music rather than research, science, or a clerical job. The Jack seems to give them an urge to reach people and give them the message that is in their hearts. They are sensitive and need much approval, which is not always forthcoming. They yearn for beauty but are not quite artists; they write, but cannot fully or easily express all they have to say. They suffer in their personal life and often retire into themselves and their own "gardens," allowing the world to call them hermits.

SEPTEMBER 26—LIBRA—RULED BY VENUS

Here the composers, writers, and actors run more true to form. They also excel in sculpture, bronze, marble, silver, and wood. Better suited for any artistic line than for business, although make good lawyers and diplomats. Idealistic, but have an eye for the main chance—and always take it.

OCTOBER 24–SCORPIO–RULED BY MARS

Whole-souled and concentrated in whatever they do. Go all out for knowledge, or for love. Much interested in the opposite sex and should marry young. Good organizers and executives. Natural creators; put the stamp of their individuality on their work. Can succeed as writers, actors, or physicians. Want to convert the world to their own ideas.

NOVEMBER 22–SCORPIO–RULED BY MARS

More interested in leadership and prominence than the other Scorpio birthdate. Self-willed and self-determined. The women have masculine minds. All should guard against a tendency to ruthlessness in the attempt to drive home what they believe in and want to force upon others. Believe they are *right,* however, and want to work for the general good. Quite the strongest of the Jack of Hearts. Very nervous. May be fanatical in religion or their own brand of philosophy. Must seek balance. Can succeed in music or writing.

DECEMBER 20–SAGITTARIUS–RULED BY JUPITER

Torn between service to humanity and an urge for personal success. Meet extremes of poverty or wealth. Religious, humanitarian. Lawyers, politicians, healers, publishers, psychologists.

JACK OF HEARTS — PLANETARY SEQUENCE OF PERSONAL RELATIONSHIPS

Horizontal Line–Venus and Mars

NINE OF CLUBS–MERCURY CARD IN THE SATURN LINE

Too risky and negative for you to spend much time with. You won't like them or how they conduct themselves, and chances are that they will never know how you feel.

Nine of Clubs birthdates: January 31, February 29, March 27, April 25, May 23, June 21, July 19, August 17, September 15, October 13, November 11, December 9.

NINE OF SPADES–VENUS CARD IN THE URANUS LINE

You'll feel this native is worth the time and effort—for love or friendship—and undoubtedly will give them both. Self-confidence is the key word. Encourage this side and you'll be friends a long time.

Nine of Spades birthdates: January 5, February 3, March 1.

TWO OF HEARTS—MARS CARD IN THE NEPTUNE LINE

You'll probably be fooled somewhat by this native. Their cry for love is very real but you'll never convince them that they have set their ideals on a pedestal. Try not to be too aggravated when it doesn't work out. Go on to a more positive relationship.

Two of Hearts birthdate: December 29.

KING OF HEARTS—JUPITER CARD IN THE MERCURY LINE

A mentor, guru, or an older man who is able to set your perspectives back into their place. Love is definitely possible and probable with understanding and good communication. A great deal can be learned from this native—both positive and negative.

King of Hearts birthdates: June 30, July 28, August 26, September 24, October 22, November 20, December 18.

KING OF DIAMONDS—SATURN CARD IN THE VENUS LINE

Too materialisitc and insecure for your thoughts and way of life. You'll appreciate them—know the whys and wherefores of what they do—and might even be tempted to show them another way. It's Karmic, so try. But there's no need to spend a great deal of time on a probably futile task.

King of Diamonds birthdates: January 14, February 12, March 10, April 8, May 6, June 4, July 2.

SIX OF HEARTS—URANUS CARD IN THE MARS LINE
(Double Mars Line on the Diagonal Lines)

A Karmic tie inasmuch as this is the Christmas Card—also symbolic of the Christ Principle. Great mental stimulation—energy—new ideas, concepts. Good for business, if you both work at it for the gain of others as well as yourselves. Can be tremendously successful, stimulating friendship, strictly on an impersonal love basis.

Six of Hearts birthdates: October 29, November 27, December 25.

FOUR OF CLUBS—NEPTUNE CARD IN THE JUPITER LINE
(Mars Line on the Vertical Line)

A totally captivating love, romance, sexual relationship that could cause you to do a complete turnabout in whatever you are involved in prior to this involvement. (The same is true on an impersonal love basis.) The caution comes in knowing the person before you make a radical move. A Double Neptune influence can create illusions that can be devastating in the light of day. Chances are you won't be disappointed.

Four of Clubs birthdates: April 30, May 28, June 26, July 24, August 22, September 20, October 18, November 16, December 14.

Vertical Line—Jupiter

TEN OF SPADES—THE MERCURY LINE

Strong communication; you may understand them when very few others do. Don't let them put themselves down in any way, they are capable people and you are capable of helping them know this. Don't attempt any personal involvements over any length of time.

Ten of Spades birthdates: January 4, February 2.

EIGHT OF DIAMONDS—CROWN LINE

You'll like and love this native and, wish they had a little more insight into their spiritual side. Romantic love is definitely possible and is a good combination for you. Encourage them to read more, study more, and not worry about money so much. Learn more about the exact meaning of values. Look for an active life if you're personally involved.

Eight of Diamonds birthdates: January 19, February 17, March 15, April 13, May 11, June 9, July 7, August 5, September 3, October 1.

EIGHT OF HEARTS—NEPTUNE LINE

Too frivolous and scatterbrained for you to make much sense of this relationship. Actually, you should stick with it. They have great power and can create energizing forces with groups or any projects you may be involved in. No personal associations are best.

Eight of Hearts birthdates: August 31, September 29, October 27, November 25, December 23.

SEVEN OF SPADES—URANUS LINE

A co-worker, friend, and confidant. You can tell them your innermost thoughts. Great for business—highly profitable for you especially if dealing with a new item or new ideas. Highly trustworthy and capable of understanding your particular quest, even if it's not quite clear to you. Romantic love possible, but not probable unless both are involved in similar humanitarian projects.

Seven of Spades birthdates: January 7, February 5, March 3, April 1.

THREE OF SPADES—SATURN LINE

One of your obligations to yourself, a native who doesn't know quite where he or she is spiritually. Willing to explore, sometimes in order to disbelieve. Spend what time you can, but don't look for overnight results. Avoid personal involvements and lengths of time spent beating a dead horse.

Three of Spades birthdates: January 11, February 9, March 7, April 5, May 3, June 1.

TEN OF DIAMONDS–JUPITER LINE

Great business involvement for you, but don't be disappointed if they don't respond to you otherwise. Materialistically oriented but may surprise you with their awareness. Good relationship on any level, but don't try to convert. Accept them as they are—they're worthy of it.

Ten of Diamonds birthdates: January 17, February 15, March 13, April 11, May 9, June 7, July 5, August 3, September 1.

FOUR OF CLUBS–MARS LINE: SEE HORIZONTAL LINE

Diagonal Lines

FIVE OF CLUBS–MERCURY AND SATURN LINES

Great communication when you're together but don't depend on this native to feel the same way tomorrow. You could spend the rest of your life explaining and exploring without anything of real substance being attained. A difficult relationship and probably best avoided.

Five of Clubs birthdates: March 31, April 29, May 27, June 25, July 23, August 21, September 19, October 17, November 15, December 13.

SIX OF HEARTS–DOUBLE MARS LINE: SEE HORIZONTAL LINE

FOUR OF SPADES–JUPITER AND VENUS LINES

Magnetism for a beautiful love and/or friendship. You cannot escape this native. They will represent everything you've ever wanted and you would be foolish to pass up any kind of involvement. Truly one of the more exquisite involvements on any level for any card.

Four of Spades birthdates: January 10, February 8, March 6, April 4, May 2.

QUEEN OF DIAMONDS–SATURN AND MERCURY LINES

A distaste for the person but an understanding of why they are like they are. Irritating, disagreeable, and unable to understand you, although physically attracted to you. Pass on the involvement unless it is of short duration.

Queen of Diamonds birthdates: January 15, February 13, March 11, April 9, May 7, June 5, July 3, August 1.

QUEEN OF CLUBS–MERCURY AND MARS LINES

Mental stimulation on a balancing level like you've never experienced it before. This native will create an atmosphere of "stop-look-listen." When you're emotionally carried away, look to the Queen of Clubs friend to place it in its proper perspective. Definitely an impersonal relationship.

Queen of Clubs birthdates: January 28, February 26, March 24, April 22, May 20, June 18, July 16, August 14, September 12, October 10, November 8, December 6.

TWO OF DIAMONDS—MARS AND SATURN LINES

You'll want to talk to them but practically everything they say irritates you. A material plane native that probably cannot be dissuaded. Don't waste valuable time. Look elsewhere.

Two of Diamonds birthdates: January 25, February 23, March 21, April 19, May 17, June 15, July 13, August 11, September 9, October 7, November 5, December 3.

ACE OF HEARTS—JUPITER AND URANUS LINES

A challenging love-romantic situation that might wind up giving you more insight—for good or ill. They will adore you, so don't miss the relationship. Friendship great—business mediocre.

Ace of Hearts birthdate: December 30.

FIVE OF DIAMONDS—SATURN AND NEPTUNE LINES

You'll never understand their motivations or anything else about this native. They'll irritate you over their concern for money, and you'll never know their state of financial affairs, even if they tell you. Best avoided on all levels.

Five of Diamonds birthdates: January 22, February 20, March 18, April 16, May 14, June 12, July 10, August 8, September 6, October 4, November 2.

JACK OF HEARTS FAMOUS BIRTHDATES

July 30	Paul Anka
	Casey Stengel
	Henry Ford
August 28	Ben Gazzara
	Donald O'Connor
	Sam Goldwyn
	Goethe
	Leo Tolstoi
September 26	Julie London
	George Gershwin

November 22   Hoagy Carmichael
               Charles De Gaulle

December 20   Irene Dunne

Clubs — Intelligence
Jack of Clubs — The Spoken Word
Eleven in Clubs — Mental Inspiration

The Venus Card in the Uranus Line. Displaces the **Jack of Diamonds** in the Natural Spread

This is a card of Memory. As a rule, those people have this gift in an extraordinary degree. Such a wealth of knowledge is stored within them, they naturally turn to teaching, writing, or speaking. They give out willingly, but apparently are none the poorer; their position in the Uranus Line keeps them well replenished.

In reality, this is a card of the future. This card comes with deviation. The Jack of Clubs is a symbol of the androgynous state toward which the race is evolving. For that reason the present manifestation is often neutral—a situa-

Planetary Sequence

			K♠	8♦	10♣			
A♠	3♦	5♣	10♠	Q♣	A♣	3♥		Mercury
2♥	9♠	9♣	J♥	5♠	7♦	7♥		Venus
8♣	J♠	2♦	4♣	6♥	K♦	K♥		Mars
A♦	A♥	8♠	10♦	10♥	4♠	6♦		Jupiter
5♦	7♣	9♥	3♠	3♣	5♥	Q♥		Saturn
J♦	K♣	2♣	7♠	9♦	J♣	Q♠		Uranus
Q♥	6♠	6♣	8♥	2♠	4♦	4♥		Neptune
Saturn	Jupiter	Mars	Venus	Mercury	Neptune	Uranus		

Neptune · Uranus · Saturn · Jupiter · Mars · Venus · Mercury

Mundane Spread

tion that causes confusion and maladjustment to present-day society. When this card belongs to a woman, this is not necessarily true at all. The Jack of Clubs is creative to a certain extent; the highly keyed or highly sensitized side is prevailed upon and brought out, and this could be the deviate side of the male Jack of Clubs. They represent neutrality more than any of the other Jacks. Can be a very inconsequential person, or can be a restless person who is driving for a certain amount of power, and because of his inability to live up to this or to touch upon it, gets easily discouraged and ends up drinking.

Of the four Jacks, the Jack of Spades and the Jack of Clubs will drink the heaviest. The Jack of Diamonds has his finger on a different pulse entirely than the Jack of Spades and the Jack of Clubs. Another keynote for the Jack of Clubs is irresponsibility, detachment, and aloofness. This is the wanderer. He wants to go from place to place. He doesn't want to be tied down to any one thing. Therefore, Jack of Clubs men and women do not make good husbands and wives. Many of the women (especially) of these dates fail to marry; the majority have masculine minds and habits of life. They are seldom domestic, never clinging vines and have little patience with pettiness or vanity. These people travel from pillar to post. They change jobs a lot and can spend money easily.

For both sexes, the lack of establishment on the side of so-called normality causes them to worry over their inability to make prescribed adjustments. They are apt to seek unusual attachments that are unwise or discrediting, as well as disappointing. These they take very seriously; their need for love is absorbing and never quite satisfied. They must cultivate good mental balance to steer clear of neuroses. Their True Place—Mars in the Jupiter Line—assures them of protection if they work for it. The only kind of work that is congenial, or endurable, is in the mental field. When they are forced into menial tasks, they are unhappy and inefficient. They must express themselves—or suffer. There is a terrific drive to give out what they know and to keep learning more and more. It is a tragic thing when these people are deprived of a good education. They will add to the knowledge they have intuitively, no matter what obstacles must be overcome, but they are helped on their way by a good educational foundation.

Negatively, there is the mentioned irresponsibility, idle curiosity, and escapism into a multitude of unfortunate or discreditable bypaths that are far removed from the wisdom they have come to seek and to preach.

They succeed best with an occupation that involves contacts. People are highly important as outlets for their abilities and as companions to fill the gap of their loneliness.

In the larger sense, the Jack of Clubs is the neophyte—the young soul seeking wisdom, the inquirer (or wanderer) who is full of uncertainty, between eighteen and thirty. They are often skeptical and shift their beliefs. They can put their knowledge to work for them or they can live by their wits. They must definitely establish themselves between thirty and sixty if they are to enjoy the remainder of their lives. The close tie with the Jack of Diamonds enables them to do this successfully. The ground on which they can rest with security is the mental ground; their weapon against all obstacles is knowledge, and cooperation with the spiritual law. Spiritual law is so exact that no one is going to get away from it. Kipling says, "The sins you commit two by two you pay for, one by one."

BIRTHDATES RULED BY THE JACK OF CLUBS

JANUARY 29–AQUARIUS–RULED BY VENUS

Born with occult knowledge. Will succeed if they like their work—not otherwise. Good knack for handling people. Humanitarians and enjoy helping others. Can reach a high place as writers, scientists, philosophers, or government officials. More attracted to these lines or to lecturing and teaching than to business.

FEBRUARY 27–PISCES–RULED BY NEPTUNE

Restless and inclined to discontent. Need contacts and variety. Not good at routine jobs. Fine promoters, receptionists, interviewers. Great mixers in any society. Inclined to a mental career: writing, poetry, journalism—but often have talent for music or acting. Very socially minded. Become depressed when shut up with their own families or deprived of active occupation. Interested in investments—property, oil, etc.

MARCH 25–ARIES–RULED BY MARS

Speedy in movement, nervous or touchy in reactions. Often feel put upon or unlucky. Have a tendency to shift blame to others. Are fine arguers and debaters but apt to become quarrelsome. Do not make adjustments easily or optimistically. Strong personalities; influential as writers, agitators, speakers. Want a voice in what goes on. May have some outstanding talent, even genius. If the latter, are stormy and erratic, difficult in private lives. Valuable people when they use balance and control.

APRIL 23–TAURUS–RULED BY VENUS

Self-concerned and self-indulgent. Have trouble (women especially) with the opposite sex. Health may be a problem. Willing to work hard for objectives, especially in art or music. Interested in politics and always dramatize their part in it. In-laws apt to present problems. Want a home of their own, and dominate it. Must watch the "rule or ruin" tendency sometimes found in Taurus. Attracted to theater or films. Can be good rulers or leaders.

MAY 21—TAURUS OR GEMINI—RULED BY VENUS OR MERCURY

The Taureans make fine actors, playwrights, or directors. Good livers and spenders; good entertainers. Gemini natives are more gifted in writing, journalism or editing, teaching, and selling. Need a fast-moving occupation. Fine trial lawyers. Slow to reach maturity and always remain young. Good linguists. Both keep late hours. Both have many friends and admirers among the opposite sex. The Gemini born take their loves lightly.

JUNE 19—GEMINI—RULED BY MERCURY

Restless and dissatisfied, but more practical than the other Gemini birthdate. Always some problems connected with love or marriage. A Karmic date, demanding philosophy and understanding—which they often lack. Home important, but often live alone or share it with one who is not congenial. Want marriage for what it will give them; take a job for what it will pay. Should cultivate a sense of service. Not favored for journeys or investments. Good brains, good writers, speakers, or actors.

JULY 17—CANCER—RULED BY THE MOON

Strong family feeling. Influenced by women of means. Sensitive and talented, especially in art and theater. Usually get good support in business. Ethical, not spiritual. Have an eye for the main chance. Can succeed with small articles for general use. Are interested in local politics and whatever affects their own community. Inclined to be too centralized and narrow-minded. Have periods of extravagance and penuriousness.

AUGUST 15—LEO—RULED BY THE SUN

The theater—as is usual for Leo—is a good avenue for success.

These people work better alone and seem to be thrown on their own resources for best accomplishment. Should be given full authority in their chosen field. If the talent lies in music, are fine orchestral directors. Family responsibilities always heavy. Can commercialize any artistic talent. Extravagant and generous—and want recognition. Protected financially. May choose banking, merchandising, publishing. Are good lawyers where oratory is an asset.

SEPTEMBER 13—VIRGO—RULED BY MERCURY

Mental and analytical. Not especially glamourous but would like to be. May be too timid for adequate faith in their own abilities. If not, make brainy, efficient directors of public affairs. Good sense of values from business angle. Good accountants, realtors, economists. Lack vision and imagination. Nervous; should avoid stimulants. Idealistic but skeptical. If talented, will make art pay. Easily bored if in a subordinate position. May be too hard-headed.

OCTOBER 11–LIBRA–RULED BY VENUS

Very intelligent. Must guard against triviality. Want popularity, and do much to deserve it. Enjoy being before the public. Usually have a sideline or hobby that is more absorbing than the chosen profession. Anxious to make money from their own efforts. Learn—through hard experience—to commercialize what they know. Illustrators, commercial painters, advertisers. Go in for sketches and impressions. Make compromises at the expense of their ideals. Can succeed as lawyers or brokers.

NOVEMBER 9–SCORPIO–RULED BY MARS

Should always avoid stimulants; become quarrelsom. Emotional and intense. Make excellent actors. Early life may bring problems in home conditions. Succeed as authors, researchers, and psychologists; also dentists and physicians. Should avoid gambling; cannot win in the long run. Have secret fears and forebodings—seldom revealed. Interested in art as dealers or patrons. Often associated with politics.

DECEMBER 7–SAGITTARIUS–RULED BY JUPITER

Original in thought and plans but need help to carry them out. Must keep all transactions strictly legitimate. Nervous, wandering, unconcentrated. Must learn to commercialize their abilities. Escape from inharmony. Skilled in stringed instruments. Good architects, politicians, sometimes actors. Popular writers and journalists. Can easily become negative and unproductive. Set in opinions. A law unto themselves. Women often found in men's jobs—and prefer them.

JACK OF CLUBS–PLANETARY SEQUENCE OF PERSONAL RELATIONSHIPS

Horizontal Line–Uranus and Neptune

NINE OF DIAMONDS–MERCURY CARD IN THE MARS LINE

Aggravation because you will feel they don't listen to you; if they did, they would profit by it. Temporary relationship, so don't spend unnecessary time.

Nine of Diamonds birthdates: January 18, February 16, March 14, April 12, May 10, June 8, July 6, August 4, September 2.

SEVEN OF SPADES—VENUS CARD IN THE JUPITER LINE

Much more attraction for this native than they for you. They feel you're not a good bet for what they have in mind for themselves. Good for friendship and business.

Seven of Spades birthdates: January 7, February 5, March 3, April 1.

TWO OF CLUBS—MARS CARD IN THE SATURN LINE

You won't want to spend more than five minutes with this native; after that you'll be tapping your foot to get away. Irritations on every level. Forget any kind of involvement.

Two of Clubs birthdates: May 30, June 28, July 26, August 24, September 22, October 20, November 18, December 16.

KING OF CLUBS—JUPITER CARD IN THE URANUS LINE

Probably representative of an older "club" man friend whom you admire and appreciate. Listen to his advice—he can be an exciting and invaluable friend to you. Opposite sexes will find friendship but are apt to tangle when it comes to a close relationship.

King of Clubs birthdates: January 27, February 25, March 23, April 21, May 19, June 17, July 15, August 13, September 11, October 9, November 7, December 5.

JACK OF DIAMONDS—SATURN CARD IN THE NEPTUNE LINE
(Jack of Clubs Displacement Card)

An attraction that, if brought to a close relationship, will bring only problems. An impasse, or checkmate in chess. Business is good if you can decide who's the boss.

Jack of Diamonds birthdates: January 16, February 14, March 12, April 10, May 8, June 6, July 4, August 2.

FOUR OF HEARTS—URANUS IN THE MERCURY LINE
(Neptune Line and Mercury Card on the Diagonals)

Great communication. It will seem as if you are best friends—for a while. Don't count on any long-term relationship on any level. Don't get involved in a business relationship.

Four of Hearts birthdates: October 31, November 29, December 27.

FOUR OF DIAMONDS—NEPTUNE CARD IN THE VENUS LINE
(Neptune Line on the Vertical Line)

This native may appear to be better off financially than he or she is, and you may be attracted by that. Don't kid yourself—see it as it is. A good relationship on any level—especially business if you're willing to work as hard as they.

Four of Diamonds birthdates: January 23, February 21, March 19, April 17, May 15, June 13, July 11, August 9, September 7, October 5, November 3, December 1.

Vertical Line—Venus

FIVE OF HEARTS—SATURN LINE

You can't possibly find love here, although you may feel drawn to this native. Take a pass. The best that can happen is that you'll spend an evening sitting up all night—talking.

Five of Hearts birthdates: October 30, November 28, December 26.

FOUR OF SPADES—JUPITER LINE

Love, romance, friendship. They can bring you the knowledge that you, yourself, have misplaced. Level-headed people, so don't be operating negatively when you meet them. Enjoy the involvement on all levels.

Four of Spades birthdates: January 10, February 8, March 6, April 4, May 2.

KING OF DIAMONDS—MARS LINE

You'll think this native can do far better if he or she tried. Although you'll admire their capabilities, it will irritate you to see talent wasted. Don't be so sure—listen closely; they know the secrets of business success.

King of Diamonds birthdates: January 14, February 12, March 10, April 8, May 6, June 6, July 2.

SEVEN OF DIAMONDS—VENUS LINE

Love, friendship, and business. This native can only bring good things to you. Don't get romantically involved unless you're serious—they can be hurt and you have the power to walk away unscathed. Friendship and business are best; you can do extremely well together.

Seven of Diamonds birthdates: January 20, February 18, March 16, April 14, May 12, June 10, July 8, August 6, September 4, October 2.

ACE OF CLUBS—MERCURY LINE

You'll feel as if you have to explain everything you do to this native—and you probably will. Short-termed situation. If it isn't—it should be.

Ace of Clubs birthdates: May 31, June 29, July 27, August 25, September 23, October 21, November 19, December 17.

FOUR OF DIAMONDS—NEPTUNE LINE: SEE HORIZONTAL LINE

Diagonal Lines

FOUR OF HEARTS—NEPTUNE AND MERCURY LINES:
SEE HORIZONTAL LINE

TWO OF SPADES—NEPTUNE AND MARS LINES
A minor sexual attraction that doesn't make sense in the light of the day. Too difficult a life pattern to hold your interest for long on any level.

Two of Spades birthdates: January 12, February 10, March 8, April 6, May 4, June 2.

QUEEN OF DIAMONDS—SATURN AND MERCURY LINES
Interesting and easy communication, but you're talking to someone who's already been there. They probably will discount your words, so don't spend a lot of time unnecessarily.

Queen of Diamonds birthdates: January 15, February 13, March 11, April 9, May 7, June 5, July 3, August 1.

THREE OF CLUBS—SATURN AND MARS LINES
Another impossible communication situation. You're talking apples and they're hearing oranges—except that this involvement could prove irritating to you. Take a pass.

Three of Clubs: May 29, June 27, July 25, August 23, September 21, October 19, November 19, December 15.

TEN OF DIAMONDS—DOUBLE JUPITER LINES
You'll jump out of your seat when you meet this native. They've got it all as far as you're concerned. You're probably right. Love, friendship, business. Pick one. Any will work and work well.

Ten of Diamonds birthdates: January 17, February 15, March 13, April 11, May 9, June 7, July 5, August 3, September 1.

TWO OF DIAMONDS—MARS AND SATURN LINES
An impossible involvement to start with. You are much too restless for this native and will become highly irritated if you ever have to sit around and just listen to them answer the telephone. Stay away from anything other than an impersonal relationship.

Your Place in the Cards

Two of Diamonds birthdates: January 25, February 23, March 21, April 19, May 17, June 15, July 13, August 11, September 9, October 7, November 5, December 3.

NINE OF SPADES–VENUS AND NEPTUNE LINES

A romantic situation that could prove to be rewarding. Similar likes and dislikes, and a definite need to "do your own thing," which should appeal to you. Good for friendship but not necessarily for business.

Nine of Spades birthdates: January 5, February 3, March 1.

ACE OF SPADES–MERCURY AND NEPTUNE LINES

A Karmic tie that will keep you forever bumping into one another. Good communication, but appearances will not necessarily be as they seem. Poor for close or romantic involvement. Best as occasional friends.

Ace of Spades birthdates: January 13, February 11, March 9, April 7, May 5, June 3, July 1.

JACK OF CLUBS FAMOUS BIRTHDATES

January 29	Paddy Chayefsky
	William McKinley
February 27	John B. Connally
	Ralph Nader
	Elizabeth Taylor
	Joanne Woodward
	Henry Wadsworth Longfellow
	John Steinbeck
March 25	Howard Cosell
	Aretha Franklin
	David Lean
	Simone Signoret
	Arturo Toscanini
April 23	Shirley Temple
	James Buchanan
May 21	Raymond Burr
	Harold Robbins
June 19	Duchess of Windsor

July 17	James Cagney
	Phyllis Diller
	Art Linkletter
August 15	Ethel Barrymore
	Napoleon Bonaparte
	Sir Walter Scott
	Princess Anne of England
October 11	Samuel W. Yorty
	Eleanor Roosevelt
November 9	Spiro Agnew
	Sargent Shriver
	Hedy Lamarr
December 7	Rudolf Friml
	Eli Wallach

Jack of Diamonds

Planetary Sequence

			K♠	8♦	10♣		
A♠	3♦	5♣	10♠	Q♣	A♣	3♥	Mercury
2♥	9♠	9♣	J♥	5♠	7♦	7♥	Venus
8♣	J♠	2♦	4♣	6♥	K♦	K♥	Mars
A♦	A♥	8♠	10♦	10♥	4♠	6♦	Jupiter
5♦	7♣	9♥	3♠	3♣	5♥	Q♦	Saturn
J♦	K♣	2♣	7♠	9♦	J♣	Q♠	Uranus
Q♥	6♠	6♣	8♥	2♠	4♦	4♥	Neptune
Neptune	Uranus	Saturn	Jupiter	Mars	Venus	Mercury	

Neptune · Uranus · Saturn · Jupiter · Mars · Venus · Mercury

Mundane Spread

Diamonds — Values

Jack of Diamonds — The Trader for Material Gain or The Worker Who Lays up Treasure in Heaven

The Neptune Card in the Uranus Line—Displaces the Three of Spades in the Natural Spread

The nature, disposition, proclivities, and qualities represented by this card take the prize for variety and peculiarity. The Jack of Diamonds is wholly material, highly spiritual, or a curious mixture of the two. If they are operating under their own Birth Card, they are well aware that hard and continuous work is a requirement for success; the displaced Three of Spades is their assurance for that. They are ready to sell anything for money or value, and there are some who will sell their own birthright.

They want money and always find a way to get it; they are mentally keen, sharp, and clever and are always looking for the thing that pays off. Spiritually, they are invariably confused. They want their own kingdom but have not reached the stage where they can assume the crown. If opportunities are not at hand, they will wander off to foreign lands to keep a sharp lookout as they go, or will drift through life and live by their wits—usually managing to get by.

Their entire Planetary Sequence is in the Neptune Line, which allows a choice between idealism and confusion. The cards in that line offer stability and power, and we seldom find a Jack of Diamonds who lacks money and protection. The Birth Card itself, a Uranus-Neptune conjunction, gives free play to the intuitions (for good or bad). An unparalleled chance for spiritual illumination; when they realize it and accept it, they are well on their way to the kingly state. When their fixed ideas get in the way, their material affairs may still flourish but their spiritual security is lost for this incarnation.

We find many who make valuable contributions along spiritual and humanitarian lines. In the case of men, it is most likely that they are operating under the King and have earned the right to their crown. The women would do better to stick to their Birth Card and avoid the emphasis on the Personality Card, (the Queen of Diamonds) with its difficult Planetary Sequence.

The majority of these natives love the sea. Many of the men follow it as a profession, but even if they make their start as deck hands, they often, by "trading," end by owning the ship.

They must have a profession that is productive; they must also have an outlet for their rare gifts of originality and creation. They are top executives in business, diplomatic agents and go-betweens, successful bankers, publishers, and advertisers. Once they learn how to judge values, they are indispensable to progress.

There is often difficulty in choosing the right profession. The idea that it must lead to financial success may block the expression of a great talent.

BIRTHDATES RULED BY THE JACK OF DIAMONDS

JANUARY 16—CAPRICORN—RULED BY SATURN

Good, practical sense of values. Associated with important business as officer or executive. If working under the King, will command a high salary. May get into a rut because of the security of their position. Travel in the interests of others, but have a voice in the decisions. Good government officials—especially ambassadors—or high-ranking officers in the armed forces—especially naval.

FEBRUARY 14—AQUARIUS—RULED BY URANUS

Attracted to the theater as actors or playwrights. Good musical or dramatic critics, but seldom kindly ones. Women may be drifters, idlers, or opportunists. Many are conscious of a message to be given. If drawn to metaphysics, should be aware of psychism; often open to invasion from wrong forces. Restless; depend on their personality to win their way. Good writers.

MARCH 12—PISCES—RULED BY NEPTUNE

Interested in spiritual growth. Poets, idealists, metaphysical teachers. Can develop direct communication. Always expressive. Interested in fraternal and occult orders. A strong card financially. Do more good with their money than the majority of the Jacks of Diamonds. Writers, composers, actors, dancers. Also druggists, steamship travel agents, restaurant managers.

APRIL 10—ARIES—RULED BY MARS

Clever at investigation. Interested in politics and like to manipulate and pull strings. Work well with others—usually with a personal motive. Know the ropes and can use them. Good promoters. Know how to use money effectively. Fluent speakers and writers. Keenly observant.

MAY 8—TAURUS—RULED BY VENUS

Writers, poets, civic leaders (political), realtors, and wholesalers. Always have money and want more. Succeed in working with the ground: oil drilling, cultivating acreage, or building and contracting. Ambitious for big business and recognized leadership. Protective of family and personal interests. Usually have an artistic or musical hobby.

JUNE 6–GEMINI–RULED BY MERCURY
Scientists, lawyers, educators, journalists. Good mixers, good talkers. Personal contacts bring the best results for business. Like to sell articles and equipment for home use. Interested in communications—telegraph, telephone, radio, etc. Often operators. Like home better than travel.

JULY 4–CANCER-RULED BY THE MOON
Must work hard for results. Like travel but can't always manage it. Deal in public utilities, food, home accessories, soda fountains, bakeries, etc. Torn between a desire for responsibility and an urge for escape through travel. Good teachers of adults. Ambitious for leadership.

AUGUST 2–LEO–RULED BY THE SUN
Actors, novelists, commentators, playwrights can succeed with this date. Make good also at banking, trading, insurance, and physical culture. Like to be their own bosses and make money through their own efforts. Can always make money by working but prefer devising systems for getting it with more speed and less effort.

JACK OF DIAMONDS–PLANETARY SEQUENCE OF PERSONAL RELATIONSHIPS

Horizontal Line–Neptune

FOUR OF HEARTS–MERCURY CARD IN THE MERCURY LINE
Fast relationship strictly on a mental level—an evening's entertainment but unable to interest you. Two different worlds. Best not to get involved on a close basis.

Four of Hearts birthdates: October 31, November 29, December 27.

FOUR OF DIAMONDS–VENUS CARD IN THE VENUS LINE
Romance, love, and a good rapport. Pushers in business; hard workers. Want to live well, the best of everything and willing to work for it. Excellent for business relationship. Good aspects for marriage until later years. You may attempt to learn the true meaning of values, this native won't. Don't underestimate the relationship and don't pass it up.

Four of Diamonds birthdates: January 23, February 21, March 19, April 17, May 15, June 13, July 11, August 9, September 7, October 5, November 3, December 1.

Your Place in the Cards

TWO OF SPADES—MARS CARD IN THE MARS LINE

Impossible to reach this native—explosive relationship leading to giant struggles and frustrations. No communication of ideas. Don't force any relationship and try not to get too personally involved.

Two of Spades birthdates: January 12, February 10, March 8, April 6, May 4, June 2.

EIGHT OF HEARTS—JUPITER CARD IN THE JUPITER LINE

Difficult for you to understand. They want a good time with no responsibilities; however, they are capable of assuming responsibility so the relationship should definitely be pursued. Love offered freely—don't be suspect of them. Look for spiritual side together—especially in later years—for a beautiful association.

Eight of Hearts birthdates: August 31, September 29, October 27, November 25, December 23.

SIX OF CLUBS—SATURN CARD IN THE SATURN LINE

Too fixed in their ideas for any kind of relationship with you. Worriers to the point of affecting you and your work if the involvement is on a personal level. Don't get involved if you can help it.

Six of Clubs birthdates: March 30, April 28, May 26, June 24, July 22, August 20, September 18, October 16, November 14, December 12.

SIX OF SPADES—URANUS CARD IN THE URANUS LINE
(Neptune and Uranus Lines on the Diagonal Lines)

An unusual and unavoidable relationship on some level: religion, metaphysics, etc. Poor for business associations unless they work for you.

Six of Spades birthdates: January 8, February 6, March 4, April 2.

QUEEN OF HEARTS—NEPTUNE CARD IN THE NEPTUNE LINE

All appearances may seem that this is the love of your life. Strong attraction on any level. Don't kid yourself—see the involvement as it really is. Your love can turn to sympathy and, eventually, pity, if this native is operating negatively.

Queen of Hearts birthdates: July 29, August 27, September 25, October 23, November 21, December 19.

Vertical Line—Neptune

FIVE OF DIAMONDS—SATURN LINE

Same goals will attract you. Money-making important to you both but your ideas can be radically different. The Five of Diamonds can be a burden to you and might try to dominate you.

Five of Diamonds birthdates: January 22, February 20, March 18, April 16, May 12, June 10, July 8, August 6, September 4, October 2.

ACE OF DIAMONDS–JUPITER LINE

A serious romantic attraction. This native will want to stand well in your estimation and will make efforts to do so, which you'll appreciate. Line up your values—this could be a forever romantic match or at least a long term, close relationship.

Ace of Diamonds birthdates: January 26, February 24, March 22, April 20, May 18, June 16, July 14, August 12, September 10, October 8, November 6, December 4.

EIGHT OF CLUBS–MARS LINE

A stimulating relationship that will irritate you—they'll seem to know it all. Listen, you may not agree but they have something worthwhile to say. Don't attempt any kind of involvement other than on an impersonal level.

Eight of Clubs birthdates: March 28, April 26, May 24, June 22, July 20, August 18, September 16, October 14, November 12, December 10.

TWO OF HEARTS–VENUS LINE

A profitable association and probably romantic as well. Strange combination (Two of Hearts and the Jack of Diamonds), but interesting and entirely possible. Especially if you are male and the Two of Hearts is a younger girl. Don't let them think your work has replaced your love for them.

Two of Hearts birthdate: December 29.

ACE OF SPADES–MERCURY LINE

A complicated person and lifestyle for you. Too secretive and seemingly untrustworthy. A wearisome person for you to be around. Best pass on any kind of involvement especially if it is not entirely on the up and up.

Ace of Spades birthdates: January 13, February 11, March 9, April 7, May 5, June 3, July 1.

QUEEN OF HEARTS–NEPTUNE LINE: SEE HORIZONTAL LINE

Diagonal Lines

SEVEN OF CLUBS–SATURN AND URANUS LINES

When you meet this native—keep on moving. It's a waste of time. You'll feel they have odd ideas and are not straightforward enough to do business with. The chances of a romantic attraction are nil.

Seven of Clubs birthdates: March 29, April 27, May 25, June 23, July 21, August 19, September 17, October 15, November 13, December 11.

EIGHT OF SPADES—JUPITER AND SATURN LINES

Great rapport. They understand your motivations and will lend support to you. Good for work and/or love; can help you overcome your difficulties.

Eight of Spades birthdates: January 6, February 4, March 2.

FOUR OF CLUBS—MARS AND JUPITER LINES

Good impersonal relationship for groups, clubs, politics—especially for the men. Not good for personal involvements; too irritating and talkative.

Four of Clubs birthdates: April 30, May 28, June 26, July 24, August 22, September 20, October 18, November 16, December 14.

FIVE OF SPADES—VENUS AND MARS LINES

Heavy sexual attraction that can lead to a long relationship. A little too pushy; may try to completely overhaul your life, but results can be good. Anxious to take trips with you. Don't let them have a say in your business—you know more than they when it comes to making money.

Five of Spades birthdates: January 9, February 7, March 5, April 3, May 1.

ACE OF CLUBS—MERCURY AND VENUS LINES

This native will find out anything you want to know, and can accomplish it quickly. Overlook emotional and temperamental outbursts; they are short-lived. Not good for a close personal involvement.

Ace of Clubs birthdates: May 31, June 29, July 27, August 25, September 23, October 21, November 19, December 17.

SIX OF SPADES—NEPTUNE AND URANUS LINES:
SEE HORIZONTAL LINE

JACK OF DIAMONDS FAMOUS BIRTHDATES

January 16	Dizzy Dean
	Ethel Merman
February 14	Jack Benny
	Hugh Downs
	John Barrymore

Jacks

March 12	Liza Minnelli
April 10	Clare Booth Luce Nikolai Lenin
May 8	Rick Nelson Roberto Rossellini Fulton J. Sheen Dante
July 4	George Murphy George M. Cohan Neil Simon Stephen Foster Louis Armstrong Nathaniel Hawthorne Garibaldi Calvin Coolidge
August 2	James Baldwin Myrna Loy Peter O'Toole

Jack of Spades

Planetary Sequence

			K♠	8♦	10♣			
A♠	3♦	5♣	10♠	Q♣	A♣	3♥		Mercury
2♥	9♠	9♣	J♥	5♠	7♦	7♥		Venus
8♣ Mercury	J♠	2♦	4♣	6♥	K♦	K♥		Mars
A♦	A♥ Neptune	8♠ Uranus	10♦ Saturn	10♥ Jupiter	4♠ Mars	6♦ Venus		Jupiter
5♦	7♣	9♥	3♠	3♣	5♥	Q♦		Saturn
J♦	K♣	2♣	7♠	9♦	J♣	Q♠		Uranus
Q♥	6♠	6♣	8♥	2♠	4♦	4♥		Neptune

Neptune · Uranus · Saturn · Jupiter · Mars · Venus · Mercury

Mundane Spread

Spades — Labor, Wisdom
Jack of Spades — A Neophyte in Wisdom
Eleven in Spades — Revelation of Wisdom

The Uranus Card in the Mars Line. Displaces the **Seven of Clubs** in the Natural Spread

This is one of the Fixed Cards, a symbol of fixed and unalterable principle. For the individuals, however, there is no sure fixity within themselves. The struggle and obstacles represented by the Seven of Clubs often are too much for their immaturity to cope with and not until they operate under the King do they acquire the wisdom that makes them *know* which are the things that "endureth forever" and which are not.

There are certain things they do know, however, and finally come to realize. They know that they must pay off all Karmic debts, and not contract new ones; that there is no admission into the Kingdom of Heaven until the accounts are settled. They know that resurrection is the thing they want and (subconsciously) they know that they are the heralds of the gospel of rebirth and the abolishment of death. They know that Jacks, Kings, and Queens are the hierarchy of authority and that they must learn to take their place among the crowned ones. They are neophytes, to be sure, but are already ordained, with the grade ahead of them clearly marked as the only road to their attainment.

Will they make it? Many there are who do, with honor and glory. Among the positive ones, no matter how gifted or successful they may be, there is a certain modesty and humility that bespeak their awareness of the fact that they are but learners and strivers. There is also a certain dignity that is born of recognition of their high calling and the sure knowledge that they will one day reach their goal. They have equipped themselves with education and training in the line in which they are best fitted to express their abilities; they have worked for the art—or the job—rather than for the pay check. They have refused to worry and strain for money for personal success for they know they are giving their best to their work and that the intentions behind their actions are right and honorable.

The negatives destroy the protection that surrounds the Jack of Spades by shiftlessness and irresponsibility. They are subject to scandal and disgrace, to misinterpretation of their motives, disappointment in their friends, and lack of achievement in their work. They fail to take advantage of the wonderful opportunities provided by their Sequence and unless they wake up in time, they end their days in loneliness and the overhanging fear of poverty.

The men of this card should always aim to reach the King. The women, unless aware of the true significance and place of the Queen, fare better when they stick to the Birth Card. There is ample room for success in the life. They usually have a masculine type of mind and they can attain their own place among the high ones if they take the trouble to provide the necessary foundation. If not, and if they choose to operate through the Personality Card, they are apt to become servants or drudges.

BIRTHDATES RULED BY THE JACK OF SPADES

JANUARY 3–CAPRICORN–RULED BY SATURN
Must overcome materialism—also personal ambition for the limelight. Despite their marked ability as writers, scientists, and physicians, a great many of these natives are attracted to the stage or films and acquit themselves well. The Birthday Number aids them in expression; the Sign and its Ruler give them seriousness and application.

FEBRUARY 1–AQUARIUS–RULED BY URANUS
Even more theater folk are found in this birthdate, as is usual for Aquarius. Here is more emotional power, more individuality, and a keener sense of progress as a part of the New Order. These are specialists in their chosen field: acting, music, writing, or science.

JACK OF SPADES–PLANETARY SEQUENCE OF PERSONAL RELATIONSHIPS

Horizontal Line—Mars and Jupiter

EIGHT OF CLUBS–MERCURY CARD IN THE NEPTUNE LINE
Communication will take precedence over everything else with this native. You will be enchanted by the tales they are able to weave. You will feel that they are charming, but you will also feel a stubbornness that will keep you from getting too personally involved. It's just as well. This might be a difficult involvement for you both on a one-to-one basis. But don't pass up the opportunity of friendship. These are definitely people worth knowing.

Eight of Clubs birthdates: March 28, April 26, May 24, June 22, July 20, August 18, September 16, October 14, November 12, December 10.

SIX OF DIAMONDS–VENUS CARD IN THE MERCURY LINE
There is a Karmic connection that will not go unnoticed. Probably a love-at-first-sight kind of romance, but the relationship will be easier if you are a male Jack of Spades and your Six of Diamonds is a female. With the reverse situation, if finances go sour, it would not be unusual to find your Six of Diamonds spending time and grocery money in the corner bar while you become the household servant. The only recourse for you both, in that case, would be to have faith. Negative life patterns are created by those who have negative thoughts. Think positive and then get into action.

Six of Diamonds birthdates: January 21, February 19, March 17, April 15, May 13, June 11, July 9, August 7, September 5, October 3, November 1.

FOUR OF SPADES—MARS CARD IN THE VENUS LINE

Like a bear to honey. That's how you'll feel about your Four of Spades. But don't forget the bees. This is a stubborn card for you, too. They think they *know* the answers, and you *think* you know the answers. Philosophy, with only questions and *no* answers might help this relationship. Under the Mars influence, this whole thing is liable to be a sexual attraction that perhaps should remain just that.

Four of Spades birthdates: January 10, February 8, March 6, April 4, May 2.

TEN OF HEARTS—JUPITER CARD IN THE MARS LINE

You will be literally swept off your feet by this native, whether it's romance or as platonic friends. They will be forceful, dynamic, and, most of all, full of more love than you've seen accumulated in one person in a long time. And, they are willing to share. But be prepared for the days when they won't be there. Some days they'll show up with presents when you least expect them and other days, when you expect them, they won't show up at all. And remember, if you're contemplating a love affair with a Ten of Hearts, when it's over, they won't be half as upset as you. So walk with your eyes open and enjoy. These are people to enjoy.

Ten of Hearts birthdates: July 31, August 29, September 27, October 25, November 23, December 21.

TEN OF DIAMONDS—SATURN CARD IN THE JUPITER LINE

Investments with a Ten of Diamonds in the fields of medicine, clinics, hospitals, etc., will probably bring you large returns. Any kind of close attachment with this native, however, will be more trouble than it's worth to you. Keeping up with a Ten of Diamonds is not the foremost thing on your mind, remember, so it's better not to get involved that way in the first place.

Ten of Diamonds birthdates: January 17, February 15, March 13, April 11, May 9, June 7, July 5, August 3, September 1.

EIGHT OF SPADES—URANUS CARD IN THE SATURN LINE
(Jupiter and Saturn Lines on the Diagonal Lines)

You'll find an affinity here without ever quite knowing why. These people *have* the power that you know is out there somewhere, waiting for you. You may feel resentment with this, subconsciously. They can open new doors for you and this can be a fulfilling relationship. If you have an unusual and difficult-to-diagnose disease, an Eight of Spades doctor *may* be able to come up with the answers.

Eight of Spades birthdates: January 6, February 4, March 2.

ACE OF HEARTS—NEPTUNE CARD IN THE URANUS LINE
(Jupiter Line on the Vertical)

You can expect this native to introduce you to a new way in metaphysical studies. They are probably going to these meetings in order to meet new people, but that doesn't mean something for you can't be learned. Don't concern yourself with their motivation. Other than a casual friend, they are not on the same plane as you and so therefore should not be considered romantically.

Ace of Hearts birthdate: December 30.

Vertical Line—Uranus

NINE OF SPADES—VENUS LINE

You will love these people. Romantic love is entirely possible as well and is recommended if you and your Nine of Spades stay on the positive plane. This could be exciting with great communication—romantic and never conventional. You are both essentially on the same trip and this native could become one of the most important people in your life, in any kind of involvement.

Nine of Spades birthdates: January 5, February 3, March 1.

THREE OF DIAMONDS—MERCURY LINE

How would you ever get this native to become dependent enough on you to have a truly lasting relationship? That's a good question. You probably can't, and just when you think you've got everything in your favor and have finally found that certain someone. This person will never think they have enough money for themselves—or for you—and they usually will fall into the role of feeling sorry for themselves, which really leaves you out in the cold. Great friends, but try to avoid that close, personal tie that you will probably never really get anyway.

Three of Diamonds birthdates: January 24, February 22, March 20, April 18, May 16, June 14, July 12, August 10, September 8, October 6, November 4, December 2.

SIX OF SPADES—NEPTUNE LINE

Don't be misled because the Displacement Card of the Six of Spades is the Nine of Spades. You'll see some of the same traits you like but it is by no means the same person. A close involvement with this native can only wind up in unhappiness. You'll be constantly subjected to dullness, day in and day out. And if you try to change it, you will be met with stronger resistance. Don't bother to get involved.

Six of Spades birthdates: January 8, February 6, March 4, April 2.

Jacks

KING OF CLUBS—URANUS LINE

Here is a happy, healthy relationship if *you* work at it. The King will not have time for your immature side and if you are a female Jack of Spades, your guy is the King of Clubs—be careful how you handle yourself. Don't try to impress him on how many things you know because he's already way ahead of you. And put on your most ladylike outfit and sweetest smile. He's *not* interested in your masculine mind. The relationship is more difficult with the roles reversed, and not really recommended unless both of you are operating under your Personality Cards, and even then, very difficult.

King of Clubs birthdates: January 27, February 25, March 23, April 21, May 19, June 17, July 15, August 13, September 11, October 9, November 7, December 5.

SEVEN OF CLUBS—SATURN LINE
(Jack of Spades Displacement Card)

A Karmic relationship. This is one of those debts you must pay off in this lifetime. No relationship of any kind is recommended with this native. But when you find yourself involved, your understanding can perhaps help this native a little more on the way. Try to know and accept this person as is.

Seven of Clubs birthdates: March 29, April 27, May 25, June 23, July 21, August 19, September 17, October 15, November 13, December 11.

ACE OF HEARTS—JUPITER LINE: SEE HORIZONTAL LINE

Diagonal Lines

TWO OF HEARTS—VENUS AND NEPTUNE LINES

You'll never know where you stand romantically with this native. It will seem to be one way and then, suddenly, it's another. Good for friendship—communication should be good—but don't put any faith into a close, personal involvement. It will probably never happen.

Two of Hearts birthdate: December 29.

EIGHT OF SPADES—JUPITER AND SATURN LINES:
SEE HORIZONTAL LINE

THREE OF SPADES—JUPITER AND SATURN LINES

This is *not* a romantic involvement for you but you'll probably take a fling anyway. The problems arise in expressing yourselves to each other. They won't believe what you *know* is the Law—they are struggling and you are waiting. The uncertainty in finding solutions that the Three of Spades encounters is apt to force them into a rut that you may feel could pull you in with them. Don't have great expectations about any kind of relationship—just take it as it comes.

Three of Spades birthdates: January 11, February 9, March 7, April 5, May 3, June 1.

NINE OF DIAMONDS—URANUS AND MARS LINES

You will find very little in common with this native. They will irritate you and try to impress you without ever taking into consideration what kind of person you may be. It is a relationship best forgotten for you.

Nine of Diamonds birthdates: January 18, February 16, March 14, April 12, May 10, June 8, July 6, August 4, September 2.

FOUR OF DIAMONDS—NEPTUNE AND VENUS LINES

You won't be able to escape this relationship, but that doesn't necessarily mean it's good for you. This Four of Diamonds will live in a dream world and, at first, be wrapped in a love bubble with you. When the bubble leaks, you may find yourself being hounded to make more money, do more things, and a general dissatisfaction with what is at hand. This, of course, really doesn't fit into your plans for yourself, so try not to be swept away too rapidly without realizing the consequences. This can also be a good friend who'll always manage to do fairly well financially, if they're willing to work at it. Try to avoid a close, day-to-day attachment. They'll probably make you too nervous.

Four of Diamonds birthdates: January 23, February 21, March 19, April 17, May 15, June 13, July 11, August 9, September 7, October 5, November 3, December 1.

ACE OF DIAMONDS—JUPITER AND NEPTUNE LINES

Communications can be strong here, especially in the realm of metaphysics. Good for friendship but, similar to the Four of Diamonds, not your trip romantically, or on a daily basis. Their needs and wants are quite different from yours.

Ace of Diamonds birthdates: January 26, February 24, March 22, April 20, May 18, June 16, July 14, August 12, September 10, October 8, November 6, December 4.

NINE OF CLUBS—VENUS AND SATURN LINES

If you're at a large party, you can bet that one of the people there who will attract you will be a Nine of Clubs. You'll find yourself drawn to this native but probably unwilling to put up with them on a full-time basis. They will need you for more than you need them and you may feel the relationship is a hardship for you.

Nine of Clubs birthdates: January 31, February 29, March 27, April 25, May 23, June 21, July 19, August 17, September 15, October 13, November 11, December 9.

TEN OF SPADES—MERCURY AND JUPITER LINES

You can work hand in hand with this person and you will probably find a romantic involvement that could be one of the finest relationships in your life. Your goals, aims, and ideals are much the same and at the same time you will find a physical attraction and many happy times. You both should take warning and avoid routines and ruts, which are easy for each of you.

Ten of Spades birthdates: January 4, February 2

TEN OF CLUBS—MARS LINE

This native will prod your mind like an electric shock. You can learn from them. And although it may be under volatile circumstances, don't let the information slip away. It's another step on the road you're on. Not recommended for personal involvements of any kind, particularly romance.

Ten of Clubs birthdates: January 30, February 28, March 26, April 24, May 22, June 20, July 18, August 16, September 14, October 12, November 10, December 8.

JACK OF SPADES FAMOUS BIRTHDATES

January 3	Cicero
	Lucretia Mott
	Clement Attlee
	Ray Milland
	J. R. R. Tolkien
February 1	John Ford
	Clark Gable

Queens

QUEENS represent the spiritual nature of man and the principle of birth—not death. Their authority is equal to that of the Kings, proving that true rulership is both masculine and feminine. They are the receptive, intuitive, and cooperative aspects of royalty.

The alliance of Queens with the twelfth position in the scale of numbers gives evidence of their importance in the plan of creation and the universal application of their symbolism. Queens are co-rulers of the twelve signs of the Zodiac and the twelve houses of the planets. Of the planets themselves, ten are known and it is prophesied that two are yet to come. The twelve simple letters of the Hebrew alphabet are also connected with the twelve signs in a relationship that is one of the secrets of the Rosicrucian doctrine—as is the full significance of the "Twelve Grand Points of Masonry." The *total* number of the Court Cards is twelve, but Queens *as Twelve* have a special significance of rulership over the twelves that deal most directly with our mundane experiences—signs, houses, and the months of the year.

In none of the pictures of the Queens do we find the swords or battle axes with which the Kings are armed. Their only "weapons" are the symbols they hold in their hands—symbols of fecundity, fertility, and the "blossoming" of prayer, desire, and hope. The privilege of conception, embodied in the Queens, applies not alone to the increase and population of the children of earth; they are the makers and projectors of the principles upon which laws are founded and upheld. Recipients of the Fires of Life, it is the Waters or "Mothers" who are to conceive and bear into form the Expressions of the Divine Mind.

Equality of rulership is as old as the "Little Book," but it took a waste of centuries for us to recognize it! In our own country it was not until 1920 that women were given the vote—and some years later that they were allowed to sit among the jurors and pass judgment. Queens *are* the true judges for they alone, by their gift of receptivity, have conceived the principles of judgment.

Your Place in the Cards

Hearts judge and rule by the principle of love. They promote dreams, conceive the desires, and see the visions of a world of joy and peace in the union of kindred hearts and the doctrine of universal brotherhood.
Clubs judge and rule by intelligence, intuition, and good judgment. Directly instructed, they are sure of their ground and secure in their knowledge.
Diamonds judge by values—apparent or unseen. They are sometimes insecure on their own thrones.
Spades judge by willingness to work and the degree of eagerness and devotion in the quest for wisdom. They are the disciplinarians.

Queen of Hearts

Hearts—Love
Queen of Hearts—A Magnet for Family and Friends
Twelve In Hearts—Love and Justice toward the Human Family
The Neptune Card in the Neptune Line. Displaces the **Ten of Spades** in the Natural Spread

This is a card of beauty, magnetism, affection, and idealism. Inherent in it is so much that is wanted and needed in the world, it is almost a pity to have to mention the faults and pitfalls that are expressed in the lives of its natives. The women represent the much-loved mother—a soft, not universal mother. The personal mother. Temperish but sweet. She loves her children and may

Planetary Sequence

			K♠ Mars	8♦ Venus	10♣ Mercury		
A♠	3♦	5♣	10♠ Neptune	Q♣ Uranus	A♣ Saturn	3♥ Jupiter	Mercury
2♥	9♠	9♣	J♥	5♠	7♦	7♥	Venus
8♣	J♠	2♦	4♣	6♥	K♦	K♥	Mars
A♦	A♥	8♠	10♦	10♥	4♠	6♦	Jupiter
5♦	7♣	9♥	3♠	3♣	5♥	Q♦	Saturn
J♦	K♣	2♣	7♠	9♦	J♣	Q♠	Uranus
Q♥	6♠	6♣	8♥	2♠	4♦	4♥	Neptune

Neptune · Uranus · Saturn · Jupiter · Mars · Venus · Mercury

Mundane Spread

not sacrifice for them like the Queen of Diamonds would, but nevertheless, she has a softness. Also represented are the sweetheart, the indispensible sister, or the adored daughter.

The men are gentle, sensitive, and creative, sympathetic and understanding. If the negative wasn't always there to deal with, this would be the most desirable card in the pack.

The women are invariably attractive, with a strong appeal to the opposite sex. When they trade on it they are flirts. They want constant flattery, good clothes, and good times. They may become lazy, frivolous, and whiners.

The men may easily be too gentle—to the point of spinelessness—too self-indulgent, too feminine, too unbalanced, and sexually indeterminate. This is a difficult card for a man. One of the boys. The soft man who is looking for a caveman friend, which creates turmoil. The escapists of both sexes have a drink problem to contend with.

All of them are popular and hospitable, social-minded or cosmic-minded, cooperative and appreciative, generous and faithful (as a rule), just and honest. They are fluent talkers. This person could charm the birds off the trees. This comes through the power of speech. They are concerned with living well, and want good clothes. And they want things peaceful. They do not like inharmony. Fact of the matter is that they can't take it. It throws them off balance. And if things are not moving pleasantly, they lose interest. Almost invariably, they are talented in some artistic line; if they cannot express it in some art form, they listen and appreciate it. They are intense and dramatic and capable of deep devotion.

They are attracted to a professional type of work or to marriage. The women seldom make a success of both at the same time. Contacts are very important and they should never live alone. They are interested in foreign lands and people, and take them to their hearts as readily as their own. They are tolerant of others' customs, ideals, and modes of life. They are "shining" people, optimistic, friendly, and comforting.

Even the undeveloped ones have their charm and usefulness. Although they may not be aware of their potentialities or the importance of their cosmic mission, or their obligation as defined by their True Place (Saturn Card in the Venus Line), they never willingly cause heartache or distress. Their flirtatiousness and triviality are harmless.

They can associate themselves with some of the most interesting people in the world since their Planetary Sequence proceeds directly to the Crown Row. (This, of course, applies only to the Birth Card, not to the heart female who may choose to operate under the Queen of Hearts as her Personality Card.)

They are impressionable and receptive; many are psychic and mediumistic. There is a strong streak of religion in all of them.

Even when we should, we don't like to find fault with them; they are too loving and desirable.

BIRTHDATES RULED BY THE QUEEN OF HEARTS

JULY 29–LEO–RULED BY THE SUN
Many of these people are ardent reformers, sincere religionists, and unselfish philanthropists—but they all have exaggerated egos and very nearly all are megalomaniacs. They simply *must* be Kings, and woe to the man (or woman) who disputes their authority, questions their opinions, or offends their ego! Those who can work off this childish complex in the theater (where many are found) or as the head of some religious or educational institution, are easier to deal with in social or family life. But with the majority, those in close association with them must toe the mark—or else! They are too high-strung for their own (or others') good. Very successful musicians, authors, and merchants, as well as actors.

AUGUST 27–VIRGO–RULED BY MERCURY
The least frivolous and flirtatious of the Queen of Hearts. Mental and critical but willing to see their own faults as well as others'. Will sacrifice for a good education. Forget themselves in working for causes or digging for facts. Good business managers for others; efficient and executive. Writers, publishers, philosophers. Overdo service.

SEPTEMBER 25–LIBRA–RULED BY VENUS
Often talented in art but have more success as patrons or dealers. Good judges of quality and value. Collectors. Good beauty operators. Can succeed in law or politics. Exacting in family life. Writers, dancers, poets. Are fond of form and ceremony, especially in religion.

OCTOBER 23–LIBRA–RULED BY VENUS
(The last degree; *may* be—but rarely—a Scorpio birthdate). The most positive of the Queen of Hearts. Stubborn and impulsive. Demand personal freedom. Retain youthful appearance to old age. Intuitional, but incline to materialism. Good government officials, agents, lawyers, salesmen. Love art but cannot commercialize it. Are successful in lines where the personality counts. Dynamic and impressive. Not well adapted for medicine. Like to feel wanted and needed. Very emotional.

NOVEMBER 21–SCORPIO–RULED BY MARS
Mentally keen. Inclined to suspicion. Disciplinary toward others. May have disturbing fears and doubts. Borrow trouble. Do not realize their own

capabilities. Are better friends than marriage partners. Should avoid selfishness and self-pity. Hard working and reliable as employees, but want key positions. Suited to educational work, music, preaching, government posts. Emotional and religious.

DECEMBER 19—SAGITTARIUS—RULED BY JUPITER
The most difficult date of all the Queens of Hearts. Suffer in the emotional life; may have some physical affliction to contend with. Good recuperative power and usually long-lived. Hardships may be overcome after maturity. Need a working philosophy to get by. Are well suited to public life. Mental and nervous. Attracted to mechanics, science, radio and television, chemistry. Can succeed in business, but always approach everything from a scientific angle. Discontented with themselves, and others. Should cultivate optimism.

QUEEN OF HEARTS—PLANETARY SEQUENCE OF PERSONAL RELATIONSHIPS

Horizontal Line—Crown and Mercury

TEN OF CLUBS—MERCURY CARD IN THE CROWN LINE
Brilliant communication, if you try; but too intense overall for you. Too complicated for a close relationship. Friendship fine, but know they'll tend to irritate you. Well worth the investment, so try to spend some time (however little) getting to know these natives.

Ten of Clubs birthdates: January 30, February 28, March 26, April 24, May 22, June 20, July 18, August 16, September 14, October 12, November 10, December 8.

EIGHT OF DIAMONDS—VENUS CARD IN THE CROWN LINE
Fabulous business associate but more than likely a romantic relationship. Ideal if you are able to cope with their viewpoints on values. Your heart can get punctured by the tips of their eight diamonds but you'll never want for anything on a material level. Spiritually inclined but you may not be interested in either. Good relationship for you under any circumstances so don't let this one get away.

Eight of Diamonds birthdates: January 19, February 17, March 15, April 13, May 11, June 9, July 7, August 5, September 3, October 1.

KING OF SPADES—MARS CARD IN THE CROWN LINE

You won't be able to see this native beyond the end of your nose. Will seem too stubborn, too fixed in ideas and probably even a little fanatical. A relationship not worth the effort. But make doubly sure before you erase them from your chalkboard. They could be (and probably are) hiding a real consciousness that could be quite rewarding to you personally.

King of Spades birthdate: January 1.

THREE OF HEARTS—JUPITER CARD IN THE MERCURY LINE
(Double Mercury Lines on the Diagonal Lines)

A good friend of mutual benefit to you both. Although tempted, don't try to reassure love through words. Actions are more important here. Most of all, this is a fun card and you'll have many good times together. Business life not the best, you're both too busy entertaining.

Three of Hearts birthdates: November 30, December 28.

ACE OF CLUBS—SATURN CARD IN THE VENUS LINE

Strong attraction but a difficult involvement on any level. They'll never quite believe that you love them better (or as much as) your other friends. Too complicated for happiness.

Ace of Clubs birthdates: May 31, June 29, July 27, August 25, September 23, October 21, November 19, December 17.

QUEEN OF CLUBS—URANUS CARD IN THE MARS LINE

Always available to tell you of a better way to run your life. This could be a relationship that leans too heavily on you. They do have new ways and their judgment is sound, so try to overcome the irritating factors and listen—even if you don't think it applies. Not good for close involvements.

Queen of Clubs birthdates: January 28, February 26, March 24, April 22, May 20, June 18, July 16, August 14, September 12, October 10, November 8, December 6.

TEN OF SPADES—NEPTUNE CARD IN THE JUPITER LINE

Business could be good here except you will never fully understand what's going on. The end result is good so if you can give them their way, they can do the job for you—especially in a fast turn-over situation that requires communications. A good agent for you if you're in show business. Personal life is more difficult because you may not always believe them even when you should.

Ten of Spades birthdates: January 4, February 2.

Your Place in the Cards

Vertical Line—Neptune

JACK OF DIAMONDS—URANUS LINE

This native can hurt you in a personal involvement by the very nature of the card. Values are usually entirely material for the first half of the life. They are much more interested in business than in having a good time. Will only participate in the good time if it leads to business. You'll spend most of your time alone. Good for business affiliations but otherwise, don't get involved.

Jack of Diamonds birthdates: January 16, February 14, March 12, April 10, May 8, June 6, July 4, August 2.

FIVE OF DIAMONDS—SATURN LINE

Love for you but doubtful if it's returned. They are too busy keeping up with their neighbors while you're planting radishes or running a boy-scout troop. If you get involved, make it brief and forgotten or be prepared to earn money for the rest of your life. Friendship is best—it's safer and saner.

Five of Diamonds birthdates: January 22, February 20, March 18, April 16, May 14, June 12, July 10, August 8, September 6, October 4, November 2.

ACE OF DIAMONDS—JUPITER LINE

Physical attraction that won't go far—and shouldn't. Not even on the same wave length as you—almost to the point of harassing your good nature. Take it all in stride, they mean well. Meanwhile, don't get involved.

Ace of Diamonds birthdates: January 26, February 24, March 22, April 20, May 18, June 16, July 14, August 12, September 10, October 8, November 6, December 4.

EIGHT OF CLUBS—MARS LINE

A stimulating attraction that is probably mostly mental, but not meant to eliminate romance. Personal involvements are difficult and this card will unwittingly dominate you. In any event, the relationship is good, and could be powerful.

Eight of Clubs birthdates: March 28, April 26, May 24, June 22, July 20, August 18, September 16, October 14, November 12, December 10.

TWO OF HEARTS—VENUS LINES

A Karmic relationship that could be fulfilling to you both if you can convince this native that you love only him or her. Chances are they will never believe you and any chances for a close involvement would wind up as history. Difficult on any level.

Two of Hearts birthdate: December 29.

ACE OF SPADES—MERCURY LINE

Unexpected meetings, conversations that surprise you. No love life and preferably no business. Friendship possible but only probable if you make it happen.

Ace of Spades birthdates: January 13, February 11, March 9, April 7, May 5, June 3, July 1.

Diagonal Lines

KING OF CLUBS—DOUBLE URANUS LINES

Many things to be learned from this native—perhaps a whole new world of ideas and things. Business and friendship all right, romance not good. A short-termed involvement.

King of Clubs birthdates: January 27, February 25, March 23, April 21, May 19, June 17, July 15, August 13, September 11, October 9, November 7, December 5.

NINE OF HEARTS—DOUBLE SATURN LINES

Fall in love and the chances are good that you'll be miserable the rest of your life, unless you're both highly evolved. Then the relationship could be Karmic and exactly what you need in each other. On the negative side, even friendship would be difficult, but probable. No business—neither of you really have what it takes to do well together.

Nine of Hearts birthdates: August 30, September 28, October 26, November 24, December 22.

TEN OF DIAMONDS—DOUBLE JUPITER LINES

Your best business involvement is right here, although you won't feel that way most of the time. You'll disapprove of everything they do; yet they can make you a lot of money. So follow them without giving them too much interference. Opposite sexes may find a strong sexual attraction but divorce could be the outcome of any marriage. Friendship will be quarrelsome but rewarding.

Ten of Diamonds birthdates: January 17, February 15, March 13, April 11, May 9, June 7, July 5, August 3, September 1.

SIX OF HEARTS—DOUBLE MARS LINES

You'll never enjoy yourself more than with this native—when there are people around. A close involvement will reveal an entirely different person when you're alone, and here is where the problems start. Friendship is great, business not bad, and romance should be out.

Six of Hearts birthdates: October 29, November 27, December 25.

Your Place in the Cards

SEVEN OF DIAMONDS—DOUBLE VENUS LINES

Somewhere, sometime in your life you'll know a Seven of Diamonds, love him or her, and yet know that to carry the relationship any farther is pure folly. A Karmic involvement based on love but beset with problems created by the combination. Look elsewhere and love this native from afar.

Seven of Diamonds birthdates: January 20, February 18, March 16, April 14, May 12, June 10, July 8, August 6, September 4, October 2.

THREE OF HEARTS—DOUBLE MERCURY LINES:
SEE HORIZONTAL LINE

QUEEN OF HEARTS FAMOUS BIRTHDATES

July 29	Benito Mussolini
	Sigmund Romberg
August 27	Lyndon B. Johnson
	Martha Raye
	Confucius
October 23	Johnny Carson
November 21	Stan Musial

Planetary Sequence

			K♠	8♦	10♣		
A♠ (Jupiter)	3♦ (Mars)	5♣ (Venus)	10♠ (Mercury)	Q♣	A♣	3♥	Mercury
2♥	9♠	9♣	J♥	5♠ (Neptune)	7♦ (Uranus)	7♥ (Saturn)	Venus
8♣	J♠	2♦	4♣	6♥	K♦	K♥	Mars
A♦	A♥	8♠	10♦	10♥	4♠	6♦	Jupiter
5♦	7♣	9♥	3♠	3♣	5♥	Q♦	Saturn
J♦	K♣	2♣	7♠	9♦	J♣	Q♠	Uranus
Q♥	6♠	6♣	8♥	2♠	4♦	4♥	Neptune

Neptune · Uranus · Saturn · Jupiter · Mars · Venus · Mercury

Mundane Spread

Clubs—Knowledge
Queen of Clubs—Mental Receptivity, Intuition
Twelve In Clubs—Mental Balance
The Mars Card in the Mercury Line. Displaces the **Three of Hearts** in the Natural Spread.

All Queens represent the receptive principle and man's spiritual nature. The Queen of Clubs emphasizes *mental* attitudes and approaches as well; whatever is received is relayed through the mind. The spirituality that is expressed is balanced, wise, and logical.

These people are far removed from the yearning aspirants who take their religion prayerfully and tearfully. They know (or they should know) that they are always in direct contact with the higher forces of intelligence who are using them as channels. They seek their knowledge from that source and they apply it to their work with all the mind-power at their command. When formulating their judgments, they use their brains rather than their emotions.

In their personal lives they cannot seem to apply this sharp cleavage between heart and mind. The displacement of the Three of Hearts makes them uncertain in their associations and often subjects them to disappointment and heartache in their closest relationships. Always positive and strong of will. When suffering comes, it is deep and lasting.

In the application of their knowledge, they are practical and decisive. Their intuitional power never fails them when it comes to work or service. Their True Place is in the exact center of the Divine Plan and from that point all that concerns their mission radiates. Their quest for knowledge is insatiable and they are impatient and intolerant of ignorance or mental laziness in others.

They want complete freedom of action and will brook no interference from others. For that reason, coupled with "heart" uncertainty, many avoid marriage—especially the women. When they make the experiment, it often fails; they are not domestic and they don't know the meaning of subservience. There is in these women, however, an element of cosmic motherhood; they symbolize Mary, mother of Jesus.

Besides the deep urge for a personal love, they want money for the respect and the freedom it brings. They are generous and good spenders, and they usually make amply money by their own efforts.

They are leaders in any profession they follow, and it usually is a profession rather than a business. Among the men, those who follow business are apt to have women associates or partners.

The majority need to cultivate tolerance—although they seldom lack sympathy—and firmness in handling their own tempers.

Intuitively, they are far ahead of their time. They are inventive, creative, and inspirational. They are essentially people of the New Age of Intelligence, scientific progress, and the ability to see through and beyond the veil that has long hidden the truths that are soon to be revealed.

BIRTHDATES RULED BY THE QUEEN OF CLUBS

JANUARY 28—AQUARIUS—RULED BY URANUS

Many of these people are subject to confusion in the home life and make a break away from home as early as possible—or desire to. Should try to clarify their sense of values. Are sensitive, set, and difficult to deal with. Feel they are not understood. Often talented but may not find an outlet and forced to work, instead, at some uncongenial occupation. Highly emotional; not well-balanced. Must control the inclination for stimulation; are dangerously over-stimulated naturally, in most cases. Should avoid dealing with earth or its products; no real estate, mining, etc. Make good dramatists, teachers, aviators, explorers. Restless.

FEBRUARY 26—PISCES—RULED BY NEPTUNE

Have an urge for travel, but seldom enjoy it. In many cases it presents obstacles or danger. Work best behind the scenes: in hospitals, secret service, as confidants, or diplomats. Good understanding of human desires and foibles. Excellent writers about people. Many are inclined to religion and philosophy. Versatile and inventive. Can succeed in pictures if talent is confirmed. Love affairs disappointing.

MARCH 24—ARIES—RULED BY MARS

Attracted to politics and finances. Make good economists, financial advisers, brokers, government officials, or officers in the armed forces. Ambitious, hard-working. Nervous and touchy. Quick to take offense. Are loyal to friends and their interests. Should have a specialty.

APRIL 22—TAURUS—RULED BY VENUS

Mainly interested in those having a special type of knowledge similar to their own. Uncertain of their own beliefs; change their viewpoints and opinions. Set in their feelings and cannot be coerced. Have an urge for service but do not know how to satisfy it. Strong likes and dislikes. Usually talented, especially in music. Will sacrifice for family and chosen favorites. Seldom contented. Indulgent—often lazy. Well fitted for public life and should give service. Good for designing, decorating, landscape gardening.

MAY 20—TAURUS—RULED BY VENUS

Many talents and abilities. Always a good business head; attract money. Legal type of mind. Intuitive and inventive. Inclined to secrecy. Intense in emotions, but hide it. Must be at the head of own affairs; never subordinate. Should avoid domination and possessiveness. Need changes and contacts. Can reach the top in their profession. Keen appreciation of music and drama; often fine performers at both. Definitely on the metaphysical wire.

JUNE 18—GEMINI—RULED BY MERCURY

Often succeed in the theater or films, but are better fitted for a mental occupation. Good for law, politics, accounting, literature. Like travel; want things to move fast. Ambitious for success rather than money, but are money-conscious and may be penurious. Often win distinction. Change home frequently.

JULY 16—CANCER—RULED BY THE MOON

A Karmic birthdate. Usually interested in humanitarian causes. Should be in public life, before the footlights, or writing on subjects that concern public interest or welfare. Must guard against selfishness—also narrowness in viewpoint. Fine journalists and commentators, novelists, or historians. Need a good education. Many study law as a step to politics. May have a strong religious bend. Interested in cults and philosophies.

AUGUST 14—LEO—RULED BY THE SUN

More mental than the majority of Leo natives. Very keen for money and like to take chances to win it. Usually successful. Want to be leaders, and may overreach themselves. Wonderful people if developed. Restless. If in the theater, should try for road engagements. Good at buying and selling. Attracted to the opposite sex but uncertain about their love affairs. Not always happy in marriage. Are creative in mental fields.

SEPTEMBER 12—VIRGO—RULED BY MERCURY

Excellent technicians—in art or the laboratory. Mental and practical. Good in journalism, architecture, botany—any science. Technical lawyers, corporation counselors. Not interested in the earth (farming, etc.) except for chemical analysis of soil or experiments with plants. Not easy or fluent writers or speakers but interested in literature. Can succeed as publishers or advertisers. Have a keen judgment of literary merit and business methods. Good theoretical psychologists—not counselors.

OCTOBER 10—LIBRA—RULED BY VENUS

Gifted as artists, actors, and composers. Are restless and ambitious. Not often contented until they reach the top. Demand personal freedom. If willing to submit to training, may become important lawyers or leaders in their special field. Less soft and amenable than the majority of Librans. May be prolific writers—especially on religion or philosophy. Are seldom domestic. If disappointed in love, will make no effort to rebuild.

NOVEMBER 8–SCORPIO–RULED BY MARS

Productive and executive. Good financiers, heads of corporations, insurance brokers. Dramatic and magnetic. Hard to convince, but when they are, become ardent converts—and to too far. Often have a sense of importance that is ill-founded. If talented in any line, will work to reach the top, and mow down anything that stands in the way. May easily become ruthless. Intense and dynamic in whatever course they follow.

DECEMBER 6–SAGITTARIUS–RULED BY JUPITER

A Cosmic Card. Interested in humanity. Fine teachers, especially of metaphysics. Have unseen protection in work but lack security in their personal lives. Money usually a problem; must work for what they get. Eager for knowledge—to pass on. Will spend for classes rather than for home or self. Connected with health problems; burdened with responsibility. If undeveloped, will be crafty and secretive. Are mental, nervous, and sensitive. Know they must serve.

QUEEN OF CLUBS–PLANETARY SEQUENCE OF PERSONAL RELATIONSHIPS

Horizontal Line–Mercury and Venus

TEN OF SPADES–MERCURY CARD IN THE JUPITER LINE

Good friend; degree of intimacy will depend on your tolerance level. This native is a plodder. Introduce them to metaphysics and the relationship can be more rewarding. Business aspects extremely good, especially as your spokesman.

Ten of Spades birthdates: January 4, February 2.

FIVE OF CLUBS–VENUS CARD IN THE SATURN LINE

Instant like for this native but be careful of romantic aspirations or you'll be setting yourself up for another disappointment. These natives won't seem to be as interesting and flighty after a while. Relationship too wearisome for romance; friendship fine but would have to be sustained by you.

Five of Clubs birthdates: March 31, April 29, May 27, June 25, July 23, August 21, September 19, October 17, November 15, December 13.

THREE OF DIAMONDS—MARS CARD IN THE URANUS LINE

Watch your temper here; this could be a real explosion. Don't feel challenged to spend time and energy on trying to convince them to stop worrying over finances. With this native it could be a way of life. Friendship could be dynamic, but as an acquaintance preferably.

Three of Diamonds birthdates: January 24, February 22, March 20, April 18, May 16, June 14, July 12, August 10, September 8, October 6, November 4, December 2.

ACE OF SPADES—JUPITER CARD IN THE NEPTUNE LINE

A good relationship that you will probably want to abandon—but don't. Look for romance and/or friendship; you might find it through metaphysics. At least give the involvement a chance.

Ace of Spades birthdates: January 13, February 11, March 9, April 7, May 5, June 3, July 1.

SEVEN OF HEARTS—SATURN CARD IN THE MERCURY LINE

One look and you'll dislike this native, and probably without knowing why. Don't get involved romantically (even if you are a masochist), or you'll find the same romantically unstable reflection that you sometimes see in the mirror. A Karmic tie—stay away from their jealous and gossipy side and don't instigate anything of this nature. If possible, don't get involved at all.

Seven of Hearts birthdates: September 30, October 28, November 26, December 24.

SEVEN OF DIAMONDS—URANUS CARD IN THE VENUS LINE
(Double Venus Lines on the Diagonal Lines)

Romance with a lot of surprises. Don't get involved if you don't like an active life. Find their spiritual side and you'll find a beautiful relationship with new and rewarding experiences. A definite must on any level: romance, friendship, business can all be profitable. Particularly good for mental stimulation—use your knowledge and their know-how.

Seven of Diamonds birthdates: January 20, February 18, March 16, April 14, May 12, June 10, July 8, August 6, September 4, October 2.

FIVE OF SPADES—NEPTUNE CARD IN THE MARS LINE
(Venus Line on the Vertical Line)

A good personal friend, especially in the public life, but don't blame them if they prove to be disappointing. Your expectations and their capabilities can be two different things. Accept the changes they may try to inflict on you and then use your own better judgment for your own decision. Travel to foreign lands and other landmarks might prove to be your best neutral topic.

Five of Spades birthdates: January 9, February 7, March 5, April 3, May 1.

Vertical Line—Mars

TEN OF CLUBS—CROWN LINE

Great mental stimulation; you'll like this native even if he or she is on an opposing side. Romantically, it's a fast love affair—you have too many things to say to each other to get hung up on any level other than mental. Good for business.

Ten of Clubs birthdates: January 30, February 28, March 26, April 24, May 22, June 20, July 18, August 16, September 14, October 12, November 10, December 8.

TWO OF SPADES—NEPTUNE LINE

Romance a la the movies—until the lights go on. You'll sometimes feel that you're speaking in two different languages. Encourage them to come out of their dream world and take a good look at practicality and you might have a chance with a happy, healthy relationship. Don't try business, but friendship is all right if you are willing to put up with them.

Two of Spades birthdates: January 12, February 10, March 8, April 6, May 4, June 2.

NINE OF DIAMONDS—URANUS LINE

They'll always seem "right"—or at least they think they are, and this will undoubtedly create an irritation. You won't like the way they like to throw their money away, and the whole relationship will be a giant quarrel (on other issues as well). Best advice: take a pass.

Nine of Diamonds birthdates: January 18, February 16, March 14, April 12, May 10, June 8, July 6, August 4, September 2.

THREE OF CLUBS—SATURN LINE

There's no way you won't like this person—in some particular fashion—but a close examination will probably reveal that you can't live with them. You'll feel sorry for them and, if it's worth it, help them to see Another Way. They are appreciative and it does sink in eventually (whether you think so or not). A friend at best—but mostly burdensome.

Three of Clubs birthdates: May 29, June 27, July 25, August 23, September 21, October 19, November 17, December 15.

TEN OF HEARTS—JUPITER LINE

Use your keen judgment on this one—it's needed. A Karmic tie that could have you married off over the weekend. But winning smiles and warm eyes alone don't sustain over the years and you'll find yourself spending time alone, wondering where your Ten of Hearts is off to now. They mean well and are sincere, but when the relationship is over (and it usually eventually is), it's really over. They are not nearly as vulnerable as you. Be a friend and be happier. Preferably no business ventures.

Ten of Hearts birthdates: July 31, August 29, September 27, October 25, November 23, December 21.

SIX OF HEARTS—MARS LINE

A close involvement here would be quarrelsome. They live in one lifestyle and you live in another. Nice people but in a rut as far as you're concerned. Friendship is possible but not on a concentrated level. Sporadic visits are enough in this case.

Six of Hearts birthdates: October 29, November 27, December 25.

FIVE OF SPADES—VENUS LINE: SEE HORIZONTAL LINE

Diagonal Lines

EIGHT OF DIAMONDS—JUPITER AND CROWN LINES

Romance, friendship, or business, this native can meet you on equal ground, and each relationship can be successful. Be careful of their greedy side because this will turn you off in a hurry. If they're into a large accumulation of money, you won't be happy on a personal basis.

Eight of Diamonds birthdates: January 19, February 17, March 15, April 13, May 11, June 9, July 7, August 5, September 3, October 1.

SEVEN OF DIAMONDS—DOUBLE VENUS LINES: SEE HORIZONTAL LINE

KING OF HEARTS—MERCURY AND MARS LINES

Romance, but go easy. They won't fall into your arms at your first meeting although you might think they will. Likable people, you'll find an immediate rapport but watch their occasional quick temper. Not a problem and soon over with, but don't overlook it. These natives tend to be too fatherly. Best if you avoid the elder ones; they'll browbeat you with smiles and advice that may not even pertain to you in any way.

King of Hearts birthdates: June 30, July 28, August 26, September 24, October 22, November 20, December 18.

JACK OF HEARTS—JUPITER AND VENUS LINES

Strong attraction but little in common. Friendship is the only way this relationship can survive. This native can only be of help to you, and the friendship can be rewarding. Avoid business unless the native is trained in a particular profession. Otherwise, they will sit around and philosophize while you're hustling the business and running the show.

Jack of Hearts birthdates: July 30, August 28, September 26, October 24, November 22, December 20.

TWO OF DIAMONDS—SATURN AND MARS LINES

Romance between you and this native would become so irritating that you could wind up in mental and physical combat. Friendship is best; you'll like them—just don't try to live with them. Business could be difficult because you'll never win an argument, even when you're right, and most of the time you will be. Too frustrating an involvement.

Two of Diamonds birthdates: January 25, February 23, March 21, April 19, May 17, June 15, July 13, August 11, September 9, October 7, November 5, December 3.

ACE OF HEARTS—URANUS AND JUPITER LINES

Strong physical attraction that could come about through unusual circumstances. Skeptics at heart, conversations can be exciting on the occult or metaphysical level. Take it easy, they're not as qualified. So enjoy the relationship—and don't get married.

Ace of Hearts birthdate: December 30.

FIVE OF DIAMONDS—SATURN AND NEPTUNE LINES

An attraction and you may feel compelled to dissuade them from their delusions of grandeur. Don't waste your time, especially if it requires money, or you're liable to get hooked into the situation. Fine friendship—not good for romance or business, mainly because of their ability to occasionally have odd ideas. Don't project something into this relationship that isn't there.

Five of Diamonds birthdates: January 22, February 20, March 18, April 16, May 14, June 12, July 10, August 8, September 6, October 4, November 2.

QUEEN OF CLUBS FAMOUS BIRTHDATES

February 26	Godfrey Cambridge
	Johnny Cash
	Jackie Gleason
	Tony Randall
	Victor Hugo
	Buffalo Bill

Your Place in the Cards

March 24	Steve McQueen Thomas Dewey
April 22	Eddie Albert
May 20	Cher Buono Moshe Dayan George Gobel James Stewart
June 18	Sammy Cahn Paul McCartney
July 16	Ginger Rogers Barbara Stanwyck
August 14	Buddy Greco John Ringling North Hermes
September 12	Maurice Chevalier
October 10	Helen Hayes Giuseppe Verdi
November 8	Alain Delon Katharine Hepburn
December 6	Dave Brubeck

Queen of Diamonds

Diamonds—Values
Queen of Diamonds—Desired Domination in the Realm of Values
Twelve in Diamonds — Balanced Judgment of Worth

The Mercury Card in the Saturn Line. Displaces the **Three of Diamonds** in the Natural Spread.

This is one of the most difficult cards of the entire fifty-two, and the leader of an exacting—often grueling—Sequence. There is a test given for every step of the way and since the main concern is judgment of values and the accepted translation of the word is *money,* these people are born with and live with an all-absorbing money-consciousness from their first breath to their last.

The entire Sequence, up to the Neptune Card, is in the Saturn Line; every card in the Displacement Line of the Natural Spread is a Diamond; the Mundane Pattern is operated from a Diamond center and Queens, in their own right, are endowed with rulership and control. Would it not be logical to expect that the Queens of Diamonds would have unlimited money at their disposal? But have they? In a few rare instances these people have acquired or inherited wealth; the majority go through life with an ever-present money problem, if not actual limitation.

The answer is in Saturn. To that agent of ageless wisdom Values do not

Planetary Sequence

			K♠	8♦	10♣			
A♠	3♦	5♣	10♠	Q♣	A♣	3♥		Mercury
2♥	9♠	9♣	J♥	5♠	7♦	7♥		Venus
8♣	J♠	2♦	4♣	6♥	K♦	K♥		Mars
A♦	A♥	8♠	10♦	10♥	4♠	6♦		Jupiter
5♦	7♣	9♥	3♠	3♣	5♥	Q♦		Saturn
Uranus	Saturn	Jupiter	Mars	Venus	Mercury			
J♦	K♣	2♣	7♠	9♦	J♣	Q♠ (Neptune)		Uranus
Q♥	6♠	6♣	8♥	2♠	4♦	4♥		Neptune

Neptune · Uranus · Saturn · Jupiter · Mars · Venus · Mercury

Mundane Spread

mean money. As soon as the natives of this card learn that priceless lesson their problems are solved. Learning lessons that are based upon laws, however, is accomplished only by those who consciously and deliberately seek that special knowledge. What they want for themselves becomes subservient to what is wanted by the plan for the whole of mankind. Hark back to the divine command—"Let the Waters (Diamonds) bring forth abundantly"; "Be fruitful and multiply and have dominion"; and finally, "Lay up for yourselves treasures in heaven." On the money level, some of the greatest philanthropists are Queens of Diamonds; in the world of art, some of the greatest poets, painters, and musicians have contributed their "wealth"; in the realm of religion and metaphysics, some of the greatest teachers and way-showers. They have all learned what Values are.

The path is a hard one, so beset with obstacles and difficulties that those who are on it must use all their strength of will and energy of body to overcome them. If they know no better and care no more than to remain on the lower levels, there is no escape from toil and disappointment. The women are the greatest sufferers, for there is no alternative for their Birth Card. The men should, if possible, follow the Jack or the King; either one of these patterns offers easier climbing.

The Queen of Diamonds is a very dominating, mercenary card, negatively. The Queen of Diamond women, who are mercenary, usually are so out of fear. The Queen of Diamonds can also represent spirituality in the highest degree of initiation. Spirituality, not just the mundane field and the material plane. This is a mature person, not the childhood sweetheart, but a person who has gone through all the fires of Initiation. With a Queen of Diamonds who is well instructed or well balanced, it is a very hard working, sacrificial type of individual. But if the person is not well integrated, then they will be constantly afraid. Substance will run away from her or him and therefore the drive is for money, money, money. And money in big letters, not small print.

For females, this is a very determined woman. She will sacrifice to the nth degree for her family, especially the July birthdays. She will go out and scrub floors if she has to for her children. Nevertheless, she is still money-conscious. There is indecision about people, about the marriage relationship and turmoil comes up because of finances. The finances are all under this Saturn Line, so all Queens of Diamonds suffer financially. They never seem to have quite enough to go around. They are always helping their children through school. All Queens of Diamonds want a home and invariably they are shoved around and pushed around from one place to the other.

These people are fitted for authority and should have it. Because of illness or responsibility, they may be forced into uncongenial work—which becomes an added burden. They are diligent and dependable, strong of character, and determined. They must guard against hardness and sharpness of tongue, domination and self-will. They have much to contend with and much should be forgiven them—but they are also much to blame.

BIRTHDATES RULED BY THE QUEEN OF DIAMONDS

JANUARY 15—CAPRICORN—RULED BY SATURN
Conformists to orthodoxy, but want enlightenment. Money much desired but always a problem. Uncertain in faith. Fear of the future and worry over it, which interferes with work and health. Strong of will and purpose. Are never weak characters. Fair, honest, and cooperative. Mental. May have unusual writing ability, especially along dramatic lines. Good head for business; good government officials. Experiment in religion.

FEBRUARY 13—AQUARIUS—RULED BY URANUS
Can never find happiness or themselves until they work for humanity. Creative and inventive. Actors, writers, musicians. Good brains and keen wit. Want changes but find them unsatisfactory. Personal life confused. Must conquer desire to escape duty or personal problems. Can succeed in science or radio.

MARCH 11—PISCES—RULED BY NEPTUNE
Love music and dancing; can often succeed at either or both. More universally minded than many Queen of Diamonds, more willing to serve without pay. Good propagandists. Write or work for causes. Seek government position for the sake of reform. Seldom given due credit for their work. Inclined to criticism. Become more positive and efficient in later years. Must be content to remain in the background.

APRIL 9—ARIES—RULED BY MARS
Must learn to keep an impersonal attitude toward work-associates. Emotional involvement destroys their power. Need stability. Want to be officers or leaders. Pioneers in politics, cultists. May be talented in music, writing.

MAY 7—TAURUS—RULED BY VENUS
The most talented of all the Queens of Diamonds—in art, music, or drama especially. Work for education or public interests. If not performers, are good directors, producers, or impresarios. Idealistic, often poetical. Intuitive. Drawn to metaphysics. Women like clubs, circles, sororities, etc. Contribute to success of those they love.

JUNE 5—GEMINI—RULED BY MERCURY
Self-concerned, fickle, restless; not always dependable or responsible.

Refuse to allow interference with personal plans or desires. Can succeed at nursing, traveling, salesmanship. Make easy contacts; want constant change and variety. Are unable to make up their minds. Good lawyers. Must have freedom, variety, and movement.

JULY 3–CANCER–RULED BY THE MOON
Want security for self and family. Good leaders in clubs, welfare movements, collections for charity. Are concerned for children (P.T.A.). Succeed in dress shops, food merchandising, teaching; often good entertainers. If in a medical line, good doctors for women and children. Can promote what they believe in.

AUGUST 1–LEO–RULED BY THE SUN
Most ambitious and self-important of all the Queens of Diamonds. Believe they are supreme in authority; think others should work for them. Like changes and business journeys. Will not take responsibility if it interferes with their plans. Good negotiators, promoters, office managers. Magnetic. May have dramatic or musical ability. Should cultivate unselfishness and strength of character. Must learn to deserve leadership.

QUEEN OF DIAMONDS–PLANETARY SEQUENCE OF PERSONAL RELATIONSHIPS

Horizontal Line–Saturn and Uranus

FIVE OF HEARTS–MERCURY CARD IN THE VENUS LINE
Too changeable in their emotions to permit you to spend valuable time here. Friendship good, communications high, but don't take on their problems too by becoming involved in their love life.
Five of Hearts birthdates: October 30, November 28, December 26.

THREE OF CLUBS–VENUS CARD IN THE MARS LINE
Strong sexual attraction that can lead to love, marriage, etc. Irritations are high with this card. Again, you don't have to take more of these burdens on. Don't get involved in business; try to stay clear of a close involvement.
Three of Clubs birthdates: May 29, June 27, July 25, August 23, September 21, October 19, November 17, December 15.

THREE OF SPADES—MARS CARD IN THE JUPITER LINE

Another strong sexual attraction that could have you in a Las Vegas wedding chapel one week and a Reno divorce court the next. Stay friends and stay out of trouble.

Three of Spades birthdates: January 11, February 9, March 7, April 5, May 3, June 1.

NINE OF HEARTS—JUPITER CARD IN THE SATURN LINE

You could make money in a business venture with this native but the price for what money you might make may be too high. Good friends and advisors but don't get involved otherwise.

Nine of Hearts birthdates: August 30, September 28, October 26, November 24, December 22.

SEVEN OF CLUBS—SATURN CARD IN THE URANUS LINE

A problem person with nerve-ending surprises. Karmic, so, therefore, an inevitable relationship. Encourage them to go on to higher education. Stay out of their personal lives.

Seven of Clubs birthdates: March 29, April 27, May 25, June 23, July 21, August 19, September 17, October 15, November 13, December 11.

FIVE OF DIAMONDS—URANUS CARD IN THE NEPTUNE LINE

Appears to be something other than what is truly the situation—usually gives the impression of affluence. Disappointing if you become closely involved. Friendship is fine, but don't always depend on this native. Business aspects are not good, so don't get involved.

Five of Diamonds birthdates: January 22, February 20, March 18, April 16, May 14, June 12, July 10, August 8, September 6, October 4, November 2.

QUEEN OF SPADES—NEPTUNE CARD IN THE MERCURY LINE
(Uranus Line on the Vertical Line)

A mysterious relationship that can flit in and out of your life. Not many things in common. Although hostility won't be prevalent, there won't be a feeling of companionship. Better forgotten other than an occasional friend.

Queen of Spades birthdate: January 2.

Vertical Line—Mercury

SIX OF DIAMONDS—JUPITER LINE

Romance and/or a close friendship would leave you both struggling for the almighty dollar. Business can work well, especially in a sales-oriented type of work. A good friend and someone you can talk to, but don't get too involved.

Six of Diamonds birthdates: January 21, February 19, March 17, April 15, May 13, June 11, July 9, August 7, September 5, October 3, November 1.

KING OF HEARTS—MARS LINE

You'll love the easy-going attitude of this native as well as being physically and sexually attracted. Can make life a little easier for you, so pursue the relationship. Let him or her have an occasional temper tantrum. Great for friendship as well.

King of Hearts birthdates: June 30, July 28, August 26, September 24, October 22, November 20, December 18.

SEVEN OF HEARTS—VENUS LINE

Don't be misled and think that this can be love. In any close association this native will think you're doing one thing when you're actually doing another, etc. They won't trust you and will cause unnecessary problems for you both. So avoid the relationship if possible.

Seven of Hearts birthdates: September 30, October 28, November 26, December 24.

THREE OF HEARTS—MERCURY LINE

A good relationship if you can ever communicate about the same things. Love is first on their list and money's on yours. Find a common meeting ground and you'll find a friend. Romance is possible if you don't pick on them in a destructive or negative manner.

Three of Hearts birthdates: November 30, December 28.

FOUR OF HEARTS—NEPTUNE LINE

Stand back and admire this happy person but don't get involved or you'll find the situation isn't what you think it is. They will unknowingly bring you more problems. Stay friends and out of business with them.

Four of Hearts birthdates: October 31, November 29, December 27.

QUEEN OF SPADES—URANUS LINE: SEE HORIZONTAL LINE

Diagonal Lines

JACK OF CLUBS—URANUS AND VENUS LINES

Business is what will attract you most of all here. The charm and new approaches that this native displays, together with your own good feelings about him or her, will prompt you to become involved. A word of caution: don't put all your eggs in one basket, so to speak. Save a little for yourself. If the business doesn't make it, you will suffer far more than this native. The same is true for personal relationships; they are temporary and best avoided to protect yourself.

Jack of Clubs birthdates: January 29, February 27, March 25, April 23, May 21, June 19, July 17, August 15, September 13, October 11, November 9, December 7.

TWO OF SPADES—NEPTUNE AND MARS LINES

A strong sexual relationship, love, and marriage are all possible—but take a good, long look because this native will not be the same person you saw in the beginning of the relationship. Don't be discouraged, it might be better. An easier life for you with this person; permit them their occasional dramatizations and exaggerations, and don't be uptight so much. A good match; enjoy it.

Two of Spades birthdates: January 12, February 10, March 8, April 6, May 4, June 2.

FOUR OF SPADES—JUPITER AND VENUS LINES

Another good relationship that can bring positive thoughts and actions. More temporary or sporadic than the Two of Spades, but definitely an involvement worth pursuing on any level. This is a good person for you to know—very positive and can help keep you on that positive plane you keep slipping off.

Four of Spades birthdates: January 10, February 8, March 6, April 4, May 2.

SIX OF HEARTS—DOUBLE MARS LINES

Probably the strongest sexual attraction in your sequence. If the same sex, a good friend who does things (or doesn't do something) that disturbs you. Can be a love/hate relationship if not watched. No business ventures.

Six of Hearts birthdates: October 29, November 27, December 25.

JACK OF HEARTS—VENUS AND JUPITER LINES

More problems; operating on an entirely different plane. You'll like this native very much but won't be able to find a way to justify their particular way of life. A possible sexual attraction on your part. Other than straight friendship, don't get involved.

Jack of Hearts birthdates: July 30, August 28, September 26, October 24, November 22, December 20.

FIVE OF CLUBS—MERCURY AND SATURN LINES
A definite physical attraction that cannot make your life easier. Good mental rapport, but their restlessness will bother you in a negative way sooner or later.

Five of Clubs birthdates: March 31, April 29, May 27, June 25, July 23, August 21, September 19, October 17, November 15, December 13.

QUEEN OF DIAMONDS FAMOUS BIRTHDATES

January 15	Martin Luther King
	Gene Krupa
	Aristotle Onassis
February 13	Tennessee Ernie Ford
	Kim Novak
March 11	Ralph Abernathy
	Lawrence Welk
April 9	Jean-Paul Belmondo
	Sol Hurok
	Paul Robeson
May 7	Gary Cooper
	Petr Ilich Tchaikovsky
	Johannes Brahms
June 5	Igor Stravinsky
July 3	Stephen Boyd
	Gina Lollobrigida
	Pete Fountain
	Virginia Graham
	Eva Marie Saint
August 1	Francis Scott Key
	Herman Melville

Queen of Spades

Spades—Labor, Wisdom
Queen of Spades—The Crown of Labor
Twelve in Spades—Organization of Service to Humanity

The Mercury Card in the Uranus Line. Displaces the **Ten of Diamonds** in the Natural Spread

The Queen of Spades is a very important card and there are two types of individuals under this card. This is in the Crown position in the Natural Spread and, along with the King of Spades and the Jack of Spades, represents the Father, Son, and Holy Ghost. This is the spiritual manifestation operating in the realm of man.

Together with the Queen of Clubs, this card represents cosmic motherhood. These two Queens are the Mary and Martha of the Bible. The Queen of Clubs sits at the feet of the Teacher that she may learn; the Queen of Spades runs His household and smooths His pathway that the Source of Wisdom may enrich the world unhampered. Both of these cards are closely connected with the Ten of Diamonds; both are centers in the Divine Plan—the Queen of Clubs as center of the Natural Spread as the pivotal principle, and the Queen of Spades as the center of the Crown Line as the highest point in this ray or these sunbeams (Crown Line equals Sun Line) that go down through all the

Planetary Sequence

			K♠	8♦	10♣		
A♠	3♦	5♣	10♠	Q♣	A♣	3♥	Mercury
2♥	9♠	9♣	J♥	5♠	7♦	7♥	Venus
8♣	J♠	2♦	4♣	6♥	K♦	K♥	Mars
A♦	A♥	8♠	10♦	10♥	4♠	6♦	Jupiter
5♦	7♣	9♥	3♠	3♣	5♥	Q♦	Saturn
J♦	K♣	2♣	7♠	9♦	J♣	Q♠	Uranus
Uranus	Saturn	Jupiter	Mars	Venus	Mercury		
Q♥	6♠	6♣	8♥	2♠	4♦	4♥	Neptune
						Neptune	
Neptune	Uranus	Saturn	Jupiter	Mars	Venus	Mercury	

Mundane Spread

rest of the cards. For the Queen of Spades, this is often the source of the troubles.

The Queen of Spades in the Mundane position is the Mercury Card in the Uranian Line. Negatively, this is a very high-strung and nervous individual. This represents a nurse, a housekeeper, a governess, any servile or domestic application. In this particular lifetime, the Queen of Spades is put on this lower level because of some Karmic neglect in the previous life; the lack of fulfillment of obligations in some form. The card is punished, so to speak, at this lifetime. This is not the True Position—the True place is in the Crown Line and, of all the Queens, the Queen of Spades is the only one that is on the upper line.

Queen of Spades people have come to lead and direct; they are corulers with the highest authority—the King of Spades. When they find themselves in a subordinate position, it is galling and irksome to them for they know they do not belong there. That, however, is exactly what happens to those who are operating negatively.

They symbolize the household drudges, caretakers, janitors, or menial servants of the world. They work hard and are ill paid. They live down to earth, ignorant of true values, incapable of intelligent judgment, lacking in vision, despairing of the future. They are jealous, antagonistic, and usually mercenary. Even among those who are aware of their supremacy, there is a conflict as to how it shall be expressed and it often results in a dictatorial attitude and disciplinary insistence when it comes to dealing with others.

The Queen of Spades is probably a very unhappy person. In German, there is a word—*Weltschmerz*. The Queen of Spades has this, the suffering of the soul that is so deep and goes beyond the individual. The later in life they marry, the better. Build your house upon the rock and not upon the sand. Queens of Spades must build solidly. They have to know that there is something under them; otherwise, the tide, so to speak, washes away the foundation.

They have good mental balance, right judgment of values, and eagerness for service, as well as a willingness to work without sparing themselves. They know where they belong and they are continually struggling to get back to the Crown.

They are usually in business for themselves and will hire anything they dislike to do. They are excellent managers for others. Intuitive, impulsive, and independent, they are valuable contributors to the highest type of accomplishment.

A religious leader that is a Queen of Spades is living up to the exact examplification of the life as it should be. There is satisfaction in the whole, knowing that the cosmic substance is not accumulative but rather circulatory. The result is the ability to cooperate with the Divine Will. This is the unification of God and man, manifested in this card. This is the union of the inner man with his God at all times. This is the True Value of the Queen of Spades.

BIRTHDATES RULED BY THE QUEEN OF SPADES

JANUARY 2–CAPRICORN–RULED BY SATURN

The best field is education, the best teaching philosophy and religion. If these people remain wholly commercial or confine their interest to economics, they fail in their destiny. May have talent for writing, seldom for art. Good servants of the people, government heads.

QUEEN OF SPADES–PLANETARY SEQUENCE OF PERSONAL RELATIONSHIPS

Horizontal Line–Uranus and Neptune

JACK OF CLUBS–MERCURY CARD IN THE VENUS LINE

Personal attraction of short duration. Communications good, business affiliations okay. Opposite sexes may think it's love but you may wind up as the "maid" or the "butler." Be careful, this native can move fast and forget (you) easily.

Jack of Clubs birthdates: January 29, February 27, March 25, April 23, May 21, June 19, July 17, August 15, September 13, October 11, November 9, December 7.

NINE OF DIAMONDS–VENUS CARD IN THE MARS LINE

Love, romance, and sex—not necessarily in that order. A Nine of Diamonds and you can pose a difficult combination, or it can be exceptionally good. No middle ground. Take the time to study the native to see whether he or she is operating positively. If they make an effort to dominate you—run.

Nine of Diamonds birthdates: January 18, February 16, March 14, April 12, May 10, June 8, July 6, August 4, September 2.

SEVEN OF SPADES–MARS CARD IN THE JUPITER LINE

Good business relationship. Watch your tendency to be bossy and negative. It's not necessary here. They know what they're doing and it will be a profitable association. Hold up your end of the work load. Friendship fine, but edgy at times. Romance aspects should be thought over carefully and avoided if possible.

Seven of Spades birthdates: January 7, February 5, March 3, April 1.

Your Place in the Cards

TWO OF CLUBS—JUPITER CARD IN THE SATURN LINE

A good friend you can count on—someone who could do research for you in business. A difficult romantic pattern but not impossible. You may outgrow this native over the years.

Two of Clubs birthdates: May 30, June 28, July 26, August 24, September 22, October 20, November 18, December 16.

KING OF CLUBS—SATURN CARD IN THE URANUS LINE

A Karmic tie, a knowledgeable person. You may feel he or she hasn't earned the respect they demand. Don't feel inhibited and (preferably) don't get into any close associations.

King of Clubs birthdates: January 27, February 25, March 23, April 21, May 19, June 17, July 15, August 13, September 11, October 9, November 7, December 5.

JACK OF DIAMONDS—URANUS CARD IN THE NEPTUNE LINE

New doors can be opened by this native, but don't necessarily walk through them. Know the person to make sure he or she isn't on a completely material plane. Any involvements on this level will not work. Don't fool yourself. Take a little time.

Jack of Diamonds birthdates: January 16, February 14, March 12, April 10, May 8, June 6, July 4, August 2.

FOUR OF HEARTS—NEPTUNE IN THE MERCURY LINE
(Neptune Line on the Vertical Line)

You'll always have a Four of Hearts somewhere in your life or in your heart. But here is another situation where you must not kid yourself and see the situation as it really is, for good or ill. Friendship is best. These natives can give you many hours of pleasure; romance is not impossible, but you may find disappointment in finances. Not the greatest business affiliation you could make, so try and stay clear of that.

Four of Hearts birthdates: October 31, November 29, December 27.

Vertical Line—Mercury

QUEEN OF DIAMONDS—SATURN LINE

Difficult relationship that should not be attempted on any level other than that of a casual acquaintance. Communications good, but it may be only to complain about the problems you both have.

Queen of Diamonds birthdates: January 15, February 13, March 11, April 9, May 7, June 5, July 3, August 1.

SIX OF DIAMONDS–JUPITER LINE

A romantic relationship that can be of great benefit to you. Perhaps difficult to adjust to society's standards in the beginning. Help this native to keep from getting discouraged. You have the power.

Six of Diamonds birthdates: January 21, February 19, March 17, April 15, May 13, June 11, July 9, August 7, September 5, October 3, November 1.

KING OF HEARTS–MARS LINE

A sexual attraction that is better off left alone. A definite argumentative involvement on any level. You won't be able to understand them nor they you. Exception would be a highly impersonal arrangement.

King of Hearts birthdates: June 30, July 28, August 26, September 24, October 22, November 20, December 18.

SEVEN OF HEARTS–VENUS LINE

Romance and/or friendship where you will have to sustain the relationship in the beginning by reassuring your love. Good for you with similar viewpoints and lifestyles.

Seven of Hearts birthdates: September 30, October 28, November 26, December 24.

THREE OF HEARTS–MERCURY LINE

A Karmic responsibility but try not to get personally involved. Guidance and advice in their love life is probably all they're looking for, so don't take on anything more. Careful that this native doesn't become a burden to you.

Three of Hearts birthdates: November 30, December 28.

FOUR OF HEARTS–NEPTUNE LINE: SEE HORIZONTAL LINE

Diagonal Lines

FIVE OF HEARTS–SATURN AND VENUS LINES

A possible romantic attraction; their busy lives will intrigue you. But don't get involved or you'll become just another face in the past. Good for friendship, fluctuating finances if attempt a business arrangement.

Five of Hearts birthdates: October 30, November 28, December 26.

TEN OF HEARTS–JUPITER AND MARS LINES

You won't know what hit you from your first meeting with this native. Love at first sight, butterflies, and bells. The problem is that they are not that stable in their love life, so be prepared to share on an impersonal, or even personal, basis. But the rewards could easily be worth the price, so stay with it.

Ten of Hearts birthdates: July 31, August 29, September 27, October 25, November 23, December 21.

FOUR OF CLUBS–MARS AND JUPITER LINES

You'll feel you can't get a word in edgewise and you're probably right, but they mean well. Take it as it comes and hold down your irritations. You shouldn't marry them, but you can learn from them.

Four of Clubs birthdates: April 30, May 28, June 26, July 24, August 22, September 20, October 18, November 16, December 14.

NINE OF CLUBS–VENUS AND SATURN LINES

A good relationship for love or friendship. Problematical for business unless both are in the teaching fields. A possible "meant to be" involvement for you both. Difficult on a day-to-day basis, but stay with the situation and don't become subservient. That isn't necessary for happiness.

Nine of Clubs birthdates: January 31, February 29, March 27, April 25, May 23, June 21, July 19, August 17, September 15, October 13, November 11, December 9.

THREE OF DIAMONDS–MERCURY AND URANUS LINES

Problems on any level, especially personal. You are traveling two different roads. Do what you have to do and then get out of the involvement.

Three of Diamonds birthdates: January 24, February 22, March 20, April 18, May 16, June 14, July 12, August 10, September 8, October 6, November 4, December 2.

FOUR OF DIAMONDS–NEPTUNE AND VENUS LINES

A temptation you may not be able to resist. Usually a short-term affiliation but not necessarily here—especially if you are involved in work together. Possible romantic tendencies, but don't be confused by the two if they are intertwined. Work is more important to this native than romance with you.

Four of Diamonds birthdates: January 23, February 21, March 19, April 17, May 15, June 13, July 11, August 9, September 7, October 5, November 3, December 1.

QUEEN OF SPADES FAMOUS BIRTHDATES

January 2	James Wolfe (1727)
	Nathaniel Bacon (1647)

Kings

KINGS symbolize the positive, masculine, activating principle in humanity. They represent aggressiveness as initiative—not combativeness. They are endowed with authority and rulership, but their number in the "Little Book" indicates that they have not sole authority. Between their one and their three stands two, the mother, or the Queen. Before initiative is expressed, it must be nurtured, formulated, and given a body as principle. The Kings, therefore, although they occupy the highest place, are but co-rulers, like the Queens. Without the spiritual vision, furnished by the Queens, their "people" would "perish."

Thirteen by reduction is Four—the builder of the foundation and the layer of the cornerstone. There are Four of these Kings, and four times thirteen equals 52, which is the number of "pages" in the "Little Book." In any Four there is always a potential twenty-two—the Master Magician, the transformer of ideals into realities.

As with the natives of these cards, mystery and misconception (as well as negative or evil expression) have been built around the number. Thirteen is the number of two Hebrew words—Love and Unity—and among the wiser ones of old, these qualities together with their number, were held to be sacred. It is only a Christian superstition, derived from the tragic deflection of Judas, that gives to Thirteen the label evil or "unlucky." In the lives of many of our "Kings" the harmful superstition has done its work, since we invariably and inevitably express what is built into our consciousness.

Kings are the Jacob of the Bible—the founders and fathers of the Twelve (tribes) who were entrusted with leading the "children" to the Source of All Good. In the Hebrew Liturgy there were 13 logical rules for interpreting the law and this is actually the task of the Kings of the four suits.

Kings are usually kindly people, sympathetic and understanding. In the sequence, they may represent the father or an older brother, not a son.

They know subconsciously that their power depends upon cooperation; in whatever line they follow their best work is done in partnership. They always have a sense of authority but it seldom leads to domination. If operating negatively, they can be very antagonistic and quarrelsome.

Hearts rule by love. They are pleased when their deeds bring blessings, but they let others take the glory.
Clubs wield their power through knowledge. They know that mind-development is the surest road to progress.
Diamonds "have dominion" over all "substance." Theirs is the power of distribution.
Spades rule by wisdom. They are the guardians of Divine Law, Initiates who have earned their crowns.

King of Hearts

Hearts – Love
King of Hearts – "The Beloved Disciple"
Thirteen in Hearts – Conjugal Fidelity, Paternal Love

The Mercury Card in the Mars Line. Displaces the **Two of Clubs** in the Natural Spread

We cannot fully understand these people without duly considering the True Place of their card—Uranus in the Venus Line. The front they present to the world is kindly, friendly, and magnetic. They give an impression not so much of power as of peace, protection, and "safe harbor." Within, however, they have power over "the greatest thing in the world"—divinely bestowed, inspirationally expressed, and they know that that kind of power is invincible. When they are living true to themselves and their mission, they never have to fight for place or recognition, nor do they want it. They are fully

Planetary Sequence

		K♠	8♦	10♣			
A♠	3♦	5♣	10♠	Q♣	A♣	3♥	Mercury
2♥	9♠	9♣	J♥	5♠	7♦	7♥	Venus
8♣ (Uranus)	J♠ (Saturn)	2♦ (Jupiter)	4♣ (Mars)	6♥ (Venus)	K♦ (Mercury)	K♥	Mars
A♦	A♥	8♠	10♦	10♥	4♠	6♦ (Neptune)	Jupiter
5♦	7♣	9♥	3♠	3♣	5♥	Q♦	Saturn
J♦	K♣	2♣	7♠	9♦	J♣	Q♠	Uranus
Q♥	6♠	6♣	8♥	2♠	4♦	4♥	Neptune

Neptune / Uranus / Saturn / Jupiter / Mars / Venus / Mercury

Mundane Spread

content to be agents and reflectors of the Everlasting Love that knowing all, forgives all. Theirs is the mission of John the Divine.

The problems they meet in life are indicated by the card that usurps their True Place, the Nine of Spades. They are brought to them by others or by circumstances beyond their control. Unlike the majority of cards (people), they seldom manufacture their own problems. The Nine of Spades can also create crippling accidents or long spells of illnesses for the King of Hearts.

The King of Hearts and the King of Diamonds are always associated together because they are more dependent on other people. The King of Hearts represents a fatherly attitude. This is a warm hearted person, but temperish. Quick in their reactions; these quick reactions sometimes come from fear. But innately, they have a good philosophy and they snap out of their temper tantrums. They never hold grudges and, after their temper is spent, they will then listen. King of Hearts people know that out of disappointment comes fulfillment; therefore, in their inner being, they are not really afraid. In fact, the King of Hearts is rather easygoing. This might be a downfall.

As a card for women, the King of Hearts would be too nervous and too bossy. And when one of these women begins to express her nervousness and bossiness, she needs to take warning—it is the signal for a hurry call for the psychologist. The true King of Hearts wants peace in his home; he wants quiet. He wants to rule through peace and he means to be fair. He means to be loving. He also means to pay his bills but there may be a tendency to take a longer time than usual.

With all their sweetness and amenability they are very positive, not from stubbornness but because they are sure of themselves and of the principles for which they stand. That is their only "fixity." The other Kings express their consciousness of rulership; not so the King of Hearts. They feel it is unnecessary to proclaim anything so self-evident and indisputable.

King of Hearts men are softies, in a way. They usually lack stamina or fortitude. On occasion, when they are quarrelsome and overbearing, it is not so much the evidence of negativity as a problem they are not facing and, therefore, they should seek professional advice. They displace the Two of Clubs, which should not be forgotten—the Two of Clubs is a fear card. They are constantly meeting with disappointment in others, are frequently deceived or betrayed. The weaker ones will naturally build up a fear neurosis and will, also naturally, express it in attempted domination and quarreling as a measure of defense. Like any other mental sickness, it needs treatment rather than condemnation. They can be readily cured.

King of Hearts people do not like a great deal of traveling. They like action and to be on the go a lot, but never off too far that they can't get back home. A warm person, but fiery. Temper first and then reason. They should be allowed to explode—with no one around—and then they are all right. By nature, they are the most desirable people on earth and the most worthy of love. They will respond to any call for help from any quarter, and you can forget to thank them if you choose; it will make no difference. They are the heart and center of family life, the friend, and harmonizer in work associations. We scarcely know if they want to be Kings; we are glad to let them be, for they play the part so beautifully. When we meet them on their own ground and tune in on their love and kindliness, they never bring us anything but joy. They are human and they can fight when confronted with hatred or ugliness, but even then they are pretty sure to make allowances. Despite all this, they are never weak.

BIRTHDATES RULED BY THE KING OF HEARTS

JUNE 30—CANCER—RULED BY THE MOON

Intuitional, sympathetic, and vital. Not lazy, like many Cancerians. Interested in service to young people. Should marry early; may become selfish later on. Good teachers, preachers, lecturers, and counselors. Have a gift for oratory; could succeed on the stage. If interested in music, better conductors than performers. Like approval and an audience. Inclined to be self-satisfied.

JULY 28—LEO—RULED BY THE SUN

Very successful as actors or directors; naturally drawn to the theater. Often have musical talent. Must be leaders in their own field, and are usually fitted for it. Good army officers; much concerned with humanity. Social welfare workers, propaganda writers, progressive group leaders. Can commercialize any talent or ability. If engaged in merchandising or publishing, will succeed at it. Like big projects.

AUGUST 26—VIRGO—RULED BY MERCURY

Torn between an urge for service and a secret desire for recognition. Are never small, but want to be bigger than their birthdate prescribes. Love nature, out-of-door life, and animals. Good veterinarians, diagnosticians, miners, contractors, chemists. Heavy writers, usually with a message. May become important in industry or as underofficials in government. Excel in scientific lines. The early years may be disturbed by the father.

SEPTEMBER 24—LIBRA—RULED BY VENUS

Law, science, and statesmanship are the best occupations for these natives. May get into a rut and stay there. Unhappy alone. Should marry young. Kindly and indulgent parents. Spiritual and emotional. Will compromise for peace. Can succeed in textile designing, architecture, or commercial drawing.

More scientific than the usual Libran, but keenly interested in art and beauty. May have talent for acting or singing.

OCTOBER 22–LIBRA–RULED BY VENUS

Mental, sensitive, and idealistic. Better actors than September 24, more dynamic. Become ill through inharmony. Good sculptors, carvers, musicians, painters. Love home, children, and dogs. Should be in public life. Need to be alone to build back their energy. Seldom orthodox but always spiritual. Psychically sensitive.

NOVEMBER 20–SCORPIO–RULED BY MARS

Strong intuitions. Go to extremes. Positive and self-assured. Fine judges or lawyer-statesmen. Dutiful, dependable, executive. Not always successful in marriage; it may bring burdens. More apt to suffer than other Kings of Hearts. Interests apt to be dual: two marriages, two homes, two occupations, etc. Succeed in real estate.

DECEMBER 18–SAGITTARIUS–RULED BY JUPITER

Restless, nervous, and undecided. Should cultivate a talent for an outlet—preferably music or acting. Interested in philosophy, religion, literature, publishing, and travel. Could succeed at any of these. Make money, but do not always keep it. Honest, just, philanthropic.

KING OF HEARTS–PLANETARY SEQUENCE OF PERSONAL RELATIONSHIPS

Horizontal Line—Mars and Jupiter

KING OF DIAMONDS–MERCURY CARD IN THE VENUS LINE

An attraction but too harsh and perhaps even crass to interest you enough to pursue. Good for business, especially if you are the "opener" and the King of Diamonds is the "closer." Communications good; a natural rapport. Stay out of male-female involvements on a romantic level—it will probably be temporary.

King of Diamonds birthdates: June 30, July 28, August 26, September 24, October 22, November 20, December 18.

Kings

SIX OF HEARTS–VENUS CARD IN THE MARS LINE

A heavy love affair that may lead nowhere. In the beginning, fun and excitement eventually leading to too many parties—too much drinking and socializing for either of you to accomplish those necessary things of life. The Six of Hearts will probably be the first to want to call a halt—or at least, put a cap on the relationship. Accept it, reevaluate and revise your involvement if you want to keep it. Good for friendship, not good for business if your paycheck relies on the other's financial prowess.

Six of Hearts birthdates: October 29, November 27, December 25.

FOUR OF CLUBS–MARS CARD IN THE JUPITER LINE

Too irritating for a close involvement. Good as your spokesman even though what they say may not always be to your liking. It will still create good end results, so stick with it.

Four of Clubs birthdates: April 30, May 28, June 26, July 24, August 22, September 20, October 18, November 16, December 14.

TWO OF DIAMONDS–JUPITER CARD IN THE SATURN LINE

An excellent doctor, nurse, healer. Someone who can help you; someone who will take care of you. Good aspects for all involvements—providing you listen, disseminate, and use the information as it is given—on a positive level.

Two of Diamonds birthdates: January 25, February 23, March 21, April 19, May 17, June 15, July 13, August 11, September 9, October 7, November 5, December 3.

JACK OF SPADES–SATURN CARD IN THE URANUS LINE

A Karmic tie that can bring you new thoughts, new ways to do things, new viewpoints. An obligatory kind of relationship that can only manifest itself on the positive level. Caution if you are male and the Jack of Spades is female, and you are romantically interested or involved. If she is operating under the Queen of Spades (her Personality Card), she will drive you from home right into the local bars. Act positively and enjoy an old debt brought to you in this life.

Jack of Spades birthdates: January 3, February 1.

EIGHT OF CLUBS–URANUS CARD IN THE NEPTUNE LINE

"Listen my children and you shall hear . . ." should be the opening phrase for this relationship. This card is a weaver of stories, a storyteller of great happenings—certainly a "don't miss" relationship on any level. They will sound as if they have validity in their stories, but you will feel a need to question it—don't worry. It may not matter if the lesson is learned, for they have much to teach.

Eight of Clubs birthdates: March 28, April 26, May 24, June 22, July 20, August 18, September 16, October 14, November 12, December 10.

SIX OF DIAMONDS—NEPTUNE CARD IN THE MERCURY LINE
(Jupiter Line on the Vertical Line)

A difficult card for you to maintain a personal, romantic relationship with. Their interests are materialistic (or at least more concern for the material plane than yours), and you wish life to be more carefree. You may be disillusioned if you get involved, so be sure of the individual before the commitment.

Six of Diamonds birthdates: January 21, February 19, March 17, April 15, May 13, June 11, July 9, August 7, September 5, October 3, November 1.

Vertical Line—Mercury

SEVEN OF HEARTS—VENUS LINE

You may think you've got it made romantically with this card, but you better take a longer, closer look. They can never understand your open, friendly ways without suspecting you of something ulterior. Your nature will never put up with that. So consider it for what it probably will be. A short-lived romantic fling and/or friendship. Business aspects not good, so keep everything in perspective.

Seven of Hearts birthdates: September 30, October 28, November 26, December 24.

THREE OF HEARTS—MERCURY LINE

An immediate like and/or love that will prove to be too demanding on you. It's doubtful if you could ever convince them that you really belong to them, so enjoy the relationship for whatever it is and don't look for anything permanent without problems.

Three of Hearts birthdates: November 30, December 28.

FOUR OF HEARTS—NEPTUNE LINE

Everytime you see this individual, you'll feel as if you've just had a shot of vitamin B 12. The same meeting could leave you just as irritated, because you'll never quite know where they are mentally or spiritually. Don't get involved romantically or in business. Be friends and you'll enjoy each other for the rest of your lives.

Four of Hearts birthdates: October 31, November 29, December 27.

QUEEN OF SPADES–URANUS LINE

Someone who will put up with your temper tantrums without saying a word and will never cease to amaze you when they sublimate their own knowledge and intuition. This is negative and not necessary. For a positive relationship, push the Queen of Spades a little. Understand that their values are not that different from your own—their search is probably more intense than yours, but the end result for you both could be a rewarding relationship on a personal level. Business is not recommended.

Queen of Spades birthdate: January 2.

QUEEN OF DIAMONDS–SATURN LINE

An unavoidable confrontation—and confrontation is probably the best word for what will happen when you meet a true Queen of Diamonds. You have radical ideas (in different directions) of what makes you, and the rest of the world, happy. Remember that one man's poison is another man's meat. You don't have to get involved with a Queen of Diamonds, and you shouldn't. But when you do—whether it be with the Birth Card or with someone operating under the Queen of Diamonds as a Personality Card—learn from the experience in a positive manner. Don't be masochistic and don't stay involved.

Queen of Diamonds birthdates: January 15, February 13, March 11, April 9, May 7, June 5, July 3, August 1.

SIX OF DIAMONDS–JUPITER LINE: SEE HORIZONTAL LINE

Diagonal Lines

SEVEN OF DIAMONDS–DOUBLE VENUS LINES

There's no doubt about the attraction here. Maybe not at first, but talk to the native a little and you'll be snuggled in their arms (or vice versa). Through communications you'll find love here, but it will be short-termed and a definite struggle if you pursue it. Your long-term goals are the same but the manner in which you may wish to get there will be radically different—to the point of not being able to live with it. Great for business and friendship but be careful of falling in love.

Seven of Diamonds birthdates: January 20, February 18, March 16, April 14, May 12, June 10, July 8, August 6, September 4, October 2.

QUEEN OF CLUBS–DOUBLE MARS LINES

A great sexual attraction that could work for you on a positive plane. If romance is on the agenda, watch out for your temper; they won't put up with too many of your outbursts and it's not necessary. They understand far more than you may give them credit for. Good for business and/or friendship. Enjoy this one.

Queen of Clubs birthdates: January 28, February 26, March 24, April 22, May 20, June 18, July 16, August 14, September 12, October 10, November 8, December 6.

EIGHT OF DIAMONDS–JUPITER AND CROWN LINES

Great stimulation to do great things as long as you're around these natives. They can inspire you to go out and accomplish all those things you've only been dreaming about. If you followed their advice, it's entirely possible that it really could happen. Don't try to get personally or romantically involved— it's too trying on your personality. Enjoy the involvement for exactly what it is, and use it. They genuinely want to help.

Eight of Diamonds birthdates: January 19, February 17, March 15, April 13, May 11, June 9, July 7, August 5, September 3, October 1.

FOUR OF SPADES–JUPITER AND VENUS LINES

A beautiful relationship that will seem to have everything, but don't be too crushed if it doesn't turn out to be a forever thing. Definitely on the romantic wire, even though it may seem to be secondary. Great for friendship and possible for business (but not as good as your King or Seven of Diamonds involvement for business).

Four of Spades birthdates: January 10, February 8, March 6, April 4, May 2.

THREE OF CLUBS–SATURN AND MARS LINES

You may feel compelled to become involved with this card but that isn't necessarily so. Good for friendship most of all, poor for business, and romantic love could be a problem (with all of their problems).

Three of Clubs birthdates: May 29, June 27, July 25, August 23, September 21, October 19, November 17, December 15.

SEVEN OF SPADES–URANUS AND JUPITER LINES

A powerfully inspiring individual who could press you to the point of argument. Keep the relationship impersonal and the conversations without anger and you could learn a lot from both the negative and positive sides of this native.

Seven of Spades birthdates: January 7, February 5, March 3, April 1.

SIX OF CLUBS—NEPTUNE AND SATURN LINES

A card, if developed and attuned to you, could be your friend for life. Definitely not someone who could hurt you or deceive you; although you may not always understand them, it may not be necessary. Listen to their advice. If they are operating positively, there is no one who has better intuition about things and people. A possible romantic affiliation but not sexually dynamic. Definitely a relationship you should not miss.

Six of Clubs birthdates: March 30, April 28, May 26, June 24, July 22,

KING OF HEARTS FAMOUS BIRTHDATES

June 30	Susan Hayward
	Lena Horne
July 28	Jacqueline Kennedy Onassis
	Rudy Vallee
	Joe E. Brown
September 24	Anthony Newley
	F. Scott Fitzgerald
October 22	Joan Fontaine
	Franz Liszt
	Leon Trotsky
November 20	Dick Smothers
December 18	Willy Brandt

King of Clubs

Clubs — Knowledge
King of Clubs — Maturity in Knowledge
Thirteen in Clubs — Discrimination and Balance in Knowledge

The Uranus Card in the Uranus Line. Displaces the **Two of Spades** in the Natural Spread

This is a card of ripe judgment. Kings have passed through the various tests imposed and are equipped for control of the field assigned to them and the ability to pass on to others the results of their training.

By nature, Kings of Clubs are spiritually minded, although forceful and often hasty and aggressive. When their knowledge is applied on the higher levels they become physicians or spiritual healers. When they are chary of their gifts and inclined to barter or debase them, they become hard, self-centered, unsympathetic, and incapable of rendering service to others or of achieving any further growth for themselves.

By position, the type of knowledge inherent in these people is not only of the conscious mind or efficient brain but is also occult in character. Uranus opens doors of understanding and when there is a power card in that position, we have only to walk through the door and discover for ourselves what lies on the other side.

The True Place, Saturn in the Jupiter Line, bespeaks the obligation to act as teacher and counselor and the mutual blessing (jupiter) to be derived

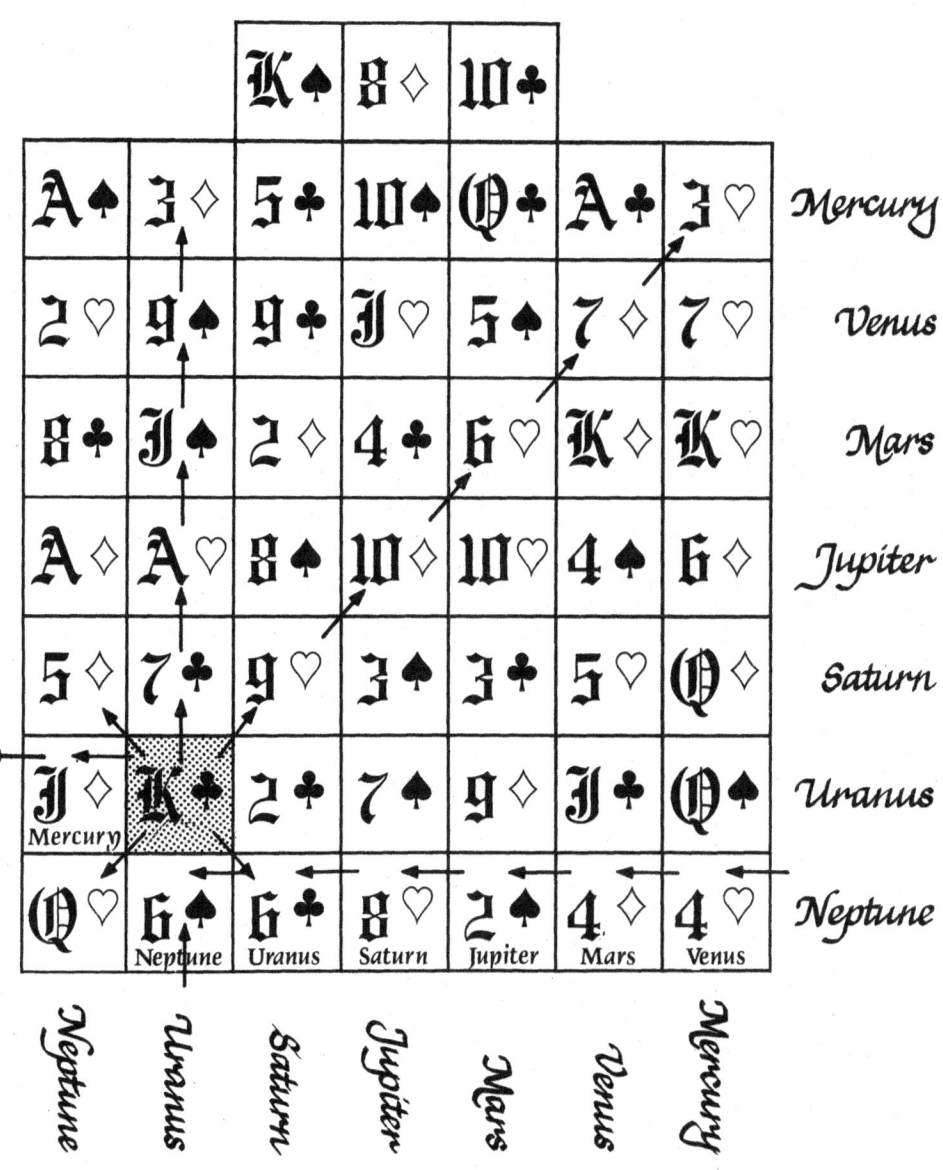

therefrom. The displacement of the Two of Spades inclines these people to business, preferably in association. Two always involves union, agreements, dickering, discussing, and exchanging ideas. There is always much detail connected with their work: papers, messages, records, and data. Among the very successful, when struggle has become a thing of the past, there is danger of getting into a rut of routine or static prosperity because of the two Sixes at the end of the sequence. These people are meant to be indefatigably progressive and they must take care that they live up to the expectation. When they detect any signs of overcontentment or self-sufficiency, they should give themselves a swift prod and a strong "shot" in the name of progress. The Club symbol, it must be remembered, is the upward-pointing clover.

As a rule, both sexes are keen in learning and quick thinkers. The women, however, are often guilty of scattering their forces because of emotional disturbance or family problems. They succeed best if happily married and can be of great help to their husbands by furnishing workable ideas or by active participation in the mental angles of their business. Both sexes are strong for family ties; they make excellent parents and will make sacrifices to provide their children with a good education.

Even the careless and negative among them have keen intelligence and insight, although they often waste themselves in idle curiosity instead of a quest for knowledge that counts. Therefore they may never attain the high place of power that is theirs by right. It is these Kings, collectively, however, that lead us to a knowledge of the why and wherefore of our being. They are the Knowers.

BIRTHDATES RULED BY THE KING OF CLUBS

JANUARY 27–AQUARIUS–RULED BY URANUS

It is the exception when these natives do not realize that they are forerunners of the New Age and have a job to do for it. If on a lower rung of the ladder, will embrace some progressive cult or movement where others do their thinking for them—often mistakenly. Always want to champion the underdog. Successful politicians, labor leaders, business men. May be very gifted in music or acting.

FEBRUARY 25–PISCES–RULED BY NEPTUNE

Healers and teachers—often mystics. Many priests or nuns in this birthdate. Want peace and spiritual assurance; apt to doubt themselves and their power unless they follow a commercial career. Love the sea and long journeys by water. Can succeed brilliantly in music, especially singing. If attracted to the theater, make better directors or producers than actors. Willing to work behind the scenes. Natural humanitarians; very service-minded. Fine assistants in institutions.

MARCH 23–ARIES–RULED BY MARS

Dynamic and progressive. Less spiritually concerned than many Kings of Clubs. Like big, successful business; ambitious; can buy or sell anything for big concerns or covering a big field. Popular; free spenders; make money easily. Get along well with men. Always take an active part. Successful in publishing or compiling information for a wide circulation. If gifted in art, may paint but usually seek the theater (or films). Clear, scientific minds.

APRIL 21–ARIES OR TAURUS–RULED BY MARS OR VENUS

Both are interested in living comfortably. A strong love of home as well as business. If Aries, must guard against selfishness and domination of will; if Taurus, watch out for possessiveness and greed. Usually well content with home and work. Often promoted or exploited. Work well with the earth; naturalists. Always lovers of art, if not performers. If gifted, can succeed in music, painting, or engraving—especially if Taurus. Both signs have writing ability.

MAY 19–TAURUS–RULED BY VENUS

More gifted in art, music, and drama than other Taurus birthdate. Very aware of unseen forces and can develop this gift to an extraordinary extent. Versatile in ability. If they choose industry, will be meticulous about the rights of employees, but will demand good service in return. A fine sense of humor. Easy and friendly people to work with. Philanthropic. Make good educators, judges, philosophical writers.

JUNE 17–GEMINI–RULED BY MERCURY

More inclined to art and music than many Geminians, but are also good writers, teachers, lawyers, interpreters, and statisticians. Know how to commercialize their knowledge. Like to own a large library but do not care for deep reading; think they know enough already. Interested in metaphysics and psychic phenomena; their approach is more from curiosity than spirituality. The women are often pleasure-loving and opportunists. Restless and changeable.

JULY 15–CANCER–RULED BY THE MOON

In whatever line of work they are, these are very impressive people—and want to be. Have a great respect for public opinion and are careful to preserve their reputation. Will work hard for comfort and appearances. Are good teachers, counselors, and priests. Good listeners. Can write on philosophical or educational topics; good journalists and commentators. May have musical ability or talent for painting. Are sympathetic, understanding, comforting.

AUGUST 13–LEO–RULED BY THE SUN

Spiritual, intuitive, often psychic. Always leaders in their chosen field. Protective toward others. Inject drama into their work. If not actors (and many are) will be playwrights, dramatic critics, or theater sponsors. Maintain good balance between mental and emotional nature; too intellectual to be swept off their feet by emotional crises. A Karmic birthday number. Life is often more difficult for these people than for many Kings of Clubs. Are sustained by their unusual spiritual qualities.

SEPTEMBER 11–VIRGO–RULED BY MERCURY

Authors, statesmen, and educators predominate in this birthdate. The birthday number produces many poets and creative prose writers. Highly nervous; anxious to know the law and teach it. Unless in the literary field, are drawn to science. Good researchers, statisticians, technicians, economists. Often found as commissioners or directors of local departments: police, charity, etc. Make good City Fathers.

OCTOBER 9–LIBRA–RULED BY VENUS

This is an exacting birthdate and often proves to be the downfall of the weaker ones. If bent on serving self instead of humanity, they invite failure and seek escape in self-indulgence. Good mixers; want adulation. Good orators and exhorters. Agents and go-betweens, diplomats. Make friends easily. Can be saints or sinners. Must learn emotional balance. Take everything personally. Suffer if thwarted in love. Better writers than artists.

NOVEMBER 7–SCORPIO–RULED BY MARS

Physicians or metaphysicians. Destined for rulership. Experimenters—in surgery or occultism. Can be black magicians, ruthless and cruel if undeveloped. Of all Kings of Clubs are in the most danger of getting off the right track. Know their power too well. Indefatigable diggers for secrets, scientific or occult. Strong views on social and governmental questions. mostly iconoclastic. Apt to believe that the end justifies any means. *Must* keep all transactions legitimate.

Kings

DECEMBER 5–SAGITTARIUS–RULED BY JUPITER

Nervous, impatient, high-strung but devoted to loved ones, generous with employees, and charitable toward the underprivileged. Demand personal freedom, but do not impose their authority or lord it over those in their environment. Have a good sense of values; can drive a good bargain. Like changes, travel, and speed. Make good salesmen, writers, talkers. May have dramatic gifts or musical talent. Like to be connected with public life.

KING OF CLUBS–PLANETARY SEQUENCE OF PERSONAL RELATIONSHIPS

Horizontal Line–Uranus and Neptune

JACK OF DIAMONDS–MERCURY CARD IN THE NEPTUNE LINE

It may seem to be difficult to recognize at first, but these people will probably prove to be too materialistic to your intellectual way of thinking. You will probably butt heads with the more mature ones as well.

Jack of Diamonds birthdates: January 16, February 14, March 12, April 10, May 8, June 6, July 4, August 2.

FOUR OF HEARTS–VENUS IN MERCURY

This friendship will get off to a fast start. You may be turned off by their conceit but use your Kingly judgment and you will find underneath the skin, a true giver.

Four of Hearts birthdates: October 31, November 29, December 27.

FOUR OF DIAMONDS–MARS IN VENUS

There is an attraction for you here, but it will probably be short-lived. You will appreciate how hard this person must work, to acquire, but you may not wish to understand why acquiring is so important to them. Eventually, it will probably become an irritating relationship.

Four of Diamonds birthdates: January 23, February 21, March 19, April 17, May 15, June 13, July 11, August 9, September 7, October 5, November 3, December 1.

TWO OF SPADES–JUPITER CARD IN THE MARS LINE
 (King of Clubs Displacement Card)

This relationship will bring good things to you, but, once again, not

505

without irritations. You will understand them better than most people since this is your Displacement Card. But they might seem to be too complicated and off-balance for you.

Two of Spades birthdates: January 12, February 10, March 8, April 6, May 4, June 2.

EIGHT OF HEARTS—SATURN CARD IN THE JUPITER LINE

You may first meet this person and feel that you have met before. There will be a definite attraction but be prepared for trials and tribulations. The highs will be high but the lows will be the bottom. Try to guide them to a better understanding of themselves and the friendship can be rewarding to you.

Eight of Hearts birthdates: August 31, September 29, October 27, November 25, December 23.

SIX OF CLUBS—URANUS CARD IN THE SATURN LINE

This person could take you down roads you've only read about. You will appreciate their keen sense of intuition. Although you may have to prod them a little, it could be worth it if they don't become a burden to you. Have patience when they seem to be worrywarts.

Six of Clubs birthdates: March 30, April 28, May 26, June 24, July 22, August 20, September 18, October 16, November 14, December 12.

SIX OF SPADES—NEPTUNE CARD IN THE URANUS LINE

This person will seem to be a drifter, the kind that would be happy to be on welfare because the "government owes it to me." A closer look might reveal a type of peace that you might be able to adapt to your own too busy schedule. Don't get disheartened with this native too quickly.

Six of Spades birthdates: January 8, February 6, March 4, April 2.

Vertical Line—Uranus

SEVEN OF CLUBS—SATURN LINE

This person may rile you to the point where you may behave immaturely. If you take the time for a closer look, you will find someone who is actually looking up at you. If not too heavy a burden, try to encourage their educational development and intuitional power.

Seven of Clubs birthdates: March 29, April 27, May 25, June 23, July 21, August 19, September 17, October 15.

ACE OF HEARTS—JUPITER LINE

This will not be an intellectual trip for you, it's strictly romance. Be prepared to give, rather than get, in this relationship. But it could be worth it all.

Ace of Hearts birthdate: December 30.

JACK OF SPADES—MARS LINE

This person won't appeal to you at all. A man may seem effeminate to you; a woman, hard. It might be better not to encourage the relationship—the only exception being if the Jack of Spades you know is highly evolved. In any case, it will be an argumentative situation at best and any marriage will probably end up in divorce.

Jack of Spades birthdates: January 3, February 1.

NINE OF SPADES—VENUS LINE

This is an extremely favorable relationship for you. But again, you will have to give somewhat. The difference here is that the gift you would give might be in the way of an encouraging word or a pat on the back.

Nine of Spades birthdates: January 5, February 3, March 1.

THREE OF DIAMONDS—MERCURY LINE

Their insecurities will probably disturb you to the point of having headaches, if you spend a lot of time around these people. Try short or spaced visits, if possible. If not, try a hobby.

Three of Diamonds birthdates: January 24, February 22, March 20, April 18, May 16, June 14, July 12, August 10, September 8, October 6, November 4, December 2.

SIX OF SPADES—NEPTUNE LINE: SEE HORIZONTAL LINE

Diagonal Lines

QUEEN OF HEARTS—DOUBLE NEPTUNE LINES

This person can stimulate your ideas and create a mental juice flow. If a man, he may, however, appear weak to you; a woman, motherly. Whatever your feelings toward this native, question it before you fall headlong into a situation that may actually be the extreme opposite of what you think it is.

Queen of Hearts birthdates: July 29, August 27, September 25, October 23, November 21, December 19.

NINE OF HEARTS—DOUBLE SATURN LINES

This would be a difficult relationship for you. Your knowledge and understanding would not necessarily be of value to these people, creating frustrations for you.

Nine of Hearts birthdates: August 30, September 28, October 26, November 24, December 22.

TEN OF DIAMONDS—DOUBLE JUPITER LINE

You will have great appreciation for these people, and, in almost all circumstances, it will be a close relationship. You may feel that they are a little too materialistic but you will be able to see beyond as well. Good for love and marriage.

Ten of Diamonds birthdates: January 17, February 15, March 13, April 11, May 9, June 7, July 5, August 3, September 1.

SIX OF HEARTS—DOUBLE MARS LINE

These people may seem to be overly friendly to the point where they force themselves on you and others. The friendship could be rewarding if you can overcome the irritations you will feel accompany it.

Six of Hearts birthdates: October 29, November 27, December 25.

SEVEN OF DIAMONDS—DOUBLE VENUS LINE

Another good relationship, but these people will seem to be flighty. That will certainly not deter you in searching for and finding a strong romance and friendship. Strengthen the bonds by maintaining your own balance and these people will keep life interesting for you.

Seven of Diamonds birthdates: January 20, February 18, March 16, April 14, May 12, June 10, July 8, August 6, September 4, October 2.

THREE OF HEARTS—DOUBLE MERCURY LINE

These people are too fickle in your eyes, in both their ideas and love life, and probably will not present a great deal of appeal to you.

Three of Hearts birthdates: November 30, December 28.

FIVE OF DIAMONDS—SATURN AND NEPTUNE LINES

These people will seem to you to want everything done yesterday. Too changeable and burdensome for a healthy romance with a King of Clubs.

Five of Diamonds birthdates: January 22, February 20, March 18, April 16, May 14, June 12, July 10, August 8, September 6, October 4, November 2.

SIX OF CLUBS: SEE HORIZONTAL LINE

KING OF CLUBS FAMOUS BIRTHDATES

January 27	Wolfgang Amadeus Mozart Lewis Carroll Samuel Gompers Troy Donahue William Randolph Hearst, Jr. Skitch Henderson Kaiser Wilhelm II
February 25	Jim Backus George Harrison Enrico Caruso
March 23	Werner von Braun Joan Crawford Erich Fromm Fannie Farmer
April 21	Queen Elizabeth II Anthony Quinn William Shakespeare
July 15	Rembrandt Van Rijn
August 13	Alfred Hitchcock Fidel Castro
September 11	Marshall Tito, Yugoslavia O. Henry
October 9	John Lennon
November 7	Billy Graham Madame Marie Curie
December 5	Otto Preminger Walt Disney

Diamonds — Values
King of Diamonds — Judgment based on Materialism
Thirteen in Diamonds — Occult Understanding of Values
   The Venus Card in the Mars Line. Displaces the **Three of Clubs** in the Natural Spread
   The accepted interpretation of this card is most uncomplimentary, but there are so many glaring exceptions in the conduct of its natives, they should be stressed even more emphatically than the run of the mill.
   There is only one one-eyed King, and that is the King of Diamonds. A person who shows one side; perhaps all that you want to see. It is not a question of shortsightedness, but it is a question of dishonesty. Some Kings of Diamonds would join a social organization specifically if he were an undertaker, so that he would be sure of all the business.
   In other words, the King of Diamonds has a method in his madness, or he has a reason back of everything that he does. He is calculating; this is the negative side.
   He doesn't want to fight in the sense of getting out and having fisticuffs, but he wants to rule and has a terrific drive for power. King of Diamonds people are victims of the materialistic trend that has characterized our

Planetary Sequence

			K♠	8♦	10♣		
A♠	3♦	5♣	10♠	Q♣	A♣	3♥	Mercury
2♥	9♠	9♣	J♥	5♠	7♦	7♥	Venus
8♣	J♠	2♦	4♣	6♥	K♦	K♥	Mars
Saturn	Jupiter	Mars	Venus	Mercury			
A♦	A♥	8♠	10♦	10♥	4♠	6♦	Jupiter
					Neptune	Uranus	
5♦	7♣	9♥	3♠	3♣	5♥	Q♦	Saturn
J♦	K♣	2♣	7♠	9♦	J♣	Q♠	Uranus
Q♥	6♠	6♣	8♥	2♠	4♦	4♥	Neptune

Neptune · Uranus · Saturn · Jupiter · Mars · Venus · Mercury

Mundane Spread

evolution for hundreds of years. Since we have set money as our goal and standard, what can its custodians do but fight to acquire it, manipulate it, and prove themselves efficient rulers and controllers of it. What, indeed, unless they are in touch with the mighty Uranian force that is granted to them in their True Place—Jupiter in the Uranus Line.

As in the case of the majority of Diamond natives, the basic error lies in the definition of values. If we are born to power, being Kings, we must equip ourselves for rulership. And if power means money, and only that, money we must get in such abundance that no one can outstrip or outdo us.

It is no wonder that only a very few accept and work on the principle so clearly defined in the Bible—"Not by might nor by power, but by My Spirit," saith the Lord of Hosts. Those who do are the Initiates; the hard-boiled materialism of the typical King of Diamonds is unknown to them. As politicians, they refuse to accept bribes; as business men, they are never ruthless—overriding the little fellow with the little business or exacting from him the grilling bonus as the only means of his continuance to function and support his family; as joiners, they do not use their club or fraternity to feather their own nests; as corporation heads, they do not contrive and connive until they get control of the stock and are able to proclaim a freeze-out for their fellow directors.

When not operating strictly on the negative side, they are successful business people who must always watch out for the tendency to grab the surplus but who are willing to take gamblers' chances because they can afford to lose—but seldom do. They are never in inferior positions; they always have ample funds at their disposal, or backers who will come to their rescue. They are always kingpins.

The women are more undecided but always positive in action; they have the troublesome Queen of Diamonds to handle and, unless they keep their personalities out of all business dealings, they will meet with emotional disappointment and frustration. Many King of Diamonds women don't marry, because they are too positive, too bossy, and can't unbend. This can be the slave driver; the office manager that squeezes every bit of work out of you.

The fight always is to keep in the driver's seat, for both the men and the women. Because of this, they deny themselves the power of love. They should be aware of the law of love manifesting in man. They can overcome any difficulty through understanding. These people know how to manifest. Even if they are materialistically minded, they still have the power to manifest.

Positively, the King of Diamonds is endowed with wisdom and occult power. They may appear cold and hard, but at heart they are strictly just and inclined to philanthropy; much depends upon the birth sign and number. With true spiritual development, the negative traits may never manifest. They all have the power of accumulation and control.

BIRTHDATES RULED BY THE KING OF DIAMONDS

JANUARY 14—CAPRICORN—RULED BY SATURN

For these people, money is everything. Their ambition for place, power, and material assets is boundless. Restless and unconcentrated, they seek one avenue after another to attain their objectives. Are primarily attracted to banking or large financial projects but will also seek government posts for the prestige and salary. Make fearless officers and fighters in the armed forces. Dramatic; will seek the stage if it offers inducement.

FEBRUARY 12—AQUARIUS—RULED BY URANUS

The best of all dates for the King of Diamonds. Humanitarian and wise; aware of their mission. Novelists, statesmen, producers, actors, patriots—always philanthropic. Fine orators. Successful as arbitrators, personnel workers, advertisers, or agents. Usually make a valuable contribution to progress and improvement. Creative; unorthodox.

MARCH 10—PISCES—RULED BY NEPTUNE

More honest and conscientious than many King of Diamonds. Are ambitious and money-minded but will not resort to trickery to gain their ends. Often talented in music, painting, or acting. Can write poetry, mysteries, or psychological fiction. If in business, prefer to own their own. Can deal successfully in perfumes, drugs, or any liquids. Like travel, especially by sea. Acquire their learning from absorption, not books.

APRIL 8—ARIES—RULED BY MARS

Good promoters and exploiters—of themselves or others. Good lawyers and bargainers. Always have an eye for profit. Dislike hard or routine work. Can act as brains behind another's business. Set things in motion and then turn them over to others until time to divide the profits. If in the theater, will do something original and distinctive. Work well in association but refuse to be dictated to. Are specialists in their field.

MAY 6—TAURUS—RULED BY VENUS

The most emotional of the King of Diamonds. Family ties and love of home strong. Usually hospitable and friendly but very set in ways and inclined to domination. Excellent actors. Always mental in any line of work. Many have beautiful voices. Creative ability sometimes expresses in poetry or musical prose. The less personally ambitious are concerned with national, social, or civic improvement.

JUNE 4—GEMINI—RULED BY MERCURY

Clever opportunists. Know all the tricks of brain and personality to achieve their ends with but little effort. The failures are due to laziness and unwillingness to use what they know. Succeed in selling or buying, as lawyers, stock brokers, or realtors. Good gamblers, good company; take everything in their stride and refuse to be downed.

JULY 2—CANCER—RULED BY THE MOON

Concerned with education, philosophy, history, and naturalism. Make good preachers of the calvinistic type. May be sincerely interested in humanity. Good teachers or leaders of large groups. Want a position of authority but have many friends and admirers. Want money for personal comfort. The men want women with a good earning capacity. Not an easy date for women.

KING OF DIAMONDS—PLANETARY SEQUENCE OF PERSONAL RELATIONSHIPS

Horizontal Line—Mars and Jupiter

SIX OF HEARTS—MERCURY CARD IN THE MARS LINE

Great stimulation, effervescence; your top salesman; the business associate who will usually agree with you because he inwardly knows you are right, etc. (When he doesn't agree, you will listen as to why.) Impossible for any kind of lasting personal relationship unless you consider a personal relationship as someone who will entertain your business associates. Friendship not only a possibility but a definite probability.

Six of Hearts birthdates: October 29, November 27, December 25.

FOUR OF CLUBS—VENUS CARD IN THE JUPITER LINE

An immediate love sensation and a lasting and growing feeling for this native over the years. Someone you will never forget; someone you will think you probably should have married—and you probably should have. Definitely love—whether romantic or friendship. Business is possible, but you will feel protective of this person and it's not really necessary. Enjoy it most of all.

Four of Clubs birthdates: April 30, May 28, June 26, July 24, August 22, September 20, October 18, November 16, December 14.

TWO OF DIAMONDS—MARS CARD IN THE SATURN LINE

A definite irritation, someone you may have to put up with whether at work or in your homelife. A complete disagreement in concepts, especially in

Kings

the financial areas. You *know* and they question your knowledge—constantly. Don't bother with the relationship on any level.

Two of Diamonds birthdates: January 25, February 23, March 21, April 19, May 17, June 15, July 13, August 11, September 9, October 7, November 5, December 3.

JACK OF SPADES—JUPITER CARD IN THE URANUS LINE

A possible romantic attraction but be careful of trying to dominate each other. Definitely better if you are male and the Jack of Spades is female. Best for friendship—possible for business, but not exceptionally good.

Jack of Spades birthdates: January 3, February 1.

EIGHT OF CLUBS—SATURN CARD IN THE NEPTUNE LINE

This could be the individual who will have the idea to help you make a million dollars. It's a Karmic tie that will always leave you in a quandary as to their motivations. Listen and learn. They have a lot to say and a lot of ideas you can convert into money. Try not to get personally involved; it shouldn't be too hard as their direction is entirely different from your own.

Eight of Clubs birthdates: March 28, April 26, May 24, June 22, July 20, August 18, September 16, October 14, November 12, December 10.

SIX OF DIAMONDS—URANUS CARD IN THE MERCURY LINE
(Mercury and Jupiter Lines on the Diagonal Line)

Great communication; they will know exactly what you want when you want it. A person who will always keep you surprised by their knowledge of True Values. Work with them and learn with them—you are both searching for the same thing and could find great rapport if you try. Business is good, but spiritual development is better.

Six of Diamonds birthdates: January 21, February 19, March 17, April 15, May 13, June 11, July 9, August 7, September 5, October 3, November 1.

FOUR OF SPADES—NEPTUNE CARD IN THE VENUS LINE
(Jupiter Line on the Vertical Line)

Another love attraction that you will never understand, and this one probably more than the other ones. Their set of values are in a different place than yours so, for a successful relationship, don't try to change them. You're not wrong, but neither are they. Enjoy the relationship and profit by it, perhaps for the rest of your life.

Four of Spades birthdates: January 10, February 8, March 6, April 4, May 2.

Vertical Line—Venus

SEVEN OF DIAMONDS—VENUS LINE

A fabulous business relationship—you can't do better. Great for communications, so learn how to execute their ideas; you are much better at this than they. Personal relationships are difficult as they are much more intense in their search for love and spirituality than you. The probable end result would be temporal. But don't miss a business venture—it could be dynamite.

Seven of Diamonds birthdates: January 20, February 18, March 16, April 14, May 12, June 10, July 8, August 6, September 4, October 2.

ACE OF CLUBS—MERCURY LINE

Someone who could virtually find out anything for you that you wanted to know and enjoy the task. A relationship that is necessary to them, and important for you. Not spiritual, strictly a knowledge and exchange of ideas, and someone you will like as well. Romantic relationships are possible, but you may be too difficult for them to handle. Know the person first.

Ace of Clubs birthdates: May 31, June 29, July 27, August 25, September 23, October 21, November 19, December 17.

FOUR OF DIAMONDS—NEPTUNE LINE

An employee who will always be willing to stay after hours; someone who will question your motivations but never your authority. Sexually stimulating for opposite sexes, but not recommended for personal relationships. You'll never quite be able to figure them out and probably won't take the time to do so anyway.

Four of Diamonds birthdates: January 23, February 21, March 19, April 17, May 15, June 13, July 11, August 9, September 7, October 5, November 3, December 1.

JACK OF CLUBS—URANUS LINE

Great business relationship; someone who can bring you new and innovative ideas that you can execute—all of which will bring profit to you in some form. Possible romanticism, but not probable nor recommended. Too aloof, untouchable, and independent (masculine to male King of Diamonds) for you. Good for friendship if you don't try to rely on them in a personal situation. They can't and won't always deliver or be there when needed in a personal involvement.

Jack of Clubs birthdates: January 29, February 27, March 25, April 23, May 21, June 19, July 17, August 15, September 13, October 11, November 9, December 7.

FIVE OF HEARTS—SATURN LINE

A romantic involvement that you should immediately dismiss and keep on an impersonal level. They will keep you hopping to the point where you may not be able to run your business. Karmic ties make the meeting unavoidable, but keep it in its proper perspective. This is a problem card for you, so keep these people at a distance as much as possible.

Five of Hearts birthdates: October 30, November 28, December 26.

FOUR OF SPADES—JUPITER LINE: SEE HORIZONTAL LINE

Diagonal Lines

FIVE OF SPADES—MARS AND VENUS LINES

Communications, stimulations, and love are all a part of this card and your relationship to it. However, you will find it to be on an impersonal level to be successful. This is your councilman who is making efforts to improve the neighborhood; or any other government and/or public service officials who are connected with you and your own personal and business concerns. Don't attempt a personal "opposite sex" involvement—it not only would be difficult, but probably temporary.

Five of Spades birthdates: January 9, February 7, March 5, April 3, May 1.

TEN OF SPADES—JUPITER AND MERCURY LINES

A good business affiliation, especially in products sold through direct mail and/or for the home. A knowledgeable person you will probably not find much in common with on a one-to-one relationship. Enjoy the involvement and don't be surprised if it turns out to be romantic—just be cautious.

Ten of Spades birthdates: January 4, February 2.

KING OF SPADES—CROWN AND SATURN LINES

Argumentative (sometimes without knowing why); too stubborn in what you may think are crazy ideas. An almost impossible relationship on any level unless both natives are highly evolved.

King of Spades birthdate: January 1.

SIX OF DIAMONDS—MERCURY AND JUPITER LINES: SEE HORIZONTAL LINE

SEVEN OF HEARTS—VENUS AND MERCURY LINES

Communication that can lead to love but be careful that the Seven of

Hearts isn't operating negatively and not believe you when you say you were "at a meeting" or "over at Mother's." This native may not be able to put up with the things you feel you have to do to gain the goals you have for yourself. Better as a friend—forget business and romance, if possible.

Seven of Hearts birthdates: September 30, October 28, November 26, December 24.

TEN OF HEARTS—JUPITER AND MARS LINES

A quick love affair that's going to cost you in one way or another. The lesson learned will probably be worth it as long as you can live with it and profit by the knowledge when it's over. Businesswise, a good salesman/spokesman for you, but seemingly plagued with problems of one kind or another. Keep the involvement on an impersonal level and you can't get too hurt.

Ten of Hearts birthdates: July 31, August 29, September 27, October 25, November 23, December 21.

THREE OF SPADES—SATURN AND JUPITER LINES

An immediate rapport; for opposite sexes, love. The relationship may be difficult to maintain. Your drive for your end goals could be disrupted by this native's need for your constant reassurance or physical attention. Personal, romantic involvements can be sustained only by "two pillars, neither touching the other, yet together holding up the Temple." You are definitely on different roads.

Three of Spades birthdates: January 11, February 9, March 7, April 5, May 3, June 1.

TWO OF CLUBS—MARS CARD IN THE URANUS AND SATURN LINES

This native could prove to be the most irritating person you have ever met, and yet he or she could be a trusted employee, a necessary relative, or your best buddy from high-school days. Not only are your perspectives entirely different, but the customs and ways of this card can irk you. Occasional meetings are best—if there are any meetings at all.

Two of Clubs birthdates: May 30, June 28, July 26, August 24, September 22, October 20, November 18, December 16.

SIX OF SPADES—NEPTUNE AND URANUS LINES

A good rapport; a good co-worker; someone who seems to understand something about you and how you operate. You may not completely understand this native, but it won't entirely matter. A possible romance, but seemingly too hard and unfeeling. A good relationship, so work on it on any level.

Six of Spades birthdates: January 8, February 6, March 4, April 2.

KING OF DIAMONDS FAMOUS BIRTHDATES

January 14	Benedict Arnold
	Albert Schweitzer
February 12	General Omar Bradley
	Lorne Greene
	Abraham Lincoln
	Charles Darwin
April 8	Mary Pickford
May 6	Willy Mays
	Rudolf Valentino
	Orson Welles
	Rosalind Russell
	Robespierre
	King George III

Planetary Sequence

			K♠	8♦	10♣		

A♠	3♦	5♣	10♠	Q♣	A♣	3♥	Mercury
Neptune	Uranus	Saturn	Jupiter	Mars	Venus	Mercury	
2♥	9♠	9♣	J♥	5♠	7♦	7♥	Venus
8♣	J♠	2♦	4♣	6♥	K♦	K♥	Mars
A♦	A♥	8♠	10♦	10♥	4♠	6♦	Jupiter
5♦	7♣	9♥	3♠	3♣	5♥	Q♦	Saturn
J♦	K♣	2♣	7♠	9♦	J♣	Q♠	Uranus
Q♥	6♠	6♣	8♥	2♠	4♦	4♥	Neptune

Neptune · Uranus · Saturn · Jupiter · Mars · Venus · Mercury

Mundane Spread

Spades — Labor, Wisdom
King of Spades — The Highest Initiate
Thirteen in Spades — High Spiritual Voltage in Practical Application
The End Card in the Crown Line. **No Displacement** — a Fixed Card.

There is only one King of Spades and the birthdate ruled by this card is January 1. This is a very powerful card. The average person born under this card would not live as the King of Spades. This is a master card, a card that belongs to a person who has the potential for great power. It is also a card of fixation and stubbornness. They have to be at the head of things; they have to rule—whether it be on the negative or positive side.

On the spiritual side, this is the *most* positive of the cards. The potential is so great that the average person cannot live up to it. The truth of the card might make them heads of departments with particular specialized work, but spiritually they cannot handle the power. This is why there is only one King of Spades. It's a person who sometimes overreaches himself; he doesn't know how to bring his potential to himself.

The King of Spades is the highest of all the cards, yet it produces many mediocre people and quite a few failures. A few hundred years from now that will probably not be the case. They shall have learned better how to handle "high spiritual voltage," what sort of obligation they are under when entrusted with a mission, and just what it means to become an initiate.

Some of these people are big enough to meet their opportunities and make the grade. The few Kings of Spades that actually would work on the destiny pattern they have would be a forerunner of something—head of a great spiritual order or some religious organization that would not necessarily be orthodox. (The average King of Spades would work either under the Jack of Spades or the Queen of Spades. The card is too great a responsibility and the average person born under it will have great difficulty in handling it.) However, through suffering and the hard road to wisdom, they have taken their degrees up to the final one—rulership. They have power because they have earned it, but they are too wise in humility to flaunt it or abuse it. Because they don't talk about it, they are called secretive; because they don't brag about it, it is often not recognized; and because they are preachers and teachers of the great truths of Resurrection, Rebirth, and Eternal Life, they are called fanatics or crackpots.

When these Spades have actually reached the King stage, it matters not at all to them what they are called or how they are treated. The King of Spades has no alternate; he is fixed and immovable, displacing nothing but himself, free to move to any line or position in the Spread for more effective operation—never separated from his great wisdom or high crown. He knows the Law, for he is the embodiment of all the laws. He is misunderstood because he has dealing with things of which the majority are as yet ignorant.

In the Natural Order, he comes directly to the Ace of Hearts—a desire for love—but since this card is displaced by the Three of Hearts in the Mundane Spread, his emotional life will be disturbed by uncertainty in relationships and unreliability in his closest associations.

These people are seldom successful in marriage because of this emotional conflict, always disturbing to the required regulation of the mental attitudes. If marriage is not entered into early in life, there is likely to be no marriage at all but rather an increase in the population of nunneries, monasteries, ashrams, or other types of holy or secret orders. A cloistered life is often voluntarily chosen as one of the disciplines of personal denial or the advantages of spiritual refuge.

A woman born the King of Spades couldn't live up to it; she is out of place to begin with; she has jumped into something where she doesn't belong. The Queen of Spades is the feminine ruler and she has no business taking over the King. If so, she is out of step with herself. She can't usually fulfill the Queen role as she isn't ready for it—because she was born the King! Negatively, she will work in a servant or menial capacity.

A man born as any Spade card would never choose the King of Spades to operate under. Spades are too little understood, in the first place. There is too much potential with the Spades and too much demand. A man actually born as the King of Spades will probably not live up to the card as well. He would find it very difficult. There is too much spirituality and potentiality, but he would have the power. However, the other Kings—the King of Hearts, Diamonds, and Clubs—all have better equipment for this plane. There is less disturbance in the life than with the King of Spades. The Bible says: "And I gave my heart to wisdom and to know madness and folly, I perceived that this also is a vexation of spirit, for in much wisdom is there much grief, and he that increases his knowledge, increases his sorrow." This is probably why they say, "The older the soul, the harder the path." This may be true, for if when we are born we knew all the experiences the soul had to make, certainly for those who are on the Path—the tendency would be to run back.

Many remain in the world and are very much a part of it. They are personally ambitious, self-protective, capable of living and enjoying life to the fullest—like other Kings or commoners. They may not go far in terms of their high calling, but they manage to leave an imprint in their chosen line and seldom sink to lowness or meanness or deliberate evil.

When we meet a real teacher whose birthdate is January 1, we shall be wise indeed if we sit at his feet and get all the instruction he is willing to give us. We are on holy ground.

BIRTHDATE RULED BY THE KING OF SPADES

JANUARY 1–CAPRICORN–RULED BY SATURN

Successful in business. Can control groups, especially workers. Never in an inferior position. Ardent patriots; fine government officials. Can write, paint, or act.

KING OF SPADES—PLANETARY SEQUENCE OF PERSONAL RELATIONSHIPS

Horizontal Line—Mercury

THREE OF HEARTS—MERCURY CARD IN THE MERCURY LINE

A relationship of rapport that always leaves this native in an inferior position; communications are more in the areas of asking advice as opposed to common ground discussions. Not anyone you would want to spend any length of time with.

Three of Hearts birthdates: November 30, December 28.

ACE OF CLUBS—VENUS CARD IN THE VENUS LINE

Romantic love is possible and probable, but can only be successful if you permit them to make knowledgeable discoveries that you may think common knowledge to you. Don't be too hard with them, they are searching and can actually surpass you if you're not on your toes and aware of evolving yourself. Good for friendship and business, but try not to combine romantic love with either one—you could make them feel inadequate and unloved even when the situation doesn't exist.

Ace of Clubs birthdates: May 31, June 29, July 27, August 25, September 23, October 21, November 19, December 17.

QUEEN OF CLUBS—MARS CARD IN THE MARS LINE

A tremendous amount of energy can come to you through this native. A high-powered attorney whom you may think doesn't have all the answers. Don't be so quick to judge; you will feel a natural inclination to disagree with this individual, on one level or another. This is negative. Use the relationship to full advantage. You both deserve to know each other. Personal involvements of any kind should not be considered, even if the sex drive is strong for opposites. It will also prove to be just as volatile as it is sexy.

Queen of Clubs birthdates: January 28, February 26, March 24, April 22, May 20, June 18, July 16, August 14, September 12, October 10, November 8, December 6.

TEN OF SPADES—JUPITER CARD IN THE JUPITER LINE

A follower; an initiate; a co-worker. Even romance is possible, depending entirely on you and how much you may try to ride roughshod over this native. Don't be overbearing; they don't require this from you for a successful relationship. They can be a tremendous help to you in almost anything you undertake and will react as positively to you as you, yourself, allow.

Ten of Spades birthdates: January 4, February 2.

FIVE OF CLUBS—SATURN CARD IN THE SATURN LINE

This native represents an old debt that you have come to resolve. Undoubtedly a difficult relationship for you both, but more frustrating for you. Seekers of information, it may be difficult for you to relate the difference between knowledge and wisdom to them. Urge them to express themselves instead of running away, which would be one step in the right direction. No other involvements are desired or necessary.

Five of Clubs birthdates: March 31, April 29, May 27, June 25, July 23, August 21, September 19, October 17, November 15, December 13.

THREE OF DIAMONDS—URANUS CARD IN THE URANUS LINE

An easy outgoing person who could successfully work for you as well as be your friend. Full of surprises, and usually to your benefit. Not too involved on the spiritual plane and therefore should not be close in your personal life. But enjoy the times you will have together.

Three of Diamonds birthdates: January 24, February 22, March 20, April 18, May 16, June 14, July 12, August 10, September 8, October 6, November 4, December 2.

ACE OF SPADES—NEPTUNE CARD IN THE NEPTUNE LINE

You will never understand this person and any length of time spent with them will leave you frustrated and more confused, if you attempt to have a personal involvement. It may seem otherwise at first, but remember that it will probably end in disillusionment. They might try but cannot grasp the things you have to say and do. Take a pass on the relationship if possible.

Ace of Spades birthdates: January 13, February 11, March 9, April 7, May 5, June 3, July 1.

Vertical Line—Saturn

SIX OF CLUBS—NEPTUNE LINE

A native that you will like immediately; find good communications and feel that they pretty much have it together. Don't live with those ideas if you're seeking any kind of long-term relationship. In essence, you are right in your feelings about this native but you may be heading for a fall if you attempt to project more than what actually meets the middle eye. Good for friendship most of all, business a possibility, romance should not be considered until you know all the facts and fictions of the person.

Six of Clubs birthdates: March 30, April 28, May 26, June 24, July 22, August 20, September 18, October 16, November 14, December 12.

TWO OF CLUBS—URANUS LINE

This native is better working for you or being your friend rather than having romance. (You may be tempted romantically.) You can find out anything you want to know through this individual, but make sure you don't reveal too much of yourself to them at the same time. Keep any involvements impersonal.

Two of Clubs birthdates: May 30, June 28, July 26, August 24, September 22, October 20, November 18, December 16.

NINE OF HEARTS—SATURN LINE

You can talk your head off with this native and they will still ask the same question over and over again. Too frustrating for any kind of involvement. Stimulating, but aggravating. Best avoided.

Nine of Hearts birthdates: August 30, September 28, October 26, November 24, December 22.

EIGHT OF SPADES—JUPITER LINE

Probably one of the best and most rewarding relationships you can find; someone who can only help you and bring good happenings into your life. Someone who can understand you and put up with your fits of stubbornness and fanaticism. Go easy on them; they only mean well and bring love to you.

Eight of Spades birthdates: January 6, February 4, March 2.

TWO OF DIAMONDS—MARS LINE

This native could be your doctor who tells you things you don't want to hear; the fabulous secretary who is always talking on the phone when you need her most, etc. Whatever the involvement, don't pursue it on a personal level or you're asking for trouble. You will meet head-on and neither of you will give an inch. Try a little flattery; they won't believe you outwardly but it will make the association much easier.

Two of Diamonds birthdates: January 25, February 23, March 21, April 19, May 17, June 15, July 13, August 11, September 9, October 7, November 5, December 3.

NINE OF CLUBS—VENUS LINE

A natural attraction for opposite sexes, but too chancy to spend a lot of time with. When they're kissing you, you'll never know if they're looking over your shoulder at someone else. Better for friendship and not recommended for business; they gamble too much in their overall lives to give you the kind of confidence you require.

Nine of Clubs birthdates: January 31, February 29, March 27, April 25, May 23, June 21, July 19, August 17, September 15, October 13, November 11, December 9.

FIVE OF CLUBS—NEPTUNE CARD IN THE MERCURY LINE: SEE HORIZONTAL LINE

Diagonal Lines

TEN OF SPADES—MERCURY AND JUPITER LINES: SEE HORIZONTAL LINE

FIVE OF SPADES—VENUS AND MARS LINES

A sexually oriented, romantic relationship that will eventually irritate you to some degree, hopefully not enough to dissolve the association. These natives mean well and want only the best for you. Listen and respond with your great ability for comprehension, and then handle it quietly, without disturbing the structure of this native's personality. Happiness is possible and probable on a personal level. Good for friendship, and good for business only if this native works for you—preferably in a sales or personal contact type of capacity for best results.

Five of Spades birthdates: January 9, February 7, March 5, April 3, May 1.

KING OF DIAMONDS—MARS AND VENUS LINES

If romance is on your mind, it can only end disastrously for you both; neither of you will give up your power. Your head is in one direction and this native's head is in another. Sexually stimulating for you, but argumentative on any level. You simply have nothing to talk about, so take a pass on any kind of involvement other than business. In the case of business, give up a little of your power; these natives have the knack more than you to make a lot of money.

King of Diamonds birthdates: January 14, February 12, March 10, April 8, May 6, June 4, July 2.

SIX OF DIAMONDS—JUPITER AND MERCURY LINES

You have a lot to teach this native and the result can be extremely rewarding for you both. The foundation for the teaching is values, and their meanings. Whatever time is needed, it cannot be wasted by an association with this card. All involvements are possible: friendship, best; business, second; romance, last.

Six of Diamonds birthdates: January 21, February 19, March 17, April 15, May 13, June 11, July 9, August 7, September 5, October 3, November 1.

THREE OF DIAMONDS—MERCURY AND SATURN LINES: SEE HORIZONTAL LINE

TWO OF HEARTS—VENUS AND NEPTUNE LINES

This is a definite romantic attraction that could leave you in a constant state of quandary as to how to please them, or what else you can do to show that you love them. You may try money, but that's not what they're looking for. Your own calling on the spiritual level is so high that you have little else to give to someone who needs so much. The same can be true of friendship, and business is not recommended. Idealistically, you won't get involved, but that's doubtful; so when you do, try to understand that you know far more than they, so it is up to you to handle and rule the relationship in the most positive fashion possible. A nice person—you'll enjoy them. Try to not be too critical.

Two of Hearts birthdate: December 29.

KING OF SPADES FAMOUS BIRTHDATES

January 1
- Barry Goldwater
- J. Edgar Hoover
- J. D. Salinger
- Lorenzo de Medici
- Paul Revere
- Betsy Ross

The Joker

The Initiate-Teachers of old deliberately concealed much of their priceless wisdom from the "profane" by words or pictures that conveyed opposite or distorted meanings to all but the serious students who, by meditation and visual impression, could see behind the veil and discover the truth. The Fool of the Tarot, which is where the Joker originated, is the pictorial statement of the One Force, the No Thing yet Everything to all men—Eternal Energy, boundless, measureless, and infinite. It is all seasons, all forms, and all activities.

If you are the Joker, it is imperative that you find out where you are, that you not fritter your time away, as the little dog on the heel of the Joker reminds him that he must accomplish. The Joker doesn't belong in the pattern; it means all things to all men.

It has the same relationship to the cards as Washington, D.C., has to the United States. The Joker can or cannot be trusted. It is very difficult to tell where these people are operating. Whether they are working under hearts, or if they are working under spades. They never choose to operate under clubs or diamonds. The only way a Joker can tell how he is operating is by work, and by contacts—to see what cards fall in the sequence of what heart or spade card, and to see if those cards correspond with any of their close relationships and contacts. A Joker can work anywhere, having no fixed position. A female Joker would be more likely to work under the Queen of Hearts or the Queen of Spades because it is Capricorn, the same as her own birthdate.

The Fool of the "Little Book" is, for some players, the "highest trump"; for the majority it is discarded and forgotten. It is, however, included as the "zero" page (or piece in the cards), for its inescapable symbolism represents the complete motion of the earth about the sun and is the sole accountant for the "remnant of days" in our solar year. It, too, is all seasons; it is the four quarters of the earth, the four suits; therefore all cards and all birthdates.

As a single card, it rules but one birthdate, December 31, the first decanate of Capricorn, ruled by Saturn. Its natives are indeed "All things to all men—or nothing to no thing."

The Joker natives are a law unto themselves. They belong in the Crown Line as much as do the King of Spades, the Eight of Diamonds, and the Ten of Clubs. The wise ones will choose their own birthdates. They can choose to operate as the King of Spades or the Ace of Hearts in the plan, not the Mundane Spread. It is impossible to analyze them; they hold the key to themselves, and guard it. Their success or failure depends on their own degrees of awareness.

There is no Planetary Sequence for the Jokers inasmuch as they choose their own.

THE JOKER FAMOUS BIRTHDATES

December 31   Henry Matisse

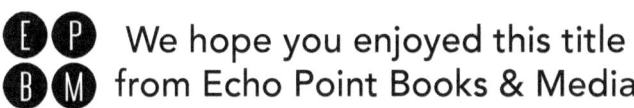

We hope you enjoyed this title from Echo Point Books & Media

Before Closing this Book, Two Good Things to Know

1. Buy Direct & Save

Go to www.echopointbooks.com (click "Our Titles" at top or click "For Echo Point Publishing" in the middle) to see our complete list of titles. We publish books on a wide variety of topics—from spirituality to auto repair.

Buy direct and save 10% at www.echopointbooks.com

DISCOUNT CODE: EPBUYER

2. Make Literary History and Earn $100 Plus Other Goodies Simply for Your Book Recommendation!

At Echo Point Books & Media we specialize in republishing out-of-print books that are united by one essential ingredient: high quality. Do you know of any great books that are no longer actively published? If so, please let us know. If we end up publishing your recommendation, you'll be adding a wee bit to literary culture and a bunch to our publishing efforts.

Here is how we will thank you:

- A free copy of the new version of your beloved book that includes acknowledgement of your skill as a sharp book scout.
- A free copy of another Echo Point title you like from echopointbooks.com.
- And, oh yes, we'll also send you a check for $100.

Since we publish an eclectic list of titles, we're interested in a wide range of books. So please don't be shy if you have obscure tastes or like books with a practical focus. To get a sense of what kind of books we publish, visit us at www.echopointbooks.com.

If you have a book that you think will work for us, send us an email at editorial@echopointbooks.com

www.ingramcontent.com/pod-product-compliance
Lightning Source LLC
Chambersburg PA
CBHW051047230426
43666CB00012B/2592